Art & Architecture Thesaurus

SUPPLEMENT 1

THE GETTY
ART HISTORY
INFORMATION
PROGRAM

The Art and Architecture Thesaurus
is a program of
The Getty Art History Information Program

Art &
Architecture
Thesaurus

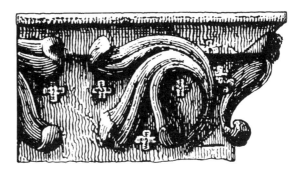

Toni Petersen
DIRECTOR

SUPPLEMENT 1

Published on behalf of
The Getty Art History Information Program

OXFORD UNIVERSITY PRESS

New York · 1992 · Oxford

Oxford University Press

Oxford   New York   Toronto
Delhi   Bombay   Calcutta   Madras   Karachi
Petaling Jaya   Singapore   Hong Kong   Tokyo
Nairobi   Dar es Salaam   Cape Town
Melbourne   Auckland

and associated companies in
Berlin   Ibadan

Published by Oxford University Press, Inc.
200 Madison Avenue, New York, New York 10016

Oxford is a registered trademark of Oxford University Press

Library of Congress Cataloging-in-Publication Data
Art & architecture thesaurus. Supplement 1 / Toni Petersen, director.
        p. 21½x28 cm.
      "Published on behalf of the Getty Art History Information
Program."
    ISBN 0-19-507656-7
      1. Subject headings—Art. 2. Art—Terminology. 3. Subject
headings—Architecture. 4. Architecture—Terminology.
I. Petersen, Toni. II. Getty Art History Information Program.
III. Title: Art and architecture thesaurus.
Z695.1.A7A76   1990 Suppl.   91-36537
025.4'97—dc20   CIP

9 8 7 6 5 4 3 2 1

Printed in the United States of America
on acid-free paper

Designed by Jonathon Nix, The Studley Press, Dalton, Massachusetts

Contents

Preface

THIS IS THE FIRST in a series of updates to the *Art and Architecture Thesaurus (AAT)*. It must be used in conjunction with the three-volume set of the *AAT* published in 1990.

A thesaurus, if it is to be useful, is a work that continually evolves and changes to reflect the changing terminology of the field and its users' requirements. Since the 1990 publication, users have submitted suggestions for new terms and comments on existing terms at the rate of approximately seventy-five per month. In addition to these suggestions from outside, there has been an impact on existing terminology through the development of new hierarchies. The result is this compilation of all changes to the *AAT* since the publication of the 1990 edition.

Each entry in this supplement includes a history note as a means of recording the changes. The history note is a permanent part of a term's record. All future publications of the *AAT* will contain this convention for the history of term changes.

Twenty-three hierarchies were published in 1990. An additional thirteen are scheduled for completion in the next year. The entire *AAT* will be published in a new edition in 1994. The new edition will contain, besides all the projected hierarchies, the changes recorded in this supplement, any further changes to the already published hierarchies, additional scope notes, and many related terms.

Acknowledgments

THE PROCESS OF PRODUCING this supplement electronically required a long period of planning and design on the part of Getty Art History Information Program (AHIP) technical staff and *AAT* staff. Special thanks go to Joseph Busch, Systems Project Manager, April Brown, Systems Analyst, and programming staff at AHIP for the implementation of the complex feature, History Note, that allowed us to process all the additions and changes to the 1990 edition of the *AAT* that have been reported here. Dagmar Jaunzems, *AAT* Production Manager, supervised the production of the supplement and saw it through publication.

We should also like to thank those colleagues who reviewed the design of the publication and made valuable suggestions for improvement. A number of catalogers and indexers were polled concerning the desirability of publishing a supplement. Those who reviewed the design in detail were Kathe Chipman, *Avery Index to Architectural Periodicals*; Bethany Mendenhall, The Getty Center for the History of Art and the Humanities; Maryly Snow, The University of California at Berkeley; Daniel Starr, The Museum of Modern Art; and Jennifer Trant, The Canadian Centre for Architecture. In addition, Michael Ester, Director of AHIP, Eleanor Fink, Program Manager at AHIP, and Nancy Bryan, Research Associate at AHIP, provided excellent advice on the design and content.

Art & Architecture Thesaurus

Supplement 1

PART I:
Introduction

Introduction

1. Scope

Supplement 1 provides changes made to the 1990 publication of the *Art and Architecture Thesaurus (AAT)*. It contains new terms, some deletions, and changes to existing terms. Many scope notes have been added and existing ones expanded. New sources that have been used to support the changes are also included. Minor spelling changes and corrections of typographical errors are not noted in this supplement.

Descriptors have been deleted primarily as a result of work on developing hierarchies or because they were compound terms that could be postcoordinated from already existing descriptors.

Since 1990 the *AAT* has begun adding related term references to existing terms. Although the task is far from complete, it was felt important to include in this publication the related terms that have been added thus far. They appear with the term changes.

New hierarchies are not included but will be part of the next full edition of the *AAT*, scheduled for publication in 1994.

1.1 Term Change Summary:

	ADDED	DELETED	CHANGED	MOVED	SPLIT
Descriptors	546	101	298	492	59
Guide Terms	62	14	14	9	
Alternate Terms	436	11	175		
Lead-in Terms	1997	131	144		
Scope Notes	522		435		
Related Terms	147				

2. Arrangement

The changes reported in this supplement are divided into three major categories: changes to terms, changes to hierarchy structure, and changes to bibliographic sources.

Information about term changes is contained in Part II and is subdivided into three categories: (a) the *Alphabetical Listing of Term Changes* contains all the changes and provides full information about each change; (b) the *Changed Terms* section provides a list of the original form of changed descriptors, guide terms, and lead-in terms along with their revisions; (c) the *Summary of Term Changes* provides an overview of the major term changes and contains descriptors, guide terms, and lead-in terms grouped according to the type of change.

Changes in hierarchical structure are in Part III. The restructured segments are arranged in hierarchy order with the broader term being given as a means of identifying the location.

Source additions are in Part IV. This is an alphabetical listing by source code of sources added to the thesaurus as a result of the term changes.

Part V includes forms for submitting new terms or commenting on existing terms.

2.1 Alphabetical Listing of Term Changes

The *Alphabetical Listing of Term Changes* in this supplement and the cumulative index of the 1990 publication look very similar in format and content. Terms are arranged alphabetically and each entry contains all the pertinent information about that term, with two noteworthy differences. The *Alphabetical Listing of Term Changes* differs from the cumulative index by including guide terms as main entries. It also does not provide a complete record for each descriptor but lists instead only the changes that were made since the 1990 publication.

The lead-in term entries are only those lead-in terms that have been added or changed. They are followed by the traditional USE convention pointing to the preferred term. Lead-in terms that have been deleted are found in the record under the descriptor.

To the already existing conventions (UF, ALT, SN) three new ones have been added in this supplement:

History Note (HN) The history note is a record of the change and immediately follows the main entry. History notes are arranged in reverse chronological order.

Broader Term (BT) The broader term is provided for new, deleted, and moved descriptors and guide terms in order to identify their hierarchical placement.

Related Term (RT) Although the addition of related terms to the 1990 publication is not complete, their significance warranted at least a partial listing. They are integrated with the other changes. A history note identifies the addition of the related terms.

A detailed description of the information provided for each type of change is listed below.

2.1.1 Changes to Descriptors and Guide Terms

2.1.1.1 Descriptors and Guide Terms Added: The entry for a descriptor or guide term that has been added contains the full record for that term. A broader term (BT) is provided to locate it in the hierarchy. Should the broader term be a guide term, its line number is given as well, since guide terms do not appear in the cumulative index of the 1990 publication. If the broader term is also a new term or has been moved to a new location, then it is necessary to consult the *Alphabetical Listing of Term Changes* for the location of the broader term. Absence of a line number for a guide term that is given as a broader term indicates that it is new.

EXAMPLES:

arboriculture
HN   April 1990 added
BT   **horticulture**
SN   Raising and care of trees and shrubs,
     usually in gardens or for ornamen-
     purposes. For the cultivation and
     and study of forest trees, use **silvi-
     culture.**
RT   **arboriculturists**

<plastics by function>
HN   April 1990 added
BT   **plastics**

printing plates
HN   February 1991 added
BT   *<printing and printmaking equipment>*
     TB.341
SN   Flat pieces (as of metal) from which
     textual or pictorial images are
     printed
UF   engraving plates
     plates, engraving
     plates, printing
     plates (printing equipment)

2.1.1.2 Descriptors and Guide Terms Moved: The entries for descriptors and guide terms that have been moved contain only the history note recording the move and a broader term identifying the new location. Since guide terms do not appear in the alphabetical index of the 1990 publication, hierarchy codes and line numbers are provided for the original location of the moved guide term as well as for any broader terms that are guide terms. If the broader term is a new term or has been moved also, then it is necessary to consult the *Alphabetical Listing of Term Changes* for the location of the broader term. Absence of a line number for a guide term that is given as a broader term indicates that it is new.

EXAMPLES:

migration
HN October 1990 moved
BT *<functions by general context text>*
  KG.2

<bases and base components> RT.65
HN June 1991 moved
BT *<column components>* RT.112

In entries for narrower terms that have been moved along with their broader term, the original broader term is retained. It is necessary to go to the change for that broader term for the new location of the entire cluster.

EXAMPLES:

migration
HN October 1990 moved
BT *<functions by general context>*
  KG.2

emigration
HN April 1990 moved
BT migration

immigration
HN November 1990 moved
BT migration

Descriptors and guide terms that have been moved from a published hierarchy to a hierarchy under development have a statement to that effect in the history note. No broader term is given since the new hierarchy is not part of the 1990 publication.

EXAMPLE:

underpainting
HN October 1990, moved to hierarchy
  under development

2.1.1.3 Descriptors and Guide Terms Deleted: The entries for descriptors and guide terms that have been deleted contain the history note and the broader term. Hierarchy codes and line numbers are provided for guide terms that are deleted or given as broader terms.

EXAMPLES:

jamba oil
HN July 1990 deleted
BT nondrying oil

<drawings by location or context>
VD.120
HN October 1990 deleted
BT drawings

Entries for descriptors that are compound terms and have been deleted because they can be postcoordinated from existing *AAT* terms are provided with an explanation to that effect in the history note.

EXAMPLES:

state maps
HN   July 1991 split, use **state** (ALT of
          states) + **maps**

ornament drawings
HN   April 1991 split, use **ornament** +
          drawings

Descriptors that were deleted and then made lead-in terms to other descriptors in the published hierarchies have this information recorded in the history note for the deleted descriptor. They appear as added lead-in terms with the other descriptor and also have a separate USE reference.

EXAMPLES:

souvenir albums
HN   June 1991 deleted, made lead-in to
          viewbooks

souvenir albums
USE   **viewbooks**

viewbooks
HN   June 1991 lead-in term added
UF   souvenir albums

If a descriptor is deleted and made a lead-in term in a hierarchy under development then the history note will state this but its location, since it is in a developing hierarchy, is not given.

EXAMPLE:

correspondence art
HN   October 1991 deleted, made lead-
          in term in hierarchy under develop-
          ment

2.1.1.4 Descriptors and Guide Terms Changed: When the form of a descriptor or guide term has been changed or replaced by a different term, the new term is used for the main entry, and the previous term is recorded in the history note. The original guide term is provided with a hierarchy code and line number.

EXAMPLES:

Destructive Art
HN   May 1990 descriptor changed, was
          Auto-destructive

<environmental concepts>
HN   April 1991 guide term changed, was
          <environmental   sciences   concepts>
          BM.416

inorganic materials
HN   February 1991 guide term changed,
          was *<inorganic materials>* MT.3

7

2.1.2 Changes to Alternate Terms and Lead-in Terms

2.1.2.1 Alternate Terms and Lead-in Terms Added: New alternate terms and lead-in terms appear as part of the record for the descriptor. The history note indicates the addition and the new term appears after the appropriate code, ALT or UF.

EXAMPLES:

analyzing
HN   February 1991 alternate term added
ALT   **analyzed**

light blue
HN   June 1990 lead-in terms added
UF   blue, Della Robbia
blue, dull
Della Robbia blue
dull blue

The added lead-in terms also have a separate entry.

EXAMPLES:

Della Robbia blue
USE   **light blue**
dull blue
USE   **light blue**

2.1.2.2 Alternate Terms and Lead-in Terms Changed: Any change to the form of an alternate term or lead-in term is recorded under the respective descriptor. The history note states the change and provides the previous form. The new term appears following the appropriate code.

EXAMPLES:

light greenish yellow
HN   April 1990 lead-in term changed,
was **canary**
UF   canary yellow

clippings files
HN   March 1990 alternate term changed,
was **clipping file**
ALT   **clippings file**

The changed lead-in term appears as a separate entry.

EXAMPLE:

canary yellow
USE   **light greenish yellow**

2.1.2.3 Alternate Terms and Lead-in Terms Deleted: Alternate terms and lead-in terms that have been deleted are recorded in the history note under the appropriate descriptor. The history note provides the deleted term. There is no separate entry for deleted lead-in terms.

EXAMPLE:

moderate blue
HN   April 1990 lead-in term **smalt blue**
      deleted

2.1.3 Changes to Scope Notes

2.1.3.1 Scope Notes Added or Changed: Additions or changes to scope notes are recorded in the history note under the descriptor. The new text of the scope note follows the scope note code.

EXAMPLE:

camouflage
HN   January 1990 scope note added
SN   The technique of disguising the appearance of beings or things so as to make them blend into the surroundings.

2.1.3.2 Scope Note Source Changed, Added, or Deleted: Scope note sources that were changed, added, or deleted are recorded in the history note of the descriptor. The changed or added source is provided in the text of the history note.

EXAMPLE:

atlantes
HN   November 1990 scope note changed, source RT deleted

2.1.4 Related Terms Those related terms that have been added to descriptors in the 1990 publication are recorded in the history note under their respective descriptor. The related terms appear following the code RT.

EXAMPLE:

fibrous plaster
HN   February 1991 related term added
RT   **fibrous composites**

2.2 Changed Terms The *Changed Terms* section provides a list of the old form and then the new or revised form of a term. If a term has been replaced by another term, it is also considered a change in form and will appear in this list.

The section is arranged alphabetically and includes descriptors, guide terms, and lead-in terms subdivided by type of term.

2.3 Summary of Term Changes The *Summary of Term Changes* is a topical arrangement of added, deleted, and moved, descriptors, guide terms, and lead-in terms. Also included are compound descriptors that have been split and made into two separate descriptors. It provides the terms alone and not their location or the details of the change.

This section may be used as an index to both the *Alphabetical Listing of Changes* in this supplement and cumulative index of the 1990 publication.

2.4 Hierarchy Changes Sections of some hierarchies have required restructuring. The *Hierarchy Changes* shows those sections in which the restructuring was complex enough to cause possible confusion if reported only on a term-by-term basis.

The restructured section may include terms that were not changed as well as those that were.

The restructured sections are arranged alphabetically by hierarchy and then by line number. The first line of each section contains the broader term, along with its hierarchy code and line number; this identifies the location of the restructured section in relation to the 1990 publication. The ellipsis represents unchanged portions of the hierarchy.

EXAMPLE:

BUILT WORKS COMPONENTS (RT)

RT.112   *<column components>*
                   <bases and base components>
                   Asiatic bases
                   Attic bases
                   <base components>
                       griffes

                       .

                       .

                       .

RT.1151   *<fireplace components>*
                   .

                   .

                   .

                   <hearths and hearth components>
                   hearths
                       hearthstones
                       <hearth components>
                       back hearths
                       front hearths

                       .

                       .

                       .

2.5 Sources Any new bibliographic sources that have been used as references for the changes listed in this supplement are recorded alphabetically by source code in this section.

2.6 Candidate Term and Comment Forms This section provides sample Candidate Term and Comment Forms that may be duplicated and used to submit suggestions to *AAT* editorial staff.

Art &
Architecture
Thesaurus

SUPPLEMENT 1

PART II:
Term Changes

Alphabetical Listing
of Term Changes
Changed Terms
Summary of Term Changes

Alphabetical Listing of Term Changes

The *Alphabetical Listing of Term Changes* includes, in alphabetical order, all types of changes and pertinent information relating to the changes.

The entries are either descriptors or guide terms with the various changes listed in the history note. In order to locate the respective term in the 1990 edition, each entry also provides either a broader term, line number, or the original form of the changed term. If the broader term is a new term or has been moved also, then it is necessary to consult the *Alphabetical Listing of Term Changes* for the location of the broader term. Absence of a line number for a guide term that is given as a broader term indicates that it is new or has also been moved.

New lead-in terms, besides being recorded in the history note of the descriptor, also have a separate entry in the *Alphabetical Listing of Term Changes* with the traditional USE reference to the descriptor.

100% cotton rag board
USE **museum board**

'Izz-al-Din Qilich Arslan III
HN October 1990 descriptor changed, was Izz-ad-Din Qilich Arslan III

à la poupée
HN April 1990 added
BT *<matrix preparation techniques>*
SN Printing technique in which color is applied to specific areas of the plate with a pad or rolled piece of felt. (PRTT)
UF dolly method
method, dolly

à trois crayons (printmaking)
USE **crayon manner**

abaci (capital components)
HN May 1991 descriptor changed, was abaci
May 1991 alternate term changed, was abacus
ALT **abacus (capital component)**

abat-jours
HN November 1990 moved
November 1990 scope note changed
BT *<openings by form>* RT.830
SN Use for beveled openings in a wall or in a roof which admit light from above.

Abbasid
April 1990 descriptor changed, was Abbasid (dynasty)

Abdülhamid II
HN April 1990 lead-in term **Abdül hamit II** deleted

Abies fraseri
USE **Fraser's balsam fir**

ablution fountains
HN August 1990 scope note added
SN Fountains for ritual cleansing, usually associated with religious buildings.

abrash
HN June 1991 added
BT *<conditions and effects: textiles>*
SN Unintentional variations in the color of a rug caused by irregular dyeing of the yarn, or by using yarn from a different dye lot.

abrasion
HN April 1991 scope note changed
SN Material removing process which results in the loss or disruption of a surface as a result of wearing, grinding, rubbing, or scraping.

absorbency
HN May 1991 added
BT *<properties of materials>* BM.936
ALT **absorbent**
SN The property by which a material is able to take up a liquid or a gas by capillary, osmotic, solvent, chemical or other means.

absorption
HN March 1991 alternate term added
ALT **absorbed**

Abstraction, Eccentric
USE **Eccentric Abstraction**

abuse of substances
USE **substance abuse**

abuse, drug
USE **drug abuse**

abuse, substance
USE **substance abuse**

abutments
HN August 1990 scope note added
SN Masses, usually of masonry, that support and receive the thrust of arches, vaults, or trusses.

academicism
HN February 1991 moved
BT *<forms of expression>* BM.171

academies
HN May 1991 scope note added
SN Organizations of learned individuals united for the advancement of art, science, or literature. (W)

acanthus
HN October 1990 lead-in terms added
UF acanthus leaf
leaf, acanthus

acanthus leaf
USE **acanthus**

accent light
USE **accent lighting**

accent lighting
HN May 1991 added
BT **local lighting**
SN Localized lighting technique designed to emphasize a particular object or area.
UF accent light
light, accent
lighting, accent

access
HN April 1990 lead-in term added
UF accessibility

access doors
HN September 1991 scope note changed
SN Doors, usually small, opening through a finished construction, as into a duct or wall, and used to provide a means of inspection of equipment or services housed behind. (DAC)

access floors
HN November 1991 lead-in term **raised flooring systems** deleted
November 1991 lead-in term **flooring systems, raised** deleted
August 1990 lead-in terms added
UF floors, raised
raised floors

accessibility
USE **access**

accolades
HN June 1991 scope note changed, source HAS deleted

achievements, funereal
USE **hatchments**

achromatic colors
USE **neutrals**

acid-biting
USE **biting**

acid precipitation
USE **acid rain**

acid rain
HN February 1991 lead-in terms added
UF acid precipitation
precipitation, acid

acid, orthophosphoric
USE **phosphoric acid**

acid, phosphoric
USE **phosphoric acid**

acid, tannic
USE **tannin**

Acolapissa
HN April 1991 added
BT *<Southeastern Native American styles>* FL.1429

acoustical insulation
HN June 1991 moved
BT *<insulation by function>*

acoustics
HN January 1991 alternate term added
ALT **acoustical**

Acra red (TM)
USE **quinacridone red**

acrylic
HN April 1990 lead-in term added
UF Acryloid (TM)

acrylic paint
HN July 1990 lead-in terms added
UF Aqua-Tec (TM)
Liquitex (TM)
magna
paint, plastic
plastic paint

acrylic painting
HN June 1990 added
BT *<painting techniques by medium>* KT.239

UF painting, acrylic
painting, polymer
polymer painting

Acryloid (TM)
USE acrylic

active solar heating
HN February 1991 scope note added
SN Use for solar heating systems that include mechanical equipment and hardware to collect and transport heat; for solar heating systems without mechanical assistance, use **passive solar heating**.

addiction
HN January 1991 added
BT disease
SN The state of being physically or psychologically habituated to a substance or practice to such an extent that its cessation causes severe trauma. For the long term or excessive use or misuse of narcotics, alcohol, or other substances, use **substance abuse**. (RHDEL2)
RT addicts
substance abuse

addiction, drug
USE drug addiction

addiction, narcotic
USE drug addiction

addicts
HN January 1991 added
BT <*people by state or condition*> HG.775
ALT addict
SN Those who are addicted to an activity, habit, or substance. (RHDEL2)
RT addiction
substance abuse

addicts, dope
USE drug addicts

addicts, drug
USE drug addicts

addicts, narcotic
USE drug addicts

additive, antistatic
USE antistatic agents

adhesion
HN October 1991 scope note changed
SN The joining of two surfaces by means of a generally viscous, sticky composition such as an adhesive or through physical or chemical force. (DAC)

adhesives
HN July 1990 lead-in term added
UF cement (adhesive)

Adja
HN June 1990 lead-in term added
UF Aja

adjudicating
HN February 1991 alternate term added
ALT adjudicated

administering
HN February 1991 scope note changed
February 1991 related term added
February 1991 alternate term added
ALT administered
SN Use for the activity of directing the business affairs and human and material resources of an organization, project, or enterprise, involving primarily the formulation of policy. When the application rather than the formulation of policy is the primary aspect, use **managing**. For directly overseeing the activities of an organization or enterprise, use **supervising**.
RT managing

admitting
HN February 1991 alternate term added
ALT admitted

adolescence
HN February 1991 added
BT <*life stages*>
SN Transitional stage between childhood and adulthood in the development of a living being; in humans, it extends mainly over the teen years and terminates legally when the official age of majority is reached.
UF teen-age

adolescents
HN February 1991 scope note added
February 1991 descriptor changed, was **teenagers**
February 1991 alternate term changed, was **teenager**
February 1991 lead-in term changed, was **adolescents**
ALT adolescent
SN People in the transitional stage of development between childhood and adulthood, commonly considered as those of 13 to 17 years of age.
UF teenagers

adsorption
HN March 1991 alternate term added
ALT adsorbed

adulthood
HN February 1991 added
BT <*life stages*>
SN Stage at which a living being is fully grown or developed.

adults
HN February 1991 scope note changed
SN People who are fully grown and developed, commonly considered to be those aged 18 years or older.

advancement
USE promoting

Advent
HN April 1991 added
BT <*religious seasons*>
SN Christian religious season lasting from the fourth Sunday before Christmas until Christmas, observed by some as a period of prayer and fasting. (WCOL9)

adventures, joint
USE joint ventures

advertising campaigns
HN May 1991 alternate term added
ALT advertising campaign

advertising design
HN March 1991 moved
BT design

advocating
HN April 1991 lead-in term added
UF promoting (advocating)

aegicranes
HN April 1991 lead-in terms added
UF goat's heads
ram's heads

Aeolic capitals
HN August 1990 lead-in terms added
UF capitals, proto-Ionic
capitals, pseudo-Ionic
proto-Ionic capitals
pseudo-Ionic capitals

aerial perspective
USE atmospheric perspective

aerodrome obstruction lights
USE obstruction lights

aeronautical ground lights
HN May 1990 added
BT <*aeronautical site elements*>
ALT aeronautical ground light
SN Any light specially provided as an aid to air navigation, other than a light displayed on an aircraft. (IESREF)
UF ground lights, aeronautical
lights, aeronautical ground

aeronautical schools
HN May 1991 descriptor split, use **aeronautical engineering + schools**

<*aeronautical site elements*>
HN August 1990 added
BT <*site elements*> RM.429

aeronautics
HN May 1991 alternate term added
ALT aeronautical

affordable housing
HN January 1991 related term added
RT Usonian houses

African Americans
HN June 1991 deleted
BT ethnic groups

afterimages
HN January 1991 alternate term added
ALT afterimage

agalmatolite
USE **pagoda stone**

age discrimination
HN February 1991 scope note added
     January 1991 alternate term added
ALT ageist
SN Discriminatory attitudes or practices toward people on the basis of their age. (ERIC12)

age, middle
USE **middle age**

age, old
USE **old age**

aged
USE **elderly**

agents, business
USE **commercial agents**

agnosticism
HN January 1991 alternate term added
ALT **agnostic**

<agricultural functions>
HN May 1991 added
BT *<functions by specific context>* KG.162

agriculture
HN February 1991 alternate term added
ALT **agricultural**

Ahmad III
USE **Ahmed III**

Ahmadnagar
HN February 1991 moved
BT **Deccani**

Ahmed III
HN November 1991 lead-in term added
     June 1990 lead-in term added
UF Ahmad III
     Ahmet III

ailerons
HN November 1990 moved
     November 1990 scope note changed
BT *<wall components by form or function>* RT.610
SN Half gables, such as those that close the end of a penthouse roof or the roof over a side aisle of a church; may be scrolled, curved, or otherwise ornamented.

air art
HN October 1991 moved to hierarchy under development

air conditioning
HN August 1990 scope note changed
SN Building systems in which air is treated to control its temperature, humidity, cleanliness, or distribution.

air cooling
HN August 1990 scope note added
SN Building system for the lowering of air temperature, as for comfort, process control, or food preservation. (MHEST)

air diffusers
HN August 1990 scope note changed
SN Outlets in an air supply duct for distributing and blending air in an enclosure, usually mounted in suspended ceilings. (MEANS)

air ducts
HN August 1990 scope note changed
SN Includes any tubes or conduits for conveying air to and from enclosed spaces or corridors within a wall or other structure used for conveying air. (STEIN)

air locks
HN July 1991 scope note changed
SN Airtight spaces permitting passage between spaces of different air pressures or qualities, or between underwater and air-filled spaces.

air-supported structures
HN November 1990 lead-in term added
     November 1990 scope note changed
SN Use for pneumatic structures supported by pressurization of the habitable space; for pneumatic structures in which closed membranes, used as building elements, are inflated, use **air-inflated structures.**
UF inflatable structures

airbrushing
HN October 1990 moved
BT *<painting techniques by application method>* KT.220

Aja
USE **Adja**

alarms, burglar
USE **burglar alarms**

albumin glue
HN June 1991 scope note added
SN Glue obtained from rapidly drying the serum from blood. (PCC)

albums, souvenir
USE **viewbooks**

alchemy
HN October 1991 scope note changed
SN Medieval chemical science and philosophy having as a main goal the transmutation of base metals into gold. (W)

alcohol dependency
USE **alcoholism**

alcohol-resin varnish
USE **spirit varnish**

alcoholics
HN January 1991 added
BT **drug addicts**
ALT alcoholic
SN Those who are addicted to alcoholic beverages.
RT alcoholism

alcoholism
HN January 1991 added
BT **addiction**
SN Addiction to alcoholic beverages.
UF alcohol dependency
     dependency, alcohol
RT alcoholics

aldanite
HN April 1990 added
BT *<minerals by composition or origin>* MT.486

alettes
HN July 1991 scope note changed
SN In Roman and later classicizing architecture, those parts of a pier that form arch abutments and flank a central engaged column or pilaster carrying an architrave.

algorithms
HN January 1991 alternate term added
ALT **algorithm**

alizarin
HN October 1991 scope note changed
SN An orange or red crystalline compound formerly prepared from the madder plant and now made synthetically from anthraquinone; used primarily in making red pigments and dyes. (W)

allées
HN April 1990 added
BT **walkways**
ALT **allée**
SN Use for walkways bordered by formally planted trees, clipped hedges, or shrubs; usually found in formal gardens or parks.

allover backing
USE **lining**

allover mounting
USE **lining**

alloys
HN February 1991 alternate term added
ALT **alloy**

alloys, mercury
USE **amalgams**

almond oil
HN October 1990 moved
BT **essential oil**

altar cavities
USE **sepulchers**

altars
HN October 1991 scope note changed
SN Use for constructions upon which religious sacrifice is offered. Includes both small, tablelike fixtures and larger, free-standing, outdoor structures. For the surface at which communion is celebrated in Protestant churches, use **communion tables.**

alternative press publications
USE **alternative publications**

alternative publications
HN May 1991 added
BT **publications**
ALT **alternative publication**
UF alternative press publications
publications, alternative
publications, alternative press

alternative spaces
HN May 1991 added
BT *<display rooms and spaces>* RM.96
ALT **alternative space**
SN Use for display and study spaces providing artists, especially new, emerging artists, the opportunity to exhibit their works outside the traditional gallery and museum context.
UF spaces, alternative
RT **exhibiting**

alto rilievo
USE **high relief**

Altoperuvian
HN June 1991 moved
BT *<Colonial Latin American styles>* FL.1707

alum
HN July 1990 added
BT *<minerals by composition or origin>* MT.486
SN Colorless-to-white crystalline potassium aluminum sulfate. Used as an additive in the leather and textile industries, in sizing paper, and as a mordant in dyeing. (MH12)
UF alum, potash
potash alum

alum, potash
USE **alum**

aluminizing
HN March 1991 alternate term added
ALT **aluminized**

aluminum alloys
HN February 1991 alternate term added
ALT **aluminum alloy**

aluminum paper
HN July 1990 added
BT *<paper by form>* MT.1903
SN Paper of silvery appearance coated with powdered aluminum. (W)
UF paper, aluminum

alumni centers
HN September 1990 added
BT *<social and civic buildings>* RK.1185
ALT **alumni center**
SN Use for college buildings housing alumni associations and having entertainment and assembly facilities for graduates.
UF centers, alumni

amalgam-gilding
HN March 1991 alternate term added
ALT **amalgam-gilded**

amalgam-silvering
HN March 1991 alternate term added
ALT **amalgam-silvered**

amalgams
HN February 1991 added
BT **nonferrous alloys**
ALT **amalgam**
SN Alloys of mercury with another metal. (W)
UF alloys, mercury
mercury alloys

ambassadors
HN December 1990 added
BT **diplomats**
ALT **ambassador**
SN Diplomats of the highest rank, sent by one sovereign or state to another or to an international organization as its chief representative. (RHDEL2)

amber (fossil resin)
HN May 1991 descriptor changed, was **amber**

ambos
HN March 1991 moved
November 1990 alternate term changed, was **ambon**
BT **pulpits**
ALT **ambo**

amboyna
USE **oil of cloves**

ambrotype
HN February 1991 moved
BT **wet collodion process**

Ambuun
USE **Mbun**

amending
HN January 1991 added
BT *<information handling functions>* KG.64
ALT **amended**
SN Officially correcting written text or recorded data by addition, deletion, or modification.

American, Mexican
USE **Mexican American**

ammoniac, sal
USE **ammonium chloride**

ammonium chloride
HN July 1990 added
BT **salt**
SN White crystalline powder used in electric batteries, in printing, as a soldering flux, and in making other compounds. (MH12)
UF ammoniac, sal
chloride, ammonium
sal ammoniac

Amol ware
HN June 1990 lead-in term added
UF Amul ware

amphitheaters
HN September 1990 scope note added
SN Use for circular or elliptical structures in which a central performance area is surrounded by rising tiers of seats.

Amstel
HN May 1990 added
BT *<modern Dutch pottery styles>*
UF Amstel porcelain
porcelain, Amstel

Amstel porcelain
USE **Amstel**

Amul ware
USE **Amol ware**

amusement arcades
HN September 1990 scope note added
SN Entertainment buildings containing a variety of games and other amusements that can be played for a nominal fee.

amusement rides
HN September 1990 scope note added
SN Recreation structures containing vehicles or other devices in or on which people may ride for amusement for a nominal fee and for a limited time.

amyl acetate
HN June 1990 lead-in term added
UF banana oil

Anachronism (Pittura Colta)
USE **Pittura Colta**

analysis, spectrum
USE **spectroscopy**

Analytic Cubist
USE **Analytical Cubist**

Analytical Cubist
HN June 1990 lead-in term added
UF Analytic Cubist

analyzing
HN February 1991 alternate term added
ALT **analyzed**

anarchism
HN January 1991 alternate term added
ALT **anarchist**

anastatic printing
HN   October 1991 moved
October 1990 scope note changed
BT   **relief etching**
SN   A process of relief etching, usually on zinc plates, used in the 19th century to reproduce existing printed material, including drawings and pages of type. (LG)

anatomical illustration
HN   May 1991 descriptor split, use **anatomical** (ALT of **anatomy**) + **illustration**

anatomical illustrations
HN   May 1991 descriptor split, use **anatomical** (ALT of **anatomy**) + **illustrations**

anatomical models
HN   March 1991 descriptor split, use **anatomical** (ALT of **anatomy**) + **models**

anatomical studies
HN   May 1991 descriptor split, use **anatomical** (ALT of **anatomy**) + **studies**

anatomy
HN   February 1991 alternate term added
ALT   **anatomical**

Andaman marblewood
USE   **marblewood**

Andhra
HN   June 1990 lead-in term changed, was **Satvahana**
UF   Satavahana

Andhra, Early
USE   **Early Andhra**

angel lights
HN   June 1991 scope note changed
SN   Small triangular lights between subordinate arches of the tracery of a window.

angle braces
HN   November 1990 deleted, made lead-in to **knee braces**

angle braces
USE   **knee braces**

angle brackets
HN   October 1991 scope note changed
SN   Use for brackets projecting from the intersection of two walls; when on the exterior, often to support a cornice; when on the interior, often to support a rafter.

angle capitals
HN   November 1990 scope note changed
SN   Capitals of corner columns.

angle columns
HN   February 1991 descriptor split, use **corner** + **columns**

angle sections
USE   **angles (rolled sections)**

angle ties
USE   **knee braces**

angled stairs
USE   **quarter-turn stairs**

angles (mathematics)
HN   May 1991 alternate term changed, was **angled**
ALT   **angle (mathematics)**

angles (rolled sections)
HN   July 1991 scope note changed
November 1990 lead-in terms added
SN   Use for metal members having an L-shaped section.
UF   angle sections
sections, angle

animal fiber
HN   June 1991 deleted
BT   **natural fiber**

animal glue
HN   June 1991 added
BT   *<animal adhesive>* MT.2344
SN   An adhesive made from a solution of degraded or denatured collagen in water.
UF   glue, animal

animal oil
HN   July 1990 scope note added
SN   Oil obtained from animal substances. (W)

animal pedigrees
USE   **studbooks**

animal size
HN   June 1991 lead-in term **animal glue** deleted

animal wax
HN   December 1990 moved
BT   *<wax by composition or origin>*

animé
USE   **East African copal**

animism
HN   July 1991 related term added
January 1991 alternate term added
ALT   **animist**
RT   **spirit houses**

annealing
HN   May 1991 moved
May 1991 scope note changed
BT   *<temperature related processes>* KT.726
SN   Process by which materials, such as metal and glass, are softened and made workable by heating and controlled cooling. (THDAT)

annexing
HN   February 1991 alternate term added
ALT   **annexed**

anniversaries
HN   May 1991 alternate term added
ALT   **anniversary**

annuals (plants)
HN   July 1991 scope note source changed to ALLAB2

annuals (publications)
HN   May 1991 descriptor changed, was **annuals**
May 1991 alternate term changed, was **annual**
ALT   **annual (publication)**

annular vaults
HN   November 1990 scope note changed
SN   Use for barrel vaults covering a space the plan of which is formed by the area between two concentric circles, or any portion of such a space.

annulated columns
HN   March 1991 scope note changed
March 1991 lead-in terms added
SN   Use for columns or clusters of shafts encircled by annulets or shaft rings, common in Medieval architecture.
UF   annulated shafts
shafts, annulated

annulated shafts
USE   **annulated columns**

annulets
HN   November 1990 moved
November 1990 scope note changed
BT   *<moldings by location or context>* RT.794
SN   Use generally for small decorative moldings, usually angular bands or fillets, encircling column shafts; specifically designates the fillets around the bottom of the echinus of a Doric capital. For the grooves encircling the bottom of a Doric capital and masking the joint between capital and shaft, use **hypotrachelia**. For molded bands around Gothic column shafts, often masking the joint between two sections of shaft, prefer **shaft rings**.

antebellum
HN   June 1991 added
BT   *<modern North American periods>*

antefixes
HN   November 1990 scope note changed
November 1990 alternate term changed, was **antefixe**
ALT   **antefix**
SN   Use for ornaments at the ridge or eaves of a roof, in classical architecture and derivatives, that close or conceal the open end of a row of cover tiles.

antennas, dish
USE   **satellite home antennas**

antennas, satellite
USE   **satellite home antennas**

antennas, satellite home
USE satellite home antennas

anthologies
HN April 1991 lead-in term added
UF miscellanies

anthro-geography
USE human geography

anthropology
HN September 1991 moved
February 1991 alternate term added
BT behavioral sciences
ALT anthropological

anthropometry
HN September 1991 moved
BT physical anthropology

anthropomorphism
HN January 1991 alternate term added
ALT anthropomorphist

anthroposophy
HN January 1991 alternate term added
ALT anthroposophist

anti semitism
USE antisemitism

anti-semitism
USE antisemitism

antifreeze
HN June 1990 lead-in term changed, was
anti-freeze solutions
UF antifreeze solutions

antifreeze solutions
USE antifreeze

antiphonals
USE antiphonaries

antiphonaries
HN December 1990 added
BT religious books
ALT antiphonary
SN Collections of psalms, anthems, or
verses to be sung responsively.
UF antiphonals

antisemitism
HN February 1991 scope note added
February 1991 lead-in terms added
January 1991 alternate term added
ALT antisemitic
SN Economic, religious, or racial dis-
crimination against Jews. (TSIT)
UF anti semitism
anti-semitism

antistatic additive
USE antistatic agents

antistatic agents
HN June 1991 alternate term added
July 1990 lead-in terms added
ALT antistatic agent
UF additive, antistatic
antistatic additive

Anyang (Nigerian)
HN August 1990 lead-in term added
UF Nyangi

apartments
HN May 1990 lead-in terms added
May 1990 scope note changed
SN Use for rooms or sets of rooms used
as dwellings or private living quarters and located in houses, hotels, or
within apartment houses.
UF domestic wings
dwelling units
family quarters, private
living quarters
living units
private family quarters
private wings
quarters, private family
residential wings
units, dwelling
units, living
wings, domestic
wings, private
wings, residential

apodyteria
HN June 1990 scope note changed
SN Dressing rooms in ancient Greek and
Roman baths and palaestrae. (W)

apophyges
HN November 1990 lead-in term
changed, was **conges**
UF congés

apothecaries (people)
USE pharmacists

appareilles
HN May 1991 deleted
BT <bastion components> RT.1172

appentices
HN June 1990 scope note changed
SN Use to designate minor structures
with roofs of single slope built against
the sides of buildings. For freestanding structures of this type, use **lean-
tos**.

applied columns
USE engaged columns

appliqué
HN June 1991 moved
BT textile working

appointing
HN February 1991 alternate term added
ALT appointed

apportioning
HN January 1991 scope note added
SN Dividing and assigning according to
some rule of proportional distribution.

appraising
HN February 1991 alternate term added
ALT appraised

approach lights
HN May 1990 added
BT aeronautical ground lights
ALT approach light
SN Aeronautical ground lights indicat-
ing a desirable line of approach to a
landing area. (MHDSTT)
UF approach-light beacons
beacons, approach-light
lights, approach

approach, global
USE globalism

approach, worldwide
USE globalism

approach-light beacons
USE approach lights

appropriated imagery
USE appropriation (critical concept)

appropriated images
USE appropriation (critical concept)

appropriation (critical concept)
HN May 1990 added
BT <historical, theoretical and critical con-
cepts> BM.285
SN In Postmodern art, the practice of
borrowing pre-existing forms or images in order to bring into question
issues of originality in art.
UF appropriated imagery
appropriated images
appropriationism

appropriationism
USE appropriation (critical concept)

apron pieces
HN November 1990 scope note changed
SN Pieces of lumber protruding from a
wall to support carriage pieces or
strings of a wooden stair at their upper ends or at landings. (MEANS)

apron pieces
USE forestages

Aqua-Tec (TM)
USE acrylic paint

aquarelle
HN July 1990 lead-in terms added
UF transparent watercolor
watercolor, transparent

aquatint
HN October 1991 moved
October 1991 scope note changed
BT etching (printing process)
SN A printing process in which resin or
other substance is applied to a plate
to make a porous ground, and the
plate is then heated and etched,
producing a range of tonal value;
often combined with line work.
(PRTT)

aquatint, sugar
USE sugar-lift

aquatint, sugar-lift
  USE **sugar-lift**

arboriculture
  HN April 1990 added
  BT **horticulture**
  SN Raising and care of trees and shrubs, usually in gardens or for ornamental purposes. For the cultivation and study of forest trees, use **silviculture**.
  RT **arboriculturists**

arboriculturists
  HN April 1990 added
  BT **horticulturists**
  ALT **arboriculturist**
  RT **arboriculture**

Arbutus menziesii
  USE **madrona**

arc brazing
  HN March 1991 alternate term added
  ALT **arc-brazed**

arc welding
  HN March 1991 alternate term added
  ALT **arc-welded**

arcades, intersecting
  USE **interlacing arcades**

arcanists
  HN March 1991 added
  BT **potters**
  ALT **arcanist**
  SN Persons professing a special secret knowledge concerning ceramics, especially the making of porcelain. (RHDEL2)

arch bands
  USE **archivolts**

archaeological illustration
  HN May 1991 descriptor split, use **archaeological** (ALT of **archaeology**) + **illustration**

archaeology
  HN February 1991 alternate term added
  ALT **archaeological**

Archaic (Greek)
  HN May 1991 descriptor changed, was **Archaic**

Arches paper
  HN July 1990 added
  BT <*paper by form*> MT.1903
  UF Arches watercolor paper
       paper, Arches
       watercolor paper, Arches

Arches watercolor paper
  USE **Arches paper**

arches, basket
  USE **three-centered arches**

arches, basket handle
  USE **three-centered arches**

arches, blunt
  USE **drop arches**

arches, broken
  USE **broken pediments**

arches, false
  USE **corbel arches**

arches, fluing
  USE **splayed arches**

arches, Palladian
  USE **Palladian windows**

arches, semi-circular stilted
  USE **surmounted arches**

arches, Serlian
  USE **Palladian windows**

arches, strainer
  USE **straining arches**

architect-designed houses
  HN January 1991 related term added
  RT **Usonian houses**

architects, garden
  USE **landscape architects**

architectural centers
  HN October 1990 moved
  BT <*information handling facilities*> RK.684

architectural design
  HN March 1991 moved
  BT **design**

architectural education
  HN October 1990 moved
  BT <*education by subject*>

architectural fantasies
  USE **fantastic architecture**

architectural firms
  HN March 1991 descriptor split, use **architecture** + **firms**

architectural lighting
  HN April 1991 scope note added
       April 1991 lead-in term **outline lighting** deleted
       April 1991 lead-in term **decorative lighting** deleted
  SN Lighting systems for the illumination of building elements, spaces, or exteriors for visual effects.

architectural psychology
  USE **environmental psychology**

architectural schools
  HN May 1991 descriptor split, use **architectural** (ALT of **architecture**) + **schools**

architectural terracotta
  HN October 1990 added
  BT **terracotta**
  SN A hard-burnt, glazed or unglazed clay unit used in building construction, machine extruded or handmade. (HAS)

architecture
  HN October 1990 alternate term added
  ALT **architectural**

architecture, bizarre
  USE **fantastic architecture**

architecture, library
  USE **libraries (buildings)**

<*architrave components*>
  HN March 1991 added
  BT <*architraves and architrave components*>

architrave cornices
  HN November 1990 lead-in terms added
  UF entablatures, friezeless
       friezeless entablatures

architraves
  HN March 1991 moved
  BT <*architraves and architrave components*>

<*architraves and architrave components*>
  HN March 1991 added
  BT <*entablature components*> RT.330

archive buildings
  USE **archives**

archives
  HN September 1990 lead-in terms added
  UF archive buildings
       buildings, archive

archivolts
  HN November 1991 lead-in terms added
       November 1990 scope note changed
  SN Molded or decorated bands around an arch, as, for example, in a series framing a tympanum.
  UF arch bands
       bands, arch

archways
  HN November 1990 scope note changed
  SN Use for openings under arches.

arena theaters
  HN September 1990 scope note added
  SN Theaters in which seating for the audience surrounds the stage in the middle. (EAA)

Arequipa
  HN June 1991 moved
  BT <*Colonial Latin American architecture styles*> FL.1710

aristocracy
  HN May 1991 moved
  BT **upper class**

Aristotelianism
  HN January 1991 alternate term added
  ALT **Aristotelian**

armed conflicts
HN   November 1990 added
BT   events
ALT   armed conflict
RT   revolutions

armed forces
HN   February 1991 related term added
RT   military personnel

aromas
USE   odors

arrangers, flower
USE   floral designers

arris gutters
HN   November 1990 scope note changed
SN   V-shaped gutters usually of wood.

art
HN   March 1991 scope note changed
SN   Use with reference to the study or practice of the fine arts or the fine and decorative arts together. With reference to the visual and performing arts together, use **arts.** For actual works or objects of the fine or decorative arts, use **works of art** or **art objects.**

art appreciation
HN   October 1990 moved
BT   <education by subject>

art education
HN   October 1990 moved
BT   <education by subject>

art for art's sake
HN   April 1990 added
BT   <historical, theoretical and critical concepts> BM.285
UF   l'art pour l'art

<art genres by medium> BM.254
HN   October 1991 deleted
BT   <art genres>

art glass
HN   January 1991 added
BT   <object genres> VB.82
SN   Glassware, of the mid- to late 19th century, that was made for ornamental more than for utilitarian purposes and that incorporated newly developed techniques for producing colors and surface textures.
UF   glass, art

art market
HN   January 1991 scope note changed
      November 1990 moved
      January 1990 lead-in terms added
BT   trade
SN   Use for the buying, selling, and trading of works of art.
UF   art trade
      trade, art

art materials
USE   artists materials

art photography
HN   April 1990 added
BT   <modern North American fine arts styles and movements> FL.1747
SN   Use for the movement in England and the U.S., from around 1890 into the early 20th century, which promoted various aesthetic approaches. Historically, has sometimes been applied to any photography whose intention is aesthetic, as distinguished from scientific, commercial, or journalistic; for this meaning, use **photography.** For discussion of photography as a fine art, use **photography** plus **art theory.** Regarding photography of art, use **photography** plus **art objects** or **works of art.**
UF   artistic photography
      fine art photography
      photography, art
      photography, artistic
      photography, fine art

art pottery
HN   October 1990 added
BT   <object genres> VB.82
SN   Ornamental pottery produced by artists and craftsmen who emphasized the artistic nature of their work; of a type closely associated with the Arts and Crafts movement.
UF   pottery, art

art schools
HN   May 1991 descriptor split, use **art** + **schools**

art trade
USE   art market

art trade
HN   January 1991 deleted, made lead-in to **art market**

art unions
HN   July 1990 added
BT   associations
ALT   art union
SN   19th-century associations for promoting the arts, especially through the distribution of paintings and prints by lottery. (W)
UF   unions, art

art, rock
USE   rock art

art, sofa
USE   sofa art

art, word
USE   visual poetry

artisans' marks
HN   March 1991 deleted
BT   <marks by maker> VW.743

artists' colors
HN   August 1990 added
BT   <paint by function> MT.2534
SN   Paints used by artists, especially as opposed to wall or bulk paints. (MAYER)
UF   colors, artists'

artists' materials
HN   July 1990 lead-in terms added
UF   art materials
      artists' supplies
      supplies, artists'

artists' statements
HN   May 1991 added
BT   <document genres by function> VW.293
ALT   artist's statement
SN   Use for texts by artists, often brief, that state, for example, explanations of the artists' work or theoretical concepts on which their work is based.
UF   statements, artists'

artists' supplies
USE   artists' materials

artists, naive
USE   naive artists

Arts and Crafts
HN   July 1991 related term added
RT   Craftsman

as-built drawings
HN   April 1990 scope note changed
SN   Use regarding the modern building trade for drawings that indicate changes made during construction from the work proposed in the working drawings. For these and other drawings or copies of drawings that are kept as file records of a completed project, use **record drawings.** For scale drawings of existing structures, generally, use **measured drawings**; for drawings that generally depict actual locations, use **topographical views.**

asarota
HN   April 1991 deleted
BT   <pavements by technique>

asbestos-cement
HN   June 1990 scope note added
SN   Fire-resistant, waterproofing material made by combining portland cement with asbestos fibers. (PUTNAM)

ash, pearl
USE   potash

ash, soda
USE   sodium carbonate

ashpits
HN   November 1990 lead-in term **ash dumps** deleted

Asiatic bases
HN   June 1991 moved
BT   <bases and base components> RT.65

asphalt prepared roofing
USE **tar paper**

assassinations
HN May 1991 alternate term added
ALT **assassination**

assemblage
HN April 1991 moved
November 1990 lead-in term added
BT **sculpture techniques**
UF assembling (sculpture technique)

assembling (sculpture technique)
USE **assemblage**

assistance
USE **assisting**

assisting
HN June 1991 lead-in term added
UF assistance

association of ideas
USE **associationism**

associationism
HN April 1990 added
BT *<psychological concepts>* BM.568
ALT **associationist**
SN The doctrine that mental and moral phenomena may be accounted for by association of ideas. (OED)
UF association of ideas

associations, educational
USE **educational associations**

astrology
HN February 1991 alternate term added
ALT **astrological**

astronomy
HN February 1991 alternate term added
ALT **astronomical**

astrophysics
HN February 1991 alternate term added
ALT **astrophysical**

asylums
HN April 1990 scope note added
SN Designates buildings used as refuges for the sick or destitute who need care rather than medical treatment; for institutional facilities treating the mentally ill, use **psychiatric hospitals** or **psychiatric clinics**, and for those treating the chronically ill, use **sanatoriums.**

asylums (psychiatric hospitals)
USE **psychiatric hospitals**

Atacameño
HN June 1990 lead-in term Atacaman deleted

ataduras
HN July 1991 scope note changed
November 1990 lead-in terms added
SN In Mayan architecture, tripartite facade moldings consisting of a central vertical band framed on top and bottom by flaring members; characteristic of Puuc architecture.
UF binder moldings
moldings, binder

atheism
HN January 1991 alternate term added
ALT **atheist**

athletic clubs
HN April 1991 scope note added
April 1991 lead-in term **health clubs** deleted
SN Buildings with sports and recreation facilities offered only on a membership basis.

atlantes
HN November 1990 scope note changed, source RS deleted
November 1990 alternate term changed, was atlante
ALT **atlas**

atlases, fire insurance
USE **fire insurance maps**

atmospheric humidity
USE **relative humidity**

atmospheric perspective
HN February 1991 scope note changed
February 1991 descriptor changed, was **aerial perspective**
February 1991 lead-in term changed, was **atmospheric perspective**
SN Use for the means of suggesting pictorial depth by depicting more distant things with less clarity of outline and detail and, where color is involved, by alteration of hue toward blue, and decrease of color saturation and value contrast. (A-Z)
UF aerial perspective

atomic wars
USE **nuclear wars**

atramentum
HN June 1991 moved
BT *<ink by composition or origin>*

Atsugewi
HN June 1990 lead-in term changed, was **Pit River Indians**
UF Pit River

Attic bases
HN June 1991 moved
BT *<bases and base components>* RT.65

attorney, letters of
USE **powers of attorney**

attribution
HN January 1991 scope note added
January 1991 alternate term added
ALT **attributed**
SN Ascription of an action or man-made object to an agent or creator, place or date; used particularly with regard to ascribing a work of art to a particular artist or school of artists. (W)

auctions
HN May 1991 alternate term added
ALT **auction**

audiences
HN May 1991 added
BT *<groups of people by activity>*
ALT **audience**
SN Use for groups of spectators or viewers.
RT **spectators**
viewers

Aurangabad
HN February 1991 moved
BT **Deccani**

authenticating
HN March 1991 alternate term added
ALT **authenticated**

Auto-destructive
USE **Destructive Art**

auto washes
USE **car washes**

automatic data processing
USE **data processing**

automatic doors
HN May 1991 scope note added
May 1991 lead-in term changed, was **automatic doors**
May 1991 descriptor changed, was **mechanically operated doors**
May 1991 alternate term changed, was **mechanically operated door**
ALT **automatic door**
SN Use for power-operated doors that open and close at the approach of a person or vehicle. (MEANS)
UF mechanically operated doors

automatic elevators
HN June 1991 scope note added
SN Use for elevators that can be operated by the passengers, having at least automatic doors and leveling at landings.

automation
HN January 1991 scope note added
January 1991 lead-in term added
January 1991 alternate term added
ALT **automated**
SN Installing mechanical or electronic devices, processes, or systems which take the place of human effort, observation, or decision, and which require minimal human intervention in their operation.
UF computerization

automatism
HN June 1991 alternate term **automatist** deleted

avalanches
HN May 1991 alternate term added
ALT avalanche

aviation
HN June 1991 added
BT aeronautics
SN Branch of aeronautics which includes the design, production, and operation of aircraft, particularly heavier-than-air aircraft. (RHDEL2)

axes (mathematics)
HN January 1991 alternate term added
ALT axis (mathematics)

axes (tools)
HN September 1991 descriptor changed, was axes
September 1991 alternate term changed, was ax
ALT ax (tool)

axial loads
HN January 1991 alternate term added
ALT axial load

axonometric drawings
HN June 1991 lead-in term added
UF axonometrics

axonometrics
USE axonometric drawings

B-ES
USE environmental psychology

babies
USE infants

Babwendi
USE Bwende

baby pink
USE moderate pink

babyhood
USE infancy

bachelors (academics)
HN April 1991 added
BT <people by degree of qualification> HG.761
ALT bachelor (academic)
SN Those who have been awarded a bachelor's degree. (RHDEL2)

back arches
HN November 1990 scope note changed
SN Use for arches that carry the primary thickness of a wall over an opening, usually a door or window, when the rest of the wall is carried by other means, such as a lintel, an arch of different form or size, or a decorated frame.

back hearths
HN November 1990 moved
November 1990 scope note added
BT <hearth components>
SN Use for that part of hearths on which the fire is built.

backing
USE lining

backlight
USE backlighting

backlighting
HN April 1991 added
BT directional lighting
SN Illumination from behind, and often above, a subject; a technique to produce highlights along edges as well as to separate an object from its background. (IESREF)
UF backlight
lighting, rim
rim lighting

backs (furniture components)
HN July 1991 alternate term changed, was backs
March 1991 descriptor changed, was backs
ALT back (furniture component)

badminton courts
HN September 1990 scope note added
SN Courts marked and equipped for playing the racket sport of badminton.

bagasse
HN June 1990 lead-in term added
UF megass

bail handles
USE bail pulls

bail pulls
HN August 1990 lead-in terms added
UF bail handles
handles, bail

baileys
HN July 1991 scope note changed
November 1990 lead-in term added
SN The enclosed open spaces within castles; especially applied to Medieval fortifications; sometimes also used to refer to the outer walls of such spaces.
UF wards

Bajun
HN June 1990 lead-in term Bajuni deleted

bake ovens
HN July 1991 added
BT ovens
ALT bake oven
SN Chambers encased in thick, fire proof vaults of clay, brick, or stone used for baking bread and other food stuffs
UF bakers' ovens
baking ovens
beehive ovens (bake ovens)
ovens, bake
ovens, baking
ovens, beehive (bake ovens)

baked enamel
HN July 1990 added
BT enamel
UF enamel, baked

bakers ovens
USE bake ovens

baking ovens
USE bake ovens

balconets
HN June 1990 lead-in term balconnettes deleted

baldachins
HN May 1991 moved
November 1990 scope note added
BT canopies
SN Use for canopies over such features as thrones, altars, tombs, or doorways; may be suspended, projecting, or free-standing. For roofed structures with columns built over altars, use ciboria. (PDARC)

balks
HN November 1990 moved
November 1990 scope note changed
BT timber
SN Use for large, squared timbers.

ball-burnishing
HN March 1991 alternate term added
ALT ball-burnished

balloon frames
HN August 1991 scope note changed
SN Wooden frameworks in which all vertical structural elements, posts and studs, of the exterior bearing walls and partitions extend the full height of the frame from sill to roof plate.

balls (parties)
HN May 1991 alternate term added
ALT ball (party)

balls, fancy
USE fancy dress balls

balls, fancy dress
USE fancy dress balls

baltei
HN November 1990 scope note changed
SN Decorative bands often encircling and seeming to constrain the middle of the bolsters on Ionic capitals.

baluster columns
HN October 1991 scope note changed
SN Columns resembling balusters, composed of a base, a potlike element, a bulbous shaft, and a capital.

Bamana
USE Bambara

Bambara
HN June 1990 lead-in terms added
June 1990 descriptor changed, was Bamana
UF Bamana
Banmana

banana oil
USE **amyl acetate**

banded columns
HN November 1991 lead-in terms added
September 1991 lead-in term **rusticated columns** deleted
September 1991 lead-in term **columns, rusticated** deleted
UF blocked columns
columns, blocked

bandleaders
USE **bandmasters**

bandmasters
HN June 1990 lead-in term added
UF bandleaders

bands, arch
USE **archivolts**

bands, chevroned
USE **zigzags**

bandstands
HN September 1990 scope note added
SN Use for structures with raised platforms on which a band or orchestra plays; often roofed when sited outdoors.

Bangombe
USE **Ngombe**

Bangongo
USE **Ngongo**

bank drafts
HN July 1991 deleted, made lead-in term in hierarchy under development

banking
HN January 1991 scope note added
SN Business of receiving and safeguarding money on deposit, loaning money, extending credit, and facilitating the transfer of funds by check, draft, or exchange.

Banmana
USE **Bambara**

banquettes (benches)
HN May 1991 descriptor changed, was **banquettes**
May 1991 alternate term changed, was **banquette**
ALT banquette (bench)

baptisms
HN February 1991 alternate term added
February 1991 descriptor changed, was **baptism**
ALT baptism

bar mitzvahs
HN May 1991 alternate term added
ALT bar mitzvah

Barba
USE **Bargu**

barbers
HN December 1990 added
BT *<people in service occupations>* HG.36
ALT barber
SN Those whose occupation is to shave or trim the beard and to cut and dress the hair of their primarily male clientele.

barge stones
HN November 1990 scope note changed
SN Stones which form the sloping edge of a gable built of masonry.

Bargu
HN October 1991 lead-in term added
June 1990 lead-in term added
UF Barba
Bongu

barite
USE **blanc fixe**

barns, cider
USE **cider mills**

barrel vaults
HN May 1991 scope note changed
May 1991 lead-in term added
May 1991 lead-in term **transverse barrel vaults** deleted
May 1991 lead-in term **barrel vaults, transverse** deleted
May 1991 lead-in term **vaults, transverse barrel** deleted
SN Vaults of plain, semicircular cross section supported by parallel walls or arcades. (DAC)
UF vaults, wagon

barrier-free design
HN May 1990 lead-in term added
UF X factor

barriers
HN November 1990 scope note added
SN Objects or sets of objects that separate, keep apart, demarcate, or serve as barricades. (W)

barriers, radiant
USE **radiant barriers**

bars (commercial buildings)
HN May 1991 descriptor changed, was **bars**
May 1991 alternate term changed, was **bar**
ALT bar (commercial building)

bars, sash
USE **muntins**

bartizans
HN November 1990 scope note added
November 1990 lead-in term **echauguettes** deleted
SN Small turrets projecting from angles on top of towers or parapets, usually as part of a fortification.

bas-relief
HN April 1991 moved
November 1990 scope note changed
BT relief
SN Sculptural relief technique in which the projection of the forms is relatively shallow.

Basal Neolithic
HN October 1990 deleted
BT *<transitional periods Stone Age to Bronze Age>* FL.18

base bid specifications
HN October 1990 lead-in term added
UF documents, base bid

<base components> RT.68
HN June 1991 moved
BT b*<bases and base components>* RT.65

base flashing
HN July 1991 scope note changed
November 1990 lead-in term added
SN Watertight membranes, along roofs or other flat surfaces, that turn up against and cover the intersection with vertical surfaces, such as chimneys or parapets; the exposed upper edge is normally covered by counterflashing.
UF under-flashing

base light
USE **base lighting**

base lighting
HN April 1991 added
BT general lighting
SN General lighting providing uniform, diffuse illumination approaching a shadowless condition acceptable for the filming of motion pictures and television programs. (IESREF)
UF base light
light, base
lighting, base

base, transparent
USE **transparent base**

baseball stadiums
HN September 1990 scope note added
SN Designates stadiums with baseball fields and stands and facilities for spectators.

baseboard units
HN November 1990 scope note changed
SN Use for heating elements that are housed in special panels placed horizontally along the baseboards of a wall.

bases (furniture components)
HN September 1991 deleted
BT *<furniture components>* TG.806

<bases and base components> RT.65
HN June 1991 moved
BT *<column components>* RT.112

<bases: furniture components>
HN   March 1991 added
   BT   *<furniture components>* TG.806

basket arches
   USE   **three-centered arches**

basket capitals
   HN   November 1990 scope note changed
   SN   Use for capitals having interlaced bands resembling the weave of a basket; found in Medieval and Byzantine architecture.

basket handle arches
   USE   **three-centered arches**

basketball courts
   HN   September 1990 scope note added
   SN   Use for courts marked and equipped for playing basketball, generally including a hard floor and one hoop raised above the ground at either end.

Bassa
   HN   August 1990 lead-in terms added
   UF   Betjek
         Koko

bastel houses
   HN   October 1991 scope note changed
   SN   Use for partly fortified houses often having a vaulted ground floor, usually for livestock, and housing domestic spaces on upper levels; generally found along the Scottish border.

bat printing
   HN   March 1991 alternate term changed, was **bat printed**
   ALT   **bat-printed**

batement lights
   HN   July 1991 scope note changed
   SN   Windows or tracery lights having a curved or inclined bottom caused by, for example, the arched heads of other lights below.

bathers
   HN   December 1990 added
   BT   *<people by activity>* HG.705
   ALT   **bather**
   SN   Use for people washing themselves with water, or immersed in water. For people actively propelling themselves through the water by natural means, use **swimmers.**

baths, shower
   USE   **shower stalls**

bathtubs
   HN   November 1990 scope note added
   SN   Plumbing fixtures, usually in the form of tubs or basins, in which baths can be taken.

batiste
   HN   July 1990 added
   BT   *<cloth by form>* MT.1856

SN   Fine, soft, sheer cloth of plain weave made of any of the principal fibers, as cotton linen, rayon, silk, or wool. (W)

bâtons rompus
   HN   November 1991 scope note changed
         August 1991 alternate term **bâton rompus** deleted
   SN   Short, straight billets or portions of molding usually of rounded section forming the zigzag molding in Romanesque architecture; for the complete molding, use **zigzag** (ALT of **zigzags**) plus **moldings.**

batt insulation
   HN   June 1991 moved
         June 1991 scope note added
         June 1991 lead-in term added
         June 1991 lead-in term **blanket insulation** deleted
   BT   *<insulation by form>*
   SN   Use for thermal or acoustical insulation available in precut, standard lengths.
   UF   batts

battened columns
   HN   May 1991 deleted
   BT   *<columns by location or context>* RT.100

battered walls
   HN   November 1990 scope note changed
   SN   Walls that incline as they rise.

battered women's shelters
   USE   **crisis shelters**

battles
   HN   November 1990 added
   BT   **armed conflicts**
   ALT   **battle**

batts
   USE   **batt insulation**

bays (bodies of water)
   HN   September 1991 descriptor changed, was **bays**
         September 1991 alternate term changed, was **bay**
   ALT   **bay (body of water)**

beach clubs
   HN   September 1990 scope note added
   SN   Use for clubhouses whose primary recreational focus is a bathing beach.

beacons, approach-light
   USE   **approach lights**

beam-and-girder constructions
   USE   **one-way beam and slab systems**

beam-and-slab floor constructions
   USE   **two-way beam and slab systems**

beam-and-slab floors
   USE   **one-way beam and slab systems**
         two-way beam and slab systems

beam and slab systems, one-way
   USE   **one-way beam and slab systems**

beams, end-supported
   USE   **simple beams**

beams, simply supported
   USE   **simple beams**

bearing walls
   HN   March 1991 lead-in term changed, was **bearing walls**
         March 1991 descriptor changed, was **loadbearing walls**
         March 1991 alternate term changed, was **loadbearing wall**
   ALT   **bearing wall**
   UF   loadbearing walls

beatifications
   HN   May 1991 alternate term added
   ALT   **beatification**

beautification
   HN   January 1991 scope note added
         January 1991 alternate term added
   ALT   **beautified**
   SN   Activity of making something beautiful or repairing or enhancing its appearance.

Beaverboard (TM)
   USE   **fiberboard**

bed moldings
   HN   November 1990 moved
         November 1990 scope note changed
   BT   *<moldings by location or context>* RT.794
   SN   Use both for small cornice moldings situated beneath the corona and above the frieze in Classical architecture and its derivatives, and for moldings located beneath an overhanging horizontal surface, as below the eaves.

beehive ovens (bake ovens)
   USE   **bake ovens**

beeswax
   HN   December 1990 moved
   BT   **insect wax**

beggars
   HN   December 1990 added
   BT   *<people by activity>* HG.705
   ALT   **beggar**
   SN   Those who subsist by asking for alms. (WCOL9)
   UF   mendicants

<behavior and mental disorders>
   HN   February 1991 added
   BT   *<psychological concepts>* BM.568

behavior disorders
   HN   January 1991 added
   BT   *<behavior and mental disorders>*
   ALT   **behavior disorder**
   UF   disorders, behavior

behavior-environment studies
USE **environmental psychology**

behavior, environment and
USE **environmental psychology**

behavioral sciences
HN September 1991 added
BT **social sciences**
ALT **behavioral science**
SN Area of study typically including anthropology, psychology, and sociology. (IESS)
UF sciences, behavioral
RT **ethics (philosophy)**

beholders
USE **spectators**
viewers

Belgian linen
HN July 1990 added
BT **linen**
UF linen, Belgian

bell capitals
HN November 1990 scope note added
SN Capitals whose basic form is shaped like a bell or an inverted bell; may be enriched with carving.

bell cotes
HN November 1990 scope note changed
November 1990 descriptor changed, was **bellcotes**
SN Use for small, open structures erected on a roof, wall, or gable of a church or other structure, carrying and sheltering bells.

bells, door
USE **doorbells**

belt sanders
HN January 1991 lead-in terms added
UF electric files
files, electric

belvederes
HN November 1990 scope note changed
SN Use for rooftop pavilions intended as lookouts or for the enjoyment of a view. For unroofed platforms, use **widow's walks**; for rooftop structures that are primarily ornamental, use **cupolas**, for small pavilions, in a garden setting, intended for enjoyment of a view, use **gazebos**.

bemas
HN October 1991 scope note changed
SN Refers to raised speaking platforms in pre-Christian and Early Christian basilicas and meeting places, in synagogues, and in Orthodox Eastern churches.

bench saws
HN January 1991 lead-in terms added
UF joiner saws
saws, joiner

Bende (Kenya)
HN June 1990 lead-in terms added
UF Kawende
Wabende

bents
HN November 1990 moved
BT **structural frames**

bequests
HN January 1991 alternate term added
ALT **bequest**

Berëzovsk phase
HN June 1990 lead-in term **Berezovo phase** deleted

berths (waterfront spaces)
HN April 1990 descriptor changed, was berths
April 1990 alternate term changed, was berth
ALT **berth (waterfront space)**

Betjek
USE **Bassa**

bicycle-wheel roofs
USE **double-cable structures**

bidding
HN January 1991 scope note added
January 1991 alternate term added
ALT **bid**
SN Offering a specific sum as the price one will pay or charge. (RHDEL2)

bidets (plumbing fixtures)
HN May 1991 descriptor changed, was bidets
May 1991 alternate term changed, was bidet
November 1990 scope note added
ALT **bidet (plumbing fixture)**
SN Bathroom fixtures used for hygenic washing of the genitals and posterior parts. (MEANS)

bigotry
USE **discrimination**

Bijapur
HN February 1991 moved
BT **Deccani**

billet moldings
HN July 1991 scope note changed
SN Used to designate moldings formed by a series of regularly spaced cubical or short cylindrical projections; found in Romanesque architecture and usually appearing in multiple rows.

binder moldings
USE **ataduras**

binding joists
HN April 1991 deleted
BT **joists**

bingo halls
HN September 1990 scope note added
SN Use for buildings, generally having large open interior spaces, that accommodate a series of tables on which bingo, and derivative games, can be played.

biochemistry
HN January 1991 alternate term added
ALT **biochemical**

biological illustration
HN May 1991 descriptor split, use **biological** (ALT of biology) + **illustration**

biological illustrations
HN May 1991 descriptor split, use **biological** (ALT of biology) + **illustrations**

biology
HN February 1991 alternate term added
ALT **biological**

birthdays
HN May 1991 alternate term added
ALT **birthday**

births
HN May 1991 alternate term added
February 1991 descriptor changed, was **birth**
February 1990 lead-in term added
ALT **birth**
UF childbirths

bistre
USE **light olive brown**

bistre brown
USE **light yellowish brown**

bistros
USE **cafés**

bite, creeping
USE **creeping bite**

bite, deep
USE **deep etching**

biting
HN March 1991 alternate term added
October 1990 moved
July 1990 scope note changed
July 1990 lead-in terms added
July 1990 descriptor changed, was **acid-biting**
BT **etching (corroding)**
ALT **bitten**
SN Use for the specific step of corroding a material by the action of acid.
UF acid-biting
biting in
etching (biting)

biting in
USE **biting**

<biting techniques>
HN October 1990 added
BT *<matrix preparation techniques>*

biting, brush
USE **spit biting**

biting, false
USE **foul biting**

biting, foul
USE **foul biting**

biting, open
USE **open biting**

biting, spit
USE **spit biting**

bits (tool components)
HN May 1991 descriptor changed, was bits
May 1991 alternate term changed, was bit
ALT **bit (tool component)**

bituminous felt
USE **tar paper**

bituminous materials
HN February 1991 alternate term added
ALT **bituminous material**

bizarre architecture
USE **fantastic architecture**

black-and-gold marble
USE **portor marble**

black-and-white photography
HN June 1991 scope note added
SN The art or practice of taking and/or processing photographs whose images are composed of gray tones, black, and white, and sometimes one hue, which may result from toning or aging.

black carbon ink
HN June 1991 moved
June 1990 lead-in term added
BT *<ink by composition or origin>*
UF carbon ink

black manner
USE **mezzotint**

black oil
HN October 1990 moved
BT **boiled oil**

blackish red
HN November 1991 lead-in term changed, was **lilac, grayish**
May 1990 lead-in term changed, was **grayish lilac**
UF gray lilac
lilac, gray

blanc fixe
HN October 1991 lead-in term added
June 1990 lead-in terms added
UF barite
enamel white
white, enamel

blanket insulation
HN June 1991 added
BT **flexible insulation**
SN Denotes flexible, lightweight, faced or unfaced thermal or acoustical in-

sulation formed in long continuous rolls.
UF blankets (insulation)
insulation, blanket
insulation, roll
roll insulation

blankets (insulation)
USE **blanket insulation**

blast-furnace slag
USE **slag**

bleached beeswax
HN December 1990 moved
BT **beeswax**

bled-to-the edge
USE **bleeding (printing technique)**

bleeding (printing technique)
HN March 1991 added
BT *<printing techniques>*
ALT **bled**
SN Printing an image so that it extends to the edge of the paper or other printing surface.
UF bled-to-the edge

bleeding (seeping)
HN September 1991 descriptor changed, was **bleeding**

blind doors
USE **false doors**

blind embossing
HN April 1990 added
BT **embossing**
ALT **blind-embossed**
SN Creating raised letters or designs without ink, foil, or other color.
UF blind intaglio
embossing, blind
embossing, uninked
inkless intaglio
intaglio, blind
intaglio, inkless
uninked embossing

blind intaglio
USE **blind embossing**

blind stamping
HN June 1991 added
BT **stamping**
ALT **blind-stamped**
SN Impressing an image into a surface using a tool that is cut intaglio with a complete design, resulting in a relief image; used especially in bookbinding.
UF blind-stamping
stamping, blind

blind windows
HN October 1991 alternate term changed, was **false window**
March 1991 moved
March 1991 scope note changed
March 1991 descriptor changed, was **false windows**
March 1991 lead-in term changed, was **blind windows**
BT *<wall components by form or function>*
RT.610

ALT **blind window**
SN Representations of windows inserted to complete a series of windows, or to give the appearance of symmetry to a facade.
UF false windows

blind-stamping
USE **blind stamping**

blizzards
HN May 1991 alternate term added
February 1991 moved
February 1991 scope note added
BT **snowstorms**
ALT **blizzard**
SN Long, severe snowstorms, often accompanied by strong winds. (WCOL9)

block printing
HN November 1991 lead-in term **block printing, relief** deleted
October 1991 moved
April 1991 scope note changed
March 1991 alternate term added
October 1990 lead-in terms added
October 1990 lead-in term **relief block printing** deleted
BT *<relief printing processes>*
ALT **block-printed**
SN Use for printing from wooden blocks, as in block books before movable type, or from wood or occasionally metal blocks on fabric. Sometimes used loosely with reference to relief printmaking processes; there prefer **relief printing**.
UF printing, wood block
wood block printing

blocked columns
HN September 1991 deleted, made lead-in to **banded columns**

blocked columns
USE **banded columns**

blocking in
USE **laying in**

blocking out
USE **stopping out**

blocks, fixing
USE **nailing blocks**

blocks, nailing
USE **nailing blocks**

bloom
HN November 1990 added
BT *<surface changing conditions and effects>* KT.916
SN Whitish or foggy effect on various types of surfaces, such as may appear on the varnish of a painting.
UF chill

blowers
HN November 1990 scope note added
SN Use for heavy-duty fans, such as those for ventilating building shafts

or forcing air through large ducted systems.

blue, Della Robbia
USE light blue

blue, dull
USE light blue
very pale blue
very pale purplish blue

blue, Thalo (TM)
USE phthalocyanine blue

blue-green
USE moderate greenish blue

bluish violet, dull
USE moderate violet

blunt arches
USE drop arches

blunt arches
HN March 1991 deleted, made lead-in to drop arches

board, 100% cotton rag
USE museum board

board, chemical wood pulp
USE conservation board

board, conservation
USE conservation board

board, corrugated
USE corrugated board

board, foamcore
USE Fome-Cor (TM)

board, mounting
USE mounting board

board, poster
USE poster board

boardwalks
HN January 1991 added
BT walkways
ALT boardwalk
SN Use for walkways of boards or planks, usually located along shores, especially beaches.

boasted work
HN November 1990 added
BT <carving techniques>
UF work, boasted

boat clubs
HN November 1991 moved
BT <club complexes>

bobsled runs
HN September 1990 scope note added
SN Use for ice-covered courses for bobsledding consisting of chutes with high walls, banked turns, and straightaways. (RHDEL2)

bodied oil
HN October 1990 moved
BT <oil by technique> MT.1995

body color
USE gouache

body color
HN June 1991 deleted, made lead-in to gouache

boiled oil
HN October 1990 moved
BT <oil by technique> MT.1995

boilers
HN November 1990 scope note added
SN Use for a wide range of pressure vessels in which water or other fluid is heated and then discharged to supply hot water for heating or steam for heating or power generation.

bolection moldings
HN November 1991 lead-in term moldings, belection deleted
November 1990 lead-in term belection moldings deleted
November 1990 scope note changed
SN Moldings or groups of moldings used to cover the joint between two surfaces on different levels and projecting beyond the surface of both.

Bolidist
HN May 1990 deleted
BT <post-1945 architecture and design styles and movements> FL.3705

bolts (fasteners)
HN September 1991 descriptor changed, was bolts
September 1991 alternate term changed, was bolt
ALT bolt (fastener)

bonding (joining)
HN July 1991 related term added
RT cladding

bonding (financial)
HN January 1991 scope note added
SN Placing under the conditions of a bond. (W)

bonds (financial records)
HN July 1991 moved to hierarchy under development

bonds (legal records)
HN July 1991 scope note changed
July 1991 scope note changed, source GAHLM deleted
SN Use for agreements pledging liability for financial or personal loss caused to another party.

bone glue
HN June 1991 moved
June 1991 scope note added
BT animal glue
SN Glue made from degraded collagen obtained from bones.

Bongu
USE Bargu

book illustration
HN May 1991 descriptor split, use book (ALT of books) + illustration

book illustrations
HN May 1991 descriptor split, use book (ALT of books) + illustrations

books, receipt (cookbooks)
USE cookbooks

border inspection stations
HN June 1991 added
BT <public buildings by location or context> RK.992
ALT border inspection station
SN Built works erected at or near border crossings where persons or vehicles are halted for examination and clearance by government officials.
UF border posts
border stations
checkpoints
customs posts
inspection stations, border
posts, border
posts, customs
stations, border
stations, border inspection
RT inspecting

border posts
USE border inspection stations

border stations
USE border inspection stations

bordering wax
HN December 1990 added
BT <wax by form or function>
SN Wax formed into an edge around a printing plate so that the plate may be bitten before immersion; used especially for extra-large plates. (PRTT)
UF walling wax
wax, bordering
wax, walling

bosses
HN October 1990 added
BT <culminating and edge ornaments> RT.1047
ALT boss

botanical illustration
HN May 1991 descriptor split, use botanical (ALT of botany) + illustration

botanical illustrations
HN May 1991 descriptor split, use botanical (ALT of botany) + illustrations

botany
HN February 1991 alternate term added
ALT botanical

Botticino marble
HN April 1990 added
BT <marble by composition or origin> MT.743
UF marble, Botticino

bottom rails
HN June 1991 descriptor split, use bottom + rails

boulle
USE **boulle work**

boulle work
HN June 1991 lead-in term added
UF boulle

boundaries
HN January 1991 alternate term added
ALT **boundary**

boundary lights
HN May 1990 added
BT **aeronautical ground lights**
ALT **boundary light**
SN Aeronautical ground lights used to indicate the limits of the landing area of an airport. (W)
UF lights, boundary

bourgeoisie
HN May 1991 moved
BT **middle class**

bousillage
HN April 1990 added
BT **building materials**
SN Mixture of mud, moss, and lime (often in the form of ground shells) used as infill between wall timbers, characteristic of French-influenced architecture of the southern United States, especially Louisiana.

bowl capitals
HN May 1991 deleted
BT **capitals**

bowling alleys
HN September 1990 scope note added
SN Designates buildings housing wooden lanes, equipped with facilities for setting bowling pins and returning balls to the user, for the indoor sport of bowling.

bowstring trusses
HN August 1991 scope note changed
March 1991 moved
BT <*trusses by form*> RT.357
SN Trusses having a bow-shaped top chord, often semicircular or parabolic, and a straight or cambered member that ties together the two ends of the bow.

box beams
HN July 1991 scope note changed
SN Use for built-up hollow beams of rectangular section, whether metal or wood.

box frames
HN November 1990 lead-in terms added
November 1990 moved
November 1990 scope note changed
BT **rigid frames**
SN Structural frames of monolithic reinforced concrete with walls and

floors in the form of slabs creating a cellular appearance.
UF cellular frames
frames, cellular

box pews
HN July 1991 scope note changed
SN Pews screened and enclosed by high backs and sides. (HAS)

boxes, press
USE **press boxes**

braced frames
HN November 1990 moved
November 1990 scope note changed
BT **structural frames**
SN Use for wooden building frames that use diagonal bracing between full-height corner posts and the plates; generally found in construction with timbers heavy enough to be mortised.

braces (supporting elements)
HN May 1991 descriptor changed, was braces
May 1991 alternate term changed, was brace
ALT **brace (supporting element)**

braces, angle
USE **knee braces**

bracket capitals
HN November 1990 scope note changed
SN Use for capitals whose upper bearing surface has been greatly extended by projecting elements placed along the planes loaded by beams or roof members, generally used to lessen the span between supports.

brackets (finish hardware)
HN May 1990 added
BT **finish hardware**
ALT **bracket (finish hardware)**

brackets (structural elements)
HN November 1991 alternate term changed, was bracket
May 1990 descriptor changed, was brackets
ALT **bracket (structural element)**

braille maps
HN January 1991 lead-in term added
UF tactile orientation models

brands
HN January 1991 lead-in terms added
UF irons, marking
marking irons

brass (alloy)
HN May 1991 descriptor changed, was brass

brass rubbing
HN July 1990 descriptor split, use brass + rubbing

braze welding
HN March 1991 alternate term added
November 1990 lead-in term added
ALT **braze-welded**
UF brazing

brazing
USE **braze welding**

breastworks
HN June 1991 scope note changed
SN Defensive walls about breast high.

breeders, livestock
USE **livestock breeders**

breeders, stock
USE **livestock breeders**

bricks, wood
USE **nailing blocks**

bridge failures
HN January 1991 alternate term added
ALT **bridge failure**

bridge trusses
HN March 1991 descriptor split, use bridge (ALT of bridges) + trusses

bridging
HN November 1990 scope note changed
SN Braces or systems of braces, placed between horizontal or vertical structural members, to stiffen them, hold them in place, and to help distribute the load. (DAC)

bridging joists
USE **joists**

briefs (legal documents)
HN May 1991 descriptor changed, was briefs
May 1991 alternate term changed, was brief
ALT **brief (legal document)**

bright violet
USE **light violet**

brilliant yellow green
HN April 1990 lead-in terms added
UF green, light lime
light lime green
lime green, light

British Colonial
HN May 1991 added
BT <*British Renaissance-Baroque styles*> FL.3190
UF Colonial, British

broaching
HN March 1991 alternate term added
ALT **broached**

Broad Manner
HN July 1990 added
BT <*Italian Renaissance-Baroque styles*> FL.3230
UF Manner, Broad

broadcasting stations
HN April 1990 scope note changed
SN Telecommunications buildings containing studios, production and technical offices, equipment spaces, and control facilities for sending and receiving microwave transmissions; for rooms and spaces designed for the origination or recording of radio or television programs, use broadcasting studios.

broadcasting studios
HN April 1990 scope note added
SN Use for rooms and spaces designed for the origination or recording of radio or television programs; for telecommunications buildings containing facilities for sending and receiving microwave transmissions, use broadcasting stations.

broken arches
HN June 1991 deleted, made lead-in to broken pediments

broken arches
USE broken pediments

broken pediments
HN July 1991 scope note changed
     June 1991 lead-in terms added
     November 1990 lead-in terms added
SN Use for pediments whose lines are interrupted either at the apex or the base, or in both locations; found especially on Late Antique, Baroque, and Mannerist architecture, and on Chippendale furniture.
UF arches, broken
     broken arches
     open pediments
     pediments, open

brokers, real estate
USE real estate agents

brokers, stock
USE stockbrokers

bronze paint
HN July 1990 added
BT metallic paint
UF paint, bronze

bronze powder
HN July 1990 added
BT <metal by form> MT.454
SN Any metal, as a copper alloy or aluminum, in fine flake form used as a pigment to give the appearance of a metallic surface. (W)
UF powder, bronze

Brosium aubletti
USE snakewood

brothels
HN July 1991 related terms added
RT prostitutes
     prostitution

brothers
HN December 1990 added
BT siblings
ALT brother
SN Male siblings.

brown, bistre
USE light yellowish brown

brown, mummy
USE moderate brown

brush biting
USE spit biting

builders guides
HN June 1991 moved
BT <books by subject> VW.522

building design, green
USE green design

building directories
HN February 1991 added
BT <directories by subject: location> VW.414
ALT building directory
SN Devices informing users of a building or complex about the location of or directions to individuals, organizations, or services within that building or complex.
UF directories, building

<building elevation attributes>
HN March 1991 moved
     November 1990 guide term changed, was <building plan attributes: number of stories> DC.96
BT <shape attributes> DC.54

building envelopes
HN January 1991 alternate term added
ALT building envelope

building failures
HN January 1991 alternate term added
ALT building failure

building lines
HN January 1991 alternate term added
ALT building line

building machinery
USE construction equipment

building services
USE building systems

building systems
HN November 1990 scope note added
     November 1990 lead-in terms added
SN Use for networks of equipment that provide nonstructural services, such as HVAC or electricity throughout a building or complex.
UF building services
     service, building

building, fast
USE fast-track method

building, slab (pottery technique)
USE slab method

buildings, archive
USE archives

buildings, library
USE libraries (buildings)

buildings, school
USE schools

built-up beams
HN November 1990 scope note changed
SN Beams, whether of metal, wood, or concrete, which are made up of separate parts fastened together.

bull's eye windows
USE oculi

bullrings
HN September 1990 scope note added
SN Arenas for bullfights. (W)

Buna S
USE styrene-butadiene rubber

bundle piers
HN May 1991 deleted
BT <piers by form>

Bunyoro
USE Nyoro

burglar alarm systems
USE burglar alarms

burglar alarms
HN October 1990 added
BT <security system components>
ALT burglar alarm
SN Use for automatic devices that give an alarm when such items as doors, windows, or safes are tampered with or opened without authorization, as by burglars. (RHDEL2)
UF alarms, burglar
     burglar alarm systems
     systems, burglar alarm

burglary
HN January 1991 added
BT crime
ALT burglarized
SN Breaking into and entering any building belonging to another with the intent to commit theft. (RHDEL2)

burial gifts
USE grave goods

burning in (painting)
HN October 1990 moved
BT <painting techniques by stage> KT.243

burnishing (polishing)
HN September 1991 alternate term changed, was burnished
     May 1991 descriptor changed, was burnishing
ALT burnished (polishing)

Burr arch trusses
HN March 1991 moved
BT <trusses by form> RT.357

bus ducts
USE **busways**

bus lanes
HN June 1990 scope note added
SN Street or highway lanes intended for use primarily by buses but also used by other traffic for such purposes as right turns. (DDT)

bus stops
HN December 1990 moved
BT **pedestrian facilities**

business
HN February 1991 moved
January 1991 scope note changed
BT *<business and related functions>*
SN Use for the broad area of commercial or mercantile activity involving the exchange of commodities, services, or financial resources. (W)

business agents
USE **commercial agents**

<business and related functions>
HN February 1991 added
BT *<functions by specific context>* KG.162

business colleges
HN July 1991 scope note changed
SN Schools for training students in the clerical aspects of business and commerce, such as typing and bookkeeping; for schools devoted to the professional study of the aspects of commercial enterprise, use **business schools.**

business schools
HN September 1990 scope note added
SN Use for schools devoted to the professional study of the organization and management of commercial enterprises, usually at the baccalaureate level and above. For schools devoted to training students in the clerical aspects of business and commerce, use **business colleges.**

<business-related functions>
HN February 1991 added
BT *<business and related functions>*

busways
HN November 1990 lead-in term changed, was **busducts**
UF bus ducts

buttery hatches
HN November 1990 scope note changed
SN Half-doors giving entrance to a pantry and over which are served out the contents of the pantry. (RS)

buttresses
HN November 1990 scope note added
November 1990 lead-in term abamuri deleted
SN Pierlike masonry elements built to strengthen or support walls or resist the lateral thrust of vaults.

Bwende
HN July 1990 lead-in term added
UF Babwendi

byre-houses
USE **housebarns**

cabañas
HN September 1990 scope note added
SN Use for small cabins, simple enclosures, or tentlike structures erected at beaches or swimming pools as bathhouses.

cabin, rustic
USE **primitive hut**

cabinet photographs
HN January 1991 lead-in terms added
UF cabinet-sized photographs
cabinets (photographs)

cabinet-sized photographs
USE **cabinet photographs**

cabinet windows
HN April 1991 scope note added
SN Use for show-windows that project outward from the principle plane of a building.

cabinets (case furniture)
HN May 1991 descriptor changed, was **cabinets**
May 1991 alternate term changed, was **cabinet**
ALT **cabinet (case furniture)**

cabinets (photographs)
USE **cabinet photographs**

cable-beam structures
USE **double-cable structures**

cable moldings
HN December 1990 scope note changed
December 1990 lead-in term added
SN Convex moldings resembling a rope or cable.
UF ropework (cable moldings)

cable net structures
HN July 1991 scope note changed
July 1991 lead-in terms added
SN Use for cable structures in which a field of crossed cables, of different and often reverse curvatures, make up the primary roof surface.
UF cable tent structures
cable-supported tents
structures, cable tent
tent structures, cable
tents, cable-supported

cable roofs
USE **cable structures**

cable-stayed structures
HN August 1991 scope note changed
August 1991 lead-in terms added
SN Cable structures that use vertical or sloping compression masts from which straight cables run to critical

points or to horizontally spanning or cantilevered members.
UF cable-supported cantilever roofs
cable-supported structures
cantilever roofs, cable-supported
guyed structures
roofs, cable-supported cantilever
structures, cable supported
structures, guyed

cable structures
HN July 1991 lead-in terms added
UF cable roofs
roofs, cable

cable structures, suspension
USE **suspension structures**

cable-supported cantilever roofs
USE **cable-stayed structures**

cable-supported roofs, double-layer
USE **double-cable structures**

cable-supported structures
USE **cable-stayed structures**

cable-supported tents
USE **cable net structures**

cable tent structures
USE **cable net structures**

cabling
HN December 1990 scope note changed, source HAS deleted

cadastral maps
HN May 1991 scope note changed
SN Maps showing boundaries of subdivisions of land, buildings, or other details for purposes of describing and recording ownership. (DOD)

cadavres exquis
HN June 1990 added
BT *<drawings by technique>* VD.122
SN Images composed by several persons where each participant is not allowed to see the previous contributions. Popular among the Surrealists.
UF corpses, exquisite
exquisite corpses

Cadioéo
USE **Caduveo**

Caduveo
HN June 1990 lead-in term added
UF Cadioéo

cafés
HN February 1991 lead-in term added
UF bistros

cafeterias
HN June 1990 scope note added
SN Self-service establishments providing prepared food and drinks from long counters for on-premise or immediate consumption.

caisson piles
HN December 1990 scope note changed
SN Piles formed by driving a hollow tube into the ground, excavating within the tube, and filling it with concrete.

caissons
HN April 1991 moved
April 1991 scope note changed
BT *\<supporting and resisting elements\>* RT.59
SN Use for watertight boxes or cylinders serving to hold out water during excavation below the water table, often used for foundations.

calamities
USE **disasters**

calamities, natural
USE **natural disasters**

calcimine
HN August 1991 moved
BT **distemper paint**

calefactories
HN June 1990 scope note added
SN Use for the heated parlors or sitting rooms in monasteries. (RHDEL2)

calendars
HN May 1991 scope note changed
SN Use for registers of days. (WCOL9)

California black oak
HN June 1990 lead-in term added
UF Kellogg's oak

Californian Middle period
USE **Middle period Californian**

call girls
USE **prostitutes**

calottes
HN December 1990 scope note added
SN Denotes hemispherical, caplike domes; the term applies to small semidomes lacking a drum or lantern, small shallow domes used in the ceilings of rooms to increase headroom, small domes not pierced by oculi, and domelike plaster surfaces suspended within double-shell domes and often decorated.

camaieu
HN July 1990 deleted, made lead-in to **monochrome**

camaieu
USE **monochrome**

camber arches
HN December 1990 moved
December 1990 scope note changed
BT *\<arches by form: construction\>* RT.218
SN Use for arches whose intrados, and possibly the extrados, has a very slight rise; for arches with no curvature, use **flat arches.**

camber windows
HN April 1991 descriptor split, use camber arch (ALT of **camber arches**) + windows

cameo glass
HN June 1990 added
BT **cased glass**
UF glass, cameo

cames
HN December 1990 scope note changed
SN Slender bars of cast lead, with or without grooves, used in casement and stained glass windows to hold the pieces of glass in place.

camouflage
HN January 1991 scope note added
January 1991 alternate term added
October 1990 moved
BT *\<protective processes and techniques\>*
ALT **camouflaged**
SN The technique of disguising the appearance of beings or things so as to make them blend into their surroundings.

campaigns
HN May 1991 alternate term added
January 1991 scope note added
ALT **campaign**
SN Systematic courses of aggressive activities designed to persuade or establish power over others.

\<Canadian Arctic Native styles\>
HN April 1991 related term added
RT *\<Pre-Columbian Arctic and Subarctic styles\>*

Canadian Eskimo
USE **Inuit**

canary yellow
USE **light greenish yellow**

canchas
HN September 1990 scope note added
SN Denotes three-walled courts marked for playing jai alai.

candelilla wax
HN December 1990 moved
BT **vegetable wax**

candle guards
USE **candle screens**

candle screens
HN August 1991 added
BT **screens**
ALT **candle screen**
SN Small screens used to protect lighted candles; of a type made in the 18th century.
UF candle guards
candles, gauze
gauze candles
guards, candle
lantern screens
screens, candle
screens, lantern
table fire screens

candlenut oil
HN October 1990 moved
BT **vegetable oil**

candles, gauze
USE **candle screens**

canephorae
HN December 1990 scope note added
December 1990 descriptor changed, was **canephores**
December 1990 alternate term changed, was **canephore**
ALT **canephora**
SN Caryatids with baskets on their heads.

canonizations
HN May 1991 alternate term added
ALT **canonization**

canopies
HN May 1991 moved
May 1991 scope note changed
BT *\<rooflike enclosing structures\>*
SN Use for small, rooflike structures, often suspended and often ornamental, that provide or suggest shelter; found, for example, at entrances or over thrones or sacred objects.

canted walls
HN April 1991 deleted
BT *\<walls by form\>* RT.571

canterburies (storage furniture)
HN May 1991 moved
May 1991 descriptor changed, was **canterburies**
May 1991 alternate term changed, was **canterbury**
BT *\<storage and display furniture\>* TG.394
ALT **canterbury (storage furniture)**

cantilever footings
HN January 1991 moved
January 1991 scope note added
January 1991 descriptor changed, was **cantilevered footings**
January 1991 alternate term changed, was **cantilevered footing**
BT **combined footings**
ALT **cantilever footing**
SN Use for combined footings in which two independent footings are connected to each other to counterbalance an assymetrical load on one of them, usually one supporting an off-center exterior wall or column.

cantilever roofs, cable-supported
USE **cable-stayed structures**

cantilevers
HN December 1990 scope note changed
SN Any projecting elements fixed at one end and free at the other.

cantons (administrative bodies)
HN May 1991 descriptor changed, was **cantons**
May 1991 alternate term changed, was **canton**
ALT **canton (administrative body)**

cantorias
USE choir lofts

cantors
HN September 1990 lead-in terms added
UF cantors, Jewish
Jewish cantors

cantors, Jewish
USE cantors

canvas
HN July 1991 scope note changed
SN A firm, closely woven cloth made in various weights, usually of linen, hemp, or cotton, and used especially for clothing, sails, tarpaulins, awnings, and for painting supports.

canvas, glass
USE fiberglass

cap moldings
HN December 1990 lead-in terms added
UF cap trim
trim, cap

cap trim
USE cap moldings

capitalism
HN January 1991 alternate term added
ALT capitalist

capitals
HN December 1990 scope note added
SN The uppermost members of columns, piers, or pilasters.

capitals, cube
USE cushion capitals

capitals, proto-Ionic
USE Aeolic capitals

capitals, pseudo-Ionic
USE Aeolic capitals

captains, ship
USE shipmasters

captions
HN March 1991 added
BT <document genres by function> VW.293
ALT caption
SN Texts identifying or explaining, and printed in close proximity to, illustrations or other images.
UF legends (captions)

car washes
HN April 1990 added
BT <service industry buildings> RK.188
ALT car wash
SN Structures with equipment and facilities for the washing, waxing, and polishing of motor vehicles.
UF auto washes
washes, car

Carancahua
USE Karankawa

carbon ink
USE black carbon ink

carbonate, sodium
USE sodium carbonate

Carborundum (TM)
HN July 1990 added
BT abrasives
SN Sharp, hard, artificial abrasive in solid or powdered form composed of silicon carbide.

carborundum paper
HN July 1990 descriptor split, use Carborundum (TM) + paper

carborundum stones
HN July 1990 descriptor split, use Carborundum (TM) + stone

card games
HN April 1991 added
BT games
ALT card game
SN Games played with playing cards.
UF games, card
RT playing cards

cardboard, corrugated
USE corrugated board

carding
HN March 1991 alternate term added
ALT carded

cards, trading
USE trading cards

Caribbean pine
USE Cuban pine

carmine, dark
USE moderate red

carnauba wax
HN December 1990 moved
BT vegetable wax

carnivals
HN May 1991 alternate term added
ALT carnival

Carpenter Gothic
HN April 1991 lead-in terms added
April 1991 descriptor changed, was Carpenter's Gothic
UF Carpenteresque
Gothic, Carpenter

Carpenteresque
USE Carpenter Gothic

carports
HN June 1990 scope note added
SN Roofed shelters for automobiles, often without walls; usually associated with or projecting from a separate building.

Carrack porcelain
USE Kraak porcelain

carriage pieces
HN December 1990 lead-in term strings, rough deleted
December 1990 lead-in term changed, was rough strings
December 1990 lead-in term changed, was horses (stair components)
UF carriages (stair components)
roughstrings

carriages (stair components)
USE carriage pieces

carthamin
USE safflower (red pigment)

carving
HN November 1990 moved
BT <carving and carving techniques>

<carving and carving techniques>
HN November 1990 added
BT cutting

<carving techniques>
HN November 1990 added
BT <carving and carving techniques>

caryophil oil
USE oil of cloves

cascades
HN December 1990 moved
BT water features

cascades, chain
USE water chains

cascades, cordonata
USE water chains

cascades, step
USE water stairs (landscaped-site elements)

cased glass
HN June 1990 scope note changed, source DAC deleted

casemates
HN November 1990 moved
November 1990 scope note added
BT <fortification elements> RT.1166
SN Use for chambers, often vaulted, in ramparts, bastions, or other outer fortification elements with openings for the firing of artillery.

casement windows
HN November 1990 lead-in term added
UF casements

casements
USE casement windows

casements, hopper
USE hopper windows

cast products
USE castings

cast shadows
HN January 1991 alternate term added
ALT cast shadow

castings
- HN January 1991 scope note added
  November 1990 moved
  August 1990 lead-in terms added
- BT <materials by technique> MT.2738
- SN Use in industrial and building trade contexts for objects made by casting. For sculptural works made by casting, use **casts.**
- UF cast products
  products, cast

castor oil
- HN October 1990 moved
- BT **vegetable oil**

cataclysms
USE **disasters**

Catalan vaults
USE **timbrel vaults**

cataloging
- HN January 1991 scope note added
- SN Systematically analyzing and describing items in a collection and arranging the information into a catalog.

cataloging, subject
USE **subject cataloging**

catalogs, sales
USE **sales catalogs**

catane dacqua
USE **water chains**

catastrophes
USE **disasters**

catches, eaves
USE **eaves boards**

cathedral ceilings
- HN April 1991 scope note added
- SN Use for ceilings formed by or suggesting open-timbered roofs, often higher than the ceilings of the other rooms in the building. (RHDEL2)

Catoquina
USE **Catukina**

Catukina
- HN June 1990 lead-in term changed, was **Catoquina Indians**
- UF Catoquina

catwalks
- HN November 1990 scope note changed
  November 1990 lead-in term **catladders** deleted
  November 1990 lead-in term **duckboards** deleted
- SN Narrow fixed walkways providing access to an otherwise inaccessible area or to lighting units, such as used above an auditorium or stage.

cauliculi
- HN November 1990 scope note changed
  November 1990 descriptor changed, was **caulicoles**
  November 1990 alternate term changed, was **caulicole**
- ALT **cauliculus**
- SN Ornamental stalks rising between the leaves of a Corinthian capital, from which the volutes spring and upon which the fleurons are sometimes supported.

cavaliers
- HN November 1990 scope note changed
- SN Use for raised, defensible works erected within a fortified place or by besiegers to command enemy positions within firing range.

cave art
- HN May 1991 scope note added
  December 1990 moved
- BT **rock art**
- SN Use for prehistoric art, especially Paleolithic, found in caves, including paintings, carvings, and certain artifacts.

cave drawings
- HN October 1990 deleted, made lead-in term in hierarchy under development

caveae
- HN June 1990 scope note added
- SN Use for the tiered, semicircular seating areas in ancient, especially Roman, theaters and amphitheaters.

cavetto moldings
- HN November 1990 scope note changed
- SN Moldings with a rounded concave surface, usually a quarter circle.

cavities, altar
USE **sepulchers**

cavity floors
USE **suspended floors**

cavity walls
- HN November 1990 scope note added
- SN Walls, usually of masonry, and usually exterior, consisting of two wythes separated by a continuous air space, the wythes held together by metal stays or wires.

cavo relievo
USE **intaglio**

CD-ROMs
- HN September 1991 added
- BT **compact disks**
- ALT **CD-ROM**
- SN Compact disks on which a large amount of digitized read-only data can be stored. (RHDEL2)
- UF compact disks read-only memory

CDCs
USE **community design centers**

cedar, oil of
USE **oil of cedar**

cedarwood oil
USE **oil of cedar**

ceiling joists
- HN March 1991 moved
- BT **joists**

ceilings
- HN November 1990 scope note changed
- SN The overhead surfaces of interior spaces, sometimes constructed to mask building systems or structural elements.

celebrations
- HN May 1991 alternate term added
- ALT **celebration**

celebrations, centennial
USE **centennials**

cellae
- HN October 1990 added
- BT <temple spaces> RM.335
- ALT **cella**
- SN Use for the sanctuaries of temples.

Cellosolve (TM)
USE **ethylene glycol monoethyl ether**

cellular frames
USE **box frames**

cellulose fiber
USE **excelsior**

cellulose fiber, wood
USE **excelsior**

Celotex (TM)
USE **fiberboard**

cement (adhesive)
USE **adhesives**

cement, plastic
USE **plastic cement**

censors
- HN May 1991 added
- BT <people by activity> HG.705
- ALT **censor**
- SN Officials who examine publications, motion pictures, correspondence, or other forms of public or private communication for the purpose of suppressing any material in them deemed objectionable on moral, political, military, or other grounds.

centenaries
USE **centennials**

centennial celebrations
USE **centennials**

centennials
- HN March 1991 added
- BT **anniversaries**
- ALT **centennial**
- SN One-hundredth anniversaries or their celebrations. (RHDEL2)

UF celebrations, centennial
centenaries
centennial celebrations

centering
HN April 1990 added
BT falsework
SN Temporary construction, usually of wood, over which arches and vaults are formed and held until they become self-supporting.

centers
HN January 1991 alternate term added
ALT center

centers, alumni
USE **alumni centers**

centers, community design
USE **community design centers**

centers, crisis
USE **crisis shelters**

centers, distribution
USE **distribution centers**

centers, fitness
USE **health clubs**

centers, job training
USE **training centers**

centers, physical fitness
USE **health clubs**

centers, skill training
USE **training centers**

centers, training
USE **training centers**

centers, world trade
USE **world trade centers**

central air conditioning
HN November 1990 scope note added
SN Air conditioning systems run from one or more centralized units that provide controlled air to an entire building or complex.

Central Asian
HN June 1990 lead-in term changed, was Transoxiana
UF Transoxianan

centrifugal casting
HN March 1991 alternate term added
ALT centrifugal-cast

ceramics, studio
USE **studio ceramics**

ceremonies
HN May 1991 alternate term added
January 1991 lead-in term added
ALT ceremony
UF rites

ceresin
HN December 1990 moved
BT ozokerite

cerography
HN July 1990 lead-in term added
UF wax engraving

certified checks
HN July 1991 moved to hierarchy under development

certifying
HN March 1991 alternate term added
ALT certified

Ch'êng-hua
USE **Chenghua**

chain cascades
USE **water chains**

chain courses
HN April 1991 scope note changed
SN Masonry courses of headers fastened together continuously by metal clamps. (RS)

chains, water
USE **water chains**

chair lifts
HN July 1991 scope note changed
November 1990 moved
BT ski lifts
SN Use for a series of chairlike elements suspended from an endless cable designed for carrying skiers up a slope. (RHDEL2)

chalcography
USE **copper engraving**
engraving (printing process)

chalice capitals
HN November 1990 deleted
BT capitals

chalk
HN November 1990 lead-in term **lime white** deleted
November 1990 lead-in term **English white** deleted

chalk engraving
USE **crayon manner**

chalk manner
USE **crayon manner**

chalk method
USE **crayon manner**

chambers, drawing
USE **drawing rooms**

chambers, withdrawing
USE **drawing rooms**

Chamula
USE **Tzotzil**

chancel screens
HN September 1991 scope note changed
November 1990 lead-in term **chancel enclosures** deleted
SN Use for partitions in Christian churches separating the chancel from the body of the church, particularly

when the chancel does not also include a choir. Use **choir screens** for the screens around the choir when the choristers are seated in the chancel area. For screens separating the sanctuary from the nave in Orthodox Eastern churches, use **iconostases**.

chancels
HN August 1991 scope note changed
SN Use for spaces in Christian churches containing the high altar and reserved for the use of the clergy. Includes the choir when present. Use **choirs** for the spaces in Christian churches, generally between the altar area and the nave, reserved for choristers.

channel beams
USE **channels (rolled sections)**

channel lights
HN May 1990 added
BT aeronautical ground lights
ALT channel light
SN Aeronautical ground lights along the sides of a channel of a water airport. (IESREF)
UF lights, channel

channels (rolled sections)
HN November 1990 scope note changed
November 1990 lead-in term added
November 1990 descriptor changed, was **channel beams**
November 1990 alternate term changed, was **channel beam**
ALT channel (rolled section)
SN Use for metal members having a C- or U-shaped section.
UF channel beams

channels (water body components)
HN September 1991 descriptor changed, was **channels**
September 1991 alternate term changed, was **channel**
ALT channel (water body component)

chapter houses
HN April 1991 lead-in terms added
UF chapter rooms
rooms, chapter

chapter rooms
USE **chapter houses**

chaptrels
HN April 1991 deleted
BT capitals

charettes
HN May 1991 alternate term added
ALT charette

charging
USE **rolling up**

charts
HN July 1991 scope note added
SN Arrangements of information in

tabular form or in a graphic representation, as by curves, of a fluctuating variable.

charts, time zone
USE time zone maps

Chavín horizon
HN September 1991 moved
BT Early horizon

check stamping
HN March 1991 alternate term changed, was check stamped
ALT check-stamped

checkpoints
USE border inspection stations

checks
HN July 1991 moved to hierarchy under development

cheeks, door
USE doorjambs

chemical closets
USE chemical toilets

chemical properties
HN January 1991 alternate term added
ALT chemical property

chemical pulp
HN July 1990 added
BT wood pulp
UF chemical wood pulp
pulp, chemical
wood pulp, chemical

chemical toilets
HN June 1991 lead-in terms added
June 1991 descriptor changed, was waterless toilets
June 1991 alternate term changed, was waterless toilet
ALT chemical toilet
UF chemical closets
closets, chemical
toilets, chemical
waterless toilets

chemical wood pulp
USE chemical pulp

chemical wood pulp board
USE conservation board

chemistry
HN January 1991 alternate term added
ALT chemical

Chêng chou
USE Zhengzhou

Chengchow
USE Zhengzhou

Chenghua
HN June 1990 lead-in term added
UF Chêng-hua

chevroned bands
USE zigzags

Chicago School
HN June 1990 added
BT <modern North American architecture styles and movements> FL.1730

Chicano
USE Mexican American

chiffoniers (chests of drawers)
HN May 1991 descriptor changed, was chiffoniers
May 1991 alternate term changed, was chiffonier
ALT chiffonier (chest of drawers)

childbirths
USE births

childhood
HN February 1991 added
BT <life stages>
SN The earliest developmental stage of a living being.

childhood, early
USE infancy

children
HN February 1991 scope note added
SN People in the earliest developmental stage of life.

children's playhouses
HN September 1990 scope note added
SN Use for small houselike structures designed for children to play in. (RHDEL2)

Chilkat
HN June 1991 added
BT Tlingit

chill
USE bloom

chilled water systems
HN November 1990 scope note added
SN Air cooling systems in which cold water is circulated between mechanical refrigeration water chilling units and remote cooling equipment.

chimes, door
USE doorbells

chimney bars
HN November 1990 scope note changed
SN Metal lintels that support the masonry above fireplace openings.

chimney breasts
HN July 1991 scope note changed
November 1990 lead-in term chimney pieces deleted
SN Use for portions of chimneys that project from the general wall plane into the room, often decorated with mantels and overmantels.

chimney caps
HN July 1991 scope note changed
SN Uppermost cornices, of masonry or other noncombustible material, atop chimneys; for extra components placed above and covering flue openings, use chimney hoods.

chimney cheeks
HN November 1990 scope note changed
SN Use for masonry on either side of a fireplace opening that supports the mantel and upper chimney construction. (MEANS)

chimney hoods
HN July 1991 scope note changed
SN Coverings that protect chimney openings; for cornicelike terminations to chimneys, use chimney caps, for extensions placed on top of chimneys to improve draft or appearance, and which generally extend the flue, use chimney pots.

chimney pieces
USE mantels

chimney pots
HN November 1990 scope note added
SN Use for metal, masonry, or ceramic extensions which continue the flue on top of chimneys to improve draft or appearance; for extensions that protect chimney openings and may serve to block rain, use chimney hoods.

chimney stacks
HN November 1990 scope note changed
November 1990 lead-in terms added
SN Use for chimneys containing a number of flues, especially when rising as shafts above a roof.
UF chimney stalks
stalks, chimney

chimney stalks
USE chimney stacks

chimneys
HN November 1990 scope note added
SN Use for vertical noncombustible structures containing flues for drawing off into the outside air products of combustion from, for example, stoves, fireplaces, and furnaces.

China clay
USE kaolin

China paper
HN July 1990 added
BT <paper by form> MT.1903
UF Chinese paper
India paper
India proof paper
paper, China
paper, India

Chinese ink
HN June 1991 moved
BT <ink by composition or origin>

Chinese insect wax
HN December 1990 moved
BT insect wax

Chinese paper
USE **China paper**

Chinese silk
HN   June 1991 moved
BT   *<cloth by composition or origin>*
      MT.1845

Chinese white
USE **kaolinite**

chloride, ammonium
USE **ammonium chloride**

chloride, ferric
USE **ferric chloride**

chloride, iron
USE **ferric chloride**

chloride, sodium
USE **sodium chloride**

chlorofluorocarbons
HN   February 1991 alternate term added
      May 1990 lead-in term added
ALT **chlorofluorocarbon**
UF   Freons (TM)

choir lofts
HN   June 1990 lead-in term changed, was
      cantoriae
UF   cantorias

choir screens
HN   August 1991 scope note changed
SN   Use for screens in Christian churches
      that separate the choir from the nave
      and aisles of a church. For partitions
      that separate the chancel from the
      nave of the church, use **chancel
      screens.**

choir stalls
HN   August 1991 scope note changed
SN   Stalls in the choir area of a church.

choirs
HN   September 1991 scope note changed
SN   Use for spaces in Christian churches,
      generally between the altar area or
      sanctuary and the nave, reserved for
      choristers. For spaces containing the
      altar area and the choir, when pre-
      sent, use **chancels.** For elevated plat-
      forms from which a choir, often
      composed of laity, sings, use **choir
      lofts.**

chop marks (printers' marks)
USE **chops**

Chopi
HN   June 1990 lead-in term added
UF   Valenge

chops
HN   April 1990 added
BT   *<marks by location or context>* VW.726
ALT **chop**
SN   Identifying marks stamped on prints
      by printers, artists, print workshops,
      or publishers; often embossed. (TY-
      LER)

UF   chop marks (printers' marks)
      marks, chop (printers' marks)

chords
HN   November 1990 scope note changed
SN   Principal members of trusses that
      extend the length of the truss. (DAC)

Chou
USE **Zhou**

CHP generating plants
USE **cogeneration plants**

chrismatories
HN   November 1990 deleted
BT   *<Christian religious building fixtures>*
      RT.1223

christenings
HN   May 1991 alternate term added
ALT **christening**

chromium alloys
HN   February 1991 alternate term added
ALT **chromium alloy**

chromolithography
HN   October 1991 moved
      October 1991 scope note changed
BT   **color lithography**
SN   A type of color lithography used
      commercially in the latter half of the
      19th century.

chronophotographs
HN   May 1991 scope note changed
SN   Use for photographs that record
      movement or change in a series of
      images, regardless of the amount of
      time intervening. For a series of im-
      ages capturing an action, as of a hu-
      man figure or animal, use **motion
      photographs.** For photographs ar-
      ranged to be seen in a specified or-
      der, use **sequences.**

chronophotography
HN   May 1991 lead-in term **serial pho-
      tography** deleted
      May 1991 lead-in term **sequential
      photography** deleted

Cibachrome (TM)
HN   May 1991 scope note changed
SN   A subtractive color process for mak-
      ing photographic prints and trans-
      parencies using a silver-dye bleach
      process. Also marketed under the
      name Cilchrome.

Ciboney
HN   June 1990 lead-in term added
UF   Siboney

ciboria
HN   July 1991 scope note changed
SN   Roofed structures with four or more
      columns built over an altar; for sus-
      pended, projecting, or freestanding
      canopies over such features as al-
      tars, thrones, or doorways, use **bal-
      dachins.** (NCE)

cider barns
USE **cider mills**

cider houses
USE **cider mills**

cider mills
HN   April 1990 added
BT   **beverage processing plants**
ALT **cider mill**
SN   Use for buildings in which apples are
      put through a press in order to pro-
      duce cider.
UF   barns, cider
      cider barns
      cider houses
      houses, cider
      mills, cider

cinctures
HN   December 1990 moved
      December 1990 scope note changed
BT   *<shaft components>* RT.143
SN   Use for moldings located at the top
      or bottom of column shafts, espe-
      cially of Classical design; for molded
      bands on shafts in Gothic architec-
      ture, not located at the ends, use
      shaft rings. For angular bands
      around the base of the Doric echinus,
      use **annulets.**

cirage
HN   July 1990 deleted
BT   **camaieu**

circles
HN   July 1991 alternate term added
ALT **circle**

circuits
HN   December 1990 scope note added
SN   Use for the complete paths taken by
      electric currents flowing through
      conductors, usually wires, from one
      terminal of a generating source
      through energy-consuming units and
      returning through different conduc-
      tors, usually wires, back to another
      terminal on the power source.
      (STEIN)

circulation (collections management)
HN   July 1991 descriptor changed, was
      circulation

circumcisions
HN   February 1991 alternate term added
      February 1991 descriptor changed,
      was circumcision
ALT **circumcision**

circuses (performances)
HN   May 1991 alternate term added
      May 1991 descriptor changed, was
      circuses
ALT **circus (performance)**

citizen participation
HN   February 1991 related term added
      April 1990 lead-in terms added
UF   participation, public
RT   public participation
      voting

citron yellow
USE **strong greenish yellow**

city maps
HN April 1991 descriptor split, use city (ALT of cities) + maps

city planning
HN November 1991 lead-in term design, urban deleted
February 1991 lead-in term urban design deleted

city plans
HN April 1991 descriptor split, use city (ALT of cities) + plans

civic design
USE **city planning**

civic improvement
HN January 1991 scope note added
SN Beautifying or improving the working condition of small-scale public amenities in a municipality, such as sidewalks, road signs, and green areas.

civil liberties
USE **civil rights**

civil rights
HN September 1991 scope note added
September 1991 lead-in terms added
September 1991 alternate term added
ALT **civil right**
SN Personal liberties that belong to each individual due to his or her status as a citizen of a particular country or community. (GALAW)
UF civil liberties
liberties, civil

civil wars
HN January 1991 scope note added
January 1991 alternate term added
November 1990 moved
January 1990 descriptor changed, was civil war
BT **wars**
ALT **civil war**
SN Wars between different sections or parties of the same nation. (W)

cladding
HN July 1991 moved
July 1991 scope note changed
July 1991 related term added
July 1991 alternate term added
BT *<metal assembling processes and techniques>* KT.788
ALT **clad**
SN Bonding one metal to another, as to protect the inner metal from corrosion or for minting coins.
RT **bonding (joining)**

clamshell buckets
HN January 1991 lead-in term added
UF clamshell grabs

clamshell grabs
USE **clamshell buckets**

clans
HN May 1991 moved
BT *<kinship groups>* HG.879

class, upper
USE **upper class**

classifying
HN March 1991 alternate term added
ALT **classified**

classroom windows
HN December 1990 scope note changed
SN Windows designed to meet the requirements of school buildings, usually featuring large multipaned glass areas.

claw hammers
HN January 1991 lead-in term added
UF khivi

clay, pipe
USE **pipe clay**

clearinghouses
HN February 1991 moved
BT **information services**

clergy
HN April 1991 alternate term added
ALT **clergyman**

clerical workers
HN September 1990 lead-in term added
UF clerks

clerks
USE **clerical workers**

clichés-glace
USE **clichés-verre**

clichés-verre
HN May 1991 lead-in term added
UF clichés-glace

climate control, indoor
USE **HVAC**

climatic charts
HN March 1991 descriptor split, use climate + charts

clippings files
HN March 1990 alternate term changed, was clipping file
ALT **clippings file**

cloister garths
HN June 1990 scope note changed
SN Open courtyards surrounded by walkways, especially in a group of buildings of a monastery or college. (W)

cloister vaults
HN October 1991 scope note changed
August 1991 lead-in term cloistered arches deleted
August 1991 lead-in term cloistered vaults deleted
August 1991 lead-in term arches, cloistered deleted
August 1991 lead-in term vaults, cloistered deleted
SN Use for vaults shaped like a pyramid with sides that bow outward.

cloisters
HN June 1990 scope note changed
SN Enclosed spaces composed of a garth and surrounding walkways, which are generally arcaded on the courtyard side and walled on the other; usually found in Christian religious building complexes. Use for such features in secular buildings only when closely resembling the prototype.

closets, chemical
USE **chemical toilets**

cloth, rubberized
USE **rubberized cloth**

cloud bands
HN June 1990 lead-in terms added
UF cloud pattern
pattern, cloud

cloud pattern
USE **cloud bands**

clove oil
USE **oil of cloves**

cloverleaf interchanges
USE **cloverleafs**

cloverleafs
HN June 1990 lead-in terms added
June 1990 scope note added
SN Road arrangements, resembling four-leaf clovers in plan, for permitting easy traffic movement between intersecting highways. (RHDEL2)
UF cloverleaf interchanges
interchanges, cloverleaf

cloves, oil of
USE **oil of cloves**

<club complexes>
HN November 1991 added
BT **recreation areas**

clubs, health
USE **health clubs**

clustered piers
USE **compound piers**

coating, roller
USE **roller painting**

cocoawood
USE **granadilla**

cocos wood
USE **granadilla**

cocuswood
USE **granadilla**

coefficient of reflection
USE **reflectance**

coefficient, reflection
USE **reflectance**

coelanaglyphic relief
HN November 1990 added
BT **relief**
SN Relief technique in which the surface of the block is allowed to remain as background and the figures are carved with positive projections within the surface. (OCA)
UF relief, sunk
sunk relief

coffering
USE **coffers (ceiling components)**

coffers (ceiling components)
HN December 1990 lead-in term changed, was **coffering (ceiling components)**
UF coffering

cogeneration facilities
USE **cogeneration plants**

cogeneration plants
HN December 1990 added
BT **power plants**
ALT **cogeneration plant**
SN Use for power plants that simultaneously generate from the same source electrical energy and useful heat energy.
UF CHP generating plants
cogeneration facilities
cogeneration systems
combined cycle power plants
combined heat and power generating plants
facilities, cogeneration
generating plants, CHP
plants, CHP generating
plants, cogeneration
plants, combined cycle power
plants, combined heat and power generating
power generating plants, combined heat and
power plants, combined cycle
systems, cogeneration

cogeneration systems
USE **cogeneration plants**

cohousing (TM)
HN April 1990 added
BT **communal housing**
SN A type of small communal housing development, designed and managed by the occupants, in which each resident family owns a home and shares with the group common fa-cilities, such as kitchens, child care centers, and laundry rooms, and their associated tasks.

coiffeuses (tables)
HN September 1991 descriptor changed, was **coiffeuses**
September 1991 alternate term changed, was **coiffeuse**
ALT coiffeuse (table)

coil building
USE **coiling**

coiling
HN November 1990 lead-in term added
UF coil building

coils
HN December 1990 scope note added
SN Piping or tubing in various configurations employed in cooling or heating systems to serve as heat exchangers.

coils (spirals)
USE **spirals**

cold-pressed paper
HN July 1990 added
BT <paper by production method> MT.1961
SN Paper having a medium to rough finish created by running the sheets through a series of coated metal cylinders.
UF paper, cold-pressed

cold welding
HN March 1991 alternate term changed, was **cold welded**
ALT cold-welded

collage
HN July 1990 scope note added
SN Use for the technique of making compositions in two dimensions or very low relief by gluing paper, fabrics, photographs, or other materials onto a flat surface. If heavy three-dimensional objects dominate, use **assemblage**. If the constituent fragments form a somewhat unified image, use **montage**.

collagraph printing
HN October 1991 moved
October 1991 scope note changed
October 1990 lead-in term added
BT <printing processes>
SN Printing process in which the printing surface is created by gluing objects to a support; can be printed in intaglio or relief or can be blind printed. (PETERD)
UF collagraphy

collagraphy
USE **collagraph printing**

collar beam roofs
HN November 1990 descriptor split, use **collar beam** (ALT of **collar beams**) + **roofs**

collar beams
HN December 1990 moved
BT <horizontal roof frame components>

colleges
HN September 1990 scope note added
SN Use for buildings or groups of buildings that house institutions of higher learning that provide general or liberal arts education leading to bachelor's degrees; may be independent or parts of universities.

colleges, military
USE **military academies**

cololches
HN December 1990 scope note changed
SN Thin wood poles used in modern Mayan building construction. (DWELL)

<Colonial Latin American architecture styles> FL.1710
HN June 1991 moved
BT <Colonial Latin American styles> FL.1707

<Colonial Latin American fine arts styles> FL.1716
HN June 1991 moved
BT <Colonial Latin American styles> FL.1707

<Colonial Latin American styles> FL.1707
HN June 1991 moved
BT **Latin American**

Colonial, British
USE **British Colonial**

colonization
HN June 1991 lead-in term added
January 1991 alternate term added
November 1990 moved
BT <governmental functions> KG.176
ALT colonized
UF colonizing

colonizing
USE **colonization**

colonnades
HN December 1990 scope note changed
SN Use for rows of columns supporting an entablature and often one side of a roof. Includes spaces behind such a feature when they are long and used for circulation.

colonnettes
HN November 1990 scope note changed
SN Use for small or slender columns; for small Medieval columns, usually attached to architectural features, use **shafts (Medieval columns)**.

color lithography
HN March 1991 added
BT **lithography**
SN Printing by lithography using a sep-

arate stone or plate for each color. (LG)
UF lithography, color

color printing
  HN October 1991 moved
  BT *<printing processes>*

color separation
  HN October 1990 moved
  BT *<printing techniques>*

color, body
USE **gouache**

color, encaustic
USE **encaustic paint**

color, scenic
USE **distemper paint**

color, size
USE **distemper paint**

colored ink
  HN June 1991 moved
  BT *<ink by property>*

colors, achromatic
USE **neutrals**

colors, artists
USE **artists colors**

colorwashing
  HN March 1991 alternate term added
  ALT **colorwashed**

colour, reflected
USE **reflected color**

column screens
USE **columnar screens**

columnae caelatae
  HN November 1990 deleted
  BT *<columns by form>* RT.84

columnar screens
  HN April 1990 added
  BT *<enclosing structural elements>* RT.387
  ALT **columnar screen**
  SN Use for rows of columns that serve primarily to separate interior spaces.
  UF column screens
      columned screens
      screens, columnar

columned screens
USE **columnar screens**

columns
  HN July 1991 scope note changed
  SN Use for cylindrical, upright masonry members, usually either giving support or appearing to give support and usually comprised of three sections: a base, capital, and shaft; common also on furniture, especially as decorative elements. Use also for all uprights in steel frame or concrete frame structures. For square or rectangular members, either in masonry construction or classically

treated, and for massive uprights in Medieval architecture, use **piers**; for wooden square uprights, use **posts**.

columns (TM), Lally
USE **Lally columns (TM)**

columns, applied
USE **engaged columns**

columns, blocked
USE **banded columns**

columns, knotted
USE **knotted columns**

columns, paired
USE **coupled columns**

combined cycle power plants
USE **cogeneration plants**

combined footings
  HN January 1991 scope note changed
  SN Use for footings that are slabs under two or more columns or columns and a wall, one of which is internal rather than on the perimeter so that the footing cannot take a beamlike form.

combined heat and power generating plants
USE **cogeneration plants**

combined loads
  HN January 1991 alternate term added
  ALT **combined load**

commencements
  HN May 1991 alternate term added
  ALT **commencement**

commercial agents
  HN April 1991 lead-in terms added
  UF agents, business
      business agents

common joists
  HN March 1991 deleted, made lead-in to **joists**

common joists
USE **joists**

common salt
USE **sodium chloride**

communicating
  HN June 1991 lead-in term added
      January 1991 scope note added
      January 1991 alternate term added
  ALT **communicated**
  SN Conveying awareness, knowledge, or information to others.
  UF communication

communication
USE **communicating**

communion records
  HN March 1991 descriptor split, use **communion + records**

communions
  HN February 1991 alternate term added
      February 1991 descriptor changed, was **communion**
  ALT **communion**

communism
  HN January 1991 alternate term added
  ALT **communist**

communities, golf course
USE **golf course communities**

community colleges
  HN September 1990 scope note added
  SN Colleges, typically without residential facilities, serving the educational needs of a specific community.

community design centers
  HN July 1990 added
  BT **social services**
  ALT **community design center**
  SN Use for multidisciplinary, nonprofit organizations comprised of professionals, generally architects and planners, and volunteers working to improve social and economic conditions in a neighborhood or community.
  UF CDCs
      centers, community design
      design centers, community

community development
  HN January 1991 scope note added
  SN Activity of solving or ameliorating a community's social and economic problems, organized and controlled mainly by the community itself. (TSIT)

community schools
  HN April 1990 added
  BT *<schools by function>* RK.794
  ALT **community school**
  SN Designates schools whose facilities and programs are closely connected with the life and needs of, and may be shared by, the whole community.
  UF schools, community

compact disks
  HN September 1991 scope note added
      July 1991 moved
  BT **optical disks**
  SN Optical disks on which programs, data, or music are digitally encoded for a laser beam to scan, decode, and transmit to a playback system, computer monitor, or television set. (RHDEL2)

compact disks read-only memory
USE **CD-ROMs**

compaction
  HN March 1991 alternate term added
  ALT **compacted**

companion pieces
USE **pendants (companion pieces)**

comparing
HN January 1991 scope note added
January 1991 alternate term added
ALT **compared**
SN Examining two or more entities in order to note relative similarities and differences.

compartments, WC
USE **toilet compartments**

compensation (economic concept)
HN April 1991 scope note added
April 1991 lead-in term added
February 1991 descriptor changed, was **compensation**
SN Something given or received in return for goods or services, or as settlement of a debt or injury. (TSIT)
UF remuneration

competitions
HN May 1991 alternate term added
ALT **competition**

competitions, invited
USE **invited competitions**

competitions, limited
USE **limited competitions**

competitions, open
USE **open competitions**

competitions, student
USE **student competitions**

complementary colors
HN January 1991 alternate term added
ALT **complementary color**

Composite order
HN December 1990 scope note added
SN Designates an architectural order characterized by capitals composed of foliate echini derived from the Corinthian order superposed by volutes derived from the Ionic order.

composites, fibrous
USE **fibrous composites**

composites, fibrous reinforced
USE **fibrous composites**

composites, filament reinforced
USE **fibrous composites**

compound piers
HN April 1991 scope note added
April 1991 lead-in terms added
SN Use for piers composed of several engaged columns or pilasters grouped around a central core.
UF clustered piers
piers, clustered

compound vaults
HN August 1991 scope note changed, RS added as source

computational linguistics
HN April 1990 scope note added
SN Branch of linguistics concerned with the use of computers for the analysis and synthesis of language data, as in translation, word frequency counts, and speech recognition and synthesis. (ERIC9)

computer-aided design
HN March 1991 moved
BT *<image-making processes and techniques>* KT.171

computer art
HN October 1991 moved
BT *<art genres>* BM.229

computer programmers
HN September 1990 lead-in term added
UF programmers

computer programming
HN January 1991 scope note added
SN Composing precise, logical sequences of instructions that direct the actions of a computer or computer system.

computerization
USE **automation**

concave relief
USE **intaglio**

concentrated loads
HN January 1991 alternate term added
ALT **concentrated load**

concentration camps
HN April 1991 scope note added
SN Designates internment centers established outside ordinary detention systems in which persons are confined for military or political security or for punishment or exploitation; persons are generally imprisoned by decree or military order, often including classes or groups of people without regard for their individual culpability. (ENCYB)

concentric arches
HN March 1991 descriptor split, use concentric + arches

concert halls
HN September 1990 scope note added
SN Use for buildings designed for musical performances.

concerts
HN May 1991 alternate term added
ALT **concert**

conches (semidomes)
USE **semidomes**

conchs
HN April 1991 scope note source changed to RK

concrete joist systems, one-way
USE **one-way joist systems**

concrete poetry
HN September 1991 scope note changed
July 1991 moved
BT **visual poetry**
SN Works of visual poetry from the 1950s and 1960s associated with the concrete poetry movement; employ language elements but often out of syntax, to be seen but not read.

concrete slab systems, waffle
USE **waffle slabs**

concrete, plastic
USE **polymer-impregnated concrete**

concrete, porous
USE **lightweight concrete**

<conditions and effects: architecture>
HN October 1990 added
BT *<conditions and effects>* KT.885

<conditions and effects: photography>
HN October 1990 added
BT *<conditions and effects>* KT.885

<conditions and effects: printing and printmaking>
HN October 1990 added
BT *<conditions and effects>* KT.885

<conditions and effects: textiles>
HN June 1991 added
BT *<conditions and effects>* KT.885

conductors (downspouts)
USE **downspouts**

conductors (materials)
HN May 1991 descriptor changed, was conductors

conductors (musicians)
HN May 1991 descriptor changed, was conductors (music)
May 1991 alternate term changed, was conductor (music)
ALT **conductor (musician)**

cones
HN January 1991 alternate term added
ALT **cone**

conferences
HN May 1991 alternate term added
ALT **conference**

confirmations
HN February 1991 alternate term added
February 1991 descriptor changed, was **confirmation**
ALT **confirmation**

congés
USE **apophyges**

Congo copal
HN June 1990 scope note added
SN A general name for fossil and other hard resins found in nearly all tropical countries and used in making varnishes and lacquers, adhesives,

and coatings, though now largely replaced by synthetic resins. (MH)

Congregational
HN   July 1991 lead-in term added
UF   Congregationalist

Congregationalist
USE **Congregational**

consecrations
HN   February 1991 alternate term added
     February 1991 descriptor changed, was consecration
ALT **consecration**

conservation board
HN   July 1990 added
BT   **cardboard**
SN   Board composed of purified cellulose pulp from wood where lignin has been removed and to which an alkaline buffer has been added. (SAITZY)
UF   board, chemical wood pulp
     board, conservation
     chemical wood pulp board

conservation scientists
HN   August 1991 added
BT   **scientists**
ALT **conservation scientist**
SN   Scientists who analyze and do research on materials and methods used in conservation.
UF   scientists, conservation

conservatism
HN   January 1991 alternate term added
ALT **conservative**

conservators
HN   November 1991 lead-in term conservation technicians deleted
     October 1991 lead-in term conservation scientists deleted
     August 1991 moved
BT   *<people in arts-related occupations>* HG.162

consolidated schools
HN   September 1990 scope note added
SN   Use for schools formed by the merging of two or more public schools, usually at the elementary level and often in rural areas. (W)

consolidation (masonry)
HN   March 1991 alternate term added
ALT **consolidated**

construction equipment
HN   April 1991 lead-in terms added
UF   building machinery
     construction machinery

construction loads
HN   January 1991 alternate term added
ALT **construction load**

construction machinery
USE **construction equipment**

construction paper
HN   July 1990 added
BT   *<paper by function>* MT.1924
SN   Inexpensive colored paper suitable for crayon and ink drawings, watercolors, and for making paper cutouts. (W)
UF   paper, construction

construction, fast-track
USE **fast-track method**

construction, incremental self-help
USE **incremental housing**

construction, metal pan
USE **one-way joist systems**

construction, one-way joist
USE **one-way joist systems**

construction, phased
USE **fast-track method**

construction, platform frame
USE **platform frames**

construction, poteaux sur solle
USE **poteaux sur solle construction**

construction, slab (pottery technique)
USE **slab method**

construction, stressed-skin
USE **stressed-skin structures**

construction, tube-in-tube
USE **tube structures**

constructions, beam-and-girder
USE **one-way beam and slab systems**

constructions, beam-and-slab floor
USE **one-way beam and slab systems**
     two-way beam and slab systems

constructions, one-way
USE **one-way structural systems**

Conté crayon (TM)
HN   July 1991 scope note changed
SN   Mixture of graphite and clay in white, sepia, sanguine, and three grades of black; used by artists in the form of a hard crayon. (W)

Conté crayons (TM)
HN   July 1990 deleted
BT   **crayons**

contests
HN   May 1991 alternate term added
ALT **contest**

contextualism
HN   January 1991 alternate term added
ALT **contextualist**

continuing education centers
HN   September 1990 scope note added
SN   Use for buildings designed to meet the needs of a continuing education program.

continuous casting
HN   March 1991 alternate term added
ALT **continuous-cast**

continuous footings
HN   December 1990 scope note changed
SN   Use for footings that support a wall or a number of columns in a line.

contracting
HN   February 1991 scope note changed
     February 1991 lead-in term contracting out deleted
SN   The entering of two or more legally competent parties into a binding agreement to do or not to do something, subject to specified terms and conditions.

contraction
HN   March 1991 alternate term added
ALT **contracted**

contrapposto
HN   April 1990 scope note changed, W added as source

control rooms
HN   June 1990 scope note changed
SN   Use for rooms containing control equipment, common examples being in broadcasting stations, auditoriums, and theaters.

control signals, traffic
USE **traffic signals**

convection heaters
USE **convectors**

convectors
HN   December 1990 scope note added
     December 1990 lead-in terms added
SN   Use for room heating units consisting of a heating device, often a finned tube, mounted in a metal enclosure with openings to allow the transfer of heat to the air, principally by convection.
UF   convection heaters
     heaters, convection

convex conoidal vaults
HN   December 1990 descriptor split, use
     convex + **conoidal vaults**

conveying systems
HN   December 1990 scope note added
SN   Use for building systems designed to move people, equipment, or goods through a building or complex; for networks of equipment designed to move similar items through and between settlements, use **transit systems**; for machinery designed for the continuous transport of material, use **conveyors**.

convicts
HN   February 1991 added
BT   *<people by state or condition>* HG.775
ALT **convict**
SN   Use for those serving a prison sen-

tence following conviction for a criminal offense. For those involuntarily confined in prison or kept in custody, use **prisoners**. For those confined to an institutional facility voluntarily or involuntarily, use **inmates**.
RT inmates
    prisoners

convocations
HN May 1991 alternate term added
ALT **convocation**

cookbooks
HN November 1991 lead-in term changed, was **books, receipt**
    August 1990 lead-in term changed, was **receipt books**
UF books, receipt (cookbooks)
    receipt books (cookbooks)

cool colors
HN January 1991 alternate term added
ALT **cool color**

cooling coils
HN May 1991 scope note added
SN Designates coiled arrangements of piping or tubing used to cool by transferring heat between one fluid and another or between a space and a refrigerant.

copies (photographic prints)
USE **copy prints**

copings
HN December 1990 alternate term added
    December 1990 descriptor changed, was **coping**
ALT **coping**

copper alloys
HN February 1991 alternate term added
ALT **copper alloy**

copper engraving
HN March 1991 added
BT **engraving (printing process)**
SN Process of engraving for printing using copper plates; replaced in the early 19th century by the use of more durable plates, either of steel or steel-faced copper.
UF chalcography
    copperplate engraving
    engraving, copper
    engraving, copperplate

Copper Eskimo
USE **Copper Inuit**

Copper Inuit
HN June 1990 lead-in terms added
UF Copper Eskimo
    Eskimo, Copper

copperplate engraving
USE **copper engraving**

coppersmiths
HN June 1990 scope note changed, W added as source

Coptic (Christian sect)
HN May 1991 descriptor changed, was Coptic

copy art
HN October 1991 moved to hierarchy under development

copy photographs
USE **copy prints**

copy photoprints
USE **copy prints**

copy prints
HN December 1990 added
BT **photographic prints**
ALT **copy print**
SN Photographic prints produced by photographing a two-dimensional work, such as a drawing or painting, or by rephotographing another photograph.
UF copies (photographic prints)
    copy photographs
    copy photoprints
    copyprints
    photographs, copy
    photoprints, copy
    prints, copy

copyediting
HN January 1991 added
BT **editing**
SN Editing a document for correctness and consistency in such matters as punctuation, spelling, grammar, or style prior to publication. (RHDEL2)
UF copyreading
RT **copyeditors**
    documents

copyeditors
HN January 1991 added
BT **editors**
ALT **copyeditor**
SN Those who edit a document for correctness and consistency in such things as punctuation, spelling, grammar, or style prior to publication. (RHDEL2)
RT **copyediting**

copyists
HN April 1991 moved
    April 1991 scope note changed
    April 1991 related term added
BT *<people by activity>* HG.705
SN Use for people who make copies, especially those who copy manuscripts, music notation, or other documents by hand.
RT **scribes**

copyprints
USE **copy prints**

copyreading
USE **copyediting**

Cor-Ten steel (TM)
HN April 1990 added
BT **high-strength low-alloy steel**
UF steel, Cor-Ten (TM)

corbel arches
HN December 1990 scope note changed
    December 1990 lead-in terms added
SN Masonry constructions whose arch-like form is created by cantilevering successive courses inward beyond the preceding until they meet at the span's midpoint; thus the courses are set horizontally, not radially; not true arches.
UF arches, false
    false arches

corbel rings
USE **shaft rings**

corbel tables
HN January 1991 scope note changed
SN May designate projecting masonry courses supported by a range of corbels, or ranges of corbels supporting cornices or other projecting courses, or ensembles of corbels and projecting courses; found especially in Medieval architecture.

corbel vaults
HN March 1991 moved
    December 1990 scope note changed
BT *<vaults by form: construction>* RT.548
SN Use for vaults constructed by corbelling, or cantilevering, successive courses inward beyond the preceding one, until they meet and are capped at the vault's midpoint.

corbels
HN December 1990 scope note changed
SN Cantilevered masonry blocks used singly or in ranges to support architectural or ornamental features or used in successive courses to form arches, domes, or vaults; when referring generally to the projecting courses of masonry, prefer **oversailing courses.**

corbie gables
HN November 1991 scope note changed
    November 1991 lead-in term changed, was **corbie gables**
    November 1991 lead-in term changed, was **gables, crow-stepped**
    December 1990 lead-in terms added
    December 1990 lead-in term **catsup gables** deleted
    December 1990 lead-in term **gables, catsup** deleted
    December 1990 lead-in term changed, was **step gables**
    December 1990 lead-in term changed, was **gables, step**
    December 1990 descriptor changed, was **crow-stepped gables**
    December 1990 lead-in term changed, was **corbiestepped gables**
    December 1990 alternate term changed, was **crow-stepped gable**
    December 1990 lead-in term changed, was **gables, corbiestepped**

ALT **corbie gable**
SN Gables having stepped edges.
UF corbiestep gables
crow gables
crowstepped gables
gables, corbiestep
gables, crow
gables, crowstepped
gables, stepped
stepped gables

corbiestep gables
USE **corbie gables**

corbiesteps
HN December 1990 scope note changed
December 1990 descriptor changed, was **crowsteps**
December 1990 alternate term changed, was **crowstep**
December 1990 lead-in term changed, was **corbiesteps**
ALT **corbiestep**
SN The component projections of corbie gables.
UF crowsteps

cord marking
HN March 1991 alternate term changed, was **cord marked**
ALT **cord-marked**

cordonata cascades
USE **water chains**

cordonate
USE **water chains**

Corinthian order
HN December 1990 scope note added
SN Use for the architectural order characterized by a capital having a bell-shaped echinus decorated with a combination of spiral and plant, usually acanthus, motifs. (FOFDA)

cork (bark)
HN May 1991 descriptor changed, was **cork**

corn oil
HN July 1990 descriptor changed, was **maize oil**
July 1990 lead-in term changed, was **corn oil**
UF maize oil

corner boards
HN December 1990 moved
BT *<wall components by location or context>* RT.666

cornice lighting
HN April 1991 scope note added
SN Lighting systems comprising light sources shielded by a panel set parallel to the wall and attached to the ceiling to distribute light over the wall; generally used for visual effect. (IESREF)

cornices
HN December 1990 lead-in term added
UF geisons

coronas (cornice components)
HN July 1991 descriptor changed, was **coronas**
July 1991 alternate term changed, was **corona**
December 1990 scope note changed
ALT **corona (cornice component)**
SN Overhanging vertical members of a cornice in classical architecture, supported by bed moldings and crowned by cymatia, usually with a drip to throw rainwater clear of the building. (DAC)

coronations
HN May 1991 alternate term added
ALT **coronation**

coronets (architectural elements)
HN July 1991 scope note changed
SN Use for ornamental features, usually in relief and triangular in form, resembling pediments and located over doors or windows.

corporate headquarters
HN May 1990 lead-in terms added
UF home offices (corporate headquarters)
offices, home (corporate headquarters)

corps de logis
HN June 1990 alternate term **corp de logis** deleted

corpses, exquisite
USE **cadavres exquis**

correspondence art
HN October 1991 deleted, made lead-in term in hierarchy under development

corrugated board
HN July 1990 added
BT **cardboard**
SN Cardboard consisting of a sheet of corrugated paper with an adherent flat board on one or both sides. (W)
UF board, corrugated
cardboard, corrugated
corrugated cardboard
corrugated paperboard
paperboard, corrugated

corrugated cardboard
USE **corrugated board**

corrugated paper
HN July 1990 added
BT *<paper by form>* MT.1903
SN Thick coarse paper formed into alternating grooves and ridges to give it elasticity. (W)
UF paper, corrugated

corrugated paperboard
USE **corrugated board**

cost accounting
HN January 1991 scope note added
SN Accounting that deals with systematically classifying, recording, analyzing, and summarizing the costs incident to production or the rendering of a service. (W)

costs
HN January 1991 alternate term added
ALT **cost**

costume
HN April 1990 added
BT **fashion**

costume design
HN March 1991 moved
BT **design**

costumers (furniture)
HN September 1991 descriptor changed, was **costumers**
September 1991 alternate term changed, was **costumer**
ALT **costumer (furniture)**

cottages, elder
USE **ECHO houses**

cotton
HN May 1991 scope note changed
SN Cloth made from cotton fiber. (WCOL9)

cotton (fiber)
USE **cotton fiber**

cotton fiber
HN July 1990 added
BT **plant fiber**
SN The white-to-yellowish fiber of the calyx, or blossom, of several species of plants of the genus Gossypium of the mallow family; used especially for making fabrics, cordage, and padding, and for producing cellulose for plastics and rayon. (MH12)
UF cotton (fiber)
fiber, cotton

cotton linters
USE **linters**

cotton rag board, 100%
USE **museum board**

cottonseed oil
HN October 1990 moved
BT **vegetable oil**

couch grass
HN February 1991 lead-in terms added
February 1991 descriptor changed, was **cutch-grass**
UF cutch-grass
quack grass

couching (embroidery)
HN May 1991 descriptor changed, was **couching**

coulisses
HN January 1991 alternate term added
ALT coulisse

counter-enameling
HN March 1991 alternate term added
ALT counter-enameled

counterflashing
HN December 1990 descriptor changed, was counter flashing

countermarks
HN January 1991 added
BT <marks by function> VW.712
ALT countermark
SN Additional marks added to something to substantiate or supersede the information given by the first marks, as a second watermark on paper, a second hallmark on gold or silver, or a mark added to a coin after issue to denote a change of value.
UF counterstamps

countermine galleries
USE countermines

countermines
HN April 1990 added
BT outworks
ALT countermine
SN Designates horizontal tunnels constructed in order to listen for and intercept and destroy attackers undermining efforts.
UF countermine galleries
galleries, countermine

counterstamps
USE countermarks

country clubs
HN November 1991 moved
BT <club complexes>

county courthouses
HN September 1990 scope note added
SN Use for public buildings in the United States that house county-level judicial and administrative facilities; for structures that house similar functions in the United Kingdom, use county halls.

county directories
HN March 1991 descriptor split, use county (ALT of counties) + directories

county government records
HN March 1991 moved
BT <government records by provenance> VW.1043

county halls
HN September 1990 scope note added
SN Use for public buildings in the United Kingdom that house various county functions, often comprising a large hall for public meetings and rooms for county courts and administration; for structures housing sim-

ilar judicial functions in the United States, use county courthouses.

county maps
HN July 1991 descriptor split, use county (ALT of counties) + maps

coupled columns
HN December 1990 scope note changed
December 1990 lead-in terms added
SN Use for groups of two columns set closer together than others in a line, or otherwise forming a visual unit; for columns with interpenetrating shafts, use doubled columns.
UF columns, paired
paired columns

coupled windows
HN January 1991 lead-in terms added
January 1991 scope note source changed to DAC
UF twin-lights
two-lights

course lights
HN May 1990 added
BT aeronautical ground lights
ALT course light
SN Aeronautical ground lights supplementing an airway beacon, used to indicate the direction of the airway and to identify by coded signal the location of the airway beacon with which it is associated. (STEIN)
UF lights, course

courtyards
HN June 1990 lead-in term cortiles deleted

cove ceilings
HN July 1991 scope note changed
SN Designates ceilings having a large concave curve at the wall-to-ceiling transition instead of a sharp angle intersection. (CHAMBD)

cove lighting
HN April 1991 scope note changed
SN Indirect lighting systems comprising light sources shielded by vertical or horizontal ledges or recesses attached to walls and distributing light over the ceiling and upper and side walls. (STEIN)

covenants
HN January 1991 alternate term added
ALT covenant

cover moldings
HN April 1991 scope note added
SN Use for wooden strips, plain or molded, that cover joints, as in paneling.

coving
HN April 1991 scope note changed
SN Concave surfaces located at the junction of a wall and ceiling.

cowls
HN December 1990 moved
December 1990 scope note changed
BT <ventilation system components> RT.1431
SN Use for caps or hoodlike devices which cover and protect the open top of pipes, stacks, or shafts while permitting the free passage of air. (RS)

Craftsman
HN July 1991 related term added
RT Arts and Crafts

crayon engraving
USE crayon manner

crayon enlargements
HN March 1991 moved
BT <photographs by processing or presentation technique> VJ.106

crayon manner
HN April 1990 added
BT <intaglio printing processes>
SN 18th-century printmaking process that imitates the appearance of chalk lines; employs etching, with the ground having been marked with a roulette, and sometimes the addition of directly engraved stippling. (OCA)
UF à trois crayons (printmaking)
chalk engraving
chalk manner
chalk method
crayon engraving
crayon method
engraving, chalk
engraving, crayon
manner, chalk
manner, crayon
method, chalk
method, crayon

crayon method
USE crayon manner

creativity
HN January 1991 alternate term added
ALT creative

Creek
HN June 1990 lead-in term added
UF Maskoki

creeping bite
HN April 1990 added
BT <biting techniques>
SN Technique of submerging a printing plate in acid in stages to produce subtle tonal gradations or other effects. (SAFF)
UF bite, creeping

Creole
HN October 1991 added
BT American Colonial

crepe
HN July 1990 added
BT <cloth by form> MT.1856

SN Lightweight cloth of various fibers with a crinkled surface obtained by using hard twisted yarns, by printing with caustic soda, by weaving with varied tensions, or by embossing. (W)

crescent moons
USE **crescents (shapes)**

crescent trusses
HN March 1991 moved
BT *<trusses by form>* RT.357

crescents (shapes)
HN May 1991 lead-in terms added
    May 1991 descriptor changed, was crescents
    May 1991 alternate term changed, was crescent
ALT **crescent (shape)**
UF crescent moons
    moons, crescent

cresting
HN December 1990 scope note changed
SN Ornamental finish, usually rhythmic and highly decorative, consisting of a regular series of motifs applied to the top of walls, roof ridges, and the like; may also be used for similar decoration on furniture or glass objects.

crevé
HN April 1990 added
BT *<conditions and effects: printing and printmaking>*
SN Use when, in etching, an area of the printing plate is too deeply bitten and lines fuse together.

crewel embroidery
USE **crewelwork**

crewelwork
HN March 1990 lead-in term added
UF crewel embroidery

criblé
USE **dotted manner**

crime
HN May 1991 related terms added
    February 1991 related term added
    January 1991 scope note added
SN The commission of acts that are forbidden by, or the omission of duties that are required by, public law and that make the offender liable to punishment by that law. (WCOL9)
RT **crime prevention**
    criminal law
    prostitution

crime prevention
HN May 1991 scope note added
    May 1991 related term added
SN Measures taken to forestall criminal or delinquent acts. (ERIC12)
RT **crime**

criminal law
HN May 1991 related term added
RT **crime**

criminology
HN February 1991 alternate term added
ALT **criminological**

crimson madder
USE **madder**

crisis centers
USE **crisis shelters**

crisis shelters
HN February 1991 added
BT **welfare buildings**
ALT **crisis shelter**
SN Denotes facilities that provide emergency social services and temporary housing in times of personal or family crisis.
UF battered women's shelters
    centers, crisis
    crisis centers
    shelters, battered women's
    shelters, crisis
    shelters, women's
    women's shelters
    women's shelters, battered
RT **emergency housing**

criticism
HN January 1991 scope note added
    January 1991 alternate term added
    October 1990 moved
BT *<analytical functions>* KG.3
ALT **criticizing**
SN Activity of analyzing and judging the quality of a man-made object, action, or plan.

critiques
HN May 1991 alternate term added
ALT **critique**

crocket capitals
HN March 1991 scope note changed, source HAS deleted

crockets
HN September 1991 scope note changed, source HAS deleted
    July 1991 scope note changed
    March 1991 moved
BT *<plant-derived motifs>* DG.50
SN In Gothic architecture and derivatives, projecting ornaments usually vegetal in form, often regularly spaced along edges of larger features, such as gables, or used on capitals.

croquet courts
HN September 1990 scope note added
SN Grass courts equipped for playing croquet.

cross-hatching
HN March 1991 alternate term added
ALT **cross-hatched**

cross springers
USE **diagonal ribs**

crossings, railroad
USE **grade crossings**

crosslight
USE **crosslighting**

crosslighting
HN April 1991 added
BT **directional lighting**
SN Method of lighting providing illumination from two directions at substantially equal and opposite angles from each other. (IESREF)
UF crosslight

crosswalks
HN December 1990 moved
BT **pedestrian facilities**

croton oil
HN October 1990 moved
BT **vegetable oil**

crow gables
USE **corbie gables**

crown posts
HN December 1990 scope note changed, RHDEL2 added as source

crown steeples
HN June 1990 scope note changed
    June 1990 lead-in term added
SN Openwork spires, the upper portion being carried over an open area by crossed arches or buttresses, thus resembling a crown.
UF crowns (spires)

crowns (spires)
USE **crown steeples**

crowstepped gables
USE **corbie gables**

crowsteps
USE **corbiesteps**

CRT's
USE **monitors (data processing equipment)**

cruciform-plan
USE **Greek cross-plan**
    Latin cross-plan

crucks
HN July 1991 scope note changed
    January 1991 moved
BT **structural frames**
SN Pairs of naturally curved timbers that rise from the ground or outer walls of buildings to support a ridge beam; joined at the top and connected by tie beams. (DAC)

Crusader
HN October 1991 scope note changed
SN European-influenced art and architecture of the eastern Mediterra-

nean, from the 12th to the 15th century.

crushed relief
USE **rilievo schiacciato**

crystals, soda
USE **sodium carbonate**

Cuban pine
HN June 1990 lead-in term added
UF Caribbean pine

cube capitals
USE **cushion capitals**

cubes
HN July 1991 alternate term added
ALT cube

cubicles, toilet
USE **toilet compartments**

cubicula
HN June 1990 scope note changed, source HAS deleted

Cuilcuilco-Ticomán
USE **Ticomán**

cul de fours
USE **semidomes**

culture, mass
USE **popular culture**

cupboards
HN July 1991 scope note changed
SN Originally boards or open structures of shelves on which cups, especially silver, might be placed for storage or display; often used interchangeably with buffets and dressers in the Middle Ages. Beginning in the 15th century, doors were added. Today a generic term for all such receptacles enclosed by doors.

cupolas
HN July 1991 scope note changed
SN Use for small structures built on the ridges of roofs, particularly common in American architecture; when these structures are intended to be used as lookouts, prefer **belvederes**; for windowed superstructures on roofs or domes used to admit light or air to the space below, use **lanterns**; for hemispherical roofs, use **domes**.

cupolas (domes)
USE **domes**

curcas oil
HN October 1990 moved
BT **vegetable oil**

curing
HN October 1991 moved
October 1991 scope note added
October 1991 descriptor changed, was **curing (leather)**
BT *<processes and techniques by specific type>* KT.5

SN A process or method involving aging, seasoning, washing, drying, heating, smoking, or otherwise treating whereby a product is preserved, perfected, or readied for use. (W)

currying
HN October 1991 moved
BT **leatherworking**

curtain walls (nonbearing walls)
HN May 1991 descriptor changed, was curtain walls
May 1991 alternate term changed, was curtain wall
ALT **curtain wall (nonbearing wall)**

curvature
USE **curved**

curved
HN May 1991 lead-in term added
UF curvature

curved dormers
HN April 1991 deleted
BT **dormers**

curvilinear tracery
HN March 1991 scope note added
March 1991 descriptor changed, was **flowing tracery**
March 1991 lead-in term changed, was **curvilinear tracery**
SN Use for tracery in which continuous compound or ogee curves predominate.
UF flowing tracery

cushion capitals
HN December 1990 scope note changed
December 1990 lead-in terms added
SN Cubic capitals with their lower angles rounded off, to make the transition to a round column; found in Medieval architecture.
UF capitals, cube
cube capitals

cusped arches
HN December 1990 scope note source changed to RS

cusps
HN December 1990 scope note changed
SN The intersection of two arcs or foils, as in Gothic tracery.

customhouses
HN September 1990 scope note added
SN Use for government office buildings where customs and duties are paid or collected and where vessels are recorded and cleared. (W)

customs
HN January 1991 alternate term added
ALT custom

customs posts
USE **border inspection stations**

cutch-grass
USE **couch grass**

Cuzco
HN June 1991 moved
BT *<Colonial Latin American fine arts styles>* FL.1716

cyclones
HN May 1991 alternate term added
ALT cyclone

cylinders (solids)
HN May 1991 descriptor changed, was cylinders
January 1991 alternate term added
ALT cylinder (solid)

cyma rectas
HN April 1991 lead-in terms added
UF moldings, ogee
ogee moldings
rectas, sima
sima rectas

cyma reversas
HN April 1991 lead-in terms added
UF reversas, sima
sima reversas

cymas
HN November 1991 lead-in term **moldings, ogee** deleted
November 1991 lead-in term **moldings, talon** deleted
April 1991 lead-in term added
April 1991 lead-in term **simas** deleted
April 1991 lead-in term **ogee moldings** deleted
April 1991 lead-in term **talon moldings** deleted
UF simas (moldings)

cymatia
HN April 1991 lead-in term added
April 1991 lead-in term **scimatia** deleted
UF simas (cornice components)

cyrtostyles
HN June 1990 scope note changed
SN Circular, projecting porticoes. (W)

Cyzican marble
USE **Proconnesian marble**

daggers (tracery components)
HN January 1991 lead-in term added
UF soufflets

Daibutsuyo
HN June 1990 lead-in term **Tenjiku yo** deleted
June 1990 lead-in term **Tenjiku-yo** deleted

damp courses
HN February 1991 moved
BT **building materials**

Dan
HN June 1990 lead-in term added
UF Gere

dark carmine
USE **moderate red**

dark gray
HN November 1991 lead-in terms added
     August 1990 lead-in term **slate color**
     deleted
UF dark purplish gray
     gray, dark purplish
     purplish gray, dark

dark greenish gray
HN April 1990 lead-in terms added
UF gray, olive
     olive gray

dark purplish gray
USE **dark gray**

dark reddish purple
HN April 1990 lead-in terms added
UF dark slate purple
     purple, dark slate
     slate purple, dark

dark slate purple
USE **dark reddish purple**

dark yellowish pink
HN April 1990 lead-in terms added
UF light red
     red, light

data processing
HN February 1991 scope note added
     January 1991 lead-in term added
SN Creating and manipulating data in
     machine-readable form by means of
     computers, including inputting,
     storage, conversion, editing, and
     printing.
UF automatic data processing

Daulatabad
HN February 1991 moved
BT **Deccani**

davenports (sofas)
HN May 1991 descriptor changed, was
     davenports
     May 1991 alternate term changed,
     was **davenport**
ALT **davenport (sofa)**

day care
HN June 1990 scope note changed, ERIC
     added as source

day care centers
HN September 1990 scope note added
SN Designates professionally run facili-
     ties that care for groups of pre-
     school children on a partial or full-
     day basis. (ERIC9)

daybooks
HN May 1991 moved
BT **bookkeeping records**

dead loads
HN January 1991 alternate term added
ALT **dead load**

Deal, New
USE **New Deal**

deaths
HN February 1991 alternate term added
     February 1991 descriptor changed,
     was **death**
ALT **death**

decagons
HN January 1991 alternate term added
ALT **decagon**

Deccani
HN February 1991 moved
BT <*Islamic Indian styles and periods*>
     FL.2224

decentralization
HN January 1991 scope note added
     October 1990 moved
     January 1990 alternate term added
BT <*organizational functions*> KG.138
ALT **decentralized**
SN Distributing the functions and pow-
     ers of an organization, governing
     body, or other authority over a less
     centralized area or among a large
     number of parties.

decision making
HN January 1991 scope note added
SN Process of making choices between
     or among alternatives.

decks
HN June 1990 scope note changed
SN Use for uncovered wood or metal
     platforms, usually attached to struc-
     tures and often raised off the ground
     or on rooftops.

décollage
HN July 1991 scope note changed
SN The tearing away of parts of post-
     ers, or other materials, that have been
     applied in layers, so that selected
     portions of the underlayers contrib-
     ute to the total image. To designate
     the resulting works, use **affiches lac-
     erérées.**

deconsecrations
HN February 1991 alternate term added
     February 1991 scope note source
     changed to OED
     February 1991 descriptor changed,
     was **deconsecration**
ALT **deconsecration**

deconstruction
HN January 1991 alternate term added
ALT **deconstructive**

decorative lighting
HN April 1991 added
BT **architectural lighting**
SN System of lights arranged for deco-
     rative purposes, as in store window

displays, on Christmas trees, or on
bushes.
UF lighting, decorative

decorative motifs
USE **motifs**

dedications (ceremonies)
HN May 1991 alternate term added
ALT **dedication (ceremony)**

dedications (documents)
HN May 1991 descriptor changed, was
     dedications
     May 1991 alternate term changed,
     was **dedication**
ALT **dedication (document)**

deep bite
USE **deep etching**

deep etch
USE **deep etching**

deep etching
HN October 1991 moved
     March 1991 alternate term added
     October 1990 scope note changed
     October 1990 lead-in terms added
BT <*biting techniques*>
ALT **deep-etched**
SN The biting of a printing plate to such
     a degree that the printing area be-
     comes substantially recessed and
     thereby productive of sharper defi-
     nition and longer runs. (W)
UF bite, deep
     deep bite
     deep etch
     etch, deep

deep red
HN April 1990 lead-in term added
UF rose

deep reddish purple
HN April 1990 lead-in terms added
UF fuchsia purple
     purple, fuchsia

deep relief
USE **high relief**

defacement
HN January 1991 alternate term added
     December 1990 moved
BT **damage**
ALT **defaced**

deficiency, mental
USE **mental retardation**

deflections
HN January 1991 alternate term added
ALT **deflection**

deformations
HN January 1991 alternate term added
ALT **deformation**

dehumidification
HN March 1991 alternate term added
ALT **dehumidified**

dehumidifying coils
HN May 1991 scope note added
SN Use for coils designed to remove moisture from the air by condensation.

delamination
HN March 1991 alternate term added
    February 1991 scope note changed
ALT **delaminated**
SN Separation into constituent layers. (GRIMMR)

Della Robbia blue
USE **light blue**

demi-relief
USE **mezzo rilievo**

demimetopes
HN March 1991 scope note changed
    March 1991 lead-in term added
SN Half or incomplete metopes in Doric friezes, usually found at corners. (RS)
UF semi-metopes

democracy
HN January 1991 alternate term added
ALT **democratic**

demographic anthropology
HN September 1991 moved
BT **anthropology**

demographics
HN January 1991 alternate term added
ALT **demographic**

demography
HN February 1991 alternate term added
ALT **demographical**

denatured alcohol
HN May 1990 lead-in term changed, was synasol
UF Synasol (TM)

dendrochronology
HN April 1991 lead-in term added
UF growth ring dating

density
HN July 1991 scope note added
    January 1991 alternate term added
ALT **dense**
SN The state or quality of being compact; the distribution of a quantity (for example, mass or energy) or entities (for example, families or shops) per unit area, such as the number of dwelling units per acre; may also be used as a measure of the mass of a substance per unit volume.

dental schools
HN September 1990 scope note added
SN Schools devoted to training dentists.

dental sinks
HN February 1991 deleted
BT **sinks**

dentils
HN March 1991 scope note changed
SN Bands of small, rectangular, tooth-like blocks, usually along the underside of a cornice; a characteristic ornament of classical and classicizing styles.

departments, maternity
USE **maternity wards**

dependency, alcohol
USE **alcoholism**

dependency, drug
USE **drug addiction**

dependency, narcotics
USE **drug addiction**

depiction
USE **representation**

depreciation
HN January 1991 alternate term added
ALT **depreciated**

depth
HN January 1991 alternate term added
ALT **deep**

describing
HN January 1991 scope note added
SN Representing in spoken, written, or signed language the attributes or qualities of something or someone. (RHDEL2)

design
HN March 1991 moved
BT *<arts-related disciplines>* KD.21

design books
HN June 1991 descriptor split, use **design** (ALT of **designs**) + **books**

design centers, community
USE **community design centers**

design, green
USE **green design**

design, urban
USE **urban design**

designers, floral
USE **floral designers**

designs
HN January 1991 alternate term added
ALT **design**

despotism
HN June 1991 related term added
    January 1991 alternate term added
ALT **despotic**
RT *<government by form>*

Destructive Art
HN May 1990 scope note added
    May 1990 lead-in term added
    May 1990 descriptor changed, was **Auto-destructive**
SN Use for art done around the early 1960s in which the process of destruction of objects or materials within the work is regarded as the work; usually associated theoretically with artists' concerns about social violence.
UF Auto-destructive

detectors, heat-actuated
USE **temperature detectors**

detectors, heat-sensing
USE **temperature detectors**

detectors, photoelectric smoke
USE **photoelectric smoke detectors**

detectors, thermal
USE **temperature detectors**

detectors, thermostatic
USE **temperature detectors**

determinism
HN January 1991 alternate term added
ALT **deterministic**

development
HN December 1990 added
BT *<functions by general context>* KG.2
ALT **developed**
SN Change over time in human activities, institutions, or settlements, usually in the sense of improvement or expansion.
RT **land use**

<development concepts> BM.1063
HN November 1991 deleted
BT *<social and economic geography concepts>*

development, linear
USE **ribbon development**

development, sustainable
USE **sustainable development**

<developmental concepts>
HN February 1991 added
BT *<health-related concepts>*

deviant behavior
HN December 1990 scope note added
SN Conduct that departs from a society's established norms, rules, standards, or expectations. (TSIT)

diagonal ribs
HN January 1991 scope note changed
    January 1991 lead-in term changed, was **cross-springers**
SN Ribs crossing a vault bay diagonally, used either to mask the groins or to support the vault.
UF cross springers

dialectic
HN January 1991 alternate term added
ALT **dialectical**

diamond-point engraving
HN October 1990 moved
BT **engraving (incising)**

diaphragm arches
HN October 1991 scope note changed
SN Use for arches built across a nave or hall that support walls rather than vaults; for such arches when they support vaults, use **transverse arches.**

diaphragm walls
HN June 1990 scope note added
SN Designates walls erected around a site to hold back wet earth to permit the construction of, for example, basements, in areas of high groundwater.

diazomata
HN July 1991 scope note changed
SN Passages or aisles in Greek theaters concentric with the outer wall. For similar features in Roman theaters, use **praecinctiones.** (RS)

die casting
HN March 1991 alternate term changed, was **die cast**
ALT **die-cast**

die stamping
HN March 1991 alternate term added
     October 1990 moved
     October 1990 scope note changed
BT **stamping**
ALT **die-stamped**
SN Shaping material, such as paper or sheet metal, between two plates, one with the design in relief and the other with the corresponding design recessed.

diffuse reflectance
HN April 1990 added
BT **reflectance**
SN Reflectance that is not specular.
UF reflectance, diffuse

diffuse reflection
HN April 1990 added
BT **reflection**
SN Reflection in which a significant portion of the light is reflected in many different directions. (ICPEP)
UF reflection, diffuse

dikkas
HN June 1991 alternate term added
     June 1991 descriptor changed, was **dikka**
ALT **dikka**

dining rooms
HN June 1990 scope note added
SN Rooms in private houses or public establishments in which dinner and other principle meals are taken and which are furnished for this purpose. (OED)

Diocletian windows
HN January 1991 lead-in terms added
UF thermal windows
     windows, thermal

diplomats
HN November 1990 scope note added
SN People employed by a national government or ruler to conduct official negotiations and maintain political, economic, and social relations with other nations or international organizations. (RHDEL2)

direct carving
HN November 1990 moved
BT *<carving techniques>*

direct lighting
HN April 1991 lead-in terms added
     April 1991 moved
     April 1991 scope note added
BT *<lighting techniques by distribution>*
SN Use for lighting techniques in which 90 to 100% of the light is directed toward the surface to be illuminated; usually downward light. (IESREF)
UF direct lighting system
     lighting system, direct

direct lighting system
USE **direct lighting**

direction indicators, landing
USE **landing direction indicators**

directional lighting
HN April 1991 moved
     April 1991 scope note added
     April 1991 lead-in term **accent lighting** deleted
BT *<lighting techniques by direction>*
SN Use for the lighting of an object or work plane primarily from a specific and preferred direction. (IESREF)

directorial photographs
USE **staged photographs**

directories
HN February 1991 scope note changed
SN Enumerations of names, addresses, and other data about specific groups of persons or organizations; may appear in alphabetic or graphic format. (AHD)

directories, building
USE **building directories**

directors (administrators)
HN September 1991 descriptor changed, was **directors**
     September 1991 alternate term changed, was **director**
ALT **director (administrator)**

disadvantaged, economically
USE **poor**

disasters
HN July 1990 added
BT **events**
ALT **disaster**
SN Sudden calamitous events producing great material damage, loss, or distress. (W)

UF calamities
     cataclysms
     catastrophes

disasters, man-made
USE **man-made disasters**

disasters, natural
USE **natural disasters**

disbursing
HN January 1991 scope note added
SN Paying out money or provisions, especially from a public fund. (RLG7)

disciplines
HN February 1991 alternate term added
ALT **discipline**

discographies
HN March 1991 moved
     March 1991 related term added
BT *<lists by form or function>* VW.252
RT **sound recordings**

discotheques
HN September 1990 scope note added
SN Entertainment buildings for dancing to recorded music or music videos and often featuring sophisticated sound systems, elaborate lighting, and other effects. (RHDEL2)

discrimination
HN July 1991 scope note changed
     February 1991 lead-in terms added
     January 1991 alternate term added
ALT **discriminatory**
SN Biased or differential attitudes toward or treatment of people on the basis of the group, class, or category to which they belong.
UF bigotry
     social discrimination

disease
HN March 1991 moved
     February 1991 scope note added
     February 1991 lead-in term added
BT *<health-related concepts>*
SN Abnormal functioning of one or more of an organism's systems, parts, or organs. (IDMB)
UF diseases

diseases
USE **disease**

diseases, mental
USE **mental disorders**

dish antennas
USE **satellite home antennas**

dishes (satellite antennas)
USE **satellite home antennas**

dishes, satellite
USE **satellite home antennas**

disinfecting
HN March 1991 alternate term added
ALT **disinfected**

dismantling
HN   March 1991 alternate term added
ALT   **dismantled**

dismissal
USE   **firing (managing)**

disorder, mental
USE   **mental disorders**

disorders, behavior
USE   **behavior disorders**

disorders, mental
USE   **mental disorders**

dispatch systems, pneumatic
USE   **pneumatic tubes**

dispensaries (health facilities)
HN   May 1991 descriptor changed, was
        dispensaries
        May 1991 alternate term changed,
        was **dispensary**
ALT   **dispensary (health facility)**

distemper paint
HN   August 1991 moved
        July 1990 lead-in terms added
BT   <*aqueous paint*> MT.2512
UF   color, scenic
        color, size
        paint, size
        scenic color
        size color
        size paint

distributed loads
HN   January 1991 alternate term added
ALT   **distributed load**

distributing
HN   January 1991 scope note added
SN   Sending out or apportioning something from a central source to a group, community, or individuals.

distribution centers
HN   February 1991 added
BT   **mercantile buildings**
ALT   **distribution center**
SN   Use for commercial buildings located regionally that combine large warehouse facilities with sales and office spaces.
UF   centers, distribution
RT   **warehouses**

distribution equipment, heat
USE   **heat-distributing units**

distribution, downfeed
USE   **downfeed systems**

district courts
HN   September 1990 scope note added
SN   Use for courthouses housing a court of general jurisdiction within a judicial district; may designate Federal or state courts.

diversifying
HN   July 1990 added
BT   <*economic and financial functions*> KG.43
ALT   **diversified**
SN   Act or practice of manufacturing a variety of products, selling a variety of merchandise, or investing in a variety of securities, for example, so that failure in or economic slump affecting one of them will not be disastrous. (RHDEL2)

divinity
HN   January 1991 alternate term added
ALT   **divine**

doctors, medical
USE   **physicians**

documenting
HN   March 1991 alternate term added
ALT   **documented**

documents
HN   January 1991 related term added
RT   **copyediting**

documents, base bid
USE   **base bid specifications**

dodecagons
HN   January 1991 alternate term added
ALT   **dodecagon**

doges
HN   June 1990 scope note changed, W added as source

dogleg stairs
HN   January 1991 scope note changed
SN   Halfpace stairs which have no well hole between successive flights; the rail and balusters of the upper and under flights fall in the same vertical plane. (DAC)

dolly method
USE   **à la poupée**

domes
HN   January 1991 scope note changed
        January 1991 lead-in term added
SN   Structural elements, usually resembling spheres or portions of spheres, constructed such that they exert equal thrust in all directions.
UF   cupolas (domes)

domestic stylebooks
HN   March 1991 deleted
BT   **stylebooks**

domestic wings
USE   **apartments**

donations
HN   January 1991 alternate term added
ALT   **donation**

Dông-Son (Indonesian)
HN   May 1991 descriptor changed, was **Dông-Son**

door bells
USE   **doorbells**

door bucks
HN   May 1991 moved
        May 1991 scope note changed
BT   <*doorway components*> RT.833
SN   Rough wood or metal subframes, set in a wall, to which finished doorframes are attached. (DAC)

door cheeks
USE   **doorjambs**

door chimes
USE   **doorbells**

door heads
USE   **doorheads**

door jambs
USE   **doorjambs**

door leaves
HN   February 1991 lead-in term added
        February 1991 lead-in term fores deleted
UF   panels (door components)

door posts
USE   **doorjambs**

door rails
HN   February 1991 scope note added
        February 1991 lead-in term added
SN   Use for the horizontal members that connect the stiles of doors. (MEANS)
UF   rails (door components)

door sills
USE   **doorsills**

door stones
USE   **doorstones**

doorbells
HN   January 1991 scope note added
        January 1991 lead-in terms added
SN   Bells, gongs, buzzers, or sets of chimes that ring inside a building when their control, usually a button located adjacent to an entrance, is activated. (PUTNAM)
UF   bells, door
        chimes, door
        door bells
        door chimes

doorheads
HN   October 1991 lead-in term added
        January 1991 lead-in term added
UF   door heads
        heads, door

doorjambs
HN   November 1991 lead-in terms added
        February 1991 scope note changed
        February 1991 descriptor changed, was **door jambs**
        February 1991 alternate term changed, was **door jamb**
ALT   **doorjamb**

SN The vertical members forming the sides of doorways. (HAS)
UF cheeks, door
    door cheeks
    door jambs
    door posts
    posts, door

doors, blind
USE **false doors**

doorsills
HN May 1991 moved
    May 1991 scope note changed
    May 1991 lead-in terms added
BT <*doorway components*> RT.833
SN Designates the lower sides and bottom of doorways; for strips fastened to the floor beneath doors to cover joints or provide weather protection, use **thresholds.** (DAC)
UF door sills
    sills, door

doorstones
HN May 1991 moved
    February 1991 lead-in terms added
BT <*doorway components*> RT.833
UF door stones
    stones, door

doorways
HN August 1991 scope note changed
SN Denotes openings, which contain or could contain a door, that provide access into or out of building spaces.

dope addicts
USE **drug addicts**

Doric order
HN March 1991 scope note added
SN Architectural order characterized by columns generally without bases, relatively simple capitals, and a frieze composed of alternating triglyphs and metopes.

dormer windows
USE **dormers**

dormers
HN February 1991 lead-in terms added
UF dormer windows
    windows, dormer

dormers, gable
USE **gable dormers**

dormers, gable-roof
USE **gable dormers**

dormers, hipped-roof
USE **hipped dormers**

dormitories (buildings)
HN May 1991 descriptor changed, was **dormitories**
    May 1991 alternate term changed, was **dormitory**
ALT **dormitory (building)**

dotted manner
HN April 1990 added
BT <*relief printing processes*>
SN Printmaking process for making relief engravings on metal, called dotted prints, using dots from punches of various shapes and sometimes including burin lines; common in the second half of the 15th century. For later, intaglio processes employing directly engraved flicks or dots for tonal areas, use **stipple engraving.** (OCA)
UF criblé
    manière criblée
    manner, dotted

double-cable structures
HN August 1991 moved
    August 1991 scope note changed
    August 1991 lead-in terms added
BT **suspension structures**
SN Use for structures supported by a series of double cables of different curvature used in the same vertical plane and held apart by struts in compression.
UF bicycle-wheel roofs
    cable-beam structures
    cable-supported roofs, double-layer
    double-layer cable-supported roofs, bicycle wheel
    roofs, double-layer cable-supported
    structures, cable beam

double-deck elevators
HN February 1991 scope note added
SN Use for tandem elevators with one car above the other riding in the same hoistway and serving two consecutive floors simultaneously.

double-gable roofs
HN February 1991 scope note changed
SN Roofs formed by the junction of two gable roofs with a valley between them, resembling the letter M in section. (DAC)

double helix stairs
USE **double spiral stairs**

double-layer cable-supported roofs
USE double-cable structures

double printing
HN October 1991 moved
    July 1990 scope note changed
    July 1990 lead-in term added
    July 1990 alternate term added
    July 1990 descriptor changed, was **double-printing**
BT <*printing techniques*>
ALT **double printed**
SN Process of reprinting a plate or block to ensure a strong, fully printed image.
UF double run

double run
USE **double printing**

double spiral stairs
HN February 1991 lead-in terms added
UF double helix stairs
    stairs, double helix

double windows
HN November 1991 lead-in term added
    February 1991 lead-in term **heat insulation windows** deleted
UF frame windows, double

dowel
HN November 1990 scope note changed
SN A pin of wood or metal used to hold or strengthen two pieces of wood where they join. (PUTNAM)

doweling
HN November 1990 added
BT **fastening**
ALT **doweled**
SN Fastening together two pieces of wood by means of dowels.

down pipes
USE **downspouts**

downfeed systems
HN February 1991 lead-in term added
    February 1991 scope note added
SN Water distribution systems in which water is pumped to holding tanks above the points of use, thereby increasing water pressure through gravity; most often employed in tall buildings where municipal water supply lacks the pressure necessary for an upfeed system.
UF distribution, downfeed

downspouts
HN July 1991 scope note changed
    December 1990 lead-in terms added
    December 1990 descriptor changed, was **conductors (piping)**
    December 1990 alternate term changed, was **conductor (piping)**
ALT **downspout**
SN Any vertical pipes, including those within a building, that convey rainwater to sewers, drains, or the ground.
UF conductors (downspouts)
    down pipes
    leader pipes
    leaders (downspouts)
    pipes, down
    pipes, leader
    pipes, rainwater
    rainwater pipes

drafting paper
USE **drawing paper**

draftsmen (artists)
HN May 1991 descriptor changed, was **draftsmen**
    May 1991 alternate term changed, was **draftsman**
ALT **draftsman (artist)**

dragging
HN July 1990 scope note changed
SN A technique of stroking paint lightly over a rough surface so that it covers the high spots and leaves the depressions untouched, thus creating a broken area of color with irregular spots of the color underneath showing through.

dragging ties
USE **dragon beams**

dragon beams
HN March 1991 scope note changed
March 1991 lead-in terms added
SN Use for short horizontal timbers bisecting the angle of a corner of a structure, at the level of the roof plate, reaching to an angle brace, and serving to support the foot of a hip rafter.
UF dragging ties
ties, dragging

dragon ties
HN August 1991 scope note changed, DAC added as source
November 1990 moved
BT **knee braces**

drains, storm water
USE **storm drains**

drama
HN April 1990 scope note changed, PG added as source

drama, sacred
USE **religious drama**

drawing (image making)
HN May 1991 descriptor changed, was drawing
April 1991 scope note added
January 1991 related term added
SN Producing visible forms primarily by delineation, usually by the direct application of material or instrument to the surface of the support.
RT **sketching**

drawing (metalworking)
HN March 1991 alternate term added
ALT **drawn**

drawing books
HN June 1991 descriptor split, use **drawing + books**

drawing chambers
USE **drawing rooms**

drawing paper
HN July 1990 lead-in terms added
UF drafting paper
paper, drafting
paper, sketching
sketching paper

drawing rooms
HN June 1990 lead-in terms added
UF chambers, drawing
chambers, withdrawing
drawing chambers
rooms, withdrawing
withdrawing chambers
withdrawing rooms

drawings
HN April 1991 scope note changed
SN Use for images produced by drawing.

<drawings by location or context> VD.120
HN October 1990 deleted
BT **drawings**

drawings of record
USE **record drawings**

drawings, mechanical (tool-aided drawings)
USE **mechanical drawings (tool-aided drawings)**

drawings, planometric
USE **plan oblique drawings**

drawings, presentation (proposals)
USE **presentation drawings (proposals)**

drawplates
HN April 1991 lead-in term added
UF wiredrawing dies

dredging
HN March 1991 alternate term added
ALT **dredged**

dressers (cupboards)
HN May 1991 descriptor changed, was dressers
May 1991 alternate term changed, was **dresser**
ALT **dresser (cupboard)**

driers
USE **dryers**

drill work
USE **drillwork**

drilling (sculpture technique)
USE **drillwork**

drillwork
HN November 1990 added
BT *<carving techniques>*
UF drill work
drilling (sculpture technique)
work, drill

drinking fountains
HN February 1991 scope note added
SN Plumbing fixtures consisting of a water jet and often a shallow basin designed to provide potable water for human consumption. (DAC)

drip and pour technique
USE **drip painting**

drip painting
HN July 1990 scope note changed
July 1990 lead-in terms added
July 1990 lead-in term **dripping** deleted
SN Use for the technique of creating paintings by dripping or pouring paint in a semi-controlled manner onto the support.
UF drip and pour technique
technique, drip

drive-in theaters
HN September 1990 scope note added
September 1990 lead-in term added
SN Designates outdoor movie theaters designed to accommodate patrons viewing from their automobiles.
UF drive-ins

drive-ins
USE **drive-in theaters**

driving machines
HN February 1991 deleted
BT *<conveying system components>* RT.1323

drop arches
HN November 1991 lead-in terms added
February 1991 moved
February 1991 scope note changed
BT **pointed arches**
SN Use for pointed arches whose radii are located within the span of the arch, whether or not the centers are above, at, or below the springing.
UF arches, blunt
blunt arches

drop tracery
HN February 1991 scope note changed
SN Tracery hanging from the intrados of an arch. (HAS)

drug abuse
HN January 1991 added
BT **substance abuse**
SN Excessive use or misuse of drugs, causing physical, emotional, mental, or sensory injury or impairment. For addiction to narcotics or other drugs, use **drug addiction**. (ERIC9)
UF abuse, drug
RT **drug addiction**

drug addiction
HN January 1991 added
BT **addiction**
SN Addiction to narcotics or other drugs. For excessive use or misuse of drugs, use **drug abuse**.
UF addiction, drug
addiction, narcotic
dependency, drug
dependency, narcotics
drug dependence
habit, narcotic
narcotic dependence
narcotic habit
narcotics addiction
RT **drug abuse**

drug addicts
HN January 1991 added
BT **addicts**
ALT **drug addict**
SN Those who are addicted to narcotics or other drugs.
UF addicts, dope
addicts, drug
addicts, narcotic
dope addicts
narcotic addicts

drug dependence
USE **drug addiction**

druggists
USE **pharmacists**

drums (column components)
HN April 1991 scope note changed
SN Use for the cylinders of stone which form the shaft of a column.

dry rot
HN December 1990 added
BT *<conditions and effects: architecture>*
SN Use for a type of decomposition of timber by fungi.
UF rot, dry

dryers
HN April 1991 lead-in term added
UF driers

drypoint
HN October 1991 moved
BT **engraving (printing process)**

dualism
HN January 1991 alternate term added
ALT **dualistic**

duchesses (chaise longues)
HN May 1991 descriptor changed, was **duchesses**
May 1991 alternate term changed, was **duchesse**
ALT **duchesse (chaise longue)**

Duco (TM)
USE **lacquer**

dull blue
USE **light blue**
very pale blue
very pale purplish blue

dull bluish violet
USE **moderate violet**

dumbwaiters (conveying systems)
HN May 1991 descriptor changed, was **dumbwaiters**
May 1991 alternate term changed, was **dumbwaiter**
February 1991 scope note added
ALT **dumbwaiter (conveying system)**
SN Hoisting or lowering mechanisms equipped with a car or platform used in buildings exclusively for carrying materials.

duplex apartments
HN June 1990 lead-in term added
UF maisonettes

dust ground
USE **rosin ground**

duststorms
HN May 1991 alternate term added
ALT **duststorm**

Dutch arches
USE **French arches**

dwarf galleries
HN June 1990 scope note changed
SN Passageways through the exterior walls of buildings and open to the outside through small-scale or slender arcades; found in Italian and German Romanesque architecture.

dwelling units
USE **apartments**

dwellings, ECHO
USE **ECHO houses**

dwellings, spirit
USE **spirit houses**

Dynastic, Early (Mesopotamian)
USE **Early Dynastic (Mesopotamian)**

Dzalamo
USE **Zaramo**

Early Andhra
HN November 1991 descriptor changed, was **Early Andra**
November 1991 lead-in term changed, was **Andra, Early**
UF Andhra, Early

early childhood
USE **infancy**

Early Dynastic (Egyptian)
HN June 1990 lead-in term added
UF Protodynastic

Early Dynastic (Mesopotamian)
HN May 1991 lead-in term added
May 1991 descriptor changed, was **Early Dynastic**
UF Dynastic, Early (Mesopotamian)

earth movements
HN May 1991 alternate term added
ALT **earth movement**

earth wax
USE **ozokerite**

earthquake loads
HN January 1991 alternate term added
April 1990 lead-in terms added
ALT **earthquake load**
UF loads, seismic
seismic loads

earthquakes
HN May 1991 alternate term added
ALT **earthquake**

earthworks (engineering works)
HN September 1991 scope note changed
September 1991 descriptor changed, was **earthworks**
September 1991 alternate term changed, was **earthwork**
ALT **earthwork (engineering work)**
SN Use generally for the results of grading, trenching, or embanking earth, for utilitarian purposes; when earth construction has more of an artistic, rather than functional, purpose, use **earthworks (sculpture)**.

easel painting
HN April 1990 added
BT **painting (image making)**
SN Use to distinguish the activity of painting portable, relatively small paintings from the painting of other types, such as mural paintings, manuscript illuminations, or decorative painting on objects.
UF painting, easel

East African copal
HN May 1990 lead-in term changed, was **anime**
UF animé

Easter sepulchers
HN August 1991 scope note changed
SN Recesses with tomb chests, usually placed in the north wall of a chancel, to hold the reserved consecrated wafers and sometimes a cross or effigy of Christ.

Eastern Luba
USE **Hemba**

eaves
HN February 1991 alternate term added
ALT **eave**

eaves boards
HN October 1991 lead-in term added
February 1991 scope note added
February 1991 lead-in terms added
SN Use for wedgeshaped boards placed at the lower edges of sloping roofs to raise slightly the lowest course of tiles or slate in order to give that course the same pitch as the courses above.
UF catches, eaves
eaves catches
eaves laths

eaves catches
USE **eaves boards**

eaves fascias
USE **fascia boards**

eaves gutters
HN February 1991 scope note added
February 1991 lead-in terms added
SN Long shallow channels positioned under and paralleling the eaves of a building for the purpose of collect-

ing and directing water from a roof. (MEANS)
UF eaves troughs
    troughs, eaves

eaves laths
USE **eaves boards**

eaves troughs
USE **eaves gutters**

Eccentric Abstraction
HN May 1991 added
BT *<post-1945 fine arts styles and movements>* FL.3712
UF Abstraction, Eccentric

eccentric loads
HN January 1991 alternate term added
ALT **eccentric load**

echini
HN September 1991 scope note changed
SN The convex moldings supporting the abaci of Doric capitals and appearing between the volutes on Ionic capitals. (DINSMR)

ECHO dwellings
USE **ECHO houses**

ECHO homes
USE **ECHO houses**

ECHO houses
HN February 1991 added
BT *<houses by occupants>* RK.323
ALT **ECHO house**
SN Designates small, free-standing, barrier-free, energy efficient, and removable dwellings that are installed adjacent to single-family homes as residences for elderly relatives, usually parents. (AARP)
UF cottages, elder
    dwellings, ECHO
    ECHO dwellings
    ECHO homes
    ECHO units
    Elder Cottage Housing Opportunity units
    elder cottages
    flats, granny
    granny flats
    homes, ECHO
    houses, ECHO
    units, ECHO
RT **temporary housing**

ECHO units
USE **ECHO houses**

eclecticism
HN January 1991 alternate term added
ALT **eclectic**

ecological psychology
USE **environmental psychology**

ecology
HN July 1991 scope note changed
    July 1991 related terms added
    February 1991 alternate term added
ALT **ecological**

SN Use for the branch of biology dealing with the relations and interactions between organisms and their habitat, including other organisms. For the aggregate of physical things, conditions, and influences surrounding and affecting a given organism or community of organisms at any time, use **environment**. For the concept of the external world, including the forces at work in it and the nonhuman life inhabiting it, perceived by human beings as separate and independent from themselves, their activities and civilization, use **Nature**.
RT **environment**
    Nature

ecology, human
USE **human ecology**

ecology, social
USE **human ecology**

economically disadvantaged
USE **poor**

economics
HN July 1991 scope note changed
    February 1991 alternate term added
ALT **economic**
SN Study concerned with the production, distribution, and consumption of money, goods, and services. (RHDEL2)

Ecuadorian
HN April 1990 added
BT **South American**

edge planes
HN October 1991 lead-in term changed, was **edge planes, piano maker's**
    October 1991 lead-in term changed, was **planes, piano maker's edge**
    April 1991 lead-in term changed, was **piano maker's edge planes**
UF edge planes, pianomaker's
    pianomaker's edge planes
    planes, pianomaker's edge

edge planes, pianomaker's
USE **edge planes**

editing
HN January 1991 scope note added
SN Collecting, preparing, and arranging materials for publication or public presentation, especially written materials, film, or tape. (RHDEL2)

educating
HN April 1991 added
BT *<educational functions>* KG.173
ALT **educated**
SN Use for the specific activities involved in deliberately conveying knowledge, skills, or social values to others. For the discipline that concerns the entire process of impart-

ing such knowledge or values, use **education**. (ERIC12)
RT **education**

education
HN May 1991 scope note added
    April 1991 related term added
    February 1991 alternate term added
ALT **educational**
SN Use for the entire discipline that concerns the entire process of imparting knowledge, attitudes, skills, or socially valued qualities of character or behavior. For the specific activities involved in deliberately conveying knowledge, skills, or social values to others, use **educating**. (ERIC12)
RT **educating**

<education by subject>
HN October 1990 added
BT **education**

education, special
USE **special education**

educational associations
HN April 1991 moved
    April 1991 descriptor changed, was **educational societies**
    April 1991 alternate term changed, was **educational society**
    April 1991 lead-in term changed, was **societies, educational**
BT **associations**
ALT **educational association**
UF associations, educational

egg crate louvers
HN July 1990 added
BT **louvers (built works components)**
ALT **egg crate louver**
UF louvers, egg crate

egg-and-oil tempera
USE **egg-oil tempera**

egg-oil paint
USE **egg-oil tempera**

egg-oil tempera
HN July 1990 added
BT **tempera**
SN Tempera made using the whole egg, with oils or resins added, having qualities of both egg tempera and oil paint. (GOTTS)
UF egg-and-oil tempera
    egg-oil paint
    paint, egg-oil
    tempera, egg-and-oil
    tempera, egg-oil

EIF systems
USE **exterior insulation and finish systems**

EIFS
USE **exterior insulation and finish systems**

Einfühling
USE **empathy**

Elder Cottage Housing Opportunity units
USE **ECHO houses**

elder cottages
USE **ECHO houses**

elderly
HN January 1991 moved
February 1990 lead-in terms added
February 1990 descriptor changed,
was **aged**
January 1990 scope note added
BT **adults**
SN Use for those in the later stage of
life, commonly considered as 65 years
of age and older.
UF aged
older adults

elections
HN May 1991 alternate term added
November 1990 moved
BT *<political events>*
ALT **election**

electric cables
HN February 1991 scope note added
SN Use both for electric conductors
comprising a number of twisted or
braided wire strands and for groups
of electric conductors bound together and insulated from one another.

electric conduits
HN February 1991 scope note added
SN Use for tubes especially constructed
for the purpose of enclosing electrical conductors. (STEIN)

electric files
USE **belt sanders**

electric furnaces
HN February 1991 scope note added
SN Furnaces in which the high temperature heat required is produced by
electricity; used especially for forging alloys and refractory materials.
(W)

electric light
USE **electric lighting**

electric lighting
HN April 1991 lead-in terms added
UF electric light
light, electric

electric switchgear
USE **switchboards**

electric wiring
HN February 1991 scope note added
SN Use for the aggregate of wires in
electrical systems. (RHDEL2)

electrical insulation
HN June 1991 moved
BT *<insulation by function>*

electricity supply, emergency
USE **emergency power supply**

electronic security systems
HN August 1990 added
BT **security systems**
ALT **electronic security system**
SN Designates security systems depen-
dent on electronic devices, such as
card readers.
UF security systems, electronic
systems, electronic security

electropolishing
HN March 1991 alternate term added
ALT **electropolished**

elementary schools
HN September 1990 scope note added
SN Use for schools generally extending
from grade 1 through grades 6 or 8
and teaching the rudiments of
learning; may house a kindergarten.

elevations (drawings)
HN May 1991 descriptor changed, was
elevations
May 1991 alternate term changed,
was **elevation**
ALT **elevation (drawing)**

elevator doors
HN March 1991 descriptor split, use **elevator** (ALT of **elevators**) + **doors**

elevators
HN February 1991 scope note added
SN Cars, cages, or platforms and associated machinery for the vertical
conveying of goods or people to and
from different levels. (W)

elevators, hydroelectric
USE **hydraulic elevators**

elevators, observation
USE **observation elevators**

elitism
HN January 1991 alternate term added
ALT **elitist**

ellipses
HN January 1991 alternate term added
ALT **ellipse**

émail en ronde bosse
USE **en ronde bosse**

emancipation
HN November 1990 added
BT **releasing**
ALT **emancipated**
UF manumission

emblem poems
USE **pattern poetry**

emblems (symbols)
HN April 1991 descriptor changed, was
emblems
April 1991 alternate term changed,
was **emblem**
ALT **emblem (symbol)**

embossing
HN August 1991 scope note changed
SN Producing raised letters or designs on
a surface.

embossing, blind
USE **blind embossing**

embossing, uninked
USE **blind embossing**

emergency electricity supply
USE **emergency power supply**

emergency exits
HN February 1991 scope note added
SN Doors, hatches, or other devices
leading to the outside, usually kept
closed and locked, and used chiefly
for emergencies when conventional
exits fail or become inaccessible.
(MEANS)

emergency housing
HN February 1991 related term added
RT **crisis shelters**

emergency lighting
HN April 1991 scope note added
SN Building lighting systems that supply illumination essential to the safety
of life and property in the event of
failure of normal supply. (IESREF)

emergency power supply
HN November 1991 scope note added
November 1991 lead-in term **power
systems, standby** deleted
February 1991 lead-in terms added
February 1991 lead-in term **standby
power systems** deleted
SN Use for electrical systems temporar-
ily produced or supplied by standby
power generators when normal electric power supply fails or is interrupted.
UF electricity supply, emergency
emergency electricity supply

emigrants
HN May 1991 added
BT *<people by state or condition>* HG.775
ALT **emigrant**
SN People who depart from their native
or usual country or region to live
elsewhere. For those who come into
a country or region from another to
settle there, use **immigrants**.
RT **emigration**
immigrants

emigrating
USE **emigration**

emigration
HN May 1991 lead-in term added
May 1991 related term added
April 1991 moved
January 1991 alternate term added
BT **migration**
ALT **emigrated**

UF emigrating
RT emigrants

empathy
HN January 1991 alternate term added
April 1990 lead-in term added
ALT empathetic
UF Einfühling

emulsion, egg/oil
USE egg-oil tempera

en camaieu
USE monochrome

en ronde bosse
HN April 1990 lead-in term changed, was email en bosse ronde
UF émail en ronde bosse

enamel paint
HN July 1990 lead-in term added
UF Ripolin

enamel white
USE blanc fixe

enamel, baked
USE baked enamel

encarnacione
HN June 1990 added
BT <painting techniques for special effects> KT.252
SN Technique used in Spanish painting which involves working the surface of a painted or carved figure to imitate flesh.
UF encarnado

encarnado
USE encarnacione

encaustic color
USE encaustic paint

encaustic paint
HN July 1990 added
BT <paint by composition or origin> MT.2510
UF color, encaustic
encaustic color
paint, encaustic
paint, wax
wax paint

encaustic painting
HN July 1990 scope note changed
SN Use for the technique of painting with pigments dispersed in molten wax. For the technique of decorating clay, use encaustic decoration.

enceintes
HN February 1991 scope note changed
SN Use for the primary line of walled fortification around forts, castles, or towns.

enclosures, toilet
USE toilet compartments

encumbrances
HN January 1991 alternate term added
ALT encumbrance

end-supported beams
USE simple beams

engaged columns
HN June 1991 lead-in terms added
UF applied columns
columns, applied

engine houses
USE powerhouses

engineering schools
HN May 1991 descriptor split, use engineering + schools

English white
USE whiting

engraving (incising)
HN October 1991 scope note changed
October 1990 moved
October 1990 descriptor changed, was engraving (surface decorating)
BT <removal processes and techniques> KT.600
SN Creating marks on the surface of a hard material such as metal or glass, by incising with a sharp tool. For printing processes that involve this technique plus intaglio printing from the surface, use engraving (printing process).

engraving (printing process)
HN October 1991 moved
October 1991 scope note changed
October 1991 descriptor changed, was engraving (printmaking)
May 1991 lead-in term added
BT <intaglio printing processes>
SN Use for the intaglio process in which the design is incised into the printing plate. Distinct from wood engraving, which is a process for relief printing. Historically, has sometimes been used to refer to printmaking processes in general, usually those employing printing plates; use the appropriate specific term. For the single step of incising the design, use engraving (incising).
UF chalcography

engraving, chalk
USE crayon manner

engraving, copper
USE copper engraving

engraving, copperplate
USE copper engraving

engraving, crayon
USE crayon manner

engraving, steel
USE steel engraving

enology
USE wine making

entablatures
HN June 1991 scope note changed
SN Use for the elaborated superstructures carried by the columns in classical architecture, horizontally divided into architrave, frieze, and cornice. Use also for similar features in other contexts, such as along the upper portions of walls.

entablatures, friezeless
USF architrave cornices

entertainment buildings
HN September 1990 scope note added
SN Distinguished from recreation buildings by more narrowly designating buildings with devices or equipment for amusement or diversion and not active sports, nor for which membership is required.

entrances
HN March 1991 scope note added
SN Use for points or places of entering. (RHDEL2)

entropy
HN January 1991 alternate term added
ALT entropic

environment
HN July 1991 related terms added
April 1990 scope note added
SN Use for the aggregate of physical things, conditions, and influences surrounding and affecting a given organism or community of organisms at any time. For the branch of biology dealing with the relations and interactions between organisms and their habitat, use ecology. For the concept of the external world, including the forces at work in it and the nonhuman life inhabiting it, perceived by human beings as separate and independent from themselves, their activities and civilization, use Nature.
RT ecology
Nature

environment and behavior
USE environmental psychology

environment-behavior studies
USE environmental psychology

environmental art
HN October 1991 moved to hierarchy under development

<environmental concepts>
HN April 1990 guide term changed, was <environmental sciences concepts> BM.416

environmental policy
HN April 1990 lead-in term state and environment deleted

environmental psychology
HN April 1990 added
BT *<psychology-related disciplines>* KD.184
SN Field of study concerned with the mutually interactive relationship between the built environment and human behavior.
UF architectural psychology
B-ES
behavior, environment and
behavior-environment studies
ecological psychology
environment and behavior
environment-behavior studies
M-ES
man-environment systems
people-environment studies
psychology, architectural
psychology, ecological
psychology, environmental
studies, behavior-environment
studies, environment-behavior
studies, people-environment
systems, man-environment

épis
HN August 1991 scope note changed
SN Use for adornments found on the terminating points of roof ridges.

episcenia
HN February 1991 descriptor changed, was episcaenia

epistemology
HN February 1991 alternate term added
ALT epistemological

equations
HN January 1991 alternate term added
ALT equation

equestrians
HN December 1990 added
BT *<people by activity>* HG.705
ALT equestrian
SN People who ride horses. (RHDEL2)
UF horseback riders
riders, horseback

Erh-li-kang
USE **Erligang**

Erligang
HN June 1990 lead-in term added
UF Erh-li-kang

erosion
HN February 1991 scope note changed
SN Process whereby materials are worn away and removed by natural causes including weathering, solution, corrosion, or transportation. (W)

escarpments (fortification elements)
USE scarps

escarps
USE **scarps**

Eskimo, Canadian
USE **Inuit**

Eskimo, Copper
USE **Copper Inuit**

estates (law)
HN January 1991 alternate term added
ALT estate (law)

estimating
HN January 1991 scope note added
SN Giving an approximate or tentative judgment regarding the value or quality of something.

estipites
HN February 1991 moved
February 1991 scope note changed
BT pilasters
SN Use for pilasters with complex ornament and low-relief sculpture that taper from top to base, as commonly encountered in Spanish post-Renaissance architecture.

estofado
HN June 1990 added
BT *<painting techniques for special effects>* KT.252
SN Technique used in Spanish painting which involves working a painted surface to create a pattern; used to embellish the robes of carved and painted figures.

etch
HN July 1990 added
BT *<materials by function>* MT.2291
SN A solution of gum arabic and acid used in desensitizing lithographic plates and stones. (TYLER)
UF etch, gum
etch, lithographic
gum arabic etch
gum etch
lithographic etch

etch, deep
USE **deep etching**

etch, gum
USE **etch**

etch, lithographic
USE **etch**

etch, open
USE **open biting**

etching (biting)
USE **biting**

etching (corroding)
HN October 1991 scope note changed
October 1990 moved
October 1990 descriptor changed, was **etching (surface decoration)**
BT *<removal processes and techniques>* KT.600
SN Creating marks on the surface of a hard material such as metal or glass, by the controlled corrosive action of acid. Use **etching (printing process)** for the series of steps that includes printing from a bitten plate.

etching (printing process)
HN October 1991 moved
October 1991 scope note changed
October 1991 descriptor changed, was **etching (printmaking)**
BT *<intaglio printing processes>*
SN Use for the intaglio process in which the design is worked into an acid-resistant substance coating the metal printing plate; the plate is exposed to acid, which etches the plate where the metal is exposed. For the single step of exposing the plate to acid, use biting.

etching ground
HN July 1990 added
BT resist
SN An acid-resistant substance applied to a surface to stop out areas that are not to be etched.
UF ground (etching)

etching, relief
USE **relief etching**

etching, sugar-lift
USE **sugar-lift**

ethics (concept)
HN January 1991 alternate term added
January 1991 descriptor changed, was ethics
ALT ethical

ethics (philosophy)
HN September 1991 related term added
RT behavioral sciences

ethnic group studies
USE **ethnic studies**

ethnic groups
HN October 1999 lead-in term added
September 1991 related term added
June 1991 scope note changed
June 1991 related term added
April 1991 moved
BT *<groups of people>*
SN Subgroups within a larger cultural or social order that are distinguished from the majority and each other by their national, religious, linguistic, cultural, or sometimes racial background. For groups that are the objects of prejudice or discrimination from the majority, use **minorities**. (ERIC12)
UF groups, ethnic
RT ethnic studies
minorities

ethnic studies
HN September 1991 added
BT social sciences
SN Use for the study of the history and culture of ethnic groups within a larger cultural or social order. For the scientific, historic, or comparative study of the origins, characteristics, and functions of human cultures and societies, use **ethnology**.

UF ethnic group studies
    studies, ethnic
    studies, ethnic group
RT ethnic groups
    ethnology

ethnocentrism
HN January 1991 alternate term added
ALT ethnocentric

ethnography
HN September 1991 moved
BT anthropology

ethnology
HN September 1991 related term added
    September 1991 scope note changed
    September 1991 moved
    February 1991 alternate term added
BT anthropology
ALT ethnological
SN Use for the scientific, historic, or comparative study of the origins, characteristics, and functions of human cultures and societies. For the study of the history and culture of ethnic groups within a larger cultural or social order, use **ethnic studies**.
RT ethnic studies

ethnopsychology
HN September 1991 moved
BT psychology

ethylene glycol monoethyl ether
HN May 1990 lead-in term changed, was cellosolve
UF Cellosolve (TM)

etymology
HN February 1991 alternate term added
ALT etymological

events
HN May 1991 alternate term added
    January 1991 scope note added
ALT event
SN Occurrences taking place during a particular interval of time.

evolutionary housing
USE incremental housing

excelsior
HN July 1990 lead-in terms added
UF cellulose fiber
    cellulose fiber, wood
    fiber, cellulose
    fiber, wood
    wood cellulose fiber
    wood fiber
    wood wool
    wool, wood

excommunications
HN May 1991 alternate term added
ALT excommunication

executing
HN February 1991 alternate term added
ALT executed

execution
HN February 1991 alternate term added
ALT executed

executions
HN May 1991 alternate term added
ALT execution

exedrae (interior spaces)
HN May 1991 descriptor changed, was exedrae
    May 1991 alternate term changed, was exedra
ALT exedra (interior space)

exhibiting
HN May 1991 related term added
RT alternative spaces

exhibitions
HN May 1991 alternate term added
ALT exhibition

existentialism
HN January 1991 alternate term added
ALT existentialist

expanded metal
HN June 1990 scope note added
SN Sheet metal that has been slit and expanded to form a mesh, which is used for reinforced-concrete work or plaster wall construction. (MH)

expatriates
HN May 1991 related term added
RT expatriation

expatriation
HN May 1991 related term added
    January 1991 scope note added
    November 1990 moved
    January 1990 alternate term added
BT emigration
ALT expatriated
SN Withdrawing voluntarily from one's native country, especially if renouncing allegiance to it or to its government. (W)
RT expatriates

expeditions
HN May 1991 alternate term added
ALT expedition

exporting
HN January 1991 scope note added
SN Carrying or sending articles of trade or commerce out of a country. (BLACKS)

exposing
USE exposure

exposure
HN April 1991 added
BT *<photographic processing and presentation techniques>* KT.404
SN The act of presenting a photosensitive surface to radiant energy, especially light; also, the total amount of radiant energy received. (RHDEL2)
UF exposing

exquisite corpses
USE cadavres exquis

exterior insulation and finish systems
HN July 1990 added
BT building materials
SN Lightweight and economical cladding system for buildings composed of insulation and wet applied finishes. (AIAENC)
UF EIF systems
    EIFS
    finish systems, exterior insulation and
    insulation and finish systems, exterior
    systems, exterior insulation and finish

exterior lighting
HN April 1991 scope note added
SN Lighting systems supplying light outdoors for safety, pleasure, or information, as for playing fields, highways, or advertising.

extradoses
HN February 1991 alternate term changed, was extradose
ALT extrados

eyebrow dormers
HN February 1991 scope note changed
    February 1991 lead-in terms added
SN Low dormers in a roof over which the roof is carried in a continuous curve. (PUTNAM)
UF eyebrow windows
    windows, eyebrow

eyebrow windows
USE eyebrow dormers

fables
HN January 1991 alternate term added
ALT fable

fabric reinforcement, wire
USE welded wire fabric

fabric, rubberized
USE rubberized cloth

fabric, welded wire
USE welded wire fabric

fabricated photographs
USE staged photographs

face strings
HN February 1991 lead-in terms added
    February 1991 scope note source changed to DAC
UF finish stair strings
    stair strings, finish
    strings, finish stair

facilities, cogeneration
USE cogeneration plants

facilities, pedestrian
USE pedestrian facilities

facility management
HN February 1991 moved
BT managing

factor, reflection
USE reflectance

factories, gunpowder
USE powder mills

faculty housing
HN April 1990 added
BT <housing by occupants> RG.81
UF housing, faculty

fading
HN March 1990 alternate term fade deleted

fairs
HN May 1991 alternate term added
ALT fair

fairy tales
HN November 1990 added
BT <document genres by form> VW.3
ALT fairy tale
UF tales, fairy

falchions
USE mouchettes

false arches
USE corbel arches

false biting
USE foul biting

false doors
HN March 1991 moved
March 1991 scope note changed
March 1991 lead-in terms added
BT <wall components by form or function> RT.610
SN Elements imitating doors, but not meant to pass through, inserted to complete a series of doors or to deceive.
UF blind doors
doors, blind

false fronts
HN March 1991 moved
BT screen facades

false thatched roofs
HN March 1991 lead-in terms added
UF roofs, simulated thatch
simulated thatch roofs
thatch roofs, simulated

false windows
USE blind windows

families
HN May 1991 moved
February 1991 related term added
BT <kinship groups> HG.879
RT siblings

family quarters, private
USE apartments

Famosa marble
USE Formosa marble

fan Fink trusses
HN March 1991 moved
March 1991 scope note added
BT Fink trusses
SN Use for Fink trusses with subdiagonals radiating outward from central points. (DAC)

fancy balls
USE fancy dress balls

fancy dress balls
HN April 1991 added
BT balls (parties)
ALT fancy dress ball
SN Balls at which those attending wear costumes departing from currently conventional style and usually representing fictional or historical characters, animals, particular occupations, or the fancy of the wearer. (W)
UF balls, fancy
balls, fancy dress
fancy balls

fanlights
HN August 1991 scope note changed
SN Semicircular windows over doors or other openings with radiating bars giving the appearance of an open fan.

fantastic architecture
HN July 1991 scope note added
July 1991 lead-in term added
May 1990 lead-in terms added
SN Use for architecture designs that are eccentric, outrageous, or unconventional, that jolt or excite the viewer, and that are generally characterized by an unusual juxtaposition of shapes or materials; may be spontaneously constructed, incomplete, or unbuilt.
UF architectural fantasies
architecture, bizarre
bizarre architecture

farmers markets
HN May 1991 alternate term added
ALT farmers market

farming
HN May 1991 added
BT <agricultural functions>
SN Operating or participating in the operation of a farm.
RT farms

farms
HN September 1991 scope note added
May 1991 related term added
SN Complexes where plants or animals are raised for livelihood or commerce.
RT farming

farms, horse
USE horse farms

farms, stud
USE horse farms

fascia boards
HN February 1991 lead-in term added
February 1991 descriptor changed, was eaves fascias
February 1991 lead-in term changed, was fascia boards
February 1991 alternate term changed, was eaves fascia
ALT fascia board
UF eaves fascias
fascias (eave components)

fascias
HN March 1991 moved
March 1991 scope note changed
BT <architrave components>
SN Use for the flat strips on Ionic and Corinthian architraves. For boards nailed across the ends of rafters in wood construction, use fascia boards.

fascias (eave components)
USE fascia boards

fascism
HN January 1991 alternate term added
ALT fascist

fashion design
HN March 1991 moved
BT design

fast building
USE fast-track method

fast-track construction
USE fast-track method

fast-track method
HN July 1990 added
BT <processes and techniques by specific type> KT.5
SN Architectural project management technique whereby construction is allowed to begin before the design and specifications are completed.
UF building, fast
construction, fast-track
construction, phased
fast building
fast-track construction
method, fast-track
phased construction

fasts
HN May 1991 alternate term added
ALT fast

fat lime
HN June 1990 scope note added
SN A pure lime either quick lime or hydrated lime; lime putty having a good spread; used to fill voids in the finish coat as it is applied and troweled. (DAC)

fauces
HN June 1990 alternate term faux deleted

feasts
HN   May 1991 alternate term added
ALT   feast

features, water
USE   **water features**

fees
HN   January 1991 alternate term added
ALT   fee

fei pai
USE   **fei po**

fei po
HN   April 1990 added
BT   **brushwork**
SN   Brushwork in Chinese painting in which the brush is pulled quickly across the paper, allowing the hairs to separate so that the ink is broken and uneven and the paper shows through. (AAC71)
UF   fei pai
flying white
white, flying

fellowships
HN   January 1991 alternate term added
ALT   **fellowship**

felt, bituminous
USE   **tar paper**

felt, tarred
USE   **tar paper**

felt-tip markers
USE   **felt-tip pens**

felt-tip pens
HN   September 1991 lead-in terms added
UF   felt-tip markers
markers, felt-tip

female
HN   January 1991 added
BT   **sex**
SN   Referring to the sex that normally produces eggs or female germ cells. (RHDEL2)
RT   **women**

females, human
USE   **women**

fenestellas
HN   March 1991 moved
BT   *<windows by location or context>* RT.957

fenestrals
HN   March 1991 scope note changed
SN   Window openings closed with cloth or translucent paper instead of glass.

ferric chloride
HN   July 1990 added
BT   **salt**
UF   chloride, ferric
chloride, iron
iron chloride
iron perchloride
iron, perchloride of
perchloride of iron
perchloride, iron

Ferrite (TM)
USE   **Mars yellow**

Ferrox (TM)
USE   **Mars yellow**

festivals
HN   May 1991 alternate term added
ALT   festival

festoon lighting
HN   June 1991 deleted
BT   *<lighting by form>*

fêtes
HN   May 1991 alternate term added
ALT   fête

fetishes
HN   October 1990 added
BT   *<object genres by function>* VB.100
ALT   fetish

feudalism
HN   January 1991 alternate term added
ALT   feudal

fiber optics
HN   July 1990 added
BT   **optics**
SN   Branch of optics that deals with the transmission of light through glass or plastic; has particular application in the transmission of textual data or images. For the actual strands of glass or plastic, use **optical fibers.**
UF   optics, fiber
RT   **optical fibers**

fiber reinforced composites
USE   **fibrous composites**

fiber, cellulose
USE   **excelsior**

fiber, cotton
USE   **cotton fiber**

fiber, wood
USE   **excelsior**

fiberboard
HN   July 1990 lead-in term added
May 1990 lead-in term changed, was beaverboard
UF   Beaverboard (TM)
Celotex (TM)

Fiberglas (TM)
USE   **fiberglass**

fiberglass
HN   July 1990 added
BT   *<glass by form>* MT.246
SN   Glass which is drawn into fibrous form and can be woven into cloth. It is strong, light, nonflammable and has a high tensile strength.
UF   canvas, glass
Fiberglas (TM)
fibrous glass
glass canvas
glass fiber
glass, fiber
glass, spun
spun glass

fibers, optical
USE   **optical fibers**

fibro-concrete
HN   February 1991 related term added
RT   **fibrous composites**

fibrous composites
HN   February 1991 added
BT   **composite materials**
ALT   **fibrous composite**
SN   Use for composite materials of fibers embedded in a matrix, as in some reinforced plastics.
UF   composites, fibrous
composites, fibrous reinforced
composites, filament reinforced
fiber reinforced composites
filament reinforced composites
reinforced composites, fibrous
reinforced composites, filament
RT   **fibro-concrete**
fibrous plaster

fibrous glass
USE   **fiberglass**

fibrous plaster
HN   February 1991 related term added
RT   **fibrous composites**

fiction, romance
USE   **romances**

field houses
HN   September 1990 scope note added
SN   Use both for buildings providing enclosed and unobstructed space adaptable for various physical education and recreation activities, such as track events and basketball, and for buildings housing equipment and dressing facilities for athletes; often located at or near athletic fields.

filament reinforced composites
USE   **fibrous composites**

files (documents)
HN   May 1991 descriptor changed, was files
May 1991 alternate term changed, was file
ALT   file (document)

files, electric
USE   **belt sanders**

fill
USE   **fill light**

fill insulation
HN   June 1991 moved
BT   **flexible insulation**

fill light
HN   June 1991 added
BT   **supplementary lighting**
SN   Supplementary lighting to reduce, soften, or eliminate shadows caused by the main source of illumination.
UF   fill
light, fill

fillers
HN May 1990 scope note changed
SN Substances added to products to increase, for example, bulk, viscosity, opacity, or strength or materials used to fill in gaps or other spaces.

filletsters
USE **fillisters**

fillisters
HN September 1991 lead-in term added
UF filletsters

film (material)
HN May 1991 descriptor changed, was film

film formers
HN May 1990 deleted
BT additives

film museums
USE **museums of moving images**

film-stencil method
HN October 1990 deleted
BT stenciling

filmmakers
HN July 1991 lead-in term **producers** deleted
    February 1991 scope note added
SN Use for makers of personal, independently produced films, who are responsible for the conception, sponsorship, and execution of all aspects of the film. (USMREL)

filmographies
HN March 1991 added
BT <lists by form or function> VW.252
ALT filmography
SN Selective or complete lists of motion pictures, typically by one director, actor, or on a specific subject.
RT motion pictures

finance
HN February 1991 moved
    February 1991 scope note changed
    January 1991 alternate term added
BT economics
ALT financial
SN Branch of economics concerning the management or use of funds and credit by a government, business, or individual. (W)

financial records
HN March 1991 lead-in terms added
    January 1991 scope note added
SN Documents pertaining to money matters.
UF fiscal records
    records, fiscal

Fine Manner
HN July 1990 added
BT <Italian Renaissance-Baroque styles> FL.3230
UF Manner, Fine

finger painting
HN February 1991 moved
BT <painting techniques by application method> KT.220

finials
HN March 1991 lead-in term changed, was **guglias (finials)**
UF guglias

finish stair strings
USE **face strings**

finish systems, exterior insulation and
USE **exterior insulation and finish systems**

Fink trusses
HN August 1991 scope note changed
    March 1991 moved
BT <trusses by form> RT.357
SN Use for a variety of symmetrical trusses: those in the form of three isoceles triangles with one triangle in the center with its base along the bottom chord and each of the outer two triangles having its base along the sloping side at an upper chord, or those in the form of triangles with diagonal members forming w-shapes, or those in the form of rectangles with few verticals in proportion to numerous diagonal web members of different lengths.

fiore di Persico
HN October 1990 scope note added
SN Variegated marble, of various shades of red, pink, and purple on a white ground-mass, quarried in ancient times principally at Epirus in Turkey.

fiorto marble
HN October 1990 scope note added
SN Variegated marble of light chocolate brown and white, from Italy. (RS)

fire detectors
HN March 1991 scope note added
SN Sensors and interconnected monitoring equipment that detect fires or the effects of fires and activate alarm systems. (MEANS)

fire detectors, ionization
USE **ionization detectors**

fire detectors, photoelectric
USE **photoelectric smoke detectors**

fire extinguishing systems
HN March 1991 scope note added
SN Use for installations of automatic sprinklers, foam distribution systems, fire hoses and/or portable fire extinguishers designed for extinguishing fires. (MEANS)

fire hydrants
HN June 1990 scope note added
    June 1990 lead-in term added
SN Supply outlets for drawing water from mains or service pipes and usually located along streets and used for firefighting.
UF hydrants

fire insurance maps
HN October 1990 lead-in term added
UF atlases, fire insurance

fire protection systems
HN March 1991 scope note added
SN Protection systems that provide safeguards to construction and exit facilities through the use of fire alarm, fire detecting, and fire extinguishing equipment to reduce the risk and spread of fire. (STEIN)

fire stations
HN September 1990 scope note added
SN Use for buildings housing firefighting apparatus and, usually, firefighters. (W)

fire stations, manual
USE **manual stations**

fire towers (building divisions)
HN June 1990 scope note added
SN Designates vertical enclosures in buildings containing a stairway and having a fire endurance rating high enough to qualify as fire escapes. (DAC)

fire towers (watchtowers)
HN May 1991 descriptor changed, was **fire towers**
    May 1991 alternate term changed, was **fire tower**
ALT fire tower (watchtower)

firebacks
HN March 1991 scope note added
SN Designates the back walls or linings of fireplaces.

fireplace cheeks
HN April 1991 scope note added
SN Designates the splayed sides of fireplaces.

fireplaces
HN March 1991 scope note changed
SN Use for openings or recesses in chimneys or walls in which fires may be built, as for heating or cooking; may also refer to low fireproof structures erected outdoors for cooking over open flames.

fires
HN May 1991 alternate term added
ALT fire

firewood
HN May 1990 lead-in term added
UF fuelwood

firing (managing)
HN May 1991 descriptor changed, was firing
    December 1990 lead-in terms added
UF dismissal
    termination (employees)

firmer gouges
HN January 1991 scope note source changed to MEANS

fiscal records
USE **financial records**

fish glue
HN June 1991 moved
    May 1990 scope note added
BT **animal glue**
SN Glue made from the degraded collagen from fish skins and wastes. Also glue made from the swim bladders of fish, a tissue composed entirely of collagen.

fish oil
HN October 1990 moved
BT **animal oil**

fitness centers
USE **health clubs**

fixed windows
HN March 1991 scope note changed, source MEANS deleted

fixing blocks
USE **nailing blocks**

fixture traps
HN March 1991 scope note added
SN Use for traps integral with or serving plumbing fixtures and for interceptors serving as such traps. (STEIN)

flagstone
HN May 1990 scope note added
SN Refers to large flat sections of slate used for paving and also bluestone cut for this purpose. (MH)

flame detectors
HN March 1991 scope note added
SN Equipment that detects fire in the flame stage.

flame spread ratings
HN January 1991 alternate term added
ALT **flame spread rating**

flammability
HN April 1991 added
BT **chemical properties**
ALT **flammable**
SN Use generally for the ability to support, or high capacity for, combustion.

Flandreau
USE **Santee Dakota**

flashing (building components)
HN May 1991 descriptor changed, was **flashing**

flat arches
HN March 1991 scope note changed
SN Use for arches in which neither intrados nor extrados has any curvature, yet is composed of voussoirs arranged so that lateral thrusts are generated from vertical loads; for arches with very slight curvature, use **camber arches.**

flat wash
HN June 1990 added
BT **wash technique**
SN Technique which involves the application of flat color over an area too large to be covered by a single brush stroke. (TPH)
UF wash, flat

flats (apartments)
HN May 1991 descriptor changed, was **flats**
    May 1991 alternate term changed, was **flat**
ALT **flat (apartment)**

flats, granny
USE **ECHO houses**

flawlessness
USE **perfection**

flea markets
HN May 1991 alternate term added
ALT **flea market**

flèches
HN June 1990 descriptor changed, was **fleches**
    June 1990 alternate term changed, was **flech**
ALT **flèche**

fletton
HN January 1991 lead-in term added
UF London brick

flexible insulation
HN June 1991 moved
BT <*insulation by form*>

flexible pavements
HN November 1991 moved
    March 1991 scope note added
BT **pavements**
SN Pavements that maintain intimate contact with and distribute loads to the subgrade and depend for stability on aggregate interlock, particle friction, and cohesion; for pavements that are more rigidly bonded, use **rigid pavements.** (MEANS)

fliers
HN March 1991 lead-in term added
    March 1991 scope note source changed to DAC
    March 1991 lead-in term **flyers (steps)** deleted
UF flyers

flights
HN March 1991 scope note source changed to DAC

floodlighting
HN April 1991 moved
    April 1991 scope note added
BT <*lighting techniques by distribution*>

SN Uniform, nearly shadowless illumination for lighting scenes or objects to a luminance greater than their surroundings. (IESREF)

floods
HN May 1991 alternate term added
ALT **flood**

floor constructions, beam-and-slab
USE **two-way beam and slab systems**

floor joists
HN March 1991 descriptor split, use **floor** (ALT of **floors**) + **joists**

floor systems, one-way
USE **one-way beam and slab systems**

floor to ceiling windows
HN May 1991 deleted
BT <*windows by form*>

floors
HN March 1991 scope note added
SN The surfaces of rooms or spaces on which one walks.

floors, beam-and-slab
USE **one-way beam and slab systems**
     two-way beam and slab systems

floors, cavity
USE **suspended floors**

floors, pan
USE **one-way joist systems**

floors, raised
USE **access floors**

floors, waffle
USE **waffle slabs**

floral designers
HN September 1990 lead-in terms added
UF arrangers, flower
    designers, floral
    flower arrangers

flower arrangers
USE **floral designers**

flowing tracery
USE **curvilinear tracery**

flue linings
HN March 1991 scope note added
SN Use for linings of chimneys constructed of special heat-resistant materials to prevent fire, smoke, and gases from spreading to surrounding spaces.

flue walls
USE **hot walls**

flues
HN March 1991 scope note added
    March 1991 lead-in terms added
SN Use for passageways constructed to control drafts in and carry away products of combustion from fireplaces and furnaces.

UF pipes, smoke
    smoke pipes

fluing arches
  USE **splayed arches**

fluorescent light
  USE **fluorescent lighting**

fluorescent lighting
  HN April 1991 lead-in terms added
  UF fluorescent light
      light, fluorescent

flyers
  USE **fliers**

flying buttresses
  HN March 1991 scope note changed
  SN Exterior arched supports transmitting the thrust of a vault or roof from the upper part of a wall outward to a pier or buttress.

flying staircases
  USE **flying stairs**

flying stairs
  HN March 1991 lead-in terms added
  UF flying staircases
      staircases, flying

flying white
  USE **fei po**

foamcore board
  USE **Fome-Cor (TM)**

foils
  HN June 1991 moved
      June 1991 scope note changed
  BT <*culminating and edge ornaments*> RT.1047
  SN Circular or nearly circular lobes tangent to the inner side of a larger arc, as of an arch, or meeting each other in projecting cusps.

folding shutters
  HN March 1991 scope note source changed to DAC

folium
  HN April 1990 added
  BT **vegetable dye**
  SN A vegetable juice, red in its natural state, used in the Middle Ages as a coloring; probably obtained from the turnsole plant. (THEOPH)

folklore
  HN March 1991 scope note changed
  SN Traditional and expressive forms of culture, such as song, story, dance, ritual, handicraft, art, food ways, costume, custom, religion, architecture, and work skills, and of the processes and meanings that underlie them. (PG)

follies
  HN October 1990 moved
  BT <*single built works by design*> RK.1372

Fome-Cor (TM)
  HN September 1991 added
  BT **board**
  SN Lightweight board with a plastic foam center faced with paper on both sides, often used for mounting or backing works of art. (ELSPAS)
  UF board, foamcore
      foamcore board
  RT **mounting board**

fonts
  HN March 1991 scope note added
  SN Basins or other vessels in which water is contained for baptisms.

<*food and beverage making processes and techniques*>
  HN January 1991 added
  BT <*processes and techniques by specific type*> KT.5

food stands
  HN April 1990 added
  BT **stands (mercantile structures)**
  ALT **food stand**
  SN Designates roadside eateries serving a limited menu at low prices, generally over a counter or through a window; may range from slight architectural structures to freestanding buildings.
  UF stands, food

football stadiums
  HN September 1990 scope note added
  SN Use for stadiums designed and equipped for playing and viewing American football.

footings, spread
  USE **spread footings**

forest fires
  HN May 1991 alternate term added
  ALT **forest fire**

forestages
  HN June 1990 lead-in terms added
  UF apron pieces
      pieces, apron

forgings
  HN May 1990 scope note added
  SN Metal parts, worked to a predetermined shape by one or more of such processes as hammering, pressing, rolling, or upset forging. (STEIN)

formal gardens
  HN July 1991 related term added
      May 1991 related term added
  RT **parterres**
      water chains

Formist
  HN April 1990 added
  BT <*modern Polish fine arts styles and movements*> FL.3409
  ALT **Formism**

Formosa marble
  HN May 1990 lead-in terms added
  UF Famosa marble
      marble, Famosa

forms (documents)
  HN May 1991 descriptor changed, was **forms**
      May 1991 alternate term changed, was **form**
  ALT **form (document)**

formulas
  HN January 1991 alternate term added
  ALT **formula**

foul biting
  HN April 1990 added
  BT <*conditions and effects: printing and printmaking*>
  SN Irregular marking of a printing plate during biting as a result of faulty grounding.
  UF biting, false
      biting, foul
      false biting

foundation walls
  HN March 1991 scope note added
  SN Use for walls partly or entirely below grade that support the exterior parts of structures.

foundations (structural elements)
  HN March 1991 scope note added
      March 1991 descriptor changed, was **foundations**
      March 1991 alternate term changed, was **foundation**
  ALT **foundation (structural element)**
  SN Use for those parts of structures, usually located below ground level, that transmit building loads to the soil or rock underneath; when specifically distinguishing the support systems and areas of structures below ground, including the foundation, from the above-ground portions, use **substructures**.

foundations, mat
  USE **raft foundations**

founders (originators)
  HN June 1991 alternate term changed, was **founder**
      March 1991 scope note added
      March 1991 lead-in terms added
      March 1991 descriptor changed, was **founders**
  ALT **founder (originator)**
  SN Those who establish or originate things such as movements, institutions, or communities.
  UF founding fathers
      foundresses

founding fathers
  USE **founders (originators)**

foundresses
  USE **founders (originators)**

foundry sand
HN May 1990 scope note added
SN Any sand employed for making molds for casting metals, but especially refers to sands that are refractory and also have binding qualities. (MH)

fountains, soda
USE **soda fountains**

Fox
HN June 1990 lead-in term added
UF Musquakie

foxing
HN August 1991 scope note changed
SN Pale, brown, diffuse spots that appear on paper or other surfaces, probably either from mold growth or metallic impurities in the paper.

fractals
HN January 1991 alternate term added
ALT **fractal**

frame construction, platform
USE **platform frames**

frame structures, space
USE **space frames**

frame windows, double
USE **double windows**

frames, cellular
USE **box frames**

framing, platform
USE **platform frames**

framing, western
USE **platform frames**

Fraser's balsam fir
HN May 1990 lead-in term changed, was **Abies Fraseri**
UF Abies fraseri

free schools
HN September 1990 scope note added
SN Designates privately run schools with programs organized as an alternative to traditional public or private schools, usually with a highly flexible or voluntaristic framework.

French arches
HN February 1991 scope note changed
    February 1991 descriptor changed, was **Dutch arches**
    February 1991 alternate term changed, was **Dutch arch**
    February 1991 lead-in term changed, was **French arches**
ALT **French arch**
SN Use for flat arches in which the joints of the voussoirs do not radiate but all slope outward from the center at the same angle on both sides.
UF Dutch arches

French doors
HN March 1991 moved
    March 1991 scope note changed
BT *<openings by form>* RT.830
SN Floor-length wall openings consisting entirely or mostly of glass panels and hinged on one side so they may function as either doors or windows; often used in pairs.

Freons (TM)
USE **chlorofluorocarbons**

frets, labyrinth
USE **meanders (patterns)**

frieze-band windows
HN November 1991 alternate term changed, was **frieze band window**
    March 1991 scope note changed
    March 1991 descriptor changed, was **frieze band windows**
ALT **frieze-band window**
SN Windows externally located in a wide band of trim just beneath cornices; found on Greek Revival houses.

friezeless entablatures
USE **architrave cornices**

friezes (entablature components)
HN June 1991 scope note changed
SN Middle horizontal members of a classical entablature, above the architrave and below the cornice; for horizontal decorated bands in general, found on architecture and furniture, use **friezes (ornamental bands)**.

frigidaria
HN June 1990 scope note changed
SN The cold rooms of Roman baths, sometimes including a cold plunge.

front hearths
HN November 1991 scope note added
    November 1990 moved
BT *<hearth components>*
SN Use for the parts of hearths that project into rooms.

frontal depiction
USE **frontality**

frontality
HN November 1990 scope note changed
    May 1990 lead-in term added
SN The quality possessed by a sculpture, building, or other structure that is designed to be viewed from directly in front; in pictorial compositions, the quality possessed by figures that face directly out of the picture.
UF frontal depiction

frost heaves
HN May 1991 alternate term added
ALT **frost heave**

frottage
HN July 1990 scope note changed
SN The technique of making a rubbing from a textured surface, especially when the rubbing is then incorporated into a collage or montage; popular among the Surrealists as a form of automatism.

fuchsia purple
USE **deep reddish purple**

fuelwood
USE **firewood**

full plate
USE **whole plate**

fun houses
HN September 1990 scope note added
SN Denotes buildings, commonly found in amusement parks, containing various devices designed to startle or amuse and arranged along a passage through which patrons walk. (W)

fun parks, water
USE **waterparks**

functions (activities)
HN June 1991 alternate term added
    May 1991 descriptor changed, was **functions**
ALT **function (activity)**

fund raising
HN January 1991 scope note added
SN Process of raising money for nonpersonal, noncommercial purposes, such as for nonprofit organizations or political concerns.

funding
HN January 1991 scope note added
SN Providing direct cash support to another person or organization. (NARA)

funeral gifts
USE **grave goods**

funerals
HN May 1991 alternate term added
ALT **funeral**

funereal achievements
USE **hatchments**

furnaces
HN March 1991 scope note added
SN Use for equipment designed for the production of heat by combustion.

gable dormers
HN November 1991 alternate term changed, was **gabled dormer**
    March 1991 lead-in terms added
    March 1991 descriptor changed, was **gabled dormers**
    March 1991 lead-in term changed, was **dormers, gabled**
ALT **gable dormer**

UF dormers, gable
    dormers, gable-roof
    gable-roof dormers

gable ends
  HN March 1991 scope note source
      changed to DAC

gable posts
  HN March 1991 scope note source
      changed to DAC

gable-roof dormers
  USE **gable dormers**

gables, corbiestep
  USE **corbie gables**

gables, crow
  USE **corbie gables**

gables, crowstepped
  USE **corbie gables**

gables, stepped
  USE **corbie gables**

gaged brick
  USE **gauged brick**

galas
  HN May 1991 alternate term added
  ALT **gala**

gallerias
  USE **shopping arcades**
      shopping malls

galleries (rooms)
  HN May 1991 descriptor changed, was
      galleries
      May 1991 alternate term changed,
      was **gallery**
  ALT **gallery (room)**

galleries, countermine
  USE **countermines**

galleries, organ
  USE **organ lofts**

galleting
  HN April 1990 added
  BT **filling**
  ALT **galleted**
  SN The insertion of stone chips into the
      joints of rough masonry to reduce the
      amount of mortar required, to wedge
      larger stones in position, or to add
      detail to the appearance. (DAC)
  UF garreting

galletted joints
  HN April 1990 descriptor split, use **gal-**
      leted (ALT of **galleting**) + **joints**

gambrel roofs
  HN March 1991 lead-in term added
  UF gambrels

gambrels
  USE **gambrel roofs**

games
  HN May 1991 alternate term added
  ALT **game**

games, card
  USE **card games**

ganosis
  HN April 1991 moved
  BT **sculpture techniques**

garage doors
  HN March 1991 scope note added
  SN Use for doors that are designed to
      allow the entry of vehicles into ga-
      rages.

garage sales
  HN May 1991 alternate term added
  ALT **garage sale**

garbage
  HN July 1991 added
  BT **refuse**
  SN Animal or vegetable refuse from the
      shipping, processing, or preparation
      of food. (W)

garden architects
  USE **landscape architects**

garden shows
  HN May 1991 alternate term added
  ALT **garden show**

gardens
  HN April 1991 related term added
  RT **horticulture**

gargoyles
  HN March 1991 scope note changed
  SN Waterspouts carved into grotesque
      figures and projecting from the roof
      gutters of buildings.

Garhwal
  HN June 1990 descriptor changed, was
      Garwhal

garreting
  USE **galleting**

gasen
  USE **gasenshi**

gasenshi
  HN July 1990 added
  BT **handmade paper**
  SN Handmade Japanese paper, made of
      10% mitsumata. (SAFF)
  UF gasen
      gasenshi echizen

gasenshi echizen
  USE **gasenshi**

gateposts
  USE **hanging posts**
      shutting posts

gates, lich
  USE **lich gates**

gauffrage
  USE **goffering**

gauged arches
  HN March 1991 scope note changed
  SN Use for arches built of bricks that are
      slightly wedge-shaped, so that the
      joints of the arches radiate from a
      common center.

gauged brick
  HN May 1990 lead-in term added
  UF gaged brick

gauze candles
  USE **candle screens**

geisons
  USE **cornices**

gender
  USE **sex**

gender identity
  USE **sex role**

gender role
  USE **sex role**

general diffuse lighting
  HN April 1991 moved
  BT *<lighting techniques by direction>*

general illumination
  USE **general lighting**

general lighting
  HN June 1991 lead-in terms added
      April 1991 moved
      April 1991 scope note added
      April 1991 lead-in term added
  BT *<lighting techniques by distribution>*
  SN Lighting techniques providing sub-
      stantially uniform levels of illumi-
      nation throughout an area exclusive
      of special local requirements. (IES-
      REF)
  UF general illumination
      general lighting system
      illumination, general
      lighting system, general

general lighting system
  USE **general lighting**

generating plants, CHP
  USE **cogeneration plants**

geniuses
  USE **gifted**

gentrification
  HN January 1991 alternate term added
      December 1990 moved
  BT **urban renewal**
  ALT **gentrified**

geochemistry
  HN February 1991 alternate term added
  ALT **geochemical**

geography
  HN February 1991 alternate term added
  ALT **geographical**

geography, human
  USE **human geography**

Geoksyur
HN June 1990 descriptor changed, was Geokysur

geology
HN February 1991 alternate term added
ALT geological

geometry
HN February 1991 alternate term added
ALT geometrical

geosynthetics
HN April 1990 added
BT <plastics by function>
SN A planar product manufactured from polymeric material used with soil, rock, earth, or any other geotechnical engineering related material, as an integral part of a man-made product, structure, or system. (ASTM)

geotextiles
HN April 1990 added
BT geosynthetics
SN Any permeable textile material used with foundation, soil, rock, earth, or any other geotechnical engineering related material, as an integral part of a man-made product, structure, or system. (ASTM)

Gere
USE Dan

gestation
USE pregnancy

gifted
HN June 1990 lead-in term added
UF geniuses

gifts
HN January 1991 alternate term added
ALT gift

gifts, burial
USE grave goods

gifts, funeral
USE grave goods

gifts, grave
USE grave goods

gifts, tomb
USE grave goods

gilding
HN April 1991 scope note changed
SN Surface application of metal in the form of leaf, powder applied directly to the surface, powder mixed with a binder, or other forms to approximate the effect of solid or inlaid metal.

girders
HN March 1991 scope note source changed to DAC

glair
HN April 1990 added
BT gold size
SN Gold size composed of beaten egg white and vinegar. (W)

glare
HN May 1990 scope note changed, W added as source

glass canvas
USE fiberglass

glass fiber
USE fiberglass

glass paste
USE paste (glass)

glass, art
USE art glass

glass, cameo
USE cameo glass

glass, fiber
USE fiberglass

glass, gold ruby
USE gold ruby glass

glass, spun
USE fiberglass

glassine
HN July 1990 added
BT <paper by form> MT.1903
SN A transparent thin paper used especially for envelope windows and for sanitary wrapping. (MH)
UF glassoid

glassoid
USE glassine

glazing (coating)
HN September 1991 moved
September 1991 scope note changed
July 1991 descriptor changed, was glazing
BT coating
SN Covering with a thin, usually glossy, sometimes transparent, surface coating.

glitter
HN July 1990 added
BT trimmings
SN Small glittering objects or tiny glittering bits. (W)

global approach
USE globalism

globalism
HN February 1991 added
BT <philosophical movements and attitudes> BM.503
SN Approach to social, cultural, scientific, and humanistic questions involving an orientation to the world as a single interacting system. (ERIC12)

UF approach, global
approach, worldwide
global approach
worldwide approach

glue, animal
USE animal glue

glycerin
HN July 1990 added
BT organic materials
SN Colorless, heavy, sweet liquid derived from natural fats and oils. It can be used as a plasticizer in certain media.
UF glycerol

glycerin development
USE glycerin process

glycerin process
HN July 1990 lead-in term added
July 1990 descriptor changed, was glycerine process
UF glycerin development

glycerol
USE glycerin

glyptic art
USE glyptics

glyptics
HN October 1990 moved
October 1990 scope note changed
October 1990 lead-in term added
BT carving
SN The art or process of carving gems or seals.
UF glyptic art

goat's heads
USE aegicranes

goffering
HN July 1990 lead-in term added
UF gauffrage

Gogo
HN June 1990 lead-in term added
UF Wagogo

Golconda
HN February 1991 moved
BT Deccani

gold ruby glass
HN March 1991 added
BT <glass by composition or origin> MT.236
SN Glass of a deep red color produced by means of a precipitate of gold or copper.
UF glass, gold ruby
goldrubinglas
rubinglas
ruby glass, gold

Golden Tartars
USE Jin (Golden Tartars)

Goldi
HN June 1990 lead-in term added
UF Nanai

goldrubinglas
USE **gold ruby glass**

golf communities
USE **golf course communities**

golf course communities
HN April 1990 added
BT *<settlements by economic base>* RD.46
ALT **golf course community**
SN Designates residential communities designed around golf courses.
UF communities, golf course
golf communities
golf course villages
villages, golf course

golf course villages
USE **golf course communities**

goods, grave
USE **grave goods**

gorges (bastion components)
HN March 1991 scope note changed, W added as source

gorges (landforms)
HN May 1991 descriptor changed, was **gorges**
May 1991 alternate term changed, was **gorge**
ALT **gorge (landform)**

Gothic Revival
HN July 1991 lead-in terms added
UF Gothic, High Victorian
Gothick

Gothic, Carpenter
USE **Carpenter Gothic**

Gothic, High Victorian
USE **Gothic Revival**

Gothick
USE **Gothic Revival**

gouache
HN October 1991 lead-in term added
June 1991 scope note added
June 1991 lead-in term added
SN Opaque water-based paint, usually composed of pigment in gum arabic plus a white material that increases opacity; may be used for heightening works in aquarelle or for whole paintings.
UF body color
color, body

<government by form>
HN June 1991 related term added
RT despotism

government office buildings
HN September 1990 scope note added
SN Designates buildings with office space for various departments or branches of government as well as space for public access to government officials.

grade crossings
HN June 1990 lead-in terms added
UF crossings, railroad
railroad crossings

grade-level elevators
HN March 1991 deleted
BT freight elevators

graining
HN July 1990 scope note changed
SN Painting to imitate a grain, as of wood or stone. (W)

granadilla
HN November 1991 lead-in term added
May 1990 lead-in term added
May 1990 lead-in term changed, was **cocus wood**
May 1990 lead-in term changed, was **wood, cocus**
UF cocoawood
cocos wood
cocuswood
wood, cocos

grand tours
HN May 1991 alternate term added
ALT **grand tour**

grange halls
USE **granges (fraternal buildings)**

granges
HN February 1991 deleted
BT associations

granges (fraternal buildings)
HN February 1991 added
BT fraternal lodges
ALT **grange (fraternal building)**
SN Designates local meeting places for members of the Order of Patrons of Husbandry, known as the Grange.
UF grange halls
halls, grange

granny flats
USE **ECHO houses**

graphic design
HN March 1991 moved
BT design

graphic designers
HN June 1990 scope note changed, DOT added as source

graphite (black pigment)
HN April 1991 deleted
BT carbon black

graphite paper
HN July 1990 added
BT transfer paper
SN Thin transfer paper coated on one side with graphite. (MAYER)
UF paper, graphite

grave gifts
USE **grave goods**

grave goods
HN May 1990 added
BT *<object genres by function>* VB.100
UF burial gifts
funeral gifts
gifts, burial
gifts, funeral
gifts, grave
gifts, tomb
goods, grave
grave gifts
tomb gifts

gravure
USE **intaglio printing**

gray lilac
USE **blackish red**

gray marble, Napoleon
USE **Napoleon gray marble**

gray, dark purplish
USE **dark gray**

gray, light purplish
USE **medium gray**

gray, olive
USE **dark greenish gray**

grayish green
USE **moderate bluish green**

Greco-Roman
HN December 1990 moved
BT *<ancient Italian styles>* FL.2728

Greek cross-plan
HN November 1990 lead-in term added
UF cruciform-plan

green building design
USE **green design**

green design
HN May 1990 added
BT *<environmental concepts>*
SN Use for design solutions that are conscious of the ozone-depleting and polluting effects of building materials and processes, that encourage energy and natural resource conservation and recyclability, and are, on the whole, ecologically sound.
UF building design, green
design, green
green building design

green, grayish
USE **moderate bluish green**

green, light lime
USE **brilliant yellow green**

greenways
HN April 1990 added
BT *<open spaces by location or context>* RK.1579
ALT **greenway**
SN Use for ribbons of protected lands and waters, primarily within or near cities, established to provide the public with access to open spaces that

mitigate the hard edges and over-developed landscapes of urban areas. (DLA)

grey dawn
USE **purplish gray**

gridirons (theater elements)
HN March 1991 scope note changed, IDTL added as source

grievers
USE **mourners**

griffes
HN June 1991 moved
    June 1991 scope note changed
BT *<base components>* RT.68
SN Foliate or clawlike ornaments that project from the round base of a column toward a corner of a plinth.

grillages
HN June 1991 moved
BT *<supporting and resisting elements>* RT.59

grinders (tools)
HN May 1991 descriptor changed, was **grinders**
    May 1991 alternate term changed, was **grinder**
ALT **grinder (tool)**

<grinding and milling equipment components>
HN October 1990 added
BT *<tool and machinery components>* TB.1093

grinding wheels
HN October 1990 moved
BT *<grinding and milling equipment components>*

grindstones
HN October 1990 moved
BT *<grinding and milling equipment components>*

grindstones (millstones)
USE **millstones**

grisaille
HN October 1990 moved
    October 1990 scope note changed
BT *<painting techniques for special effects>* KT.252
SN Painting of images in monochrome, usually gray tones; employed in paintings, stained glass, enamels, and on pottery and other objects.

groined vaults
HN March 1991 scope note changed, source DAC deleted

groins (vault components)
HN May 1991 descriptor changed, was **groins**
    May 1991 alternate term changed, was **groin**
ALT **groin (vault component)**

ground (material)
HN July 1990 scope note changed
SN Substance used to prepare the surface on which or from which an image is made.

ground (etching)
USE **etching ground**

ground lights, aeronautical
USE **aeronautical ground lights**

ground wood
USE **mechanical wood pulp**

ground, dust
USE **rosin ground**

ground, hard
USE **hard ground**

ground, liquid
USE **spirit ground**

ground, resin
USE **rosin ground**

ground, rosin
USE **rosin ground**

ground, spirit
USE **spirit ground**

grounds, parade
USE **parade grounds**

groundwood pulp
USE **mechanical wood pulp**

group homes
HN August 1991 scope note changed
SN Use for residential dwellings that are single housekeeping units, provide care for small groups of unrelated residents requiring supervision, and are intended to reproduce the circumstances of family life; for temporary residences of former convicts, drug users, or mental patients awaiting a return to society, use **halfway houses.**

grouped columns
HN March 1991 scope note changed
SN Use for three or more closely spaced columns which form a distinct group; when two columns form a distinct group, use **coupled columns** or **doubled columns.**

<groups of people>
HN May 1991 added
BT **people**

<groups of people by activity>
HN May 1991 added
BT *<groups of people>*

<groups of people by state or condition>
HN May 1991 added
BT *<groups of people>*

groups, ethnic
USE **ethnic groups**

groups, minority
USE **minorities**

groups, social
USE **social groups**

groups, working
USE **task forces**

growth ring dating
USE **dendrochronology**

Guangxu
HN July 1990 lead-in term changed, was **Kuang-hsu**
UF Kuang-hsü

Guarao
USE **Warrau**

guards, candle
USE **candle screens**

Guastavino system
USE **Guastavino vaults**

Guastavino vault system
USE **Guastavino vaults**

Guastavino vaults
HN April 1990 scope note changed
    April 1990 lead-in terms added
SN Use for the tile timbrel vaults erected by the Guastavino family between about 1800 and 1950, especially in the United States since 1881.
UF Guastavino system
    Guastavino vault system
    system, Guastavino
    system, Guastavino vault
    vault system, Guastavino

guerrilla warfare
HN October 1991 lead-in term changed, was **warfare, guerilla**
    January 1991 scope note added
    January 1991 descriptor changed, was **guerilla warfare**
    November 1990 moved
    January 1990 lead-in terms added
BT **wars**
SN Wars characterized by hit-and-run tactics by small, mobile groups of irregular forces operating in territory controlled by a hostile regular force. (RHDEL2)
UF guerrilla wars
    warfare, guerrilla
    wars, guerrilla

guerrilla wars
USE **guerrilla warfare**

guesthouses
HN August 1990 alternate term added
ALT **guesthouse**

guglias
USE **finials**
    pinnacles

guidance, career
USE **vocational guidance**

guidance, occupational
USE **vocational guidance**

guides, light
USE **optical fibers**

guilloche
HN June 1990 lead-in term changed, was **water-pattern**
UF water pattern

gum
HN May 1990 scope note source changed to MAYER

gum arabic etch
USE **etch**

gum etch
USE **etch**

gunpowder factories
USE **powder mills**

gunpowder mills
USE **powder mills**

gunpowder works
USE **powder mills**

guttae
HN August 1991 scope note changed
June 1991 lead-in term added
SN Pendant ornaments in the form of truncated cones found on the underside of mutules and regulae of Doric entablatures.
UF trunnels

gutters (building drainage components)
HN November 1991 alternate term changed, was **gutter (storm water system)**
March 1991 scope note changed
March 1991 lead-in term **eave troughs** deleted
March 1991 descriptor changed, was **gutters (storm water systems)**
ALT **gutter (building drainage component)**
SN Shallow channels positioned on a building for the purpose of collecting and diverting water from a roof.

guyed structures
USE **cable-stayed structures**

gymnasiums
HN September 1990 scope note added
SN Use for buildings designed and equipped for indoor sports, exercise, or physical education and training.

gypsum board
HN May 1990 lead-in term changed, was **sheetrock**
UF Sheetrock (TM)

habit, narcotic
USE **drug addiction**

habitat
HN July 1990 added
BT *<biological concepts>* BM.715
SN Use for the traditional and usual locality of a plant or animal; for the aggregate of influences affecting an organism, use **environment**. (DLA)

hagioscopes
USE **squints**

hail
HN October 1990 moved
BT *<water by form>*

half-relief
USE **mezzo rilievo**

half-round moldings
HN April 1991 lead-in term added
April 1991 scope note source changed to DAC
UF half rounds

half rounds
USE **half-round moldings**

half stereographs
HN December 1990 added
BT **stereoscopic photographs**
ALT half stereograph
SN Use for photographs originally taken as one of a pair of stereoscopic photographs but then printed or mounted as a single image.
UF half stereos
one-half stereographs
stereographs, half
stereographs, one-half
stereos, half

half stereos
USE **half stereographs**

halfway houses
HN April 1990 scope note added
SN Use for temporary residences of former convicts, drug users, or mental patients that serve as a transition environment between confinement and a return to society; for long-term residential environments, which reproduce the circumstances of family life for persons requiring continuing supervision due to special needs, use **group homes**.

halite
USE **salt**

halls
HN August 1991 scope note changed
SN Use generally for rooms large in proportion to rooms for domestic functions, circulation, or storage; use also for the principal rooms of a Medieval house and for large central rooms in certain 19th- and 20th-century English and American houses.

halls, grange
USE **granges (fraternal buildings)**

halls, pillared
USE **hypostyle halls**

hammer-beam trusses
HN March 1991 moved
BT *<trusses by form>* RT.357

hammer beams
HN March 1991 scope note changed
SN Short, horizontal members projecting inward at the top of interior walls, attached to the foot of principal rafters in a roof and generally supporting arched roof braces.

hand coloring
HN May 1991 scope note added
SN Applying color by a manual process.

handball courts
HN September 1990 scope note added
SN Courts marked for playing handball and including at least one smooth wall.

handles, bail
USE **bail pulls**

handling, waste
USE **waste management**

hanging posts
HN October 1991 lead-in term **posts, gate** deleted
October 1991 lead-in term **posts, hinge** deleted
March 1991 lead-in term changed, was **gate posts**
March 1991 lead-in term changed, was **hinge posts**
UF gateposts
hinging posts

hanging stiles
HN March 1991 scope note added
March 1991 descriptor changed, was **hinge stiles**
March 1991 alternate term changed, was **hinge stile**
March 1991 lead-in term changed, was **hanging stiles**
ALT hanging stile
SN Use for the stiles on doors to which the door hinges are attached.
UF hinge stiles

Hanukkah
HN April 1991 moved
BT *<religious seasons>*

hard ground
HN July 1990 added
BT **etching ground**
SN Etching ground which is applied to a warm printing plate and hardens upon drying.
UF ground, hard

hard light
HN April 1991 added
BT *<lighting techniques by distribution>*

SN Method of distributing light to produce sharply defined shadows.
UF light, hard

harems
HN June 1990 scope note added
SN Use for the women's quarters of Islamic houses.

Harlem Renaissance
HN July 1991 moved
BT African American

hatches
HN March 1991 lead-in term hatchways deleted

hatchments
HN April 1990 added
BT <identifying symbols> VW.697
ALT hatchment
SN Diamond-shaped tablets or panels exhibiting the coat of arms of a deceased person, displayed upon their death.
UF achievements, funereal
funereal achievements

haunches
HN March 1991 scope note changed
SN The middle part between the crown and the springing of arches. (DAC)

hawkers
USE peddlers

haylofts
HN June 1990 scope note added
SN Upper-story storage spaces for hay in stables or barns.

headers (masonry units)
HN June 1990 descriptor changed, was headers

heads, door
USE doorheads

health
HN November 1991 moved
BT <health and related concepts>

<health and related concepts>
HN February 1991 added
BT <biological concepts> BM.715

health boards
HN June 1990 lead-in term added
UF health departments

health clubs
HN April 1991 added
BT health facilities
ALT health club
SN Use for establishments offering facilities for exercise and active physical conditioning, whether or not on a membership basis.
UF centers, fitness
centers, physical fitness
clubs, health
fitness centers
physical fitness centers
RT recreation buildings

health departments
USE health boards

health, mental
USE mental health

<health-related concepts>
HN February 1991 added
BT <health and related concepts>

hearings
HN May 1991 alternate term added
ALT hearing

<hearth components>
HN November 1990 added
BT <hearths and hearth components>

hearths
HN March 1991 scope note added
November 1990 moved
BT <hearths and hearth components>
SN Use for the floors of fireplaces and the immediately adjacent floor areas.

<hearths and hearth components>
HN November 1990 added
BT <fireplace components> RT.1151

hearthstones
HN March 1991 moved
March 1991 scope note added
BT hearths
SN Single, large stones forming the floors of fireplaces. (DAC)

heat-actuated detectors
USE temperature detectors

heat-distributing units
HN May 1991 scope note added
May 1991 lead-in terms added
SN Use generally for the components of heating systems that distribute heat within rooms and spaces, usually by radiation or convection.
UF distribution equipment, heat
heat distribution equipment
heating terminals
terminals, heating

heat distribution equipment
USE heat-distributing units

heat pumps
HN March 1991 scope note added
SN Equipment used in systems that heat or cool areas and that have compression cycles and reverse refrigeration cycles. (STEIN)

heat-sensing detectors
USE temperature detectors

heaters, convection
USE convectors

heating systems
HN March 1991 lead-in term added
March 1991 scope note added
SN Assemblies of interrelated equipment designed to provide heat to buildings and other structures.
UF plants, heating

heating terminals
USE heat-distributing units

heaven
HN October 1990 added
BT <doctrinal concepts> BM.680
SN Place or state of eternal bliss and ideal relationship with God or the gods, usually accorded as the reward for virtue and true religious faith.

Hebrew schools
HN May 1991 scope note changed
SN Use for children's day schools teaching Jewish subject matter or the Hebrew language or both, usually synagogue-based and operated under Conservative or Reform Jewish auspices. For Orthodox Jewish day schools, use yeshivas.

heel stones
HN March 1991 deleted
BT <gate components>

heiaus
HN March 1991 added
BT <religious structures> RK.1082
ALT heiau
SN Use for Hawaiian, pre-Christian, outdoor temples or sanctuaries.

heliarc welding
USE shielded metal arc welding

helical vaults
USE spiral vaults

heliotype
HN July 1991 added
BT collotype
SN A modified version of collotype in which the alum-hardened gelatin layer is transferred from glass to the metal plate; allows for the making of many more prints than ordinary collotype.
UF heliotypgraphy

heliotypes
HN July 1991 added
BT collotypes
ALT heliotype
SN Photomechanical prints produced by the process called heliotype.

heliotypgraphy
USE heliotype

hell
HN October 1990 added
BT <doctrinal concepts> BM.680
SN Place or state of extreme or eternal suffering, usually inflicted as punishment upon the wicked or the nonbelieving.

Hemba
HN July 1990 lead-in term added
UF Eastern Luba

hemispheres
HN   July 1991 alternate term added
ALT   hemisphere

hempseed oil
HN   October 1990 moved
BT   vegetable oil

herbals
HN   October 1990 added
BT   <books by subject> VW.522
ALT   herbal
SN   Books containing names and descriptions of herbs, or of plants in general. (OED)

herd-books
USE   studbooks

heritage zones
USE   historic districts

heroic
USE   over life-size

Herreran
HN   May 1991 moved
BT   <Spanish Renaissance-Baroque styles> FL.3242

hewing
HN   October 1990 added
BT   cutting
ALT   hewn
SN   Cutting with blows of a heavy cutting instrument. (WCOL9)

hexagons
HN   July 1991 alternate term added
ALT   hexagon

hide glue
HN   June 1991 moved
     June 1991 scope note changed
BT   animal glue
SN   Animal glue made from degraded collagen obtained from skin and hide.

high altars
HN   March 1991 scope note source changed to DAC

high relief
HN   April 1991 moved
     November 1990 lead-in terms added
BT   relief
UF   alto rilievo
     deep relief
     relief, deep

high schools
HN   September 1990 scope note added
SN   Use for schools providing education beyond the elementary school level, usually from grades 9 to 12 but sometimes including grades 7 and 8. (DAC)

hinge stiles
USE   hanging stiles

hinging
HN   May 1991 added
BT   fastening

ALT   hinged
SN   Mounting or fastening with a hinge.

hinging posts
USE   hanging posts

hip jack rafters
USE   jack rafters

hip rafters
HN   March 1991 scope note added
SN   Use for rafters placed at the juncture of the inclined planes forming hip roofs. (DAC)

hip roofs
HN   March 1991 scope note changed
SN   Use for roofs which rise to a peak or ridge by inclined planes on all, usually four, sides, therefore requiring hip rafters.

hipped dormers
HN   March 1991 lead-in terms added
UF   dormers, hipped-roof
     hipped-roof dormers

hipped-roof dormers
USE   hipped dormers

Hissar
HN   July 1990 lead-in term added
UF   Tepe Hissar

historia
USE   istoria

historic districts
HN   July 1990 lead-in terms added
UF   heritage zones
     zones, heritage

historic landscapes
HN   April 1991 added
BT   <cultural landscapes by function> RD.281
ALT   historic landscape
SN   Cultural landscapes that are significant in the history of landscape architecture or gardening or that were developed as a result of historic use of natural features; includes shaped areas of land and sometimes structures.
UF   landscapes, historic

historic structure reports
HN   October 1991 added
BT   technical reports
ALT   historic structure report
SN   Use for reports that comprehensively document and analyze immovable constructed works in terms of such factors as the evolution of their form, current condition, materials, and structural stability in order to establish priorities and costs for renovation or preservation.
UF   HSRs
     reports, historic structure

historical sociology
HN   September 1991 moved
BT   sociology

historicism
HN   May 1990 alternate term added
ALT   historicist

Hlengwe
USE   Thonga

holidays
HN   May 1991 alternate term added
ALT   holiday

holism
HN   April 1990 added
BT   <philosophical movements and attitudes> BM.503
SN   Theory according to which a whole cannot be analyzed without residue into the sum of its parts or reduced to discrete elements. (W)

hollow newel stairs
USE   open newel stairs

hollow newel stairs
HN   March 1991 deleted, made lead-in to open newel stairs

hollow relief
USE   intaglio

home antennas, satellite
USE   satellite home antennas

home offices
HN   May 1990 added
BT   offices
ALT   home office
SN   Workspaces in the home set aside exclusively for income-producing businesses; for reading and writing spaces used for household accounting or recreational purposes, use studies (rooms).
UF   offices, home

home offices (corporate headquarters)
USE   corporate headquarters

homeless persons
HN   March 1991 lead-in terms added
UF   people, homeless
     people, street
     street people

homes, ECHO
USE   ECHO houses

hood moldings
HN   August 1991 scope note changed
SN   Use for projecting moldings carried over door and window openings, sometimes to deflect rainwater from the openings; common in Medieval architecture. For rectangular hood moldings, use labels (moldings).

hoods (enclosing structures)
HN   May 1991 moved
     May 1991 descriptor changed, was hoods (roofs)

May 1991 alternate term changed, was **hood (roof)**
March 1991 scope note changed
BT *<rooflike enclosing structures>*
ALT **hood (enclosing structure)**
SN Includes small projecting covers serving to carry off the fumes from stoves, fireplaces, or laboratory benches.

hook ladders
HN May 1990 lead-in terms added
UF ladders, scaling
scaling ladders

hookers
USE **prostitutes**

hooks
HN May 1991 deleted
BT *<holding and gripping tools>*

hooks
HN May 1991 descriptor changed, was **hooks (hardware)**
May 1991 alternate term changed, was **hook (hardware)**
ALT **hook**

Hopi
HN September 1991 lead-in term added
UF Moqui

hopper casements
USE **hopper windows**

hopper ventilators
USE **hopper windows**

hopper windows
HN March 1991 lead-in terms added
UF casements, hopper
hopper casements
hopper ventilators
hospital lights
hospital windows
lights, hospital
ventilators, hopper
windows, hospital

<horizontal roof frame components>
HN December 1990 guide term changed, was *<roof beams>* RT.504

horse farms
HN October 1991 added
BT *<farms by function>* RG.7
ALT **horse farm**
SN Use for farms primarily engaged in the keeping, feeding, or breeding of horses for by-products, livestock increase, or investment.
UF farms, horse
farms, stud
stud farms

horseback riders
USE **equestrians**

horticulture
HN April 1991 related term added
February 1991 alternate term added
ALT **horticultural**
RT **gardens**

hosho
HN July 1990 added
BT **handmade paper**
SN Thick, absorbent, handmade paper made primarily of kozo.

hospital lights
USE **hopper windows**

hospital wards
HN June 1990 scope note added
June 1990 lead-in term added
SN Divisions, floors, or rooms of hospitals for a particular type or group of patients. (RHDEL2)
UF wards

hospital windows
USE **hopper windows**

hot-pressed paper
HN July 1990 added
BT *<paper by production method>*
MT.1961
SN Paper having a smooth finish created by running the sheets through a series of heated metal cylinders.
UF paper, hot-pressed

hot walls
HN April 1990 added
BT *<walls by function>* RT.581
ALT **hot wall**
SN Use for garden walls provided with heating channels, or flues, which create an artificial microclimate for assisting in the growth or ripening of fruit tress or shrubs trained against the walls; popular in the 18th and 19th centuries.
UF flue walls
walls, flue
walls, hot

hotel registers
HN March 1991 descriptor split, use **hotel (ALT to hotels)** + **registers (lists)**

hotels (public accommodations)
HN May 1990 descriptor changed, was **hotels**

hôtels (town houses)
HN May 1990 descriptor changed, was **hôtels**

hôtels de ville
HN September 1990 scope note added
SN Use for municipal buildings in France and other French-speaking countries.

house traps
HN July 1991 scope note added
SN Use for traps installed in building drains to prevent circulation of air between the plumbing system of the building and the building sanitary drainage system.

housebarns
HN April 1990 added
BT *<houses by form: plan>* RK.255

ALT **housebarn**
SN A broad class of rectangular buildings sheltering under one roof two different functions at opposite ends, often with a common entry, one end housing a family, the other usually livestock; used since the Neolithic period, especially in the colder climates of Europe and North America.
UF byre-houses
houses, long (housebarns)
houses, mixed
long houses (housebarns)
mixed houses

houses, cider
USE **cider mills**

houses, ECHO
USE **ECHO houses**

houses, long
USE **longhouses**

houses, long (housebarns)
USE **housebarns**

houses, mixed
USE **housebarns**

houses, neighborhood
USE **settlement houses**

houses, settlement
USE **settlement houses**

houses, spirit
USE **spirit houses**

houses, tower
USE **tower houses**

houses, Usonian
USE **Usonian houses**

housing discrimination
HN February 1990 scope note added
SN Restriction or denial of residential occupation, tenancy, or ownership because of prejudice based on such factors as age, sex, sexual preference, race or ethnic group, or social or economic status.

housing, evolutionary
USE **incremental housing**

housing, faculty
USE **faculty housing**

housing, incremental
USE **incremental housing**

housing, step-by-step
USE **incremental housing**

Howe trusses
HN March 1991 moved
March 1991 scope note changed
BT *<trusses by construction>*
SN Use for planar trusses of various configurations in which the diagonal members are in compression and the

vertical members are in tension; when the diagonals are in tension and the verticals are in compression, use **Pratt trusses.**

Hsien-fêng
USE **Xianfeng**

HSRs
USE **historic structure reports**

Hsüan-tung
USE **Xuantong**

Hsüan-tê
USE **Xuande**

Huari
HN July 1990 lead-in term added
UF Wanka

Hum
HN July 1990 lead-in term added
UF Humbu

human ecology
HN May 1990 added
BT **sociology**
SN The interdisciplinary study of the mutually adaptive interrelationship of individuals and their near environment; involves aspects of demographics, home economics, housing, design, social services, and family behavior. For the study of the broader spatial and organizational patterns of people across the landscape, use **human geography.**
UF ecology, human
ecology, social
social ecology
RT **human geography**

human females
USE **women**

human geography
HN July 1991 related term added
May 1990 scope note added
May 1990 lead-in terms added
May 1990 descriptor changed, was **urban geography**
SN Study and explanation of the spatial, organizational, and behavioral patterns of people across the natural and built landscapes; includes the methods and theories of behavioral geography, cognitive geography, economic geography, marketing and decision theory, and locational analysis. For the sociological study of individuals and their near environment, use **human ecology.**
UF anthro-geography
geography, human
urban geography
RT **human ecology**

human males
USE **men**

Humbu
USE **Hum**

humidity, atmospheric
USE **relative humidity**

humidity, relative
USE **relative humidity**

hurricanes
HN May 1991 alternate term added
ALT **hurricane**

hut, primitive
USE **primitive hut**

huts
HN April 1990 scope note added
SN Simply constructed or small and humble dwellings, generally of natural materials. (RHDEL2)

HVAC
HN March 1991 lead-in term added
March 1991 scope note added
SN Systems that supply the heating, ventilation, and air conditioning to buildings and complexes.
UF climate control, indoor

HVAC systems, incremental
USE **incremental air conditioning**

Hyderabad
HN February 1991 moved
BT **Deccani**

hydrants
USE **fire hydrants**

hydraulic elevators
HN March 1991 lead-in terms added
UF elevators, hydroelectric
hydroelectric elevators

hydraulics
HN February 1991 alternate term added
ALT **hydraulic**

hydroelectric elevators
HN March 1991 deleted, made lead-in to **hydraulic elevators**

hydroelectric elevators
USE **hydraulic elevators**

hydrostone
HN May 1990 scope note changed, MH added as source

Hyper-Mannerism
USE **Pittura Colta**

hyperbolas
HN July 1991 alternate term added
ALT **hyperbola**

hyperthyra
HN March 1991 deleted, made lead-in to **overdoors** and **lintels**

hyperthyra
USE **lintels**
overdoors

hypocausts
HN June 1991 moved
June 1991 scope note added
BT **warm air heating**
SN Ancient Roman heating systems that circulate hot air from furnaces through subfloor spaces and through flues in walls.

hypostyle halls
HN June 1990 scope note added
June 1990 lead-in terms added
SN Use for halls whose roof is supported by rows of columns giving a forestlike appearance. (PDARC)
UF halls, pillared
hypostyle rooms
hypostyles
pillared halls
rooms, hypostyle

hypostyle rooms
USE **hypostyle halls**

hypostyles
USE **hypostyle halls**

hypotrachelia
HN April 1991 scope note changed
SN Use for the grooves beneath the necking of Doric capitals masking the joint between capital and shaft; for the fillets encircling the Doric capital at the bottom of the echinus, use **annulets.**

I-beams
HN March 1991 scope note added
SN Rolled or extruded structural metal beams having a cross section resembling the letter I. (DAC)

ice hockey rinks
HN September 1990 scope note added
SN Use for ice-skating rinks specially marked and equipped for playing ice hockey.

ice skaters
HN December 1990 added
BT **skaters**
ALT **ice skater**
UF skaters, ice

ice-skating rinks
HN September 1990 scope note added
SN Use for bounded areas of ice suitable for skating, usually artificially frozen and enclosed.

ice storms
HN May 1991 alternate term added
ALT **ice storm**

iconostases
HN August 1991 moved
August 1991 scope note changed
BT *<screens in Christian religious buildings>* RT.1248
SN Screens in Orthodox Eastern churches that separate the sanctuary from the nave, usually pierced by

three doors and, since the 14th or 15th century, covered with icons. (ODCC)

identity, gender
USE **sex role**

identity, sex
USE **sex role**

ill
HN January 1991 added
BT *<groups of people by state or condition>*
SN Those who are afflicted with illness or disease.
UF sick
RT **illness**

ill health
USE **illness**

illness
HN February 1991 added
BT *<health-related concepts>*
SN State of poor health, of being subject to a disease, disorder, or other malfunctioning of the mind or body.
UF ill health
sickness
RT **ill**

illumination (illustration)
USE **manuscript illumination**

illumination, general
USE **general lighting**

illuminators
HN May 1991 scope note changed
SN Artists who paint or draw pictures or other decorative forms in manuscripts. For those who create works in miniature, such as paintings, photographs, furniture, and other objects, use **miniaturists.**

illusion
HN May 1990 added
BT *<psychological concepts>* BM.568

illustration
HN May 1991 scope note added
SN The art or process of providing illustrations.

Image, New
USE **New Figuration**

immigrants
HN May 1991 scope note added
May 1991 related terms added
SN People who come into a country or region from another to settle there. For those who depart from their native or usual country or region to live elsewhere, use **emigrants.**
RT **emigrants**
immigration

immigrating
USE **immigration**

immigration
HN May 1991 lead-in term added
May 1991 related term added
January 1991 alternate term added
November 1990 moved
BT **migration**
ALT **immigrated**
UF immigrating
RT **immigrants**

impact loads
HN January 1991 alternate term added
ALT **impact load**

impasto
HN October 1990 scope note added
SN Application of paint in thick, opaque masses, usually with a well-loaded brush or a palette knife. (OCA)

imperfection
HN April 1990 added
BT *<aesthetic concepts>* BM.487

importing
HN January 1991 scope note added
SN Bringing articles of trade or commerce into a country from abroad.

impost blocks
HN March 1991 lead-in term added
March 1991 scope note changed, GARD86 added as source
UF superabaci

imposts
HN March 1991 scope note changed, IGA added as source

impoverished people
USE **poor**

in register
HN April 1990 added
BT *<conditions and effects: printing and printmaking>*
SN Use when, in printing, each successive plate or block was positioned accurately. (THDAT)
UF register, in

inaugurations
HN May 1991 alternate term added
ALT **inauguration**

incarcerating
HN January 1991 scope note added
SN Imprisoning or putting in a place of confinement. (RHDEL2)

incentive zoning
HN April 1990 added
BT **zoning**
SN Systems whereby developers are granted concessions in exchange for providing amenities a community feels are desirable.
UF zoning, incentive

incised relief
USE **intaglio**

inclined elevators
HN September 1991 moved
March 1991 scope note added
March 1991 descriptor changed, was **slant elevators**
March 1991 alternate term changed, was **slant elevator**
March 1991 lead-in term changed, was **inclined elevators**
BT *<diagonal and multi-directional conveying systems>* RT.1294
ALT **inclined elevator**
SN Use for elevators whose cars or platforms move at a degree less than completely vertical.
UF slant elevators

Inconel (TM)
HN April 1990 added
BT **nickel alloys**

incremental air conditioning
HN August 1991 scope note added
August 1991 lead-in terms added
August 1991 lead-in term **incremental air conditioning systems** deleted
August 1991 lead-in term **systems, incremental air conditioning** deleted
SN Air conditioning systems in which units can operate independently without the need for a central distribution system.
UF HVAC systems, incremental
incremental HVAC systems
systems, incremental
systems, incremental HVAC

incremental construction
USE **incremental housing**

incremental housing
HN December 1990 added
BT **affordable housing**
SN Use for housing built by a slow step-by-step process whereby building components are added or altered by owner-builders as money, time, or materials become available.
UF construction, incremental self-help
evolutionary housing
housing, evolutionary
housing, incremental
housing, step-by-step
incremental construction
incremental self-help construction
self-help construction, incremental
step-by-step housing

incremental HVAC systems
USE **incremental air conditioning**

incremental self-help construction
USE **incremental housing**

indexes, KWAC
USE **key-word-and-context indexes**

indexes, KWIC
USE **key-word-in-context indexes**

indexes, KWOC
USE **key-word-out-of-context indexes**

indexes, KWOT
USE **key-word-out-of-title indexes**

India ink
HN June 1991 moved
BT *<ink by composition or origin>*

India paper
USE **China paper**

India proof paper
USE **China paper**

indicators, landing direction
USE **landing direction indicators**

indicting
HN January 1991 scope note added
SN Formally accusing of an offense, crime, wrong, or fault.

indigo
HN January 1991 lead-in term **indigo blue** deleted

indirect lighting
HN August 1991 scope note changed
May 1991 moved
BT *<lighting techniques by distribution>*
SN Lighting achieved by directing 90 to 100% of the light toward a ceiling, wall, or other reflecting surface, rather than directly at the area to be illuminated. (MEANS)

indoor tennis courts
HN September 1990 scope note added
SN Use for tennis courts enclosed within buildings or other structures.

industrial design
HN March 1991 moved
BT **design**

industrial expositions
HN May 1991 alternate term added
ALT **industrial exposition**

industrial housing
HN May 1991 scope note added
SN Use for housing provided by an industry to its employees. (LCSH)

industrial paint
HN July 1990 added
BT *<paint by function>* MT.2534
UF paint, industrial

industrial safety
USE **occupational safety**

industrialization
HN January 1991 scope note changed
December 1990 moved
January 1990 alternate term added
BT **economic development**
ALT **industrialized**
SN Activity of developing an economic organization of a society or community based on mechanized industry. (RHDEL2)

industries
HN June 1990 scope note changed, W added as source

infancy
HN February 1991 added
BT **childhood**
SN Stage of early childhood, commonly considered to be the period before being able to walk. (RHDEL2)
UF babyhood
childhood, early
early childhood

infants
HN January 1991 added
BT **children**
ALT **infant**
SN Children in the earliest stage of their lives, before being able to walk. (RHDEL2)
UF babies

infill
HN January 1991 scope note changed
December 1990 moved
BT **real estate development**
SN Real estate development which aims to maintain the character of an older area by adding new buildings which are architecturally similar to those already there.

inflatable structures
USE **air-supported structures**

influence
HN May 1991 scope note added
May 1991 related term added
SN Use for the effect exercised by someone or their work upon the creative thought or work of others. For the activity of affecting the actions, behavior, opinions, or work of others use **influencing**.
RT **influencing**

influencing
HN May 1991 added
BT *<communication functions>* KG.32
ALT **influenced**
SN Affecting the actions, behavior, opinions, or work of others, possibly unconsciously. For the effect produced by someone or their work upon the creative thought or work of others, use **influence**.
RT **influence**

information management
HN January 1991 lead-in terms added
UF information processing
processing, information

information processing
USE **information management**

information science
HN April 1990 scope note changed, source PG deleted

informing
HN April 1991 added
BT *<communication functions>* KG.32
ALT **informed**
SN Communicating information, particularly of facts or occurrences, to others. (WCOL9)

infrared spectrometry
USE **infrared spectroscopy**

infrared spectroscopy
HN April 1990 added
BT **spectroscopy**
UF infrared spectrometry
IR
spectrometry, infrared
spectroscopy, infrared

Ingalik
HN June 1990 lead-in term changed, was **Tena**
UF Tena

initialing
HN January 1991 added
BT **signing**
ALT **initialed**
SN Affixing the initials of one's name to something.

initials (abbreviations)
HN January 1991 moved
January 1991 scope note added
January 1991 related term added
January 1991 descriptor changed, was **initials**
January 1991 alternate term changed, was **inital**
BT **inscriptions**
ALT **initial (abbreviation)**
SN The first letter of each word in a name (as of a person or organization) used to stand for that name.
RT **monograms**

initiations
HN May 1991 alternate term added
ALT **initiation**

<ink by composition or origin>
HN December 1990 added
BT **ink**

<ink by function>
HN December 1990 added
BT **ink**

<ink by property>
HN December 1990 added
BT **ink**

ink, lithographic
USE **lithographic ink**

ink, printer's
USE **printing ink**

ink, printing
USE **printing ink**

ink, rubbing
USE **rubbing ink**

inkless intaglio
USE **blind embossing**

inlay, wood
USE **marquetry**

inlets
HN November 1990 added
BT *<bodies of water by location>* RD.142
ALT **inlet**
SN Use generally for narrow openings of rivers into riverbanks or lakes and seas into shores.
RT **riverbanks**
    shores (landforms)

inmates
HN February 1991 added
BT *<people by state or condition>* HG.775
ALT **inmate**
SN Use for those confined, voluntarily or involuntarily, to an institutional facility. Use **prisoners** for those involuntarily confined in prison or kept in custody. Use **convicts** for those serving a prison sentence following conviction for a criminal offense.
RT **convicts**
    prisoners

inorganic materials
HN February 1991 scope note added
    February 1991 guide term changed, was *<inorganic materials>* MT.3
SN Substances that contain no hydrocarbons or their derivatives. (RHDEL2)

inpainting
HN July 1990 scope note changed
SN In the conservation of paintings, coloring or painting an area that has been damaged or obliterated so that it blends with the surrounding colors. For restoration work that covers over original paint, use **overpaint**. (MAYER)

insanity
HN February 1991 moved
BT **mental disorders**

inscriptions
HN January 1991 scope note added
SN Use for lettering or other characters marked on something, including prints, especially to communicate certain official information, and generally not part of a larger text. Regarding material from the ancient period, includes most preserved written matter of any length, other than papyri.

insect wax
HN December 1990 moved
BT **animal wax**

inspecting
HN June 1991 related term added
RT **border inspection stations**

inspection stations, border
USE **border inspection stations**

installations (exhibitions)
HN July 1990 added
BT *<architectural elements by building type>* RT.1165
ALT **installation (exhibition)**
SN Use collectively for the physical elements that constitute an exhibition, including the exhibit design, graphics, labels, lighting, audiovisual components, and exhibit cases, as well as the objects on display.

institutions
HN February 1991 scope note added
SN Formally structured organizations devoted to the promotion of a particular cause or project.

instructing
USE **teaching**
    training

instructional materials
HN May 1991 scope note added
SN Print or nonprint materials used for the purpose of imparting knowledge, attitudes, or skills to others.

insulation and finish systems, exterior
USE **exterior insulation and finish systems**

<insulation by form>
HN June 1991 added
BT **insulation**

<insulation by function>
HN June 1991 added
BT **insulation**

insulation, blanket
USE **blanket insulation**

insulation, roll
USE **blanket insulation**

insurance surveys
HN July 1991 scope note added
SN Collections of data gathered and examined for the purpose of formulating insurance policies.

intaglio
HN November 1990 added
BT **sculpture techniques**
SN Technique of creating a design that is sunken into the surface, by carving or incising.
UF cavo relievo
    concave relief
    hollow relief
    incised relief
    relief, concave
    relief, hollow
    relief, incised
    relief, sunk
    sunk relief

intaglio printing
HN January 1991 scope note changed
    October 1990 moved
    October 1990 lead-in term added
BT **printing**
SN Use for printing processes in which the image prints from ink held in the recessed areas of the plate or block, which have been cut or etched away.
UF gravure

<intaglio printing processes>
HN October 1991 added
BT *<printing processes>*

intaglio, blind
USE **blind embossing**

intaglio, inkless
USE **blind embossing**

intensive care units
HN June 1990 scope note added
SN Areas in hospitals for critically ill patients requiring especially close surveillance and special life-support equipment. (AIAENC)

inter-media works
USE **intermedia**

interchanges, cloverleaf
USE **cloverleafs**

intercom systems
HN March 1991 scope note added
SN Two-way direct communication systems for communicating within limited areas, such as office buildings or airplanes. (W)

interior decoration
HN March 1991 moved
BT **design**

interior design
HN March 1991 moved
BT **design**

interior lighting
HN April 1991 scope note added
SN Lighting arrangements to illuminate indoor spaces.

interlacing arcades
HN March 1991 scope note changed
    March 1991 lead-in terms added
SN Use for arcades in which arches overlap and cross one another.
UF arcades, intersecting
    intersecting arcades

intermedia
HN February 1991 added
BT *<historical, theoretical and critical concepts>* BM.285
SN Use for the concept that certain 20th-century works merge already known art forms to inaugurate a new type. If the resulting art form gains currency and acquires a name, it becomes a new medium and is no longer intermedia. For works that

employ several distinct art forms, such as sculpture and music, use **multimedia works**. To indicate that works are composed of a variety of materials, use **mixed media**.
UF inter-media works
    intermedia works
    intermedial works
    works, intermedia
RT mixed media

intermedia works
USE **intermedia**

intermedial works
USE **intermedia**

intermission alarm systems
HN May 1991 deleted
BT communication systems

internal migration
HN January 1991 scope note changed
    January 1991 lead-in term added
    January 1991 lead-in term **mobility** deleted
    November 1990 moved
BT **migration**
SN Migration within a country or region.
UF population redistribution

Internationale Situationiste
USE **Situationist**

interns residences
HN August 1990 alternate term changed, was **intern's residence**
ALT interns residence

intersecting arcades
USE **interlacing arcades**

intersections, rotary
USE **traffic circles**

intradoses
HN March 1991 scope note source changed to DAC

Inuit
HN June 1990 lead-in terms added
UF Canadian Eskimo
    Eskimo, Canadian

invisible ink
HN June 1991 moved
BT <ink by property>

invited competitions
HN July 1990 added
BT competitions
ALT invited competition
SN Design competitions in which entry is restricted to a small number of participants specifically invited to offer solutions; usually for complex projects or projects for which particular technical expertise is required.
UF competitions, invited
    invited contests

invited contests
USE **invited competitions**

Ionic order
HN June 1991 scope note added
SN Use for the architectural order characterized by capitals with volutes, richly carved moldings, and columns with bases. (BOETH)

ionization detectors
HN October 1991 lead-in term added
    March 1991 lead-in terms added
UF fire detectors, ionization
    ionization fire detectors
    ionization particle detectors
    particle detectors, ionization

ionization fire detectors
USE **ionization detectors**

ionization particle detectors
USE **ionization detectors**

IR
USE **infrared spectroscopy**

iron alloys
HN February 1991 alternate term added
ALT iron alloy

iron chloride
USE **ferric chloride**

iron gall ink
HN June 1991 moved
BT <ink by composition or origin>

iron perchloride
USE **ferric chloride**

iron, perchloride of
USE **ferric chloride**

irons (tools)
HN October 1990 added
BT <surface working and finishing tools and accessories> TB.499
ALT iron (tool)
SN Heated metal implements used for branding and cauterizing. (W)

irons, marking
USE **brands**

isinglass
HN June 1991 moved
BT fish glue

Islamic Revival
HN October 1991 deleted
BT <modern European revival styles>

isometric drawings
HN June 1991 lead-in term added
UF isometrics

isometrics
USE **isometric drawings**

Israeli
HN July 1991 added
BT <West Asian>
SN Use only with reference to post-1948 art and architecture.

istoria
HN June 1990 added
BT <historical, theoretical and critical concepts: visual arts> BM.315
SN A manner of composing pictorial narratives. The expression usually refers to Renaissance and Baroque paintings.
UF historia

Italianist
USE **Romanist**

jack rafters
HN March 1991 scope note added
    March 1991 lead-in terms added
SN Use for rafters that do not extend from the roof plates to the ridgeboards; employed in hip roofs to reach from roof plates to hip rafters. For rafters spanning between valley rafters and ridgeboards, use **valley jacks**.
UF hip jack rafters
    jack rafters, hip
    rafters, hip jack

jack rafters, hip
USE **jack rafters**

jack trusses
HN March 1991 moved
BT <trusses by location or context> RT.377

jalousie windows
HN March 1991 scope note changed
SN Windows consisting of a series of horizontal glass louvers that pivot simultaneously in a common frame. (DAC)

jamb posts
HN March 1991 scope note changed, DAC added as source

jamb shafts
HN June 1991 scope note changed, PDARC added as source

jamba oil
HN July 1990 deleted
BT nondrying oil

jambs
HN March 1991 lead-in term postis deleted
    March 1991 lead-in term casings deleted

Japan wax
HN December 1990 moved
BT vegetable wax

Japanese ink
HN June 1991 moved
BT <ink by composition or origin>

Japanese tung oil
HN October 1990 moved
BT tung oil

jetties (erosion protection works)
HN May 1991 descriptor changed, was jetties
May 1991 alternate term changed, was jetty
ALT jetty (erosion protection work)

Jewish cantors
USE **cantors**

jib doors
HN March 1991 scope note source changed to DAC

jib-headed windows
HN May 1991 deleted
BT *<hung windows>*

Jicaque
HN July 1990 lead-in term added
UF Xicaque

Jin (Golden Tartars)
HN March 1991 lead-in terms added
March 1991 descriptor changed, was Jin
UF Golden Tartars
Ju-chên

job training
USE **vocational training**

job training centers
USE **training centers**

jockeys
HN December 1990 added
BT **equestrians**
ALT jockey
SN Those who ride horses in races. (WCOL9)

joiner saws
USE **bench saws**

joinery
HN September 1991 scope note changed
SN Light forms of woodwork, including furniture constructed with dovetail or other joints, and features such as doors or staircases in buildings.

joint adventures
USE **joint ventures**

joint occupancy
HN May 1990 lead-in terms added
UF joint tenancy
tenancy, joint

joint tenancy
USE **joint occupancy**

joint undertakings
USE **joint ventures**

joint ventures
HN October 1991 lead-in terms added
May 1990 lead-in terms added
UF adventures, joint
joint adventures
joint undertakings
undertakings, joint

joist construction, one-way
USE **one-way joist systems**

joist systems, one-way
USE **one-way joist systems**

joists
HN March 1991 lead-in terms added
March 1991 scope note source changed to DAC
UF bridging joists
common joists
joists, bridging
joists, common

joists, bridging
USE **joists**

joists, common
USE **joists**

joists, open web steel
USE **open web joists**

journalism
HN February 1991 alternate term added
ALT journalistic

journals
HN August 1991 scope note changed
SN Use for books containing accounts of an individual's or organization's occurrences or transactions, including records of financial transactions. Use **diaries** when referring to personal accounts of the writer's experiences, attitudes, or observations.

journals (bookkeeping records)
HN May 1991 deleted
BT **bookkeeping records**

journeys
HN May 1991 alternate term added
June 1990 lead-in term added
ALT journey
UF voyages

Ju-chên
USE **Jin (Golden Tartars)**

judas windows
USE **peepholes**

judas-holes
USE **peepholes**

judases
USE **peepholes**

juries
HN May 1991 alternate term added
ALT jury

Kang-chu
USE **Sogdian**

kakemono
HN July 1990 added
BT **scrolls (documents)**
SN Japanese scrolls containing calligraphy and/or pictures, intended to be unrolled occasionally and hung on the wall.

kangs
HN June 1991 moved
BT **warm air heating**

kaolin
HN June 1990 lead-in term changed, was China-clay
UF China clay

kaolinite
HN June 1990 lead-in term added
June 1990 lead-in term China clay deleted
June 1990 lead-in term white bole deleted
May 1990 lead-in term pipe clay deleted
UF Chinese white

kapok oil
HN October 1990 moved
BT **vegetable oil**

Kara-Kuyunli
USE **Karakoyunlu**

Karakoyunlu
HN July 1990 lead-in terms added
UF Kara-Kuyunli
Qara Qoyunlu
Turkoman of the Black Sheep

Karankawa
HN July 1990 lead-in term changed, was Carancahua Indians
UF Carancahua

Kasama
HN April 1990 added
BT *<Japanese pottery styles>* FL.2012

Kauma
HN July 1990 added
BT **Mijikenda**

Kawende
USE **Bende (Kenya)**

Kellogg's oak
USE **California black oak**

kernel oil
HN October 1990 moved
BT **vegetable oil**

ketubahs
HN July 1990 added
BT *<contracts by party>* VW.893
ALT ketubah
SN Traditional Jewish marriage contracts, traditionally written in Aramaic and signed by witnesses, setting out reciprocal duties of husband and wife, including the husband's obligation to pay the wife a certain sum in the event of divorce, and the wife's property rights upon his death.
UF ketubot

ketubot
USE **ketubahs**

key (color)
HN May 1990 scope note changed, MAYER added as source

key consoles
HN March 1991 scope note changed, DAC added as source

key light
HN June 1991 added
BT light
SN Use to designate the apparent principal source of illumination of a subject or area, especially in relation to photography and film.
UF key lighting
light, key
lighting, key

key lighting
USE **key light**

key-word-and-context indexes
HN April 1990 lead-in term added
UF indexes, KWAC

key-word-in-context indexes
HN April 1990 lead-in term added
UF indexes, KWIC

key-word-out-of-context indexes
HN April 1990 lead-in term added
UF indexes, KWOC

key-word-out-of-title indexes
HN April 1990 lead-in term added
UF indexes, KWOT

keys (documents)
HN March 1991 added
BT *<document genres by function>* VW.293
ALT key (document)
SN Lists of words, names, or phrases explaining or giving the value of conventions or symbols used on a map, chart, or other image.
UF legends (keys)

keys (hardware)
HN September 1991 descriptor changed, was **keys**
September 1991 alternate term changed, was **key**
ALT key (hardware)

khivi
USE **claw hammers**

kindergartens
HN September 1990 scope note added
SN Use for schools below first grade serving pupils four to six years old.

king-post trusses
HN March 1991 moved
March 1991 scope note changed
BT *<trusses by form>* RT.357
SN Use for triangular frames with a vertical central strut (the king post) extending from apex to tie beam.

<kinship groups> HG.879
HN May 1991 moved
BT social groups

Kitara
USE **Nyoro**

knee braces
HN November 1990 lead-in terms added
November 1990 moved
BT braces (supporting elements)
UF angle braces
angle ties
braces, angle
knees (braces)
ties, angle

kneelers (gable components)
HN March 1991 scope note added
SN Shaped building stones, with a flat bottom and sloping top, cut to conform to and support the copings of gables; for the more general meaning of blocks of stone placed in masonry walls to distribute the loads of beams, use **padstones.**

knees (braces)
USE **knee braces**

knotted columns
HN June 1991 scope note changed
June 1991 lead-in term added
SN Use for columns with shafts intertwined as if tied in a knot.
UF columns, knotted

Koko
USE **Bassa**

kozo
HN July 1990 lead-in terms added
UF mulberry, paper
paper mulberry

kozo paper
USE **mulberry paper**

Kpe
HN August 1990 lead-in terms added
UF Kweli
Kwiri

Kraak porcelain
HN July 1990 lead-in terms added
UF Carrack porcelain
porcelain, Carrack

Krapplack
USE **madder**

Kuang-hsü
USE **Guangxu**

Kwagiutl
USE **Kwakiutl**

Kwakiutl
HN September 1991 lead-in term added
UF Kwagiutl

Kweli
USE **Kpe**

Kwiri
USE **Kpe**

l'art pour l'art
USE **art for art's sake**

labels (documentary artifacts)
HN October 1991 descriptor changed, was **labels**
October 1991 alternate term changed, was **label**
ALT label (documentary artifact)

labels (moldings)
HN April 1991 scope note changed
April 1991 lead-in term **moldings, label** deleted
April 1991 descriptor changed, was **label moldings**
April 1991 alternate term changed, was **label molding**
ALT label (molding)
SN Moldings or dripstones that extend horizontally across the top of openings and frequently vertically part way down the sides.

labor mobility
HN October 1990 moved
BT demographics

labor, unskilled
USE **laborers**

laborers
HN June 1990 lead-in terms added
UF labor, unskilled
unskilled labor
workers, unskilled
unskilled workers

labyrinth frets
USE **meanders (patterns)**

lac (resin)
HN May 1991 descriptor changed, was **lac**

lacquer
HN July 1990 lead-in term added
UF Duco (TM)

ladders, scaling
USE **hook ladders**

laid down
USE **lining**

laid paper
HN May 1991 scope note changed
May 1991 related term added
SN Paper that shows thick and thin lines at right angles to each other, which are produced in the manufacturing; distinguished from **wove paper,** which has a more even appearance. (BATCOB)
RT wove paper

laity
HN September 1990 lead-in term added
September 1990 alternate term added
ALT layman
UF laymen

lakes (bodies of water)
HN May 1991 descriptor changed, was lakes
May 1991 alternate term changed, was lake
ALT lake (body of water)

lakes (pigments)
HN June 1990 descriptor changed, was lake pigment

Lally columns (TM)
HN March 1991 lead-in term added
March 1991 descriptor changed, was lally columns
March 1991 alternate term changed, was lally column
ALT Lally column (TM)
UF columns (TM), Lally

lamella roofs
HN October 1991 alternate term changed, was lamella structure
June 1991 lead-in terms added
June 1991 lead-in term changed, was lamella roofs
June 1991 descriptor changed, was lamella structures
ALT lamella roof
UF lamella structural systems
lamella structures
structural systems, lamella

lamella structural systems
USE lamella roofs

lamella structures
USE lamella roofs

lampposts
HN November 1991 lead-in terms added
UF light standards
standards, light

lancet windows
HN August 1991 scope note changed
March 1991 lead-in term added
SN Slender windows with lancet arches at the top, common in Gothic architecture.
UF lancets

lancets
USE lancet windows

land art
HN October 1991 deleted, made lead-in term in hierarchy under development

land grants
HN April 1990 scope note changed
SN Official documents from a government to an individual conveying fee simple title to public lands.

land reclamation works
HN August 1990 alternate term land reclamation work deleted

land reform
HN January 1991 scope note changed
October 1990 moved
BT <governmental functions> KG.176
SN Activity of effecting a more equitable distribution of agricultural land especially by dividing large estates into small holdings. (W)

land subdivision
HN January 1991 scope note added
January 1991 lead-in term added
SN Activity of dividing an area of land into smaller parcels for lots, blocks, streets, open spaces, and public areas, and the designation of the location of utilities and other services. (LOFZ)
UF subdivision

land use
HN January 1991 related term added
RT development

landing direction indicators
HN May 1990 added
BT aeronautical ground lights
ALT landing direction indicator
SN Aeronautical devices used to indicate visually the direction designated for landing and take-off. (IESREF)
UF direction indicators, landing
indicators, landing direction

landings (stair components)
HN March 1991 descriptor changed, was landings
March 1991 alternate term changed, was landing
ALT landing (stair component)

landscape architects
HN September 1990 lead-in terms added
UF architects, garden
garden architects

landscapes, historic
USE historic landscapes

landslides
HN May 1991 alternate term added
ALT landslide

lanes (roads)
HN May 1991 descriptor changed, was lanes
May 1991 alternate term changed, was lane
ALT lane (road)

language schools
HN May 1991 descriptor split, use language + schools

lanolin
HN December 1990 moved
BT animal wax

lantern screens
USE candle screens

lanterns (roof appendages)
HN March 1991 scope note changed
SN Windowed superstructures crowning a roof or dome, and serving to give light or air to the space below; in certain circumstances, such structures, whether they provide light or not; for small structures built on the ridges of roofs, common in American architecture, use cupolas.

laque de garance
USE madder

large span structures
HN March 1991 scope note added
SN Use for specially designed structures made to span great lengths.

laser art
HN October 1991 moved to hierarchy under development

Late Hittite
USE Neo-Hittite

later prints
HN January 1991 added
BT photographic prints
ALT later print
SN Photographic prints made much later than the negative and usually not by the original photographer. For prints made by the original photographer relatively soon after the picture was taken, use vintage prints.
UF prints, later
prints, reissue
reissue prints
reissues

lateral loads
HN January 1991 alternate term added
ALT lateral load

Latin American
HN June 1991 moved
BT <The Americas> FL.702

Latin cross-plan
HN November 1990 lead-in term added
UF cruciform-plan

Latinos
HN June 1991 deleted
BT ethnic groups

lattice windows
HN March 1991 scope note source changed to DAC

laundresses
HN December 1990 added
BT <people in service occupations> HG.36
ALT laundress
SN Women whose occupation is the washing and ironing of clothes and linen.
UF washerwomen

laundry rooms
HN June 1990 scope note added
SN Rooms or groups of rooms equipped

for washing, drying, and ironing clothes.

laundry trays
HN August 1991 scope note changed
SN Deep, large sinks used for washing laundry; for deep, large sinks used predominantly in factories and hospitals for washing the arms and upper body, use **wash sinks**.

laurel (wood)
HN May 1991 descriptor changed, was **laurel**

lavatories (sinks)
HN September 1991 scope note changed
SN Sinks used for washing the hands and face. For deep, relatively large sinks used for washing the arms and upper body, use **wash sinks**; for deep, large sinks used for washing laundry, use **laundry trays**.

lavender, spike
USE **spike oil**

law enforcing
HN January 1991 scope note added
SN Carrying out the provisions of or compelling compliance with public laws.

law schools
HN May 1991 descriptor split, use **law** + **schools**

lawns
HN June 1990 scope note added
SN Areas of cultivated grass or other ground cover maintained for aesthetic quality or recreation. (DLA)

laying in
HN October 1990 moved
   July 1990 scope note changed
   July 1990 lead-in term added
BT *<painting techniques by stage>* KT.243
SN The technique or activity of executing the lay-in of a painting.
UF blocking in

laylights
HN March 1991 scope note changed, W added as source

laymen
USE **laity**

lazy lines
HN June 1991 added
BT *<conditions and effects: textiles>*
SN Diagonal lines formed in textiles by the meeting points of successive rows of discontinuous wefts.
UF lines, lazy

leader heads
HN March 1991 scope note added
SN Use for enlargements at the top of downspouts to receive large volumes of rainwater from gutters or roofs.

leader pipes
USE **downspouts**

leaders (downspouts)
USE **downspouts**

leaf, acanthus
USE **acanthus**

leaves (plant materials)
HN May 1991 descriptor changed, was **leaves**
   May 1991 alternate term changed, was **leaf**
ALT leaf (plant material)

ledger boards
HN March 1991 lead-in term added
UF ribbons (ledger boards)

legal holidays
HN May 1991 alternate term added
ALT legal holiday

legends
HN March 1991 scope note added
   March 1991 alternate term added
ALT legend
SN Stories handed down by tradition from earlier times, usually concerned with a real person, place, or event, and popularly regarded as historical although not entirely verifiable.

legends (captions)
USE **captions**

legends (keys)
USE **keys (documents)**

legislating
HN January 1991 scope note added
SN Making or enacting legislation. (W)

legislation
HN January 1991 scope note changed
   January 1991 lead-in term **enacting** deleted
SN Declarations that have the force of authority by virtue of their passing or enactment by an official organ of a state or other governing body, such as laws, regulations, fund allocations, and international treaties.

<leisure events>
HN June 1991 added
BT events

lemon (color)
USE **moderate yellow**

lemon, oil of
USE **oil of lemon**

lemongrass oil
USE **oil of lemon**

Lent
HN April 1991 moved
BT *<religious seasons>*

leopardwood
USE **snakewood**

letterpress printing
HN April 1990 added
BT *<relief printing processes>*
SN Use for the process of relief printing in the context of book and other text printing.
UF printing, letterpress

letters of attorney
USE **powers of attorney**

letters of credit
HN August 1991 moved to hierarchy under development

letters of introduction
HN March 1991 deleted
BT letters

letterwood
USE **snakewood**

Lettrist
HN November 1991 alternate term added
   August 1990 descriptor changed, was **Lettrism**
ALT Lettrism

levels, split
USE **split-level houses**

liberal arts (cross-disciplinary studies)
HN May 1991 descriptor changed, was **liberal arts**

liberal arts (Medieval studies)
HN April 1990 scope note changed, source RHDEL2 deleted

liberties, civil
USE **civil rights**

libraries (buildings)
HN May 1991 descriptor changed, was **libraries**
   May 1991 alternate term changed, was **library**
   September 1990 lead-in terms added
ALT library (building)
UF architecture, library
   buildings, library
   library architecture
   library buildings

libraries (rooms)
HN September 1991 alternate term changed, was **library**
   June 1990 scope note added
ALT library (room)
SN Spaces set aside and equipped for the keeping, arrangement, and reading of books.

library architecture
USE **libraries (buildings)**

library buildings
USE **libraries (buildings)**

librettos
HN March 1990 scope note source changed to RHDEL2

lich gates
HN March 1991 lead-in terms added
March 1991 scope note source changed to DAC
March 1991 descriptor changed, was **lich-gates**
March 1991 alternate term changed, was **lich-gate**
ALT **lich gate**
UF gates, lich
lych gates

liens
HN January 1991 alternate term added
ALT **lien**

life drawings
HN February 1991 moved
BT *<drawings by subject type>* VD.144

life-size, over
USE **over life-size**

<life stages>
HN January 1991 added
BT *<biological concepts>* BM.715
RT *<people by age group>*

lift-etching
USE **lift-ground**

lift-ground
HN November 1991 lead-in term **aquatint, sugar-lift** deleted
October 1991 moved
March 1991 lead-in term added
March 1991 lead-in term **sugar-lift aquatint** deleted
BT **aquatint**
UF lift-etching

lifting (transporting)
HN May 1991 descriptor changed, was **lifting**

light art
HN October 1991 moved to hierarchy under development

light blue
HN April 1990 lead-in terms added
UF blue, Della Robbia
blue, dull
Della Robbia blue
dull blue

light greenish yellow
HN April 1990 lead-in term added
April 1990 lead-in term changed, was **canary**
UF canary yellow
yellow, canary

light guides
USE **optical fibers**

light lime green
USE **brilliant yellow green**

light olive brown
HN April 1990 lead-in term added
UF bistre

light purplish gray
USE **medium gray**

light red
USE **dark yellowish pink**

light standards
USE **lampposts**

light violet
HN November 1991 lead-in term changed, was **mauve, bright**
April 1990 lead-in term changed, was **bright mauve**
UF bright violet
violet, bright

light wells
HN June 1990 descriptor changed, was **lightwells**
June 1990 alternate term changed, was **lightwell**
ALT **light well**

light yellowish brown
HN April 1990 lead-in terms added
UF bistre brown
brown, bistre

light, accent
USE **accent lighting**

light, base
USE **base lighting**

light, electric
USE **electric lighting**

light, fill
USE **fill light**

light, fluorescent
USE **fluorescent lighting**

light, hard
USE **hard light**

light, key
USE **key light**

light, side
USE **side lighting**

light, top
USE **top lighting**

lighting
HN June 1991 scope note added
June 1991 lead-in terms added
SN Use for the arrangements and installation systems of lighting devices for particular effects.
UF lighting systems
systems, lighting

<lighting by form> RT.1353
HN June 1991 deleted
BT **lighting**

<lighting by method of illumination>
HN April 1991 guide term changed, was *<lighting by light source>* RT.1369

lighting system, direct
USE **direct lighting**

lighting system, general
USE **general lighting**

lighting systems
USE **lighting**

<lighting techniques>
HN April 1991 added
BT *<processes and techniques by specific type>* KT.5

<lighting techniques by direction>
HN April 1991 added
BT *<lighting techniques>*

<lighting techniques by distribution>
HN April 1991 added
BT *<lighting techniques>*

lighting, accent
USE **accent lighting**

lighting, base
USE **base lighting**

lighting, decorative
USE **decorative lighting**

lighting, key
USE **key light**

lighting, outline
USE **outline lighting**

lighting, rim
USE **backlighting**

lighting, side
USE **side lighting**

lighting, top
USE **top lighting**

lights
HN June 1991 scope note changed
June 1991 lead-in term **window panes** deleted
June 1991 lead-in term **panes, window** deleted
SN Use for the compartments of windows or window sashes through which daylight may pass; for the divisions of openings each consisting of a single plate of glass, use **panes.**

lights, aeronautical ground
USE **aeronautical ground lights**

lights, approach
USE **approach lights**

lights, boundary
USE **boundary lights**

lights, channel
USE **channel lights**

lights, course
USE **course lights**

lights, hospital
USE **hopper windows**

lights, obstruction
USE **obstruction lights**

lights, runway
USE **runway lights**

lights, taxiway
USE **taxiway lights**

lights, threshold
USE **threshold lights**

lightweight concrete
HN July 1990 lead-in terms added
UF concrete, porous
porous concrete

lignin
HN July 1990 added
BT **wood products**
SN Impure colorless-to-brown crystalline matter found in wood pulp. (RHDEL2)

lilac, gray
USE **blackish red**

lilac, rose
USE **moderate purplish pink**

lime green, light
USE **brilliant yellow green**

limited competitions
HN July 1990 added
BT **competitions**
ALT limited competition
SN Design competitions offering a compromise between open and invited competitions; entry is available only to a portion of a profession, for example only to those within a limited geographic area.
UF competitions, limited

line drawings
HN April 1991 scope note added
SN Drawings in which forms are indicated primarily by lines, with few or no areas of continuous tone.

line engraving
HN October 1991 moved
October 1991 scope note changed
BT **engraving (printing process)**
SN Printing process that produces images in line and with little tonal quality; the plate, usually of copper, is incised using a burin, the slight burr produced is scraped away, and the plate is inked for intaglio printing. (OCA)

linear development
HN February 1991 deleted, made lead-in to **ribbon development**

linear development
USE **ribbon development**

linen, Belgian
USE **Belgian linen**

lines, lazy
USE **lazy lines**

lines, plate
USE **plate marks**

linguistics
HN February 1991 alternate term added
ALT linguistic

lining
HN July 1991 lead-in terms added
UF allover backing
allover mounting
backing
laid down

linkage
HN May 1990 alternate term **linkages** deleted

linocut
USE **linoleum-block printing**

linocutting
USE **linoleum-block printing**

linoleum-block printing
HN November 1991 lead-in term **linoleum block-printing** deleted
October 1991 moved
January 1991 scope note changed
October 1990 lead-in term added
October 1990 lead-in term changed, was **block-printing, linoleum**
October 1990 descriptor changed, was **linocut**
October 1990 lead-in term changed, was **linoleum cut**
BT <*relief printing processes*>
SN Printing process that uses linoleum mounted on a wood block as the printing surface.
UF linocut
linocutting
printing, linoleum-block

linseed oil
HN October 1990 moved
BT **vegetable oil**

lintel courses
HN March 1991 scope note source changed to DAC

lintels
HN March 1991 lead-in term added
March 1991 scope note source changed to DAC
UF hyperthyra

linters
HN July 1990 added
BT **cotton fiber**
SN Short cotton fibers useful in papermaking and upholstery.
UF cotton linters

liquid ground
USE **spirit ground**

Liquitex (TM)
USE **acrylic paint**

literature (humanities)
HN July 1991 descriptor changed, was literature
November 1990 alternate term added
ALT literary

literature (writings)
HN May 1990 added
BT <*document genres*> VW.2
RT **writings**

literature, romance
USE **romances**

litho tusche
USE **tusche**

litho varnish
HN July 1990 lead-in term added
UF lithographic varnish

lithographic etch
USE **etch**

lithographic ink
HN December 1990 added
BT <*ink by function*>
SN Ink used in the printing of lithographs.
UF ink, lithographic

lithographic oil
USE **stand oil**

lithographic tusche
USE **tusche**

lithographic varnish
USE **litho varnish**

lithography
HN October 1991 moved
October 1991 scope note changed
BT <*planographic printing processes*>
SN Planographic printing process in which a design is deposited on the stone or plate with a greasy substance and the surface is chemically treated to accept ink only in the greasy areas.

lithography, color
USE **color lithography**

lithography, colour
USE **color lithography**

lithography, offset
USE **offset lithography**

lithotine
HN July 1990 added
BT **terpenes**
SN Lithographic solvent used as a substitute for turpentine because it is less irritating to the skin.

live loads
HN January 1991 alternate term added
ALT live load

livestock breeders
 HN September 1990 lead-in terms added
 UF breeders, livestock
  breeders, stock
  stock breeders

living quarters
 USE **apartments**

living units
 USE **apartments**

loadbearing walls
 USE **bearing walls**

loads
 HN January 1991 alternate term added
 ALT load

loads, seismic
 USE **earthquake loads**

local fire alarm systems
 HN March 1991 lead-in terms added
 UF local systems
  systems, local

local government records
 HN March 1991 descriptor split, use local government + records

local lighting
 HN May 1991 moved
  May 1991 scope note added
 BT <lighting techniques by distribution>
 SN Lighting technique that distributes illumination over a relatively limited area or confined space without significantly altering the illumination of its general surroundings.

local systems
 USE **local fire alarm systems**

locker rooms
 HN June 1990 scope note added
 SN Rooms equipped with lockers, often having showers and toilets and sometimes used as dressing rooms, as in clubhouses and gymnasiums. (DOS)

lockouts
 HN May 1991 alternate term added
 ALT lockout

locust bean pod
 HN May 1990 scope note changed, OLIVER added as source

loggers
 HN October 1990 lead-in term added
  July 1990 scope note changed, source WCOL9 deleted
 UF woodcutters (loggers)

London brick
 USE **fletton**

long houses (housebarns)
 USE **housebarns**

longhouses
 HN July 1991 lead-in term added
  December 1990 moved
  December 1990 scope note added
 BT **multiple dwellings**
 SN Use for large, rectangular, multi-family dwellings housing related families in separate compartments entered off long corridors; equipped with individual or communal hearths.
 UF houses, long

longitudinal ridge ribs
 HN May 1991 descriptor split, use longitudinal + ridge ribs

loop windows
 HN March 1991 moved
  March 1991 scope note changed
  March 1991 lead-in term added
 BT <windows by form> RT.907
 SN Vertical slitlike windows; often found in Medieval structures.
 UF loops

loopholes
 HN March 1991 scope note changed
  March 1990 lead-in term added
  March 1990 lead-in term **aleois** deleted
 SN Small openings (as in walls or parapets), often with deeply splayed jambs, through which small arms may be discharged; for similar openings to admit light and air or to permit observation, use **loop windows.**
 UF loops

loops
 USE **loop windows**
  loopholes

lotteries
 HN August 1990 added
 BT **contests**
 ALT lottery
 SN Gambling contests in which prizes are distributed to the winners among those persons who have paid for a chance to win them. (W)

lounges
 HN June 1990 scope note added
 SN Informal sitting rooms, as in hotels, theaters, and institutional buildings. (DAC)

louver windows
 HN March 1991 scope note source changed to DAC

louvers (built works components)
 HN March 1991 descriptor changed, was **louvers**
  March 1991 alternate term changed, was **louver**
 ALT **louver (built works component)**

louvers, parabolic
 USE **parabolic louvers**

lovers
 HN December 1990 added
 BT <people by activity> HG.705
 ALT lover
 SN People in love.
 UF paramours

low income people
 USE **poor**

low income persons
 USE **poor**

lug sills
 HN August 1991 scope note changed, PUTNAM added as source

lugs (furniture components)
 USE **wings (furniture components)**

Luna marble
 HN May 1990 lead-in term changed, was **lunense macchiato**
 UF Luniense marble

lunettes
 HN March 1991 moved
  March 1991 scope note source changed to DAC
 BT <wall components by form or function> RT.610

Luniense marble
 USE **Luna marble**

lyceums
 HN September 1990 scope note added
 SN Use for buildings housing institutions providing, for example, public discussions, lectures, and concerts for furthering general education.

lych gates
 USE **lich gates**

lye
 USE **sodium hydroxide**

M-ES
 USE **environmental psychology**

Ma-Xia
 HN August 1990 lead-in term changed, was **Maxia jia**
 UF Maxiajia

Macgilp
 USE **megilp**

machines, traction
 USE **traction elevators**

Mackenzie Eskimo
 USE **Western Arctic Inuit**

madder
 HN May 1990 lead-in terms added
 UF crimson madder
  Krapplack
  laque de garance
  rose madder
  Rubia

Madinka
 USE **Malinke**

madrasas
HN May 1991 moved
BT *<schools by subject>* RK.801

madrona
HN April 1990 added
BT **softwood**
UF Arbutus menziesii
pacific madrone

magi
HN December 1990 added
BT **clergy**
ALT **magus**
SN Members of a hereditary priestly caste among the ancient Medes and Persians. (WCOL9)

magilp
USE **megilp**

magna
USE **acrylic paint**

mahallas
HN June 1991 added
BT **residential districts**
ALT **mahalla**
SN Use for clearly defined residential quarters of traditional Islamic towns, each district characterized by a community related in religion, occupation, or ethnic or socio-cultural or tribal background.

maisonettes
USE **duplex apartments**

maisons de plaisance
HN September 1990 added
BT **country houses**
ALT **maison de plaisance**
SN Use for country or suburban retreats offering comfort and simplicity, combining the design of town houses with the needs of country living; less elaborate than châteaux; popular in 17th- and 18th-century France. (KALNEI)

maize oil
USE **corn oil**

male
HN January 1991 added
BT **sex**
SN Referring to the sex that in reproduction normally produces sperm cells or male gametes. (RHDEL2)
RT **men**

males, human
USE **men**

Malinke
HN August 1990 lead-in term added
UF Madinka

malleability
HN May 1990 scope note changed, MH added as source

man-environment systems
USE **environmental psychology**

man-made disasters
HN July 1990 added
BT **disasters**
ALT **man-made disaster**
UF disasters, man-made

management, risk
USE **risk management**

management, waste
USE **waste management**

managing
HN February 1991 scope note changed
February 1991 related term added
SN Use generally to include organizing, supervising, and carrying out the activities of a person, group, organization, or enterprise, and controlling its human and material resources, involving primarily the application rather than the formulation of policy. When the formulation of policy is the primary aspect, use **administering**.
RT **administering**

Manchu
USE **Qing**

manganese violet
HN November 1991 lead-in term changed, was **violet, Nürnburg**
May 1990 lead-in term changed, was **Nürnburg violet**
UF Nuernberg violet
violet, Nuernberg

manhole covers
HN June 1990 scope note added
SN Removable cast iron covers for manholes. (MEANS)

manière anglaise
USE **mezzotint**

manière criblée
USE **dotted manner**

manière noire
USE **mezzotint**

Mankato stone
HN April 1990 added
BT **magnesian limestone**
UF stone, Mankato

manlifts
HN April 1991 scope note added
SN Devices consisting of a powerdriven endless belt provided with steps or platforms and handholds for the transportation of persons in a vertical position through successive floors or levels of a building or structure. (STEIN)

manner, black
USE **mezzotint**

Manner, Broad
USE **Broad Manner**

manner, chalk
USE **crayon manner**

manner, crayon
USE **crayon manner**

manner, dotted
USE **dotted manner**

Manner, Fine
USE **Fine Manner**

Mannerist
HN August 1990 alternate term added
ALT **Mannerism**

mantels
HN August 1991 scope note changed
March 1991 lead-in terms added
SN Use for decorative frames around fireplace openings.
UF chimney pieces
pieces, chimney

manual fire stations
USE **manual stations**

manual stations
HN March 1991 lead-in terms added
UF fire stations, manual
manual fire stations

manumission
USE **emancipation**

manuscript illumination
HN July 1991 lead-in term added
UF illumination (illustration)

maps
HN April 1991 scope note changed
SN Documents depicting in graphic or photogrammetric form, normally to scale and usually on a flat medium, a selection of material or abstract features on or in relation to the surface of the earth or of a heavenly body, and generally emphasizing arterial or regional relationships. For similar representations on a horizontal plane but for depicting smaller scale objects and spaces, use **plans**. (ICA)

maps, meteorological
USE **weather maps**

marbelite
HN May 1990 scope note changed, MH added as source

marble, black-and-gold
USE **portor marble**

marble, Botticino
USE **Botticino marble**

marble, Cyzican
USE **Proconnesian marble**

marble, Famosa
USE **Formosa marble**

marble, Napoleon gray
  USE **Napoleon gray marble**

marble, Proconnesian
  USE **Proconnesian marble**

marble, Synadicum
  USE **pavonazzetto**

marbled ware
  HN April 1990 added
  BT **earthenware**
  SN Pottery made in imitation of the sur-
      face appearance of colored marble by
      means of wedging tinted or colored
      clays, or by employing colored slips
      or glazes. (SAVAGE)
  UF ware, marbled

marblewood
  HN May 1990 lead-in term changed, was
      andaman marblewood
  UF Andaman marblewood

marbling
  HN October 1990 moved
  BT **graining**

mariners
  USE **seamen**

marionette theaters
  USE **puppet theaters**

markers, felt-tip
  USE **felt-tip pens**

markets (buildings)
  HN May 1991 descriptor changed, was
      markets
      May 1991 alternate term changed,
      was **market**
  ALT **market (building)**

markets (events)
  HN May 1991 alternate term added
  ALT **market (event)**

marking irons
  USE **brands**

marks, chop (printers' marks)
  USE **chops**

marks, plate
  USE **plate marks**

Maroger medium
  HN June 1990 lead-in term added
      June 1990 descriptor changed, was
      maroger medium
  UF medium, Maroger

marquees
  HN May 1991 moved
      May 1991 scope note changed
  BT <*rooflike enclosing structures*>
  SN Cantilevered or suspended roofs over
      the entrances to buildings, of metal
      or metal and glass; in the 19th and
      20th centuries, common over the
      entrances to theaters. For smaller,
      often ornamental, rooflike struc-
      tures at entrances, use **canopies**.

marquetry
  HN October 1990 lead-in terms added
  UF inlay, wood
      wood inlay

marriage applications
  HN March 1991 deleted
  BT **marriage records**

Mars yellow
  HN November 1991 lead-in term added
      May 1990 lead-in term changed, was
      ferrox
      May 1990 lead-in term changed, was
      ferrite
  UF Ferrite (TM)
      Ferrox (TM)
      yellow oxide

martial arts training centers
  HN September 1990 scope note added
  SN Use for facilities equipped for teach-
      ing and practicing traditional Ori-
      ental combat and self-defense skills.

martyrs
  HN December 1990 added
  BT <*people by state or condition*> HG.775
  ALT **martyr**
  SN Those who sacrifice their lives for the
      sake of religion or principle.
      (WCOL9)
  RT **saints**

masa
  HN July 1990 added
  BT **machine-made paper**
  SN Inexpensive machine-made oriental
      paper.

mashrabiyahs
  USE **meshrebeeyehs**

Maskoki
  USE **Creek**

masks (performances)
  USE **masques**

masques
  HN February 1991 added
  BT **performances (events)**
  ALT **masque**
  SN Short allegorical dramatic entertain-
      ments performed by masked per-
      formers, popular in the 16th and
      17th centuries. (WCOL9)
  UF masks (performances)

mass (physical sciences concept)
  HN May 1991 descriptor changed, was
      mass

mass culture
  USE **popular culture**

mass production
  HN January 1991 scope note changed
      October 1990 moved
      January 1990 alternate term added
  BT **manufacturing**
  ALT **mass-produced**
  SN Manufacturing goods in large quan-

tities so as to attain high rates of
output at decreasing unit cost.

masterpiece
  HN May 1990 scope note changed, OCA
      added as source

mat board
  HN September 1991 scope note changed
  SN Stiff cardboard faced with decora-
      tive paper, foil, cloth, and some-
      times having a textured surface, used
      for matting two-dimensional art work
      or documents.

mat foundations
  USE **raft foundations**

Matengo
  HN June 1990 lead-in term added
  UF Wamatengo

material culture
  HN September 1991 moved
  BT **anthropology**

materials, mixed
  USE **mixed media**

maternity departments
  USE **maternity wards**

maternity wards
  HN June 1990 lead-in terms added
  UF departments, maternity
      maternity departments

mathematics
  HN February 1991 alternate term added
  ALT **mathematical**

<*matrix preparation techniques*>
  HN October 1991 added
  BT <*printing techniques*>

matter, organic
  USE **organic materials**

matting (supporting)
  HN September 1991 scope note changed
      July 1991 moved
      May 1991 descriptor changed, was
      matting
  BT **supporting**
  SN The preparation of a flat, two-
      dimensional art work or document
      for display by securing it inside a
      window mat. (REILLY)

mauve, pale
  USE **very pale purple**

Maxiajia
  USE **Ma-Xia**

Mbun
  HN July 1990 lead-in term added
  UF Ambuun

McGuilp
  USE **megilp**

MDs
  USE **physicians**

meanders (patterns)
HN June 1990 lead-in terms added
UF frets, labyrinth
labyrinth frets

meanders (water body components)
HN September 1991 descriptor changed, was **meanders**
September 1991 alternate term changed, was **meander**
ALT **meander (water body component)**

mechanical drawings (tool-aided drawings)
HN September 1991 descriptor changed, was **mechanical drawings**
September 1991 lead-in term changed, was **drawings, mechanical**
September 1991 alternate term changed, was **mechanical drawing**
ALT **mechanical drawing (tool-aided drawing)**
UF drawings, mechanical (tool-aided drawings)

mechanical pulp
USE **mechanical wood pulp**

mechanical systems
HN March 1991 scope note changed
SN Generally includes the HVAC and plumbing of buildings or complexes; in some contexts may also include electrical systems and electricity-based systems, such as protection systems and communication systems.

mechanical wood pulp
HN July 1990 added
BT **wood pulp**
SN Wood that is ground into a pulp without any additional purification. (SAITZY)
UF ground wood
groundwood pulp
mechanical pulp
pulp, groundwood
pulp, mechanical wood
wood pulp, mechanical
wood, ground

mechanically operated doors
USE **automatic doors**

mechanics (physics)
HN January 1991 alternate term added
ALT **mechanical**

mechanization
HN January 1991 scope note added
January 1991 alternate term added
ALT **mechanized**
SN Equipping with machinery, especially to replace human or animal physical labor. (W)

media
HN November 1990 moved
BT **artists materials**

media rooms
HN April 1990 added
BT <*entertainment and recreation spaces*> RM.121
ALT **media room**
SN Domestic spaces, often windowless, designed solely for viewing and listening to prerecorded materials, such as films and music.
UF rooms, media

media, mixed
USE **mixed media**

median (statistics)
HN May 1991 descriptor changed, was **median**

median strips
HN June 1990 lead-in term added
June 1990 descriptor changed, was **medians**
June 1990 alternate term changed, was **median**
ALT **median strip**
UF strips, median

medical doctors
USE **physicians**

medical illustration
HN May 1991 descriptor split, use **medical** (ALT of **medicine**) + **illustration**

medical illustrations
HN April 1991 descriptor split, use **medical** (ALT of **medicine**) + **illustrations**

medical schools
HN September 1990 scope note added
SN Designates schools or colleges of medicine, usually professional schools of universities, that prepare students who have completed baccalaureate programs to be physicians and that award doctor of medicine degrees. (ERIC9)

medicine
HN January 1991 alternate term added
ALT **medical**

medium gray
HN April 1990 lead-in terms added
UF gray, light purplish
light purplish gray
purplish gray, light

medium relief
USE **mezzo rilievo**

medium, Maroger
USE **Maroger medium**

mediums, mixed
USE **mixed media**

meetings
HN May 1991 alternate term added
ALT **meeting**

megass
USE **bagasse**

megilp
HN July 1990 lead-in terms added
May 1990 lead-in term added
UF Macgilp
magilp
McGuilp

Mehmeh
HN August 1990 descriptor changed, was **Memeh**

melting
HN November 1990 added
BT <*temperature related processes*> KT.726

membrane structures
HN March 1991 scope note changed, DS added as source

men
HN January 1991 related term added
September 1990 lead-in terms added
UF human males
males, human
RT **male**

mendicants
USE **beggars**

menologions
HN October 1990 added
BT **religious calendars**
ALT **menologion**

mensas
HN March 1991 alternate term changed, was **mensae**
ALT **mensa**

mental deficiency
USE **mental retardation**

mental diseases
USE **mental disorders**

mental disorders
HN July 1991 related term added
June 1991 alternate term added
February 1991 moved
February 1991 scope note added
February 1991 lead-in terms added
February 1991 descriptor changed, was **mental illness**
BT <*behavior and mental disorders*>
ALT **mental disorder**
SN General term for any emotional or organic mental impairments, manifested in maladaptive behavior, psychological problems, or impairment in one or more significant areas of functioning.
UF diseases, mental
disorder, mental
disorders, mental
mental diseases
mental illness
mental pathology
pathology, mental
RT **mentally handicapped**

mental health
HN February 1991 added
BT health
SN State of psychologic well-being or adequate adjustment to society and the ordinary demands of life.
UF health, mental
RT <psychological concepts>

mental health facilities
HN February 1991 lead-in term added
UF mental retardation facilities

mental illness
USE mental disorders

mental pathology
USE mental disorders

mental retardation
HN January 1991 added
BT <developmental concepts>
SN Intellectual functioning that is significantly below average and is associated with impairment in social adjustment, manifested prior to maturity, usually early in life. (IDMB)
UF deficiency, mental
    mental deficiency
    retardation
    retardation, mental

mental retardation facilities
USE mental health facilities

mentally handicapped
HN July 1991 related term added
    February 1991 lead-in term mentally retarded deleted
RT mental disorders

mentally ill
HN February 1991 added
BT mentally handicapped
SN Those subject to mental disorders.

mentally retarded
HN February 1991 added
BT mentally handicapped
SN Those whose intellectual functioning is significantly below average and are impaired in their social adjustment. (IDMB)
UF retarded, mentally

mercury alloys
USE amalgams

merry-go-rounds
HN September 1990 scope note added
SN Structures consisting of a revolving circular platform with seats, often in the form of horses or other animals, on which people may ride, usually to the accompaniment of mechanical or recorded music.

mesh reinforcement
USE welded wire fabric

mesh, welded wire
USE welded wire fabric

meshrebeeyehs
HN October 1991 lead-in term changed, was mushrebiyeh
    August 1991 lead-in term added
    February 1991 moved
    February 1991 scope note changed
    February 1991 alternate term added
    February 1991 descriptor changed, was meshrebeeyeh
    February 1991 lead-in term changed, was moucharaby
BT <windows by form> RT.907
ALT meshrebeeyeh
SN In Islamic architecture, windows filled with screens or grilles of turned wood.
UF mashrabiyahs
    moucharabies
    mushrebiyehs

mess halls
HN June 1990 scope note changed
SN May be either rooms or separate buildings, as on army bases, serving chiefly as dining halls. (W)

metal pan construction
USE one-way joist systems

metallic paint
HN July 1990 added
BT <paint by composition or origin> MT.2510
SN Paint in which the pigment is a metal. (W)
UF paint, metallic

metallic paper
HN July 1990 added
BT <paper by form> MT.1903
UF paper, metallic

metallurgy
HN February 1991 alternate term added
ALT metallurgical

metaphysics
HN February 1991 alternate term added
ALT metaphysical

meteorological maps
USE weather maps

meteorology
HN February 1991 alternate term added
ALT meteorological

Metepec
HN August 1990 lead-in term changed, was Teotihuacan IV
UF Teotihuacán IV

method, chalk
USE crayon manner

method, crayon
USE crayon manner

method, dolly
USE à la poupée

method, fast-track
USE fast-track method

method, mixed (painting)
USE mixed technique

method, slab
USE slab method

metopes
HN June 1991 scope note source changed to DAC

metropolises
HN July 1991 scope note source changed to ALLAB2

Mexican American
HN June 1991 added
BT <modern North American styles and movements> FL.1720
UF American, Mexican
    Chicano

Mexican Americans
HN June 1991 deleted
BT Latinos

mezzo relievo
USE mezzo rilievo

mezzo rilievo
HN November 1990 added
BT relief
SN Sculptural relief technique in which figures and objects project by about one-half their full roundness.
UF demi-relief
    half-relief
    medium relief
    mezzo relievo
    middle relief
    relief, medium

mezzotint
HN October 1991 moved
    October 1991 scope note changed
    July 1990 lead-in terms added
BT engraving (printing process)
SN Intaglio process in which the surface of the plate is methodically roughened with a rocker to produce a dark background; areas may then be lightened using various scrapers. Produces a printed image having a continuous tonal range. (PRTT)
UF black manner
    manière anglaise
    manière noire
    manner, black

mica (mineral)
HN May 1991 descriptor changed, was mica

Miccaotli
HN November 1991 lead-in term added
    August 1990 lead-in term changed, was Teotihuacan II
UF Teotihuacán II
    Teotihuán II

microcrystalline wax
HN December 1990 moved
BT paraffin

middle age
HN February 1991 added
BT **adulthood**
SN Stage of adult life between young adulthood and old age; in humans, commonly defined as extending from 45 to 65.
UF age, middle
midlife

middle class
HN May 1991 moved
June 1990 alternate term added
BT **social classes**
ALT **middle-class**

Middle period Californian
HN August 1990 lead-in term changed, was **Californian, Middle period**
UF California Middle period

middle relief
USE **mezzo rilievo**

midlife
USE **middle age**

migrant workers
HN April 1991 lead-in term added
September 1990 lead-in terms added
UF transient labor
transient workers
workers, transient

migration
HN October 1990 moved
BT *<functions by general context>* KG.2

military academies
HN September 1990 scope note added
September 1990 lead-in terms added
SN Use both for schools that train people for careers in the armed forces and for private schools organized following the discipline and dress codes of military life; both offer courses in military training and both are generally at university level with degree-granting programs.
UF colleges, military
military colleges
military training schools
schools, military training
training schools, military

military colleges
USE **military academies**

military installations
HN April 1991 related term added
RT **parade grounds**

military personnel
HN May 1991 related term added
April 1991 lead-in term added
February 1991 related terms added
September 1990 lead-in term added
UF military servicemen
servicemen
RT **armed forces**
officers
veterans

military servicemen
USE **military personnel**

military training schools
USE **military academies**

mills, cider
USE **cider mills**

mills, gunpowder
USE **powder mills**

mills, powder
USE **powder mills**

millstones
HN October 1990 added
BT *<grinding and milling equipment components>*
ALT **millstone**
SN Designates circular stones, usually paired and sometimes built up of several pieces, used for grinding grain or other substances fed through a central hole in the upper stone. (W)
UF grindstones (millstones)

mineral oil
HN July 1990 scope note added
SN Oils derived from petroleum or shale. (MH12)

mineral painting
HN April 1990 added
BT *<painting techniques by medium>* KT.239
SN Painting technique used occasionally in the 19th century, employing pigments in water painted on plaster and coated with water glass potassium or sodium silicate. (OCA)
UF painting, mineral
painting, water-glass
stereochromy
water-glass painting

mineral spirits
HN May 1990 lead-in term changed, was **varnolene**
UF Varnolene (TM)

mineral wax
HN December 1990 moved
BT *<wax by composition or origin>*

mineralogy
HN February 1991 alternate term added
ALT **mineralogical**

minorities
HN June 1991 scope note changed
June 1991 moved
June 1991 related term added
September 1990 lead-in terms added
BT *<groups of people>*
SN Use for smaller groups within a larger society that are the objects of prejudice or discrimination from the majority. For groups distinguished from the majority by their national, religious, linguistic, cultural, or sometimes racial background, use **ethnic groups.**
UF groups, minority
minority groups
RT **ethnic groups**

minority groups
USE **minorities**

mints
HN September 1990 scope note added
SN Use for buildings where currency and special medals are produced under government authority. (RHDEL2)

miscellanies
USE **anthologies**

misericords
HN July 1990 scope note added
SN In monastic architecture, rooms, groups of rooms, or separate buildings where monastic rule was relaxed. (DAC)

misregistration
USE **out of register**

mixed houses
USE **housebarns**

mixed materials
USE **mixed media**

mixed media
HN February 1991 scope note changed
February 1991 related terms added
November 1990 moved
July 1990 lead-in terms added
February 1990 lead-in term added
BT **media**
SN Use for combinations of a variety of materials used in the making of a single work of art. In printmaking, use when more than one technique, such as both etching and engraving, are used in one print. In painting, use **mixed technique** when oil paint glazes are laid over tempera paint or tempera paint glazes over oil paint. For 20th-century works that employ several distinct art forms, such as sculpture and music, use **multimedia works.** For the concept that certain 20th-century works merge known art forms to inaugurate a new type, use **intermedia.**
UF materials, mixed
media, mixed
mediums, mixed
mixed materials
mixed mediums
mixed method (printmaking)
RT **intermedia**
mixed technique

mixed mediums
USE **mixed media**

mixed method (painting)
USE **mixed technique**

mixed method (printmaking)
USE **mixed media**

mixed technique
HN April 1990 added
BT *<painting techniques by medium>* KT.239
SN The use in painting of oil paint glazes over tempera paint, or of tempera paint glazes over oil paint. For other combinations of materials and techniques, use **mixed media**.
UF method, mixed (painting)
mixed method (painting)
technique, mixed
technique, wet-into-wet
wet-into-wet technique
RT **mixed media**

Mizui-e
HN October 1991 deleted, made lead-in term in hierarchy under development

moats
HN March 1991 scope note added
SN Trenches around fortified places that are intended to be filled with water. (W)

mobile home parks
HN January 1991 related term added
RT **mobile homes**

mobile homes
HN January 1991 added
BT *<movable dwellings>* RK.350
ALT **mobile home**
SN Use for portable residential units that possess their own chassis with wheels, are designed for year-round living, are infrequently moved, and are larger than travel trailers; use **travel trailers** for portable vehicles designed for travel and recreational purposes and for frequent towing.
UF trailers (mobile homes)
RT **mobile home parks**
portable buildings
travel trailers

moderate blue
HN April 1990 lead-in term added
April 1990 lead-in term **smalt blue** deleted
UF smalt

moderate bluish green
HN April 1990 lead-in terms added
UF grayish green
green, grayish

moderate brown
HN April 1990 lead-in terms added
UF brown, mummy
mummy brown

moderate greenish blue
HN April 1990 lead-in term added
UF blue-green

moderate pink
HN April 1990 lead-in terms added
UF baby pink
pink, baby

moderate purplish pink
HN November 1991 lead-in term changed, was **violet, rose**
April 1990 lead-in term changed, was **rose violet**
UF lilac, rose
rose lilac

moderate red
HN April 1990 lead-in terms added
UF carmine, dark
dark carmine

moderate violet
HN April 1990 lead-in terms added
UF bluish violet, dull
dull bluish violet
violet, dull bluish

moderate yellow
HN August 1990 lead-in term changed, was **lemon**
UF lemon (color)

<modern American styles and periods>
HN July 1990 guide term changed, was *<modern American styles and movements>* FL.1719

<modern Dutch decorative arts styles and movements>
HN May 1990 added
BT *<modern Dutch styles and movements>* FL.3349

<modern Dutch pottery styles>
HN May 1990 added
BT *<modern Dutch decorative arts styles and movements>*

<modern North American periods>
HN July 1990 added
BT *<modern American styles and periods>*

<modern Polish decorative arts styles and movements>
HN April 1990 added
BT *<modern Polish styles and movements>*

<modern Polish fine arts styles and movements> FL.3409
HN April 1991 moved
BT *<modern Polish styles and movements>*

<modern Polish styles and movements>
HN April 1991 added
BT *<modern European regional styles and movements>* FL.3307

<modern Yugoslav styles and movements>
HN May 1991 added
BT *<modern European regional styles and movements>* FL.3307

modular coordination
HN November 1990 moved
BT *<technology-related concepts>* BM.1137

moldings, binder
USE **ataduras**

moldings, ogee
USE **cyma rectas**

moldings, rake
USE **raking moldings**

mollahs
USE **mullahs**

monarchy
HN January 1991 alternate term added
ALT **monarchic**

money orders
HN August 1991 moved to hierarchy under development

monitors (data processing equipment)
HN September 1991 descriptor changed, was **monitors**
September 1991 alternate term changed, was **monitors**
June 1990 lead-in terms added
ALT **monitor (data processing equipment)**
UF CRT's
VDU's

monochrome
HN October 1990 lead-in terms added
UF camaieu
en camaieu

monograms
HN January 1991 related term added
RT **initials (abbreviations)**

monotype
HN October 1991 moved
BT *<planographic printing processes>*

monsoons
HN May 1991 alternate term added
ALT **monsoon**

montage
HN April 1990 added
BT *<image-making processes and techniques>* KT.171
SN Use for the technique of making compositions from portions of existing images, such as drawings or photographs, arranged into somewhat unified images. When pieces of various relatively flat materials are pasted together to form less unified images, use **collage**. Used also in film when two or more shots are superimposed to form a single image.

montan wax
HN December 1990 moved
BT **mineral wax**

Monterey Style
HN April 1990 added
BT *<modern North American architecture styles and movements>* FL.1730

moons, crescent
USE **crescents (shapes)**

Moorish Revival
HN October 1991 added
BT *<modern European revival styles>* FL.3262
UF Revival, Moorish

Moqui
USE **Hopi**

moriki
HN July 1990 added
BT **handmade paper**
SN Delicate handmade paper made of kozo.

Mormon Church
USE **Mormonism**

Mormonism
HN September 1991 added
BT **Christianity**
ALT **Mormon**
UF Mormon Church

morning rooms
HN July 1990 scope note added
SN Use for sitting rooms, sometimes reserved for women, used during the early part of the day; popular from the early 19th century to the early 20th century, especially in England.

mortgaging
HN March 1991 alternate term added
ALT **mortgaged**

motifs
HN April 1991 lead-in terms added
UF decorative motifs
motifs, decorative

motifs, decorative
USE **motifs**

motion-picture museums
USE **museums of moving images**

motion pictures
HN March 1991 related term added
RT **filmographies**

moucharabies
USE **meshrebeeyehs**

mouchettes
HN March 1991 lead-in term added
March 1991 scope note source changed to DAC
UF falchions

mounting board
HN July 1990 added
BT **cardboard**
SN Cardboard made of either wood pulp or cotton fibers used as a backing or mat for prints and drawings. (COMPRI)
UF board, mounting
RT **Fome-Cor (TM)**

mounts (hardware)
HN May 1991 descriptor changed, was **mounts**
May 1991 alternate term changed, was **mount**
ALT **mount (hardware)**

mourners
HN December 1990 added
BT *<people by activity>* HG.705
ALT **mourner**
SN People who feel or express grief or sorrow.
UF grievers

movements, resistance
USE **resistance movements**

movie theaters
HN September 1990 scope note added
SN Use for theaters designed and equipped for the presentation of motion pictures to the public.

moving loads
HN January 1991 alternate term added
ALT **moving load**

moving ramps
HN March 1991 scope note added
SN Use for continuously moving belts designed to carry passengers or goods either horizontally or up inclines; for similar devices moving only horizontally, use **moving walkways.**

moving walkways
HN August 1991 scope note changed
May 1991 lead-in term added
SN Conveying systems having a moving surface on which passengers stand or walk and that remains parallel to its direction of travel; for similar devices designed to carry passengers or goods either horizontally or up inclines, use **moving ramps.**
UF people-movers

Mudejar Revival
HN October 1991 deleted
BT **Islamic Revival**

mudflows
HN May 1991 alternate term added
ALT **mudflow**

mukarnas
USE **muqarnas**

mulberry paper
HN July 1990 added
BT **handmade paper**
SN Opaque white handmade paper made of kozo fibers.
UF kozo paper
paper, kozo
paper, mulberry

mulberry, paper
USE **kozo**

mullahs
HN September 1990 lead-in term added
UF mollahs

mullions
HN August 1991 scope note changed
SN Slender, vertical, usually nonstructural bars or piers forming a division between doors, screens, or lights of windows; for the small members that divide glazing areas and support the panes or the verticals that separate the panels in panel doors, use **muntins.**

mummy brown
USE **moderate brown**

municipal buildings
HN September 1990 scope note added
SN Buildings occupied by the principal offices and departments of city or town governments.

municipal finance
HN February 1991 moved
BT **finance**

municipal government records
HN March 1991 moved
BT *<government records by provenance>* VW.1043

muntins
HN March 1991 scope note added
March 1991 lead-in term added
March 1991 lead-in term changed, was **sash-bars**
SN Use both for the horizontal or vertical members dividing glazing areas into lights and supporting the panes, and for the vertical members separating panels in panel doors; for the uprights that divide openings set in a series, use **mullions.**
UF bars, sash
sash bars

muqarnas
HN April 1990 lead-in term added
UF mukarnas

mural painting
HN April 1990 added
BT **painting (image making)**
SN Use for the activity of composing and executing mural paintings.
UF painting, mural
painting, wall
wall painting

murders
HN May 1991 alternate term added
ALT **murder**

Muscovite (style)
HN May 1991 descriptor changed, was **Muscovite**

museology
HN February 1991 alternate term added
ALT **museological**

museum board
HN October 1990 moved
July 1990 lead-in terms added
BT **mat board**
UF 100% cotton rag board
board, 100% cotton rag
cotton rag board, 100%
rag mat board

museums of moving images
- HN   April 1990 lead-in terms added
- UF   film museums
  motion-picture museums
  museums, film
  museums, motion-picture

museums, film
- USE   **museums of moving images**

museums, motion-picture
- USE   **museums of moving images**

mushrebiyehs
- USE   **meshrebeeyehs**

music conservatories
- HN   September 1990 scope note added
- SN   Generally designates independent professional schools of music emphasizing advanced instruction in performance for singers, conductors, and musicians; usually granting certificates.

music halls
- HN   September 1990 scope note changed
- SN   Public buildings, with seating for an audience, emphasizing musical and variety entertainment but also serving drinks.

music rooms
- HN   July 1990 scope note added
- SN   Use for rooms devoted to the playing of musical instruments or the giving of recitals, as in houses and hotels. (RS)

music schools
- HN   September 1990 scope note added
- SN   Use for schools, generally associated with universities, sponsoring degree-granting programs in a broad range of subjects pertaining to the field of music.

musicology
- HN   February 1991 alternate term added
- ALT   musicological

Musquakie
- USE   **Fox**

mustard oil
- HN   October 1990 moved
- BT   vegetable oil

mutes (physically handicapped)
- HN   September 1991 alternate term added
  September 1991 descriptor changed, was **mutes**
- ALT   mute (physically handicapped)

mutilating
- USE   **mutilation**

mutilation
- HN   June 1991 lead-in term added
  January 1991 scope note added
  January 1991 alternate term added
  December 1990 moved
- BT   destruction

- ALT   mutilated
- SN   Alteration of something, often the destruction of an essential part, to a degree that it is considered imperfect.
- UF   mutilating

mystery plays
- HN   May 1991 alternate term added
- ALT   mystery play

nailing blocks
- HN   April 1990 added
- BT   wood products
- ALT   nailing block
- SN   Wooden blocks or pegs set into construction, usually of masonry or steel, to facilitate nailing.
- UF   blocks, fixing
  blocks, nailing
  bricks, wood
  fixing blocks
  nogs
  wood bricks

naive artists
- HN   October 1990 added
- BT   artists
- ALT   naive artist
- UF   artists, naive

Nan-ga
- USE   **Nanga**

Nanai
- USE   **Goldi**

Nanga
- HN   August 1990 lead-in term changed, was **Na-ga**
  August 1990 lead-in term **Naga School** deleted
- UF   Nan-ga

naoi
- HN   October 1990 moved
- BT   cellae

Napoleon gray marble
- HN   April 1990 added
- BT   gray marble
- UF   gray marble, Napoleon
  marble, Napoleon gray

narcotic addicts
- USE   **drug addicts**

narcotic dependence
- USE   **drug addiction**

narcotic habit
- USE   **drug addiction**

narcotics addiction
- USE   **drug addiction**

narratives
- HN   October 1990 added
- BT   <document genres by function> VW.293
- ALT   narrative
- RT   romances

national guidebooks
- HN   March 1991 deleted
- BT   <guidebooks by location or context>

national holidays
- HN   May 1991 alternate term added
- ALT   national holiday

National Socialism
- HN   January 1991 alternate term added
- ALT   National Socialist

nationalism
- HN   May 1991 alternate term added
- ALT   nationalist

natural calamities
- USE   **natural disasters**

natural disasters
- HN   July 1990 added
- BT   disasters
- ALT   natural disaster
- UF   calamities, natural
  disasters, natural
  natural calamities

natural landscapes
- HN   May 1991 lead-in term added
- UF   scenery

natural ventilation
- HN   March 1991 scope note added
- SN   Use for ventilation systems that depend on natural atmospheric conditions and the manual operation of building openings, such as windows, doors, and transoms.

Nature
- HN   April 1990 added
- BT   <philosophical concepts> BM.486
- SN   Use for the concept of the physical world, including the forces at work in it and the nonhuman life inhabiting it, perceived by human beings as separate and independent from themselves, their activities, and civilization. For the aggregate of physical things, conditions, and influences surrounding and affecting a given organism or community of organisms at any time, use **environment**. For the branch of biology dealing with the relations and interactions between organisms and their habitat, use **ecology**.
- RT   ecology
  environment

nature preserves
- USE   **nature reserves**

nature printing
- HN   October 1991 moved
- BT   <printing processes>

nature reserves
HN November 1990 descriptor changed, was **nature preserves**
November 1990 lead-in term changed, was **nature reserves**
November 1990 alternate term changed, was **nature preserve**
ALT **nature reserve**
UF nature preserves

Naugahyde (TM)
HN April 1990 added
BT *<cloth by composition or origin>*
MT.1845
SN Brand of strong vinyl-coated fabric made to look like leather. (RHDEL2)

naumachias
HN May 1991 alternate term added
ALT **naumachia**

near-infrared spectroscopy
HN April 1990 added
BT **infrared spectroscopy**
UF spectroscopy, near-infrared

neckings
HN April 1991 alternate term added
April 1991 descriptor changed, was **necking**
April 1991 scope note changed, source HAS deleted
ALT **necking**

negotiable instruments
HN August 1991 moved to hierarchy under development

neighborhood houses
USE **settlement houses**

Néo-Grec
HN October 1991 scope note added
August 1990 descriptor changed, was **Neo-Grec**
SN Use for certain Neoclassical architecture of the mid-19th century, especially French.

Neo-Hittite
HN August 1990 lead-in term added
UF Late Hittite

Neo-Plastic
HN April 1991 lead-in term added
UF Nieuwe Beelding

neon
HN May 1990 added
BT **inorganic materials**
SN Inert gaseous element; used as the medium in some electric discharge lamps.

net vaults
HN March 1991 scope note changed
SN Denotes ribbed barrel vaults covered by squares set on the diagonal so that the diagonal ribs cross adjacent bays and so that by the resulting network of ribs the autonomy of individual bays is lost. (BONYED)

neutrals
HN April 1990 lead-in terms added
UF achromatic colors
colors, achromatic

New Deal
HN July 1990 added
BT *<modern North American periods>*
SN Use with reference to projects sponsored by any of the U.S. government programs established under the New Deal administration and operating at various times between 1933 and 1943.

New Figuration
HN September 1990 lead-in terms added
UF New Image

New Image
USE **New Figuration**

new towns
HN July 1990 lead-in terms added
UF planned towns
villes neuves

New Year cards
HN May 1991 added
BT **greeting cards**
SN Greeting cards given at the time of the new year.

newel caps
HN March 1991 scope note source changed to DAC

newel collars
HN March 1991 scope note source changed to DAC

newspaper illustration
HN May 1991 descriptor split, use **newspaper** (ALT of **newspapers**) + **illustration**

newspaper illustrations
HN May 1991 descriptor split, use **newspaper** (ALT of **newspapers**) + **illustrations**

Ngombe
HN October 1990 lead-in term added
UF Bangombe

Ngongo
HN October 1990 lead-in term added
UF Bangongo

nickelodeons
HN September 1990 scope note added
SN Use for early movie theaters, usually small and simple, where motion pictures, and sometimes variety shows, could be seen at inexpensive prices, usually a nickel.

niello
HN March 1991 scope note changed
SN A technique of decorating metal, usually gold or silver, by engraving it with designs that are then filled with a black inlay.

Nieuwe Beelding
USE **Neo-Plastic**

nightclubs
HN September 1990 scope note added
SN Use for establishments offering evening entertainment, such as floor shows or comedy acts, providing space and music for dancing, and usually serving liquor and meals.

Nishga
USE **Niska**

Niska
HN October 1990 lead-in term added
UF Nishga

nobility
HN May 1991 moved
February 1991 lead-in term added
February 1991 scope note changed
BT **aristocracy**
SN Ruling or highly privileged social class, whose rank, property, and privileges are maintained and passed on by heredity.
UF nobles (nobility)

nobles (nobility)
USE **nobility**

nogging
HN April 1990 added
BT **building materials**
SN Masonry, usually brickwork or stone, used as nonstructural fill in the spaces between major wood wall members in timber construction.

nogging pieces
HN April 1990 added
BT **braces (supporting elements)**
ALT **nogging piece**
SN Use for horizontal wood members between the principal timbers of half-timber construction for lateral support, especially when nogging is used.
UF nogs
pieces, nogging

nogs
USE **nailing blocks**
nogging pieces

nonbearing walls
HN March 1991 lead-in term added
UF nonloadbearing walls

nonferrous alloys
HN February 1991 alternate term added
ALT **nonferrous alloy**

nonloadbearing walls
USE **nonbearing walls**

normal schools
USE **teachers colleges**

nosings
HN March 1991 scope note changed, source PDARC deleted

novelists
HN   April 1990 added
BT   **authors**
ALT **novelist**

nuclear warfare
USE **nuclear wars**

nuclear wars
HN   January 1991 scope note added
     January 1991 lead-in terms added
     November 1990 moved
     January 1990 alternate term added
     January 1990 descriptor changed,
        was **nuclear war**
BT   **wars**
ALT **nuclear war**
SN   Wars characterized by the substantial use of nuclear weapons.
UF   atomic wars
     nuclear warfare
     wars, atomic
     wars, nuclear

nudes
HN   September 1990 added
BT   <*subject genres*> VB.69
ALT **nude**
SN   Representations of unclothed human figures.

Nuernberg violet
USE **manganese violet**

nursery schools
HN   September 1990 scope note added
SN   Schools for children usually between 2 1/2 and 5 1/2 years of age. (ERIC9)

nurses' stations
HN   July 1990 scope note added
SN   Control centers for on-call nursing staff in health facilities.

nursing schools
HN   May 1991 descriptor split, use **nursing** + **schools**

Nyangi
USE **Anyang (Nigerian)**

Nyoro
HN   August 1990 lead-in terms added
UF   Bunyoro
     Kitara

oblique arches
USE **skew arches**

observation car elevators
USE **observation elevators**

observation elevators
HN   April 1991 scope note added
     April 1991 lead-in term added
     April 1991 lead-in term changed, was **observation elevators**
     April 1991 descriptor changed, was **observation car elevators**
     April 1991 alternate term changed, was **observation car elevator**
ALT **observation elevator**

SN   Use for elevators with glass-enclosed cars with operating mechanisms so located as to maximize viewing area for the passengers.
UF   elevators, observation
     observation car elevators

observers
USE **viewers**

obstruction lights
HN   May 1990 added
BT   **aeronautical ground lights**
ALT **obstruction light**
SN   Aeronautical ground lights indicating the presence of an obstruction. (MHDSTT)
UF   aerodrome obstruction lights
     lights, obstruction

occupational safety
HN   April 1990 added
BT   **safety**
UF   industrial safety
     safety, industrial
     safety, occupational
     safety, work
     work safety

occupational therapists
HN   January 1991 added
BT   **therapists**
ALT **occupational therapist**
SN   Those whose work is occupational therapy.
UF   therapists, occupational

occupational therapy
HN   January 1991 added
BT   **health sciences**
SN   Therapy which uses forms of work or creative activity as medical or psychiatric treatment.
UF   therapy, occupational

occupational training
USE **vocational training**

Oceanian
USE **Oceanic**

Oceanic
HN   May 1990 lead-in term added
     May 1990 descriptor changed, was **Pacific**
     May 1990 lead-in term changed, was **Oceanic**
UF   Oceanian
     Pacific

oceanography
HN   February 1991 alternate term added
ALT **oceanographic**

octagons
HN   July 1991 alternate term added
ALT **octagon**

octopartite vaults
HN   March 1991 scope note changed
SN   Ribbed vaults divided into eight vaulting cells.

oculi
HN   November 1991 lead-in term changed, was **windows, bull's-eye**
     March 1991 lead-in term changed, was **bull's-eye windows**
UF   bull's eye windows
     windows, bull's eye

odors
HN   April 1990 added
BT   **environment**
ALT **odor**
UF   aromas
     scents
     smells

office automation
HN   May 1991 descriptor split, use **office** (ALT of **offices**) + **automation**

officers
HN   February 1991 added
BT   <*people in government and administration*> HG.649
ALT **officer**
SN   Those who hold offices of trust, authority, or command. (WCOL9)
RT   **military personnel**

officers, police
USE **policemen**

offices, home
USE **home offices**

offices, home (corporate headquarters)
USE **corporate headquarters**

offset lithography
HN   June 1991 added
BT   **lithography**
SN   Printing method in which an image is created by lithographic technique, using the disaffinity of greasy and watery substances, and is then transferred from the stone or plate to an intermediary, such as a rubber blanket, and then offset onto the final surface. If this transfer process is used but the original image is other than lithographic, use the more general term **offset printing**.
UF   lithography, offset
RT   **offset printing**

offset printing
HN   October 1991 moved
     June 1991 related term added
     June 1991 alternate term added
     June 1991 lead-in term **offset lithography** deleted
     October 1990 scope note added
BT   <*planographic printing processes*>
ALT **offset printed**
SN   Printing method in which the image is transferred from a plate, block, or stone to an intermediary, such as a rubber blanket, then onto the final surface. If the original image is created by lithographic technique specifically, use **offset lithography**.
RT   **offset lithography**

offsets
HN March 1991 added
BT *<conditions and effects: printing and printmaking>*
ALT **offset**
SN Use for images or marks that result from an unintentional transfer of ink or other medium. For images intentionally transferred from a print or drawing to another sheet of paper, use **counterproofs.**

ogee arches
HN March 1991 scope note changed
SN Pointed arches composed of two reversed curves.

ogee moldings
USE **cyma rectas**

oil furnaces
HN April 1991 scope note added
SN Use for apparatus for the production of heat by the combustion of oil.

oil of cedar
HN July 1990 added
BT **essential oil**
UF cedar, oil of
cedarwood oil
oil, cedarwood

oil of cloves
HN July 1990 lead-in terms added
July 1990 descriptor changed, was **clove oil**
July 1990 lead-in term changed, was **oil of cloves**
UF amboyna
caryophil oil
clove oil
cloves, oil of
oil, caryophil

oil of lemon
HN July 1990 added
BT **essential oil**
UF lemon, oil of
lemongrass oil
oil, lemongrass

oil of spike
USE **spike oil**

oil painting
HN April 1990 added
BT *<painting techniques by medium>*
KT.239
UF painting, oil

oil, caryophil
USE **oil of cloves**

oil, cedarwood
USE **oil of cedar**

oil, lemongrass
USE **oil of lemon**

oil, lithographic
USE **stand oil**

oil, paraffin
USE **paraffin oil**

oil, rapeseed
USE **rape oil**

oil, stillingia
USE **stillingia oil**

oil, sun-bleached
USE **sun-refined oil**

oil, sun-refined
USE **sun-refined oil**

oil, tallowseed
USE **stillingia oil**

oil, turpentine
USE **turpentine**

oiticica oil
HN October 1990 moved
BT **vegetable oil**

old age
HN February 1991 added
BT **adulthood**
SN Final stage of the normal life span, now commonly considered to be the years after 65.
UF age, old

older adults
USE **elderly**

olive (hardwood)
HN May 1991 descriptor changed, was **olive**

olive gray
USE **dark greenish gray**

olive oil
HN October 1990 moved
BT **vegetable oil**

on-dols
HN June 1991 moved
BT **warm air heating**

one-direction spanning slabs
USE **one-way solid slab systems**

one-half stereographs
USE **half stereographs**

one-turn stairs
HN March 1991 scope note changed
SN Stairs which pass through four right-angle turns as they progress from the bottom to top.

one-way beam and slab systems
HN August 1991 lead-in terms added
August 1991 scope note changed
SN Use for one-way structural systems in which reinforced concrete slabs are supported on beams or girders that run in one direction only.

UF beam and slab systems, one-way
beam-and-girder constructions
beam-and-slab floors
constructions, beam-and-girder
constructions, beam-and-slab floor
floor systems, one-way
floors, beam-and-slab
one-way floor systems
one-way slabs
slabs, one-way
systems, one-way floor

one-way concrete joist systems
USE **one-way joist systems**

one-way constructions
USE **one-way structural systems**

one-way floor systems
USE **one-way beam and slab systems**

one-way joist construction
USE **one-way joist systems**

one-way joist floors
USE **one-way joist systems**

one-way joist systems
HN August 1991 lead-in terms added
UF concrete joist systems, one-way
construction, metal pan
construction, one-way joist
floors, pan
joist construction, one-way
joist systems, one-way
metal pan construction
one-way concrete joist systems
one-way joist construction
one-way joist floors
pan floors
ribbed slabs
slabs, ribbed
systems, one-way concrete joist

one-way slabs
USE **one-way beam and slab systems**
one-way solid slab systems

one-way solid slab systems
HN August 1991 scope note changed
August 1991 lead-in terms added
August 1991 lead-in term **solid slabs** deleted
August 1991 lead-in term **slabs, solid** deleted
SN Use for structural systems in which the primary reinforcing steel runs in one direction only; may or may not include one-way supporting beams.
UF one-direction spanning slabs
one-way slabs
one-way solid slabs
slabs, one-direction spanning
slabs, one-way
solid slabs, one-way
spanning slabs, one-direction

one-way solid slabs
USE **one-way solid slab systems**

one-way structural systems
HN   August 1991 lead-in terms added
      August 1991 lead-in term **one-direction spanning slabs** deleted
      August 1991 lead-in term **spanning slabs, one-direction** deleted
UF   constructions, one-way
      one-way constructions
      one-way systems

one-way systems
USE   **one-way structural systems**

onion domes
HN   March 1991 scope note changed
SN   Pointed bulbous domes.

online reference services
HN   September 1990 lead-in term added
UF   reference services, online

open-air theaters
HN   September 1990 scope note added
SN   Use for theaters designed with facilities for outdoor performing arts productions.

open biting
HN   April 1990 added
BT   *<biting techniques>*
SN   Exposing to acid relatively large, unbounded areas of a printing plate, as opposed to relatively small, restricted areas, such as lines.
UF   biting, open
      etch, open
      open etch

open competitions
HN   July 1990 added
BT   **competitions**
ALT   **open competition**
SN   Design competitions in which entry is available to all in a profession.
UF   competitions, open

open composition
HN   May 1990 lead-in term added
UF   open form

open etch
USE   **open biting**

open form
USE   **open composition**

open newel stairs
HN   March 1991 moved
      March 1991 scope note changed
      March 1991 lead-in terms added
BT   *<stairs by form>* RT.1069
SN   Use for rectangular or spiral stairs that wind around an open wellhole.
UF   hollow newel stairs
      open well stairs
      stairs, hollow newel
      stairs, open well

open pediments
USE   **broken pediments**

open-timbered roofs
HN   March 1991 scope note changed
SN   Roofs in which the wooden structure is exposed to the rooms below

open web joists
HN   August 1991 scope note changed
      March 1991 lead-in terms added
SN   Trusslike joists having an open web whose component parts are either hot-rolled structural shapes or cold-formed light-gauge steel shapes. (DAC)
UF   joists, open web steel
      open web steel joists
      steel joists, open web

open web steel joists
USE   **open web joists**

open well stairs
HN   March 1991 deleted, made lead-in to **open newel stairs**

open well stairs
USE   **open newel stairs**

openings (architectural elements)
HN   March 1991 scope note added
      March 1991 descriptor changed, was openings
      March 1991 alternate term changed, was **opening**
ALT   **opening (architectural element)**
SN   Generally denotes apertures or breaks in the surface of a wall or other architectural element.

openings (events)
HN   May 1991 alternate term added
ALT   **opening (event)**

opera houses
HN   September 1990 scope note added
SN   Use for concert halls designed specifically to accommodate the production needs of opera performances.

operating rooms
HN   July 1990 scope note added
SN   Use for specially equipped rooms, usually in hospitals, where surgical procedures are performed. (RHDEL2)

optical correction
HN   May 1991 lead-in terms added
UF   optical refinement
      refinement, optical

optical fibers
HN   July 1990 added
BT   **synthetic fiber**
ALT   **optical fiber**
SN   Very thin, flexible glass or plastic strands along which large quantities of textual data and images can be transmitted in the form of light pulses; for the branch of optics dealing with the transmission of light through optical fibers, use fiber optics.
UF   fibers, optical
      guides, light
      light guides
RT   **fiber optics**

optical refinement
USE   **optical correction**

optics, fiber
USE   **fiber optics**

opus tesselatum
HN   November 1991 deleted
BT   *<pavements by technique>*

orchestra pits
HN   July 1990 scope note changed
SN   Sunken spaces in front of the forestage from which an orchestra plays.

ordinations
HN   May 1991 alternate term added
ALT   **ordination**

organ galleries
USE   **organ lofts**

organ lofts
HN   July 1990 lead-in terms added
UF   galleries, organ
      organ galleries

organic compounds
HN   February 1991 alternate term added
ALT   **organic compound**

organic materials
HN   February 1991 alternate term added
      July 1990 lead-in terms added
ALT   **organic material**
UF   matter, organic
      organic matter

organic matter
USE   **organic materials**

ornament drawings
HN   April 1991 descriptor split, use ornament + drawings

ornamentalists
USE   **ornamentists**

ornamentists
HN   July 1991 added
BT   **artists**
ALT   **ornamentist**
SN   Designers of ornament especially those artists who specialized in engraved designs of ornament, eg. J. Bérain and Owen Jones.
UF   ornamentalists

orthophosphoric acid
USE   **phosphoric acid**

Osman II
HN   October 1990 lead-in term added
UF   Uthman II

ostraka
HN October 1990 added
BT *<documentary artifacts by form>* VW.481
ALT ostrakon
SN Fragments of pottery or stone containing inscriptions.
RT papyrology

out of register
HN October 1990 added
BT *<conditions and effects: printing and printmaking>*
SN Use when, in printing, not all successive plates or blocks were positioned accurately. (THDAT)
UF misregistration
register, out of

outlets, power
USE **power outlets**

outline lighting
HN April 1991 added
BT **architectural lighting**
SN System of lights arranged to define the outline of architectural features, such as doors, windows, or rooflines.
UF lighting, outline

ovens
HN July 1991 moved
March 1991 scope note added
BT *<heating equipment>* TB.87
SN Generally designates chambers used for baking, heating, or drying; for heating equipment used to harden, bake, or char various specific materials, use **kilns**.

ovens, bake
USE **bake ovens**

ovens, baking
USE **bake ovens**

ovens, beehive (bake ovens)
USE **bake ovens**

over life-size
HN October 1990 added
BT *<size attributes>* DC.119
UF heroic
life-size, over

overbiting
HN April 1990 added
BT *<biting techniques>*
ALT overbitten
SN Excessive biting of a printing plate.

overdoors
HN March 1991 lead-in terms added
UF hyperthyra
sopraporte
soprapportas

overhead doors
HN March 1991 scope note changed
SN Doors of several hinged horizontal sections, that slide up along tracks to end in a horizontal position over the space to be entered; common in the United States as garage doors.

overmantels
HN March 1991 scope note added
SN Use for panels or ornamental structures situated above mantels.

overpainting
HN July 1990 scope note changed
SN The technique or activity of applying overpaint.

overprinting
HN October 1991 moved
July 1990 scope note changed
July 1990 alternate term added
BT *<printing techniques>*
ALT overprinted
SN Use for any process of printing new matter over, or on the same sheet as, already printed matter, including one color over another to produce a mixture of the two.

oversailing courses
HN March 1991 scope note changed
SN Masonry courses which project beyond the courses below; when referring to projecting structural elements, especially when used in a series to form arches, domes, or vaults, prefer **corbels**.

oxbow lakes
HN July 1991 scope note source changed to ALLAB2

oxidative-reductive deterioration
HN October 1990 moved
BT *<conditions and effects: photography>*

ozokerite
HN December 1990 moved
June 1990 lead-in term added
June 1990 lead-in term **galician earth wax** deleted
BT **mineral wax**
UF earth wax

PA systems
USE **public address systems**

Pacific
USE **Oceanic**

pacific madrone
USE **madrona**

padstones
HN March 1991 scope note changed
SN Use for blocks of stone placed in masonry walls under girders or other beams or trusses in order to distribute the load; for shaped stones placed on sloping walls to support the copings of gables, use **kneelers (gable components)**.

pageants
HN May 1991 alternate term added
ALT pageant

pagoda stone
HN June 1990 lead-in term added
UF agalmatolite

paint, bronze
USE **bronze paint**

paint, egg-oil
USE **egg-oil tempera**

paint, encaustic
USE **encaustic paint**

paint, industrial
USE **industrial paint**

paint, metallic
USE **metallic paint**

paint, plastic
USE **acrylic paint**

paint, size
USE **distemper paint**

paint, tempera
USE **tempera**

paint, vinyl
USE **vinyl paint**

paint, water-base
USE **water-base paint**

paint, wax
USE **encaustic paint**

painting (coating)
HN October 1990 scope note added
SN The application of paint to a surface primarily for protection. For the application of pigments to a surface to create an expressive or communicative image, use **painting (image making)**.

painting (image making)
HN October 1990 scope note added
October 1990 alternate term added
October 1990 descriptor changed, was **painting**
ALT painted
SN Use for the art and practice of applying pigments to a surface to create an expressive or communicative image. For the application of paint primarily to protect a surface, use **painting (coating)**.

painting books
HN June 1991 descriptor split, use **painting + books**

<painting techniques by tool> KT.248
HN February 1991 deleted
BT **painting techniques**

painting, acrylic
USE **acrylic painting**

painting, easel
USE **easel painting**

painting, mineral
USE **mineral painting**

painting, mural
  USE **mural painting**

painting, oil
  USE **oil painting**

painting, panel
  USE **panel painting**

painting, polymer
  USE **acrylic painting**

painting, stain
  USE **soak-stain technique**

painting, tempera
  USE **tempera painting**

painting, water-glass
  USE **mineral painting**

paintng, wall
  USE **mural painting**

paired columns
  USE **coupled columns**

Palau
  HN September 1990 lead-in term added
  UF Western Caroline

palazzi pubblichi
  HN September 1990 scope note added
  SN Italian municipal buildings, often combining the residence of the local ruler with the offices of community government. (GIRCIT)

pale mauve
  USE **very pale purple**

Paleo-Indian (Pre-Columbian North American)
  HN May 1991 descriptor changed, was Paleo-Indian

paleoanthropology
  HN September 1991 moved
  BT **physical anthropology**

paleography
  HN May 1991 related term added
       February 1991 alternate term added
  ALT **paleographic**
  RT **wax tablets**

palette
  HN May 1990 scope note changed, GCT added as source

palisades (outworks)
  HN March 1991 scope note changed
  SN Barriers composed of long stakes, usually with pointed tops, driven into the earth close together, sometimes connected by horizontal beams. (RS)

Palladian arches
  USE **Palladian windows**

Palladian windows
  HN March 1991 lead-in terms added
       March 1991 lead-in term changed, was **serliana**
  UF arches, Palladian
       arches, Serlian
       Palladian arches
       Serlian arches
       Serlian windows
       Serliana
       windows, Serlian

pan floors
  USE **one-way joist systems**

panel heating
  HN March 1991 lead-in term added
       March 1991 scope note added
  SN Use for heating systems utilizing floor, wall, or roof panels containing electrical conductors or heating pipes.
  UF panel heating, radiant

panel heating, radiant
  USE **panel heating**

panel painting
  HN April 1990 added
  BT **painting (image making)**
  SN Use to distinguish the activity of painting portable paintings on wood from the painting of other types, such as mural paintings and manuscript illuminations, especially with reference to the Medieval and Early Renaissance periods.
  UF painting, panel

panels (door components)
  USE **door leaves**

panels (surface components)
  HN May 1991 alternate term changed, was **panel**
       March 1991 descriptor changed, was **panels**
       March 1991 lead-in term changed, was **tables (panels)**
  ALT **panel (surface component)**
  UF tables (surface components)

paper mulberry
  USE **kozo**

paper, aluminum
  USE **aluminum paper**

paper, Arches
  USE **Arches paper**

paper, China
  USE **China paper**

paper, cold-pressed
  USE **cold-pressed paper**

paper, construction
  USE **construction paper**

paper, corrugated
  USE **corrugated paper**

paper, drafting
  USE **drawing paper**

paper, graphite
  USE **graphite paper**

paper, hot-pressed
  USE **hot-pressed paper**

paper, India
  USE **China paper**

paper, kozo
  USE **mulberry paper**

paper, metallic
  USE **metallic paper**

paper, mulberry
  USE **mulberry paper**

paper, pastel
  USE **pastel paper**

paper, pulp
  USE **wood pulp paper**

paper, sketching
  USE **drawing paper**

paper, stencil
  USE **stencil paper**

paper, typewriter
  USE **typewriter paper**

paper, waterleaf
  USE **waterleaf**

paper, wax
  USE **waxed paper**

paper, waxed
  USE **waxed paper**

paper, Whatman
  USE **wove paper**

paperboard, corrugated
  USE **corrugated board**

papers
  HN October 1991 added
  BT *<document genres by form>* VW.3
  SN Brief written compositions, as for example on scientific or historical topics, especially those to be read at a public meeting.

papyrology
  HN January 1991 added
  BT *<history-related disciplines>* KD.147
  SN The discipline aiming at deciphering and editing Greek and Latin texts as written on papyrus or other easily portable material. (GALLO)
  RT **classics**
       ostraka

parables
  HN October 1990 added
  BT *<document genres by function>* VW.293
  ALT **parable**
  SN Use for short, fictitious stories that illustrate a moral attitude or religious principle. (W)

parabolas
HN July 1991 alternate term added
ALT parabola

parabolic louvers
HN July 1990 added
BT louvers (built works components)
ALT parabolic louver
UF louvers, parabolic

parade grounds
HN April 1991 added
BT <open spaces by function> RK.1449
ALT parade ground
SN Designates extensive, flat, open spaces used for military exercises, marching, or riding. (DLA)
UF grounds, parade
RT military installations

parades
HN May 1991 alternate term added
ALT parade

paraffin
HN December 1990 moved
BT mineral wax

paraffin oil
HN July 1990 added
BT mineral oil
UF oil, paraffin

paramours
USE lovers

parascenia
HN August 1991 scope note changed
SN In ancient theaters, projecting structures or wings flanking the stage on either side, and with the scaena, or background, enclosing the stage on three sides. (RS)

parish maps
HN July 1991 descriptor split, use parish (administrative body) (ALT of parishes (administrative bodies) + maps

parishes (religious districts)
HN May 1991 descriptor changed, was parishes
May 1991 alternate term changed, was parish
ALT parish (religious district)

Parker trusses
HN March 1991 moved
BT Pratt trusses

parking meters
HN July 1990 scope note added
SN Coin-operated timing devices for regulating the parking of motor vehicles. (W)

parks, water fun
USE waterparks

parlatories
HN July 1990 scope note added
SN Rooms in monasteries or convents where visitors may be received. (DAC)

parliament buildings
HN September 1990 scope note added
SN Use for legislative buildings in countries with parliamentary forms of government.

parlors, smoking
USE smoking rooms

parodoi
HN July 1990 scope note changed
July 1990 descriptor changed, was parodoses
SN Side entrances in ancient Greek theaters between the audience and scaena affording access for spectators.

parolees
HN February 1991 added
BT convicts
ALT parolee
SN Convicts conditionally released from prison prior to the end of their sentence.

parterres
HN September 1990 added
BT <landscaped-site elements> RM.449
ALT parterre
SN Use for formally arranged flower beds, planters, or boxed sections of gardens, often set with raised borders and in different shapes.
RT formal gardens

participation, public
USE citizen participation

participatory design
HN March 1991 moved
BT architectural design

particle detectors, ionization
USE ionization detectors

parties
HN May 1991 alternate term added
ALT party

partitions
HN August 1991 scope note changed
SN Interior walls separating one portion of a space from another; sometimes permanent inside walls that divide buildings into various rooms, sometimes designed to move aside and open up a space. For entities other than walls that divide interior spaces, often incorporating bookshelves, cabinets, or drawers, use room dividers.

party walls
HN March 1991 scope note changed, DAC added as source

pas-de-souris
HN April 1991 scope note changed
SN In a fortification, the steps leading from walls down to water.

passenger elevators
HN March 1991 scope note added
SN Designates elevators primarily used to convey people.

passion plays
HN May 1991 alternate term added
ALT passion play

passive solar heating
HN April 1991 scope note added
April 1991 lead-in term passive solar heating systems deleted
SN Use for solar heating systems collecting and transferring heat by the natural laws of convection, conduction, and radiation with little or no mechanical assistance; for solar heating systems utilizing mechanical devices to transfer heat, use active solar heating.

paste (glass)
HN June 1991 lead-in terms added
UF glass paste
pâte-de-verre

paste (adhesive)
HN May 1991 descriptor changed, was paste

pastel paper
HN July 1990 added
BT drawing paper
SN Paper with a fibrous structure that will take and hold pastel, often coated with a dusting of pumice or sand. (MAYER)
UF paper, pastel

pastels (chalk)
HN October 1990 moved
October 1990 descriptor changed, was pastels (crayons)
BT chalk

pastels (works)
HN September 1991 descriptor changed, was pastels
September 1991 alternate term changed, was pastel
ALT pastel (visual work)

pâte-de-verre
USE paste (glass)

pâte-sur-pâte
HN April 1990 added
BT <pottery decorating techniques> KT.864

pathology, mental
USE mental disorders

patients
HN January 1991 added
BT <people by state or condition> HG.775
ALT patient
SN People awaiting or under medical care and treatment. (WCOL9)

patriotism
HN June 1991 alternate term added
ALT patriotic

patrons
HN August 1991 scope note changed
July 1991 related term added
SN Those who use their means or influence to benefit individuals, institutions, or causes; especially those who support the work of artists and writers, and including those who commission and pay for individual works. For supporters who assume primary responsibility for projects or activities, use **sponsors**.
RT **sponsors**

pattern books
HN June 1991 moved
May 1991 scope note added
BT *<books by subject>* VW.522
SN Books of designs or plans circulated or published to enable widespread copying. May be used for collections of drawings or prints which serve as artists' models.

pattern poetry
HN July 1991 added
BT **visual poetry**
SN Works of visual poetry in which the words or lines of a poem are arranged to form a visual image, usually of the subject of the poem. (HIGPP)
UF emblem poems
picture writing
poems, emblem
poetry, pattern
poetry, shaped
shaped poetry
writing, picture

pattern, cloud
USE **cloud bands**

pavements
HN April 1991 scope note changed, source RS deleted

<pavements by property> RT.812
HN November 1991 deleted
BT **pavements**

<pavements by technique> RT.815
HN November 1991 deleted
BT **pavements**

pavilions (garden structures)
HN May 1991 descriptor changed, was **pavilions**
May 1991 alternate term changed, was **pavilion**
ALT **pavilion (garden structure)**

pavonazzetto
HN November 1991 lead-in term changed, was **marble, Synnadicum**
June 1990 lead-in term changed, was **Synnadicum marble**
UF marble, Synadicum
Synadicum marble

peanut oil
HN October 1990 moved
BT **vegetable oil**

pearl ash
USE **potash**

peasantry
HN May 1991 moved
BT **social classes**

peddlers
HN September 1990 lead-in term added
UF hawkers

pedestal stands
USE **pedestals**

pedestal supports
USE **pedestals**

pedestals
HN September 1991 scope note changed
September 1991 related term added
September 1991 lead-in terms added
SN Use for solid, fixed supports found under such architectural elements as columns or balustrades, or built in to hold sculpture; may also be used for freestanding furniture supports, usually for decorative objects, sometimes incorporating cabinets or shelves; usually classically divided by tripartation into base, dado, and cap.
UF pedestal stands
pedestal supports
stands, pedestal
supports, pedestal
RT **plate warmers (furniture)**

pedestals (furniture)
HN September 1991 deleted
BT *<support furniture>*

pedestrian facilities
HN December 1990 added
BT *<road and roadside elements>* RM.469
ALT **pedestrian facility**
SN Use for elements of the cultural landscape designed for the convenience and safety of pedestrians.
UF facilities, pedestrian

pedigrees, animal
USE **studbooks**

pediments, open
USE **broken pediments**

peel towers
USE **tower houses**

peels
USE **tower houses**

peepholes
HN October 1991 lead-in term changed, was **windows, Judas**
April 1991 lead-in term added
April 1991 lead-in term changed, was **Judas holes**
April 1991 lead-in term changed, was **Judas windows**
UF judas windows
judas-holes
judases
windows, judas

pendant posts
HN April 1991 lead-in term **pendent posts** deleted

pendants (companion pieces)
HN April 1990 added
BT *<object genres by function>* VB.100
ALT pendant (companion piece)
SN Use for pairs of works of art that were designed, or purposefully chosen, to be displayed together.
UF companion pieces

pendentive domes
HN April 1991 lead-in term **handkerchief vaults** deleted

pendentives
HN April 1991 scope note source changed to DAC

Pennsylvania Dutch
USE **Pennsylvania German**

Pennsylvania German
HN May 1991 descriptor changed, was **Pennsylvania Dutch**
May 1991 lead-in term changed, was **Pennsylvania German**
UF Pennsylvania Dutch

penny arcades
HN September 1990 scope note added
SN Denotes amusement facilities that contain mechanical entertainment devices originally operated for a penny per play.

pensions (compensation)
HN June 1991 alternate term added
May 1991 descriptor changed, was **pensions**
ALT **pension (compensation)**

pent roofs
USE **skirt-roofs**

pentagons
HN July 1991 alternate term added
ALT **pentagon**

penthouse roofs
USE **shed roofs**
skirt-roofs

pentimenti
HN February 1991 moved to hierarchy under development

<people by age group>
HN July 1991 related term added
RT *<life stages>*

people-environment studies
USE **environmental psychology**

people, homeless
USE **homeless persons**

people, impoverished
USE **poor**

people, low income
USE **poor**

people-movers
HN May 1991 deleted, made lead-in to
moving walkways and **personal rapid transit**

people-movers
USE **moving walkways**
personal rapid transit

people, street
USE **homeless persons**

perception
HN May 1991 scope note added
SN The process of becoming aware of objects, qualities, or relations via the sense organs; involves the reception, processing, and interpretation of sensory impressions. (ERIC12)

perception, visual
USE **visual perception**

perchloride of iron
USE **ferric chloride**

perchloride, iron
USE **ferric chloride**

perfection
HN April 1990 added
BT *<aesthetic concepts>* BM.487
UF flawlessness

perforating
HN May 1991 added
BT *<processes and techniques by specific type>* KT.5
ALT **perforated**
SN The making of holes through an object; may be done purposefully, either when the object is made or later, or may be the result of natural processes.

performance art
HN October 1991 moved to hierarchy under development

performances
HN November 1990 alternate term added
ALT **performance**

performing artists
HN November 1991 related term added
July 1991 related term added
RT **performances (events)**
performing arts

performing arts centers
HN September 1990 scope note added
SN Use for buildings or groups of buildings containing auditoriums, multipurpose spaces, and auxiliary facilities suitable for the presentation of various performing arts, such as concerts, operas, and plays.

periaktoi
HN April 1991 scope note changed
SN In Greek theaters, the revolving tri-angular devices with differing scenery painted on each of the three faces.

perilla oil
HN October 1990 moved
BT **vegetable oil**

periodic markets
HN May 1991 alternate term added
ALT **periodic market**

periodical illustration
HN May 1991 descriptor split, use **periodical** (ALT of **periodicals**) + **illustration**

periodical illustrations
HN July 1991 descriptor split, use **periodical** (ALT of **periodicals**) + **illustrations**

peripheries
USE **urban fringes**

peristyle houses
HN April 1991 scope note added
SN Use for houses that have internal courtyards with colonnades; for ancient Roman or similarly styled courtyard houses without colonnades but with impluvia, use **atrium houses**.

perpendicular tracery
HN April 1991 descriptor split, use **Perpendicular Style** + **tracery**

perrons
HN April 1990 added
BT *<stairs by location or context>* RT.1091
ALT **perron**
SN Stairs, usually located outdoors, leading up to the entrances of large buildings, such as churches, public halls, or mansions.

personal rapid transit
HN July 1991 lead-in term added
UF people-movers

personnel evaluations
HN March 1991 deleted
BT **personnel records**

persons, low income
USE **poor**

PES-tp
USE **thermoplastic polyester**

petitioning
HN December 1990 added
BT *<communication functions>* KG.32
SN Making a formal written request to a higher authority. (WCOL9)
RT **petitions**

petitions
HN July 1991 related term added
RT **petitioning**

petrolatum
USE **petroleum jelly**

petroleum jelly
HN May 1990 lead-in term added
UF petrolatum

pharmaceutics
USE **pharmacy**

pharmacists
HN December 1990 added
BT *<people in health and medicine>* HG.380
ALT **pharmacist**
SN Those engaged in pharmacy. (WCOL9)
UF apothecaries (people)
druggists

pharmacologists
HN February 1991 added
BT *<people in health and medicine>* HG.380
ALT **pharmacologist**
SN Those who practice pharmacology.

pharmacology
HN February 1991 alternate term added
ALT **pharmacological**

pharmacy
HN February 1991 lead-in term added
February 1991 alternate term added
ALT **pharmaceutical**
UF pharmaceutics

phased construction
USE **fast-track method**

philology
HN February 1991 alternate term added
ALT **philological**

philosophical anthropology
HN September 1991 moved
BT **anthropology**

philosophy
HN February 1991 alternate term added
ALT **philosophical**

phosphoric acid
HN October 1990 added
BT **acid**
UF acid, orthophosphoric
acid, phosphoric
orthophosphoric acid

phosphorus
HN May 1991 added
BT **inorganic materials**

photoelectric detectors
USE **photoelectric smoke detectors**

photoelectric fire detectors
USE **photoelectric smoke detectors**

photoelectric smoke detectors
HN April 1991 lead-in terms added
April 1991 descriptor changed, was **photoelectric detectors**
April 1991 alternate term changed, was **photoelectric detector**
ALT **photoelectric smoke detector**

UF detectors, photoelectric smoke
    fire detectors, photoelectric
    photoelectric detectors
    photoelectric fire detectors
    smoke detectors, photoelectric

photographers, press
USE **photojournalists**

photographic postcards
HN May 1991 added
BT **picture postcards**
ALT **photographic postcard**
SN Postcards that have on one side an
    image produced with light-sensitive
    materials directly on the card.
UF postcards, photographic

<photographic reversal effects> KT.910
HN October 1990 deleted
BT *<conditions and effects>*

photographs
HN August 1991 scope note changed
SN Use for still images produced from
    radiation-sensitive materials (sensi-
    tive to light, electron beams, or nu-
    clear radiation), with the exception
    of reproductive prints of documents
    and technical drawings; for these use
    terms from the Document Types hi-
    erarchy, such as **blueprints**. Photo-
    graphs may be positive or negative,
    opaque or transparent.

photographs, copy
USE **copy prints**

photographs, directorial
USE **staged photographs**

photographs, fabricated
USE **staged photographs**

photographs, staged
USE **staged photographs**

photography
HN November 1990 alternate term added
ALT **photographic**

photography, Subjective
USE **Subjective photography**

photojournalists
HN September 1990 lead-in terms added
UF photographers, press
    press photographers

photoluminescence
HN April 1990 added
BT **luminescence**
SN Luminescence induced by the ab-
    sorption of infrared radiation, visi-
    ble light, or ultraviolet radiation.
    (RHDEL2)

photoprints, copy
USE **copy prints**

photosculpture
HN April 1991 added
BT **sculpture techniques**

SN Use for techniques for translating
    camera images into solid, three-
    dimensional representations.

phrenology
HN September 1991 moved
BT *<psychology-related disciplines>* KD.184

Phthalocyaninblau
USE **phthalocyanine blue**

phthalocyanine blue
HN November 1991 lead-in term
    changed, was **blue, Thalo**
    May 1990 lead-in term changed, was
    phthalocyaninblau
    May 1990 lead-in term changed, was
    Thalo blue
UF blue, Thalo (TM)
    Phthalocyaninblau
    Thalo blue (TM)

physical anthropology
HN September 1991 moved
BT **anthropology**

physical education buildings
HN September 1990 scope note added
SN Use for buildings in which individ-
    uals can learn and develop skills in
    sports, exercises, and hygiene.

physical fitness centers
USE **health clubs**

physicians
HN September 1990 lead-in terms added
UF doctors, medical
    MDs
    medical doctors

physiognomy
HN September 1991 moved
BT *<psychology-related disciplines>* KD.184

physiology
HN February 1991 alternate term added
ALT **physiological**

pianomaker's edge planes
USE **edge planes**

picture postcards
HN May 1991 scope note added
    May 1991 lead-in term **photo-
    graphic postcards** deleted
SN Postcards having a pictorial image on
    one side.

picture writing
USE **pattern poetry**

pieces, apron
USE **forestages**

pieces, chimney
USE **mantels**

pieces, nogging
USE **nogging pieces**

pierced walls
HN April 1991 scope note added
SN Use for masonry walls in which ma-

terial has been removed without
jeopardizing structural integrity,
either for decorative or structural
reasons.

piers (foundation components)
HN · June 1991 lead-in term added
    June 1991 lead-in term **pillars
    (foundation components)** deleted
UF pillars

piers (supporting elements)
HN May 1991 descriptor changed, was
    piers
    May 1991 alternate term changed,
    was **pier**
ALT **pier (supporting element)**

piers, clustered
USE **compound piers**

pietre dure
HN July 1990 descriptor changed, was
    pietra dure

pilaster strips
HN August 1991 scope note changed
SN Engaged piers, of only slight projec-
    tion, without a capital and base.

pilastrades
HN April 1991 scope note source
    changed to DAC

pile foundations
HN May 1991 scope note changed,
    source MHDSTT deleted

piles
HN April 1991 lead-in term added
UF pilework

pilework
USE **piles**

pilgrimages
HN May 1991 alternate term added
ALT **pilgrimage**

pillared halls
USE **hypostyle halls**

pillars
USE **piers (foundation components)**

pink, baby
USE **moderate pink**

pink, salmon
USE **strong yellowish pink**

pinnacles
HN April 1991 lead-in term changed, was
    guglias (pinnacles)
UF guglias

pipe clay
HN May 1990 added
BT *<clay by composition or origin>* MT.52
UF clay, pipe
    terre de pipe
    terre de pipe ware

pipes, down
USE **downspouts**

pipes, leader
USE **downspouts**

pipes, rainwater
USE **downspouts**

pipes, smoke
USE **flues**

piping (plumbing systems)
HN April 1991 scope note added
SN In plumbing and storm water systems, assemblies of pipes, tubes, and fittings.

Pisquow
USE **Wenatchi**

Pit River
USE **Atsugewi**

pitched roofs
HN April 1991 scope note added
April 1991 lead-in terms added
SN Designates roofs with one or more surfaces that have a pitch greater than 10 degrees from the horizontal.
UF roofs, sloping
sloping roofs

pits (earthworks)
HN May 1991 descriptor changed, was **pits**
May 1991 alternate term changed, was **pit**
ALT **pit (earthwork)**

Pittura Colta
HN May 1991 lead-in terms added
UF Anachronism (Pittura Colta)
Hyper-Mannerism

pivoted windows
HN April 1991 descriptor changed, was **pivoting windows**
April 1991 alternate term changed, was **pivoting window**
ALT **pivoted window**

plagiarism
HN January 1991 scope note added
SN Passing off the ideas or words of another as one's own, or deliberately using the work of another without crediting the source. (WCOL9)

plain sawed lumber
HN June 1990 descriptor changed, was **plain-sawed lumber**

plan (formal concept)
HN May 1990 scope note added
SN Use for the formal concept of the layout of spaces and elements in the built environment, such as of a building or city.

plan oblique drawings
HN August 1990 lead-in terms added
UF drawings, planometric
planometric drawings
planometric projections
projections, planometric

planar trusses
HN March 1991 deleted
BT *<trusses by form>* RT.357

planes (tools)
HN May 1991 descriptor changed, was **planes**
May 1991 alternate term changed, was **plane**
ALT **plane (tool)**

planes, pianomaker's edge
USE **edge planes**

planned towns
USE **new towns**

planographic printing
HN January 1991 scope note added
October 1990 moved
October 1990 lead-in terms added
BT **printing**
SN Use for printing processes in which the image is printed from a flat surface.
UF planography
printing, surface
surface printing

<planographic printing processes>
HN October 1991 added
BT *<printing processes>*

planography
USE **planographic printing**

planometric drawings
USE **plan oblique drawings**

planometric projections
USE **plan oblique drawings**

plans (drawings)
HN September 1991 descriptor changed, was **plans**
September 1991 alternate term changed, was **plan**
April 1991 scope note changed
ALT **plan (drawing)**
SN Use for orthographic drawings in the horizontal plane, generally depicting discrete objects or spaces. Can also be used for a set of drawings for a project. For general reference to depictions or photographs showing structures or sites seen from directly above, use **plan views**. For representations in plan view of portions of the earth's surface, emphasizing arterial or regional relationships and using larger scales, prefer **maps**.

plant materials
HN February 1991 alternate term added
ALT **plant material**

plantation owners
HN September 1990 lead-in term added
UF planters

planters
USE **plantation owners**

plants, CHP generating
USE **cogeneration plants**

plants, cogeneration
USE **cogeneration plants**

plants, combined cycle power
USE **cogeneration plants**

plants, combined heat and power generating
USE **cogeneration plants**

plants, heating
USE **heating systems**

plastic cement
HN July 1990 added
BT **fillers**
SN Material in a plastic state used to seal narrow openings. (W)
UF cement, plastic

plastic concrete
USE **polymer-impregnated concrete**

plastic design
HN May 1990 lead-in term added
UF ultimate-strength design

plastic paint
USE **acrylic paint**

Plastic Wood (TM)
HN February 1991 lead-in term added
February 1991 scope note added
February 1991 descriptor changed, was **plastic wood**
SN A paste of wood flour or wood cellulose compounded with a synthetic resin used for filling cavities or seams in wood products.
UF wood, plastic

plastics
HN August 1991 lead-in term **polymers** deleted

<plastics by function>
HN April 1990 added
BT **plastics**

plastisol
HN April 1990 added
BT **vinyl**

plate lines
USE **plate marks**

plate marks
HN March 1990 added
BT *<conditions and effects: printing and printmaking>*
SN Imprints of the edges of the plate on intaglio prints. (PRTT)
UF lines, plate
marks, plate
plate lines

plate warmers (furniture)
HN September 1991 moved
September 1991 related term added
BT *<support furniture>* TG.606
RT **pedestals**

plates (printing equipment)
 USE **printing plates**

plates, engraving
 USE **printing plates**

platform frame construction
 USE **platform frames**

platform frames
 HN April 1991 lead-in terms added
 UF construction, platform frame
  frame construction, platform
  framing, platform
  framing, western
  platform frame construction
  platform framing
  western framing

platform framing
 USE **platform frames**

platforms
 HN March 1991 scope note changed
 SN Flat surfaces or floors, generally
  raised above the adjoining floor or
  surface.

plating
 HN March 1990 alternate term added
 ALT **plated**

play schools
 HN May 1991 moved
  May 1991 scope note added
 BT <schools by function> RK.794
 SN Use for children's summer schools
  with facilities and structured program activities devoted to play; established as an emergency measure
  during World War I; used both as
  places for children of working parents and as places for parents and
  teachers to study the playing habits
  of children.

playing cards
 HN May 1991 related term added
 RT **card games**

plinth courses
 HN March 1991 scope note changed
 SN Masonry courses which form a con-
  tinuous plinth. (DAC)

plinths
 HN November 1990 moved
 BT <supporting and resisting elements>
  RT.59

plumbing fixtures
 HN March 1991 scope note added
 SN Use for receptacles in plumbing or
  drainage systems, other than traps,
  intended to receive or discharge liquid or waste.

plumbing systems
 HN March 1991 lead-in term water systems deleted

pneumatic dispatch systems
 USE **pneumatic tubes**

pneumatic tubes
 HN March 1991 scope note added
  March 1991 lead-in terms added
 SN Systems for conveying papers or
  small objects through tubes in specially designed receptacles by means
  of air pressure.
 UF dispatch systems, pneumatic
  pneumatic dispatch systems
  systems, pneumatic dispatch
  systems, pneumatic tube

Poblano
 HN June 1991 moved
 BT <Colonial Latin American architecture
  styles> FL.1710

poems, emblem
 USE **pattern poetry**

poetry, pattern
 USE **pattern poetry**

poetry, shaped
 USE **pattern poetry**
  visual poetry

poetry, visual
 USE **visual poetry**

pointed arches
 HN March 1991 scope note added
 SN Arches composed of arcs struck from
  an even number of centers, usually
  two, so that the apex of the arch is a
  point.

pointed arches, segmental
 USE **pointed segmental arches**

pointed segmental arches
 HN October 1991 lead-in term added
  March 1991 lead-in term added
 UF pointed arches, segmental
  segmental pointed arches

pointing (filling)
 HN May 1991 descriptor changed, was
  pointing

pointing (transferring technique)
 HN April 1991 scope note changed
  November 1990 moved
  November 1990 alternate term
  pointed (sculpture) deleted
  November 1990 descriptor changed,
  was **pointing (sculpture)**
 BT <transferring techniques> KT.739
 SN A technique used by sculptors to re-
  produce a clay or plaster model or
  to copy a finished work through
  measurements. (MAYER)

police stations
 HN September 1990 scope note added
 SN Headquarters for the police of a
  particular district, from which police
  officers are dispatched and to which
  persons under arrest are brought.
  (RHDEL2)

policemen
 HN September 1990 lead-in term added
 UF officers, police

Polish (European region)
 HN September 1991 descriptor changed,
  was **Polish**

political campaigns
 HN May 1991 alternate term added
 ALT **political campaign**

<political events>
 HN November 1990 added
 BT **events**

polo clubs
 HN November 1991 moved
 BT <club complexes>

polygons
 HN July 1991 alternate term added
 ALT **polygon**

polyhedra
 HN January 1991 alternate term added
 ALT **polyhedron**

polymer-impregnated concrete
 HN May 1990 lead-in terms added
 UF concrete, plastic
  plastic concrete

polymer painting
 USE **acrylic painting**

polysulfide elastomer
 HN May 1990 lead-in term changed, was
  thiokol
 UF Thiokol (TM)

polyurethane
 HN May 1990 lead-in term added
 UF urethane

pommels (finials)
 HN March 1991 scope note source
  changed to DAC

pony trusses
 HN March 1991 moved
  March 1991 scope note changed
 BT <trusses by location or context> RT.377
 SN Bridge trusses supporting loads on
  their lower chords and having no
  lateral bracing between their top
  chords.

pools, reflecting
 USE **reflecting pools**

poor
 HN January 1991 added
 BT <groups of people by state or condition>
 SN People who have little or no money,
  goods, or other means of support.
  (RHDEL2)

UF disadvantaged, economically
economically disadvantaged
impoverished people
low income people
low income persons
people, impoverished
people, low income
persons, low income
poverty stricken
RT **proletariat**

poppy-seed oil
HN October 1990 moved
BT **vegetable oil**

popular culture
HN October 1991 lead-in term added
May 1990 lead-in term added
UF culture, mass
mass culture

population redistribution
USE **internal migration**

porcelain enamel
HN July 1990 added
BT **enamel**
SN Generally an opaque, vitreous surface finish fused at high temperatures and used on metals. (HORNB)

porcelain, Amstel
USE **Amstel**

porcelain, Carrack
USE **Kraak porcelain**

porous concrete
HN October 1991 deleted, made lead-in to **lightweight concrete**

porous concrete
USE **lightweight concrete**

portable buildings
HN January 1991 related term added
RT **mobile homes**

portals
HN April 1990 scope note added
SN Use for impressive, monumental entrances, gateways, or doorways usually to buildings or courtyards, especially those emphasized by stately architectural treatment.

portcullises
HN March 1991 scope note source changed to DAC

porters
HN September 1990 lead-in term added
UF redcaps

portfolios (groups of works)
HN April 1990 added
BT *<object genres by form>* VB.89
ALT **portfolio (group of works)**
SN Use when a group of works is brought together such as to exemplify the work of an artist or student, or if the works (usually by one

artist) are issued or housed together in a portfolio.

portor marble
HN May 1990 lead-in terms added
UF black-and-gold marble
marble, black-and-gold

portrayal
USE **representation**

post offices
HN September 1990 scope note added
SN Use for public buildings within a government postal system at which mail is received and sorted, from which it is distributed, and at which stamps are sold and other services rendered.

post-on-sill
USE **poteaux sur solle construction**

postal cards
HN May 1991 scope note changed
SN Cards sold by the post office with postage stamps already printed on them. (RHDEL2)

postal code maps
HN March 1991 deleted
BT *<maps by subject>*

postcards
HN May 1991 scope note changed
SN Cards on which a message may be written or printed for mailing without an envelope, usually at a lower rate than that for letters in envelopes.

postcards, photographic
USE **photographic postcards**

poster board
HN July 1990 added
BT **cardboard**
UF board, poster

poster color
HN August 1991 moved
BT **distemper paint**

posts, border
USE **border inspection stations**

posts, customs
USE **border inspection stations**

posts, door
USE **doorjambs**

potash
HN July 1990 added
BT **alkali**
UF ash, pearl
pearl ash

potash alum
USE **alum**

potato printing
HN October 1991 moved
BT *<relief printing processes>*

poteaux sur solle construction
HN April 1990 added
BT *<construction by form>* KT.27
ALT **poteaux sur solle**
SN Timber frame construction in which the upright posts are raised above damp ground on individual foundation blocks to avoid rotting the frame members and to facilitate replacement of foundation pieces without rebuilding the frame; common in the vernacular architecture of the Lower Mississippi Valley.
UF construction, poteaux sur solle
post-on-sill

potlaches
HN May 1991 alternate term added
ALT **potlach**

<pottery glazing techniques>
HN July 1991 added
BT *<pottery decorating techniques>* KT.864

pottery, art
USE **art pottery**

pottery, studio
USE **studio ceramics**

pounce
HN July 1990 added
BT *<materials by function>* MT.2291
SN Fine powders of various materials used to treat or protect the surface of a drawing or of parchment, or to transfer a design through a pricked drawing.

poverty stricken
USE **poor**

powder mills
HN October 1990 added
BT *<processing plants>* RK.620
ALT **powder mill**
SN Use for factories in which gunpowder is made. (RHDEL2)
UF factories, gunpowder
gunpowder factories
gunpowder mills
gunpowder works
mills, gunpowder
mills, powder
works, gunpowder

powder, bronze
USE **bronze powder**

power generating plants, combined heat and
USE **cogeneration plants**

power lines
HN July 1990 scope note added
SN Wires used for transmitting a supply of electrical energy to buildings.

power outlets
HN March 1991 lead-in term added
March 1991 scope note added
SN Use for points in electrical systems

at which current is supplied to an appliance or device. (MEANS)
UF   outlets, power

power plants, combined cycle
USE   cogeneration plants

powerhouses
HN   May 1991 lead-in term added
UF   engine houses

powers of attorney
HN   March 1991 lead-in terms added
UF   attorney, letters of
     letters of attorney

praecinctiones
HN   July 1990 scope note changed
SN   Use for the walkways, concentric with the rows of seats, between the upper and lower seating tiers in a Roman theater. For similar features in Greek theaters, use diazomata.

Pratt trusses
HN   March 1991 moved
BT   <trusses by construction>

prayer halls
USE   sanctuaries

<Pre-Columbian Arctic and Subarctic styles> FL.782
HN   April 1991 related term added
RT   <Canadian Arctic Native styles> FL.1205

precast piles
HN   August 1991 scope note changed
SN   Reinforced concrete piles manufactured in a casting plant or at the site prior to placement in their final positions.

precipitation, acid
USE   acid rain

predictors
USE   prophets

pregnancy
HN   February 1991 added
BT   <biological concepts> BM.715
SN   State of carrying unborn young within the body. (WCOL9)
UF   gestation

premieres
HN   May 1991 alternate term added
ALT   premiere

presentation drawings (proposals)
HN   September 1991 descriptor changed, was presentation drawings
     September 1991 lead-in term changed, was drawings, presentation
     September 1991 alternate term changed, was presentation drawing
ALT   presentation drawing (proposal)
UF   drawings, presentation (proposals)

preservation
HN   April 1991 alternate term added
     March 1991 alternate term added
ALT   preserved
      preserving

press boxes
HN   April 1990 added
BT   <work and instructional spaces> RM.220
ALT   press box
SN   Use for the quarters assigned as working space for media personnel, as at sporting events and political conventions, and usually equipped with communications facilities.
UF   boxes, press

press photographers
USE   photojournalists

pressboard
HN   July 1990 added
BT   fiberboard
SN   Strong, highly glazed board resembling vulcanized fiber. (W)

preventing
HN   January 1991 added
BT   maintaining
SN   Keeping something undesirable from happening, or someone from doing something undesirable.
UF   prevention

prevention
USE   preventing

previews
HN   May 1991 alternate term added
ALT   preview

primer
HN   July 1990 lead-in term added
UF   priming (material)

priming
HN   November 1990 moved
BT   coating

priming (material)
USE   primer

primitive hut
HN   May 1991 added
BT   <historical, theoretical and critical concepts: visual arts> BM.315
SN   Use for the rationalist model of the ideal building type based on the construction of the hypothetical first dwelling and its use of materials in response to function and climate; used as a basis for various architectural theories since the 18th century.
UF   cabin, rustic
     hut, primitive
     rustic cabin

principal rafters
HN   March 1991 scope note changed
SN   Diagonal members of a roof truss

which support the purlins on which rafters are laid. (MEANS)

principals
HN   October 1990 lead-in terms added
UF   principals, school
     school principals

principals, school
USE   principals

printer's ink
USE   printing ink

printers (output devices)
HN   May 1991 descriptor changed, was printers
     May 1991 alternate term changed, was printer
ALT   printer (output device)

printing
HN   October 1990 moved
BT   <printing and printing processes and techniques>

<printing and printing processes and techniques>
HN   October 1990 added
BT   <image-making processes and techniques> KT.171

printing ink
HN   November 1990 added
BT   <ink by function>
UF   ink, printer's
     ink, printing
     printer's ink

printing plates
HN   February 1991 added
BT   <printing and printmaking equipment> TB.341
SN   Flatpieces (as of metal) from which textual or pictorial images are printed.
UF   plates (printing equipment)
     plates, engraving

<printing processes>
HN   October 1991 added
BT   <printing and printing processes and techniques>

<printing techniques>
HN   October 1990 added
BT   <printing and printing processes and techniques>

printing, letterpress
USE   letterpress printing

printing, linoleum-block
USE   linoleum-block printing

printing, screen
USE   screen printing

printing, stencil
USE   stenciling

printing, surface
USE   planographic printing

printmaking
HN October 1991 moved
October 1991 scope note changed
BT *<image-making processes and techniques>* KT.171
SN Use for the activity of producing prints as works of art; for the specific processes employed, use such terms as **intaglio printing** or **mezzotint**. For the production of other types of printed material, use **printing**.

<printmaking and printmaking techniques> KT.439
HN October 1991 deleted
BT *<image-making processes and techniques>*

printmaking techniques
HN October 1991 descriptor split, use **printmaking + techniques**

prints, copy
USE **copy prints**

prints, later
USE **later prints**

prints, reissue
USE **later prints**

prints, work
USE **work prints**

prisoners
HN February 1991 scope note added
February 1991 related terms added
February 1991 lead-in term **convicts** deleted
SN Use for those involuntarily confined in prison or kept in custody. Use **convicts** for those serving a prison sentence following conviction for a criminal offense. Use **inmates** for those confined, voluntarily or involuntarily, to an institutional facility.
RT **convicts**
inmates

private family quarters
USE **apartments**

private wings
USE **apartments**

process, relief
USE **relief printing**

process, screen
USE **screen printing**

processing, information
USE **information management**

processions
HN May 1991 alternate term added
ALT **procession**

Proconnesian marble
HN June 1991 added
BT **variegated marble**

UF Cyzican marble
marble, Cyzican
marble, Proconnesian

procuring
HN January 1991 scope note changed
SN Acquisition of goods or services through purchase, lease, hiring, or trade.

producers
HN September 1991 added
BT *<people in the performing arts>* HG.59
ALT **producer**
SN People who manage the financial and artistic resources of productions in the performing arts. (BOXCF)

products, cast
USE **castings**

profiles (orthographic drawings)
HN April 1991 descriptor changed, was **profiles**
April 1991 alternate term changed, was **profile**
February 1991 scope note changed
ALT **profile (orthographic drawing)**
SN Use for orthographic drawings of an object or structure seen in a vertical plane. In architecture, most often sections; in shipbuilding may be sections or elevations, but always showing the vessel broadside.

programmers
USE **computer programmers**

projections, planometric
USE **plan oblique drawings**

proletariat
HN May 1991 moved
January 1991 related term added
June 1990 scope note added
June 1990 alternate term added
BT **working class**
ALT **proletarian**
SN That portion of the working class at the lowest end of the social and economic scale.
RT **poor**

promissory notes
HN July 1991 moved to hierarchy under development

promoting
HN April 1991 added
BT **managing**
SN Advancing someone to a higher level in rank, position, grade or job level, or honor.
UF advancement
promotion

promoting (advocating)
USE **advocating**

promotion
USE **promoting**

promotions
HN May 1991 alternate term added
ALT **promotion**

prophets
HN December 1990 added
BT *<people by activity>* HG.705
ALT **prophet**
SN Those who foretell future events, especially divinely inspired revelations. (WCOL9)
UF predictors

proprietors
HN September 1991 lead-in term **owners** deleted

prostitutes
HN January 1991 added
BT *<people in service occupations>* HG.36
ALT **prostitute**
SN People who practice prostitution.
UF call girls
hookers
streetwalkers
RT **brothels**
prostitution

prostitution
HN January 1991 added
BT **selling**
SN Business of engaging in sexual activity for money.
RT **brothels**
crime
prostitutes
social issues

protecting
HN January 1991 moved
January 1991 lead-in term **preserving** deleted
BT **maintaining**

<protective processes and techniques>
HN October 1990 guide term changed, was *<protective processes>* KT.594

protesting
HN January 1991 scope note added
SN Openly expressing objection, disapproval, or dissent. (RHDEL2)

proto-Ionic capitals
USE **Aeolic capitals**

Protodynastic
USE **Early Dynastic (Egyptian)**

provenance
HN July 1991 scope note added
SN A record of previous ownership or previous locations of a work.

proverbs
HN December 1990 added
BT *<document genres by function>* VW.293
SN Use for short, concise sayings in common use that are often metaphorical or aliterative. (OED)

Provincial Highland
HN June 1991 moved
BT <*Colonial Latin American architecture styles*> FL.1710

psalmodia
USE **psalters**

psalmody
USE **psalters**

psalters
HN February 1991 lead-in terms added
UF psalmodia
psalmody

pseudo-Ionic capitals
USE **Aeolic capitals**

psychiatric hospitals
HN April 1990 lead-in term added
UF asylums (psychiatric hospitals)

psychiatry
HN February 1991 alternate term added
ALT **psychiatric**

psychoanalysis
HN September 1991 moved
BT **psychology**

psychohistory
HN September 1991 moved
BT <*psychology-related disciplines*> KD.179

<*psychological concepts*>
HN February 1991 related term added
RT **mental health**

psychology
HN September 1991 moved
September 1991 scope note added
February 1991 alternate term added
BT <*psychology and related disciplines*>
ALT **psychological**
SN Science of human and animal mind and behavior, with the focus on individuals in interaction with their environment.

<*psychology and related disciplines*> KD.179
HN September 1991 moved
BT **behavioral sciences**

psychology, architectural
USE **environmental psychology**

psychology, ecological
USE **environmental psychology**

psychology, environmental
USE **environmental psychology**

<*psychology-related disciplines*> KD.184
HN September 1991 moved
BT <*psychology and related disciplines*>

pteromata
HN July 1990 lead-in term **peridromes** deleted

public address systems
HN March 1991 scope note added
March 1991 lead-in term added
SN Use for a combination of devices designed to transmit, amplify, and reproduce sound, so as to make it audible to an audience in a public space.
UF PA systems

public officers
HN February 1991 moved
September 1990 scope note added
BT **officers**
SN People holding posts to which they have been legally elected or appointed and exercising government functions. (W)

public participation
USE **citizen participation**

public schools
HN September 1990 scope note added
SN Use for schools maintained at public expense for the education of children of a community or district as part of a free education system; generally includes elementary and high schools. (RHDEL2)

publications, alternative
USE **alternative publications**

publications, alternative press
USE **alternative publications**

publishing
HN January 1991 scope note added
SN Issuing printed, taped, or otherwise reproduced records of knowledge in any medium for sale or distribution to the public.

Puebla
HN June 1991 moved
BT <*Colonial Latin American styles*> FL.1707

pulp paper
USE **wood pulp paper**

pulp, chemical
USE **chemical pulp**

pulp, groundwood
USE **mechanical wood pulp**

pulp, mechanical wood
USE **mechanical wood pulp**

<*pulpit components*> RT.1245
HN March 1991 deleted
BT <*pulpits and pulpit components*>

pulpits
HN March 1991 moved
BT <*Christian religious building fixtures*> RT.1223

<*pulpits and pulpit components*> RT.1241
HN March 1991 deleted
BT <*Christian religious building fixtures*>

pumice (lava)
HN May 1991 descriptor changed, was **pumice**

pumping stations
HN July 1991 scope note source changed to ALLAB2
April 1990 lead-in term **pump houses** deleted

punch work
USE **punchwork (carving technique)**

punching
USE **punchwork (carving technique)**

punchwork (carving technique)
HN November 1990 added
BT <*carving techniques*>
UF punch work
punching

punchwork (metalwork)
HN May 1991 descriptor changed, was **punchwork**

punic wax
HN December 1990 moved
BT **bleached beeswax**

puppet stages
USE **puppet theaters**

puppet theaters
HN May 1991 moved
September 1990 scope note added
September 1990 lead-in terms added
BT <*performing arts structures*> RK.921
SN Use for portable or mobile structures designed for the presentation of puppet shows.
UF marionette theaters
puppet stages
stages, puppet
theaters, marionette

purchasing
HN January 1991 scope note added
SN Obtaining something by the payment of money or its equivalent. (W)

purlins
HN March 1991 scope note added
SN Use for the horizontal timbers laid across the principal rafters and supporting the common rafters in a roof.

purple, dark slate
USE **dark reddish purple**

purple, fuchsia
USE **deep reddish purple**

purplish gray
HN April 1990 lead-in term added
UF grey dawn

purplish gray, dark
USE **dark gray**

purplish gray, light
USE **medium gray**

pyramids (geometric figures)
HN July 1991 alternate term added
ALT **pyramid (geometric figure)**

pyramids (tombs)
HN May 1991 descriptor changed, was pyramids
May 1991 alternate term changed, was pyramid
ALT pyramid (tomb)

pyrography
HN November 1990 moved
BT *<surface coating and decorating processes and techniques>* KT.655

Qara Qoyunlu
USE **Karakoyunlu**

Qing
HN October 1990 lead-in term added
UF Manchu

quack grass
USE **couch grass**

quality
HN April 1990 added
BT *<aesthetic concepts>* BM.487
SN Use in the context of aesthetic judgment for the concept of inherent merit, worthiness, or excellence in something. For the function of selecting quality standards for a project and monitoring the finished work to assure compliance with those standards, use **quality control**.
RT **quality control**

quality control
HN February 1991 moved
February 1991 related term added
May 1990 scope note changed
BT *<business-related functions>*
SN Selecting the quality standards required for a project, and monitoring the properties of the finished work to assure compliance with those standards. For the concept of inherent merit, worthiness, or excellence in the context of aesthetic judgment, use **quality**.
RT **quality**

quantity surveyors
HN September 1990 scope note added
SN People who estimate or measure quantities of materials and equipment necessary to construct a project.

quarter-turn stairs
HN March 1991 scope note changed
March 1991 lead-in term changed, was angle stairs
March 1991 lead-in term changed, was stairs, angle
SN Stairs that, as they progress from bottom to top, turn 90 degrees; for stairs with landings at which the stair turns 90 degrees, use **quarterpace stairs**.
UF angled stairs
stairs, angled

quarterpace stairs
HN March 1991 scope note changed
SN Stairs with landings at which the stair turns 90 degrees; for stairs that turn 90 degrees as they progress from bottom to top, use **quarter-turn stairs**.

quarters, private family
USE **apartments**

queen-post roofs
HN March 1991 scope note changed
SN Roofs supported by pairs of queen posts. (DAC)

queen-post trusses
HN March 1991 moved
BT *<trusses by form>* RT.357

queen posts
HN March 1991 scope note changed
SN Use for pairs of vertical, or near vertical, symmetrically placed tie beams in a truss.

quinacridone red
HN November 1991 lead-in term changed, was red, acra
May 1990 lead-in term changed, was acra red
UF Acra red (TM)
red, Acra (TM)

Quito
HN June 1991 moved
BT *<Colonial Latin American fine arts styles>* FL.1716

quoins
HN March 1991 lead-in term cunes deleted

quotations (texts)
HN September 1991 descriptor changed, was quotations
September 1991 alternate term changed, was quotation
ALT quotation (text)

rabbinical seminaries
HN May 1991 moved
May 1991 scope note added
BT *<schools by subject>* RK.801
SN Use for educational facilities with higher education curricula specifically designed to train rabbis; for schools providing training in Talmudic law generally, but not necessarily specifically for the rabbinate, use **yeshivas**. For schools providing education for the priesthood, use **theological seminaries**.

race discrimination
HN February 1991 scope note added
SN Discriminatory attitudes and denial of rights, privileges, or choice because of race.

raceways
HN March 1991 scope note changed
SN Furrows or channels constructed to

house electrical conductors. (MEANS)

racks (support furniture)
HN November 1991 alternate term changed, was rack
May 1990 descriptor changed, was racks
ALT rack (support furniture)

racquetball courts
HN September 1990 scope note added
SN Use for four-walled enclosed courts marked for the game of racquetball.

radiant barriers
HN April 1990 added
BT **building materials**
ALT radiant barrier
SN Highly reflective building material, usually aluminum-foil-faced kraft paper or plastic film, with nonradiating properties placed in an airspace to block only radiant transfer from a heat-radiating surface, such as a hot roof, to a heat-absorbing surface, such as conventional attic insulation.
UF barriers, radiant

radiant heating
HN March 1991 scope note added
SN Systems for heating by radiation from a surface, especially from a surface heated by means of electricity, hot air, or hot water. (RHDEL2)

radiators
HN March 1991 scope note changed
SN Use to designate a nest of pipes containing circulating water or steam for heating a room.

radio stations
HN April 1990 scope note added
SN Broadcasting stations for sending and receiving radio programming transmissions; for rooms and spaces designed for the origination or recording of radio programs, use **radio studios**.

radio studios
HN April 1990 scope note added
SN Broadcasting studios designed for radio programs; for larger facilities, including offices and equipment, from which the transmissions are sent and received, use **radio stations**.

raft foundations
HN March 1991 lead-in terms added
UF foundations, mat
mat foundations

rafters
HN March 1991 scope note changed
SN Parallel sloping members that support the roof covering.

rafters, hip jack
USE **jack rafters**

rag mat board
USE **museum board**

rail fences
HN July 1990 scope note changed
SN Fences of posts and usually two or three split rails. (W)

railroad crossings
USE **grade crossings**

railroad yards
HN June 1990 lead-in term added
UF railyards

rails
HN March 1991 scope note added
SN Use for horizontal members in paneling or frames, such as a door or window.

ls (door components)
SE **door rails**

lyards
USE **railroad yards**

ain
HN October 1990 moved
BT *<water by form>*

rainbow roofs
HN March 1991 scope note changed
SN Gable roofs in the form of a pointed arch, with a gently sloping convex surface. (RHDEL2)

rainwater pipes
USE **downspouts**

raised floors
USE **access floors**

rake moldings
USE **raking moldings**

raking cornices
HN August 1991 scope note source changed to DAC

raking moldings
HN August 1991 lead-in terms added
UF moldings, rake
rake moldings

raku
HN May 1990 lead-in term added
UF raku pottery

raku pottery
USE **raku**

ram's heads
USE **aegicranes**

Ramadan
HN April 1991 moved
BT *<religious seasons>*

ramps, water
USE **water stairs (landscaped-site elements)**

rape oil
HN October 1990 moved
July 1990 lead-in terms added
BT **vegetable oil**
UF oil, rapeseed
rapeseed oil

rapeseed oil
USE **rape oil**

Rashtrakutan
HN October 1990 descriptor changed, was **Rashtrakuta**

rathäuser
HN September 1990 scope note added
SN German municipal government buildings also housing public function rooms.

ravison oil
HN May 1991 deleted
BT **nondrying oil**

raw linseed oil
HN July 1990 deleted
BT **linseed oil**

real estate agents
HN September 1990 lead-in terms added
UF brokers, real estate
real estate brokers
realtors

real estate brokers
USE **real estate agents**

realtors
USE **real estate agents**

receipt books (cookbooks)
USE **cookbooks**

receipting
HN December 1990 added
BT *<economic and financial functions>*
KG.43
ALT **receipted**
SN Acknowledging in writing the payment of a bill, or the delivery of money, articles, or goods. (RHDEL2)

receptions
HN May 1991 alternate term added
ALT **reception**

recitals
HN May 1991 alternate term added
ALT **recital**

reconstruction
HN February 1991 alternate term added
ALT **reconstructing**

record drawings
HN April 1990 scope note changed
April 1990 lead-in term added
SN In the context of the modern building trade, use for drawings or copies of drawings that are kept as file records after completion of a project; may include as-built drawings, which indicate changes made during construction. In historical contexts, use

for copies of architects' design drawings, often on a reduced scale, whether executed or unexecuted designs, kept as records of their work. For scale drawings made from existing structures, generally, use **measured drawings**; for drawings that generally depict actual locations, use **topographical views**.
UF drawings of record

records, fiscal
USE **financial records**

recovery, resource
USE **recycling**

recreation buildings
HN April 1991 related term added
September 1990 scope note added
SN Distinguished from **entertainment buildings** by more broadly designating buildings designed for or containing equipment for amusement, exercise, sports, or some pastime.
RT **health clubs**

recreation centers
HN September 1990 scope note added
SN Buildings having facilities for various recreational activities, often provided by or associated with specific groups or organizations.

recreation rooms
HN July 1990 scope note added
SN Use for rooms in homes or public buildings furnished and reserved for recreation and informal entertaining.

rectangles
HN July 1991 alternate term added
ALT **rectangle**

rectas, sima
USE **cyma rectas**

recycling
HN April 1991 added
BT **waste management**
SN Recovery and reuse of materials and energy from waste. (ALLAB3)
UF recovery, resource
resource recovery

red ocher (pigment)
HN May 1991 descriptor changed, was **red ocher**

red, Acra (TM)
USE **quinacridone red**

red, light
USE **dark yellowish pink**

red-polished ware (Cypriote)
HN May 1990 descriptor changed, was **red polished ware**

red-polished ware (Egyptian)
HN May 1990 descriptor changed, was **red-polished ware**

redcaps
USE **porters**

reference services, online
USE **online reference services**

refinement, optical
USE **optical correction**

reflectance
HN   April 1990 added
BT   *<light-related concepts>* BM.852
SN   A measure of the degree to which a surface reflects light usually expressed as the ratio of reflected light to the incident light of a reference surface.
UF   coefficient of reflection
coefficient, reflection
factor, reflection
reflection coefficient
reflection factor

reflectance, diffuse
USE **diffuse reflectance**

reflected color
HN   August 1990 lead-in term added
May 1990 scope note added
SN   Color of surface that is altered by light reflected from another colored surface.
UF   colour, reflected

reflecting pools
HN   April 1990 added
BT   **water features**
ALT **reflecting pool**
SN   Designates artificial areas of water, usually of geometric shape, specifically designed and located so as to mirror buildings or other structures.
UF   pools, reflecting

reflection
HN   April 1990 added
BT   *<light-related concepts>* BM.852
SN   The return of light, heat, or sound after striking a surface. (RHDEL2)

reflection coefficient
USE **reflectance**

reflection factor
USE **reflectance**

reflection, diffuse
USE **diffuse reflection**

reflective insulation
HN   June 1991 moved
June 1991 scope note changed
BT   **thermal insulation**
SN   Building material usually comprised of two or more layers of reflective material containing a dead air space between them and which acts as a unit to block conducted, convected, and radiated heat.

refrigerant systems
HN   March 1991 lead-in term added
UF   refrigeration

refrigeration
USE **refrigerant systems**

refugee camps
HN   May 1991 related term added
RT   **resettlement**

refuse
HN   July 1991 added
BT   *<materials by function>* MT.2291
SN   Matter or material rejected as useless and fit only to be thrown away. (W)

refuse disposal
HN   April 1991 moved
BT   **waste disposal**

regalia
HN   November 1990 added
BT   *<object genres by function>* VB.100
ALT **regale**
SN   Emblems, symbols, or paraphernalia indicative of a royal state or of an office or membership in a group.

regents
HN   September 1990 scope note added
SN   Those who govern a kingdom in the minority, absence, or disability of the sovereign. (W)

regions
HN   June 1990 added
BT   *<social and economic geography concepts>* BM.1041
SN   Cohesive areas that are homogeneous in terms of selected natural, historic, economic, political, or cultural characteristics that distinguish them from other areas. Prefer the more specific terms found under *<administrative bodies>*, such as **counties** or **nations**, or under **districts** or **landscapes** (environments).

register (transferring technique)
USE **registration (transferring technique)**

register, in
USE **in register**

register, out of
USE **out of register**

registering (information handling)
HN   May 1990 lead-in term changed, was registration
UF   registration (information handling)

registers (HVAC components)
HN   March 1991 scope note added
SN   Use for grille and damper assemblies covering the outlets of air distribution systems. (STEIN)

registrars (museology)
HN   May 1991 descriptor changed, was registrars
May 1991 alternate term changed, was registrar
ALT **registrar (museology)**

registration (information handling)
USE **registering (information handling)**

registration (transferring technique)
HN   October 1990 moved
October 1990 lead-in terms added
October 1990 descriptor changed, was **registering**
BT   *<transferring techniques>* KT.739
UF   register (transferring technique)
registry

registry
USE **registration (transferring technique)**

reinforced composites, fibrous
USE **fibrous composites**

reinforced composites, filament
USE **fibrous composites**

reinforcement, mesh
USE **welded wire fabric**

reinforcement, wire fabric
USE **welded wire fabric**

reissue prints
USE **later prints**

reissues
USE **later prints**

relative humidity
HN   April 1991 added
BT   **humidity**
SN   The ratio of the amount of water vapor in the air to the amount which would be present at the same temperature were the atmosphere to be fully saturated. (BATCOB)
UF   atmospheric humidity
humidity, atmospheric
humidity, relative

relief
HN   April 1991 moved
BT   **sculpture techniques**

relief etching
HN   April 1990 added
BT   *<relief printing processes>*
SN   Printing process in which the plate is etched, but unlike in most etching, the design is relief printed rather than intaglio printed.
UF   etching, relief

relief printing
HN   October 1990 moved
October 1990 lead-in terms added
October 1990 lead-in term **surface printing** deleted
BT   **printing**
UF   process, relief
relief process

<relief printing processes>
HN   October 1991 added
BT   *<printing processes>*

relief process
USE **relief printing**

relief, concave
USE **intaglio**

relief, crushed
USE **rilievo schiacciato**

relief, deep
USE **high relief**

relief, hollow
USE **intaglio**

relief, incised
USE **intaglio**

relief, medium
USE **mezzo rilievo**

relief, sunk
USE **coelanaglyphic relief**
　　intaglio

relievo stiacciato
USE **rilievo schiacciato**

religious drama
HN May 1990 lead-in terms added
UF drama, sacred
　　sacred drama

<religious events>
HN April 1991 related term added
RT *<religious holidays>*

<religious holidays>
HN April 1991 related term added
RT *<religious events>*

<religious seasons>
HN April 1991 added
BT **events**

remarques
HN July 1990 added
BT **annotations**
ALT **remarque**
SN Notes or sketches made by the printmaker or printer in the margins of the plate and visible in prints called **remarque proofs**. (OCA)

remote-station fire alarm systems
HN March 1991 scope note added
SN Use for fire alarm systems in which the alarm signals are transmitted to an off-premises station, and then to a fire department. (MSR7)

remuneration
USE **compensation (economic concept)**

rent control
HN October 1990 lead-in terms added
　　October 1990 moved
BT *<economic and financial functions>*
　　KG.43
UF rent restriction
　　restriction, rent

rent restriction
USE **rent control**

reports, historic structure
USE **historic structure reports**

representation
HN June 1990 lead-in terms added
UF depiction
　　portrayal

representing
HN May 1990 scope note changed, source WCOL deleted

republics
HN April 1990 added
BT **nations**
ALT **republic**
SN Nations in which political power resides in a body of citizens entitled to vote and is exercised by elected officers and representatives who are responsible to them and who govern according to law. (W)

researching
HN January 1991 scope note added
SN Conducting diligent and systematic inquiry or investigation into a subject or question, especially in order to discover or revise facts or theories. (RHDEL2)

resettlement
HN May 1991 related term added
　　January 1991 scope note added
　　October 1990 moved
　　October 1990 alternate term added
BT **relocating**
ALT **resettled**
SN Setting people in a new place or a new way of life. (W)
RT **refugee camps**

residential mobility
HN October 1990 moved
BT **demographics**

residential wings
USE **apartments**

resin ground
USE **rosin ground**

resist
HN July 1990 lead-in term added
UF stop-out

resistance movements
HN May 1991 added
BT *<political concepts>* BM.530
ALT **resistance movement**
UF movements, resistance

resource recovery
USE **recycling**

resources, water
USE **water resources**

responds
HN March 1991 scope note changed
SN Use for supports, usually pilasters or colonettes, engaged to a wall, that carry one end of an arch, a groin, or a vault rib.

restoration (process)
HN May 1991 descriptor changed, was restoration

restriction, rent
USE **rent control**

restrictive covenants
HN January 1991 alternate term added
ALT **restrictive covenants**

retaining walls
HN August 1991 scope note changed
SN Use for walls that are constructed to resist lateral loads, such as walls that hold back banks of earth.

retardation
USE **mental retardation**

retardation, mental
USE **mental retardation**

retarded, mentally
USE **mentally retarded**

reticulated tracery
HN March 1991 scope note added
SN Use for tracery consisting in large part of netlike arrangements of repeated geometrical motifs. (RHDEL2)

retreats
HN May 1991 moved
　　May 1991 alternate term added
BT **events**
ALT **retreat**

retrochoirs
HN July 1990 scope note added
SN Use to designate those areas of a church situated behind the high altar; often found in English Medieval architecture.

retroussage
HN April 1990 added
BT *<matrix preparation techniques>*
SN Lightly rubbing an intaglio printing plate with a soft rag, after it has been inked in the normal way, to produce a blurred, fuzzy effect in the print. (COMPRI)

revales
HN March 1991 deleted
BT **struck moldings**

reversas, sima
USE **cyma reversas**

revisers
HN July 1991 related term added
RT **revising**

revising
HN March 1991 added
BT *<information handling functions>*
　　KG.64
SN Making a new, amended, improved, or up-to-date version.
RT **revisers**

Revival, Moorish
USE **Moorish Revival**

revolutions
HN   January 1991 scope note added
       January 1991 related terms added
       January 1991 descriptor changed,
         was **revolution**
       November 1990 moved
       January 1990 alternate term added
BT   *<political events>*
ALT **revolution**
SN   Occasions of sweeping change in es-
       tablished patterns of government or
       social organization. (TSIT)
RT   **armed conflicts**
       social conflict

revolving doors
HN   March 1991 scope note added
SN   Use for doors intended to limit the
       passage of air through an entrance,
       consisting of leaves revolving on a
       central pivot.

revolving stages
HN   July 1990 scope note added
SN   Use for circular platforms divided
       into segments enabling multiple
       theater sets to be in place in advance
       and in turn rotated into view of the
       audience. (RHDEL2)

rhombuses
HN   July 1991 alternate term added
ALT **rhombus**

Rhythmist
HN   April 1990 added
BT   *<modern Polish decorative arts styles and*
       movements>
ALT **Rhythmism**

ribbed arches
HN   March 1991 deleted
BT   *<arches by form: construction>* RT.247

ribbed slabs
USE **one-way joist systems**

ribbed vaults
HN   March 1991 scope note changed
       May 1990 lead-in term added
SN   Vaults that include ribs either as
       supporting or decorative elements.
UF   **vaults, ribbed**

ribbed vaults, star
USE **stellar vaults**

ribbon development
HN   February 1991 lead-in terms added
UF   development, linear
       linear development

ribbon windows
USE **strip windows**

ribbons (ledger boards)
USE **ledger boards**

rice bran oil
USE **rice oil**

rice oil
HN   October 1990 moved
       July 1990 lead-in term added
BT   **vegetable oil**
UF   rice bran oil

riders, horseback
USE **equestrians**

ridgeboards
HN   March 1991 lead-in term changed,
         was **roof trees**
UF   rooftrees

ridges (roof components)
HN   April 1991 scope note added
       April 1991 descriptor changed, was
         ridges
       April 1991 alternate term changed,
         was **ridge**
ALT **ridge (roof component)**
SN   Use for the intersections of the slop-
       ing sides of roofs.

riding clubs
HN   November 1991 moved
BT   *<club complexes>*

riding schools
HN   September 1990 scope note added
SN   Use for schools where equitation is
       taught; usually including an arena,
       seating, and housing for horses and
       equipment.

rigid arches
HN   March 1991 deleted
BT   *<arches by form: construction>* RT.247

rigid insulation
HN   June 1991 moved
BT   *<insulation by form>*

rigid pavements
HN   November 1991 moved
       July 1991 scope note changed
BT   **pavements**
SN   Pavements that provide high bend-
       ing resistance and that distribute
       loads to the foundation over a rela-
       tively large area; for pavements that
       depend for stability on aggregate in-
       terlock, friction, and cohesion, use
       flexible pavements. (DAC)

rilievo schiacciato
HN   November 1990 added
BT   **relief**
SN   Sculptural relief technique in which
       projection of the forms is extremely
       shallow.
UF   crushed relief
       relief, crushed
       relievo stiacciato

rim lighting
USE **backlighting**

rings, corbel
USE **shaft rings**

Ripolin
USE **enamel paint**

risers (piping)
HN   March 1991 scope note added
SN   Use for vertical or return piping in
       plumbing systems; for vertical mains
       for soil, waste, or venting, use **stacks.**

risers (step components)
HN   March 1991 descriptor changed, was
         risers
       March 1991 alternate term changed,
         was **riser**
       March 1991 scope note changed,
         DAC added as source
ALT **riser (step component)**

risk management
HN   April 1990 added
BT   *<analytical functions>* KG.3
SN   Planning how to conduct affairs by
       assessing, minimizing, and prevent-
       ing potential losses, injuries, or other
       damages.
UF   management, risk

rites
USE **ceremonies**

roadside improvement
HN   December 1990 moved
BT   **civic improvement**

roadways
HN   July 1990 scope note added
SN   Use for those portions of thorough-
       fares over which vehicular traffic
       passes. (MHDSTT)

robbers
USE **thieves**

robotics
HN   April 1990 added
BT   **science**

rock art
HN   July 1990 added
BT   *<art genres>* BM.229
SN   Use for paintings or carvings worked
       on living rock.
UF   art, rock

rodeos
HN   May 1991 alternate term added
ALT **rodeo**

role, gender
USE **sex role**

roll insulation
USE **blanket insulation**

roll insulation
HN   June 1991 deleted, made lead-in to
         blanket insulation

roll up
USE **rolling up**

roller coasters
HN   September 1990 scope note added
SN   Use for amusement park rides hav-
       ing a gravity train that moves along
       a closed loop on a sharply winding
       trestle built with steep inclines that

produce sudden speedy plunges for thrill-seeking passengers. (RHDEL2)

roller coating
USE **roller painting**

roller painting
HN October 1990 moved
October 1990 lead-in terms added
BT **painting (coating)**
UF coating, roller
roller coating
rolling (painting)

roller-skating rinks
HN September 1990 scope note added
SN Use for buildings with large unobstructed spaces specially surfaced usually with hardwood or another smooth durable material for roller skating.

rolling (painting)
USE **roller painting**

rolling up
HN July 1990 scope note added
July 1990 lead-in terms added
July 1990 descriptor changed, was **rolling-up**
SN Applying ink to a printing plate or block or through a stencil with a roller.
UF charging
roll up

Roman sepia
HN June 1991 moved
BT **sepia**

romance fiction
USE **romances**

romance literature
USE **romances**

romances
HN March 1991 added
BT *<document genres by function>* VW.293
ALT **romance**
SN Verse or prose narratives depicting heroic, fantastic, or supernatural events, primarily in Medieval times.
UF fiction, romance
literature, romance
romance fiction
romance literature
RT **narratives**

Romanist
HN November 1990 lead-in term added
UF Italianist

Ronga
USE **Thonga**

rood lofts
HN August 1991 scope note added
SN Use for platforms above rood screens from which choirs sing or readings are made.

rood screens
HN October 1991 scope note changed
SN Use for chancel screens surmounted by a cross or crucifix; generally found in English church architecture. (RS)

roof trusses
HN March 1991 descriptor split, use **roof** (ALT of **roofs**) + **trusses**

roofing, asphalt prepared
USE **tar paper**

<rooflike enclosing structures>
HN May 1991 added
BT **membrane structures**

roofs
HN March 1991 scope note added
SN Use for the outside, overhead enclosures of buildings or other structures, including the roofing and its structural framing.

roofs, bicycle wheel
USE **double-cable structures**

roofs, cable
USE **cable structures**

roofs, cable-supported cantilever
USE **cable-stayed structures**

roofs, double-layer cable-supported
USE **double-cable structures**

roofs, lean-to
USE **shed roofs**

roofs, pent
USE **skirt-roofs**

roofs, penthouse
USE **shed roofs**
skirt-roofs

roofs, simulated thatch
USE **false thatched roofs**

roofs, sloping
USE **pitched roofs**

roofs, suspension
USE **suspension structures**

rooftrees
USE **ridgeboards**

rooms, chapter
USE **chapter houses**

rooms, hypostyle
USE **hypostyle halls**

rooms, media
USE **media rooms**

rooms, showers
USE **shower rooms**

rooms, withdrawing
USE **drawing rooms**

ropework (cable moldings)
USE **cable moldings**

rose
USE **deep red**

rose lilac
USE **moderate purplish pink**

rose madder
USE **madder**

rose windows
HN August 1991 scope note changed
SN Circular windows containing patterned tracery. (ACLAND)

rosemary
USE **rosemary oil**

rosemary oil
HN October 1991 scope note changed
June 1990 lead-in term added
SN A pungent essential oil obtained from the flowering tops of rosemary and used chiefly in soaps, colognes, hair lotions, pharmaceutical preparations, and as a retardant in oil paints.
UF rosemary

rosin ground
HN April 1990 added
BT **etching ground**
SN The acid-resistant substance used for aquatint, made by dusting rosin particles onto a plate and heating. (PRTT)
UF dust ground
ground, dust
ground, resin
ground, rosin
resin ground

rosin-sized paper
HN July 1990 deleted
BT **building paper**

rot, dry
USE **dry rot**

rotary intersections
USE **traffic circles**

rotundas (interior spaces)
HN May 1991 descriptor changed, was **rotundas**
May 1991 alternate term changed, was **rotunda**
ALT **rotunda (interior space)**

rough sills
HN August 1991 scope note changed
SN Horizontal members laid across the bottom of an unfinished opening to act as a base during construction of window frames or door frames. For the horizontal members that rest on the foundation at the bottom of a wood structure, use **sill plates**.

roughstrings
USE **carriage pieces**

rowlock arches
HN September 1991 scope note changed
March 1991 moved
BT *<arches by form: construction>* RT.247

SN Arches in which bricks or other small voussoirs are arranged in separate concentric rings. (PDARC)

royalty
HN December 1990 added
BT **nobility**
ALT **royal**
SN Those who are descendent from or related to a king or queen or line of kings and queens.
RT **rulers (people)**

rubber stamps
HN October 1991 added
BT **stamps (tools)**
ALT **rubber stamp**
SN Devices with a rubber printing surface that becomes coated by being pressed on an ink-saturated pad, used for imprinting by hand. (RHDEL2)
UF stamps, rubber

rubberized cloth
HN July 1990 added
BT <*cloth by surface treatment*> MT.1879
UF cloth, rubberized
   fabric, rubberized
   rubberized fabric

rubberized fabric
USE **rubberized cloth**

rubbing
HN April 1990 added
BT <*transferring techniques*> KT.739
SN Transferring an image from a relief surface to a material such as paper or cloth, either by placing the material over the surface and applying pressure and friction with a medium such as chalk or pencil, or by inking the surface, placing the material, and applying pressure and friction.

rubbing ink
HN December 1990 added
BT <*ink by function*>
SN Slabs of ink used in lithography to obtain soft tones. (PRTT)
UF ink, rubbing

rubbish
HN July 1991 added
BT **refuse**
SN Used up, worn out, or broken things that are not garbage or ash. (W)
UF trash

Rubia
USE **madder**

rubinglas
USE **gold ruby glass**

ruby glass, gold
USE **gold ruby glass**

rulers (people)
HN August 1991 lead-in term changed, was **sovereigns**
   February 1991 related term added
UF sovereigns (rulers)
RT **royalty**

rummage sales
HN May 1991 alternate term added
ALT **rummage sale**

runway lights
HN May 1990 added
BT **aeronautical ground lights**
ALT **runway light**
SN Aeronautical ground lights arranged along a runway indicating its direction or boundaries. (MHDSTT)
UF lights, runway

rural development
HN March 1991 scope note added
SN Basic development of rural regions emphasizing improvements in the standard of living and the active participation of the local population. (LCSH)

rural sociology
HN September 1991 moved
BT **sociology**

rural to urban migration
USE **rural-urban migration**

rural-urban migration
HN April 1991 moved
   January 1991 scope note added
   January 1991 lead-in term added
BT **internal migration**
SN Migration within a country or region from rural areas to towns or cities.
UF rural to urban migration

rustic arches
HN March 1991 descriptor split, use **rusticated** (ALT of **rustication**) + **arches**

rustic cabin
USE **primitive hut**

Rustic order
HN March 1991 descriptor split, use **rusticated** (ALT of **rustication**) + **orders**

Sabattier effect
HN October 1990 moved
BT <*conditions and effects: photography*>

sacramentaries
HN April 1991 added
BT **religious books**
ALT **sacramentary**

sacred drama
USE **religious drama**

safety, industrial
USE **occupational safety**

safety, occupational
USE **occupational safety**

safety, work
USE **occupational safety**

safflower (red pigment)
HN June 1990 lead-in term added
UF carthamin

safflower oil
HN October 1990 moved
BT **vegetable oil**

saffron
HN July 1990 lead-in term added
UF saffron yellow

saffron yellow
USE **saffron**

sailors
USE **seamen**

sails
HN November 1990 added
BT **power producing equipment**
ALT **sail**
SN Sheets or panels of material, designed to catch the wind and convert its energy, as to propel a sailing vessel or drive a windmill.

saints
HN December 1990 related term added
RT **martyrs**

sal ammoniac
USE **ammonium chloride**

sal soda
USE **sodium carbonate**

sales catalogs
HN May 1991 scope note added
   May 1991 descriptor changed, was **sale catalogs**
   May 1991 lead-in term changed, was **catalogs, sale**
   May 1991 alternate term changed, was **sale catalog**
ALT **sales catalog**
SN Use for catalogs that enumerate items that are for sale.
UF catalogs, sales

sally ports
HN March 1991 moved
   March 1991 scope note changed
BT <*fortification openings*> RT.1195
SN Large gates or passages generally linking the inner and outer works of fortresses and suitable for the use of troops making a sortie.

salmon pink
USE **strong yellowish pink**

salomónicas
USE **spiral columns**

salt
HN July 1990 added
BT **organic compounds**
SN Any compound derived from an acid by replacing hydrogen atoms of the acid with atoms of a metal. (MH12)
UF halite

salt, common
USE **sodium chloride**

salt, table
USE **sodium chloride**

salted paper prints
HN   October 1991 lead-in term added
UF   salted silver prints

salted paper processes
HN   October 1991 lead-in term added
UF   salted silver print process

salted silver print process
USE **salted paper processes**

salted silver prints
USE **salted paper prints**

sanctuaries
HN   September 1991 scope note changed
     May 1991 lead-in term added
SN   Use for the most sacred spaces of religious buildings; in a Christian church, the area containing the main altar.
UF   prayer halls

sanding wheels
HN   October 1990 moved
BT   *<grinding and milling equipment components>*

sandstorms
HN   May 1991 alternate term added
ALT **sandstorm**

sanitary drainage systems
HN   September 1991 scope note changed
SN   Use for parts of building plumbing systems that carry away waste; for sewers designed to carry away waste in larger drainage systems, use **sanitary sewers.**

sanitary sewers
HN   April 1991 scope note changed
SN   Use for sewers that carry industrial or residential liquid and solid wastes but not ground, surface, or storm waters. For parts of building plumbing systems designed to dispose of similar wastes, use **sanitary drainage systems.**

Santa Fe Style
HN   April 1990 added
BT   *<modern North American architecture styles and movements>* FL.1730

Santa Maria (period)
HN   October 1990 descriptor changed, was **Santa Maria**

Santee Dakota
HN   November 1990 lead-in term added
UF   Flandreau

sap green
HN   July 1990 lead-in term added
UF   sucus

sash bars
USE **muntins**

sash windows, sliding
USE **sliding windows**

sashes, sliding
USE **sliding windows**

sashes, storm
USE **storm windows**

Satavahana
USE **Andhra**

satellite antennas
USE **satellite home antennas**

satellite dishes
USE **satellite home antennas**

satellite home antennas
HN   February 1991 added
BT   *<communication system components>* RT.1290
ALT **satellite home antenna**
SN   Use for parabolic, dish-shaped reflectors placed on or near residences in order to receive radio, television, or microwave signals via satellite.
UF   antennas, dish
     antennas, satellite
     antennas, satellite home
     dish antennas
     dishes (satellite antennas)
     dishes, satellite
     home antennas, satellite
     satellite antennas
     satellite dishes

saunas
HN   August 1990 scope note added
SN   Rooms for bathing in which steam is produced from water thrown on heated stones or other similar materials.

saws, joiner
USE **bench saws**

scaenae
HN   April 1991 scope note changed
SN   In ancient Greek and Roman theaters, the structures facing the audience, forming the background before which performances were given and providing space for the players behind the acting area. (BOETH)

scaenae frontes
HN   April 1991 scope note changed
SN   Use for the facades of the stage buildings of ancient Greek and Roman theaters.

scale
HN   April 1991 scope note added
SN   Use for the concept of relative size, especially of one element to another or of one element to the whole; also, the proportional relation that a representation of an object or area bears to the object or area itself.

scaling ladders
USE **hook ladders**

scarcements
HN   April 1991 scope note source changed to DAC

scarifiers (masonry and plastering tools)
HN   May 1991 descriptor changed, was **scarifiers**
     May 1991 alternate term changed, was **scarifier**
ALT **scarifier (masonry and plastering tool)**

scarps
HN   February 1991 scope note changed
     February 1991 lead-in terms added
     February 1991 descriptor changed, was **escarpments**
     February 1991 alternate term changed, was **escarpment**
ALT **scarp**
SN   Steep slopes immediately in front of and below a fortification; for the outer slopes of encircling ditches of fortifications, use **counterscarps.** (W)
UF   escarpments (fortification elements)
     escarps

scenery
USE **natural landscapes**
     sets (architectural elements)

scenic color
USE **distemper paint**

scents
USE **odors**

schedules (architectural records)
HN   May 1991 descriptor changed, was **schedules (contract documents)**
     May 1991 alternate term changed, was **schedule (contract document)**
ALT **schedule (architectural record)**

schedules (timetables)
HN   May 1991 descriptor changed, was **schedules**
     May 1991 alternate term changed, was **schedule**
ALT **schedule (timetable)**

scholarships
HN   January 1991 alternate term added
ALT **scholarship**

school
HN   September 1991 scope note changed
SN   Group or succession of persons who in some area of thought or practice are disciples of the same master or are united by a general similarity of principles, methods, or artistic style.

school buildings
USE **schools**

school principals
USE **principals**

schools
HN October 1991 lead-in terms added
September 1990 scope note added
SN Individual buildings or groups of buildings designed or used as places of instruction.
UF buildings, school
school buildings

schools, community
USE **community schools**

schools, military training
USE **military academies**

schools, normal
USE **teachers colleges**

science
HN January 1991 alternate term added
ALT **scientific**

sciences, behavioral
USE **behavioral sciences**

scientists, conservation
USE **conservation scientists**

scientists, social
USE **social scientists**

scissors trusses
HN March 1991 moved
BT <trusses by form> RT.357

scores
HN October 1990 lead-in term added
UF scores, music

scores, music
USE **scores**

scrapers (finishing tools)
HN October 1991 descriptor changed, was **scrapers**
October 1991 alternate term changed, was **scraper**
ALT **scraper (finishing tool)**

screen doors
HN April 1991 scope note added
SN Use for lightweight exterior doors with small mesh screening in place of the panels, which permits ventilation, but bars insects.

screen printing
HN October 1991 scope note changed
October 1990 moved
October 1990 lead-in terms added
October 1990 descriptor changed, was **serigraphy**
BT **printing**
SN Printing by forcing ink or dye through a mesh on which a design has been formed by stopping out certain areas.
UF printing, screen
process, screen
screen process
serigraphy

screen process
USE **screen printing**

screens, candle
USE **candle screens**

screens, columnar
USE **columnar screens**

screens, lantern
USE **candle screens**

scribes
HN April 1991 related term added
RT **copyists**

scrolls (documents)
HN May 1991 descriptor changed, was **scrolls**
May 1991 alternate term changed, was **scroll**
ALT **scroll (document)**

sculpture
HN October 1991 moved to hierarchy under development

<sculpture and sculpture techniques> KT.531
HN April 1991 deleted
BT <object-making processes and techniques> KT.512

sculpture techniques
HN April 1991 moved
BT <object-making processes and techniques> KT.512

scumbling
HN July 1990 scope note changed
SN The technique or activity of applying scumbles.

seamen
HN September 1990 lead-in terms added
UF mariners
sailors

secret doors
HN March 1991 deleted
BT <doors by function> RT.860

secretaries (furniture)
HN May 1991 descriptor changed, was **secretaries**
May 1991 alternate term changed, was **secretary**
ALT **secretary (furniture)**

sections, angle
USE **angles (rolled sections)**

<security system components>
HN October 1990 added
BT <security systems and security system components>

security systems
HN April 1991 scope note added
September 1990 moved
BT <security systems and security system components>
SN Use for building systems that secure or protect a premises from unwanted intruders.

<security systems and security system components>
HN October 1990 added
BT <protection systems> RT.1502

security systems, electronic
USE **electronic security systems**

Seders
HN May 1991 alternate term added
ALT **Seder**

sedilia
HN April 1991 scope note changed
SN Use for series of seats, usually three and of stone, usually located to the south of the altar for the officiating clergy.

segmental arches
HN April 1991 lead-in term **segment arches** deleted

segmental pointed arches
USE **pointed segmental arches**

seismic loads
USE **earthquake loads**

selecting
HN January 1991 scope note added
SN Picking out or choosing in preference to another or others. (W)

selective bibliographies
HN October 1990 lead-in term **select bibliographies** deleted

self-help construction, incremental
USE **incremental housing**

selling
HN January 1991 scope note added
SN Exchanging property or services for money.

semantics
HN February 1991 alternate term added
ALT **semantic**

semi-circular stilted arches
USE **surmounted arches**

semi-metopes
USE **demimetopes**

semiarches
HN April 1991 scope note source changed to RS

semicircles
HN July 1991 alternate term added
ALT **semicircle**

semidomes
HN April 1991 lead-in term added
April 1991 lead-in term changed, was **cul-de-fours**
UF conches (semidomes)
cul de fours

semiellipses
HN July 1991 alternate term added
ALT **semiellipse**

seminars
HN   May 1991 alternate term added
ALT   **seminar**

semiotics
HN   February 1991 alternate term added
ALT   **semiotic**

sepia
HN   June 1991 moved
BT   *<ink by composition or origin>*

sepulchers
HN   November 1991 lead-in terms added
      August 1991 scope note changed
SN   Use for cavities in altars or altar-
      pieces for containing relics.
UF   altar cavities
      cavities, altar

sequins
HN   July 1990 added
BT   **trimmings**
ALT   **sequin**

serigraphy
USE   **screen printing**

Serlian arches
USE   **Palladian windows**

Serlian windows
USE   **Palladian windows**

Serliana
USE   **Palladian windows**

serpentine (shape)
HN   May 1991 descriptor changed, was
      serpentine

service elevators
HN   April 1991 scope note added
SN   Elevators intended for combined
      freight and passenger use. (MEANS)

service pipes
HN   April 1991 scope note changed
SN   Use for water or gas supply pipes
      which lead from supply sources to
      the buildings.

service, building
USE   **building systems**

servicemen
USE   **military personnel**

services, sites and
USE   **sites and services**

Setchuyo
HN   November 1990 descriptor changed,
      was **Settchuyo**

sets (architectural elements)
HN   December 1990 added
BT   *<architectural elements by building type>*
      RT.1165
ALT   **set (architectural element)**
SN   Use for the assemblage scenery,
      props, and lighting and sound sys-
      tems created to represent a setting
      used in dramatic performances.

UF   scenery
      settings

settings
USE   **sets (architectural elements)**

settlement houses
HN   April 1990 added
BT   **welfare buildings**
ALT   **settlement house**
SN   Use for buildings housing a variety
      of individual and family social, edu-
      cational, and recreational facilities
      provided for recent immigrants or
      residents of underpriviledged
      neighborhoods; especially in En-
      gland and the United States since the
      late 19th century.
UF   houses, neighborhood
      houses, settlement
      neighborhood houses
      settlements (welfare buildings)

settlements (welfare buildings)
USE   **settlement houses**

sewage disposal
HN   April 1991 moved
BT   **waste disposal**

sewage treatment
HN   April 1991 added
BT   **waste management**
SN   Treating sewage in order to remove
      its objectionable constituents and
      render it less offensive or danger-
      ous. (ENCYES)
UF   treatment, sewage
RT   **water quality management**

sewers (drainage structures)
HN   May 1991 descriptor changed, was
      sewers
      May 1991 alternate term changed,
      was **sewer**
      April 1991 scope note added
ALT   **sewer (drainage structure)**
SN   Use for underground conduits for
      carrying away waste and storm water.

sex
HN   January 1991 scope note added
      January 1991 lead-in term added
      January 1991 related term added
      January 1990 related term added
SN   Concept describing the physiologi-
      cal traits that distinguish the males
      and females of a species. For the
      pattern of attitudes and behavior that
      in any society is deemed appropriate
      to one sex rather than another, use
      sex role. For the sum of an individ-
      ual's sexual emotions, ideas, and be-
      havior, use **sexuality**. (ERIC9)
UF   gender
RT   **sex role**
      sexuality

sex identity
USE   **sex role**

sex role
HN   November 1991 related term added
      January 1991 scope note added
      May 1990 lead-in terms added
      January 1990 related term added
SN   Pattern of attitudes and behavior that
      in any society is deemed appropriate
      to one sex rather than another. For
      the concept of physiological traits that
      distinguish the males and females of
      a species, use **sex**. For the sum of an
      individual's sexual emotions, ideas,
      and behavior, use **sexuality**. (ERIC9)
UF   gender identity
      gender role
      identity, gender
      identity, sex
      role, gender
      sex identity
RT   **sex**
      sexuality

sexuality
HN   January 1991 scope note added
      January 1991 related terms added
SN   Use generally for the sum of an in-
      dividual's sexual emotions, ideas, and
      behavior. For the pattern of atti-
      tudes and behavior that in any soci-
      ety is deemed appropriate to one sex
      rather than another, use **sex role**. For
      the concept of the physiological traits
      that distinguish the males and fe-
      males of a species, use **sex**.
RT   **sex**
      sex role

shacks
HN   April 1990 scope note added
SN   Roughly and often crudely built
      dwellings. (W)

shaft rings
HN   April 1991 scope note added
      April 1991 lead-in terms added
SN   Use for bands or moldings found
      most often in Gothic architecture
      encircling shafts of columns or en-
      gaged columns at locations other
      than their ends, often to hide or to
      strengthen the joint between two
      sections of a shaft.
UF   corbel rings
      rings, corbel

shafts, annulated
USE   **annulated columns**

Shang
HN   November 1990 lead-in terms added
UF   Shang-Yin
      Yin

Shang-Yin
USE   **Shang**

Shangana
USE   **Thonga**

shaped dormers
HN   April 1991 deleted
BT   **dormers**

shaped poetry
USE **pattern poetry**
visual poetry

shear walls
HN April 1991 scope note changed
SN Use for rigid planar surfaces that inherently resist lateral thrusts of shear.

shed roofs
HN November 1991 lead-in term changed, was **roof, lean-to**
November 1991 lead-in term changed, was **roofs, penthouse (shed roofs)**
April 1991 lead-in term **pent roofs (shed roofs)** deleted
April 1991 lead-in term changed, was **penthouse roofs (shed roofs)**
UF penthouse roofs
roofs, lean-to
roofs, penthouse

sheepherders
USE **shepherds**

sheet shears
HN August 1990 scope note changed
SN Large, foot operated machines that cut sheet metal square to a fence with a guillotinelike action. (PC)

Sheetrock (TM)
USE **gypsum board**

sheets (papers)
HN February 1991 added
BT *<documentary artifacts by form>* VW.481
ALT **sheet (paper)**
SN Single pieces of paper, other than broadsides, with material written, printed, or drawn on one or both sides.

shell structures
HN April 1991 lead-in term added
UF thin shells

shelters, battered women's
USE **crisis shelters**

shelters, crisis
USE **crisis shelters**

shelters, women's
USE **crisis shelters**

shepherds
HN September 1990 lead-in term added
UF sheepherders

shielded metal arc welding
HN March 1990 lead-in terms added
UF heliarc welding
welding, heliarc

ship captains
USE **shipmasters**

shipmasters
HN September 1990 lead-in terms added
UF captains, ship
ship captains

shipwrecks
HN December 1990 added
BT **disasters**
ALT **shipwreck**
SN Occasions of the severe damage or loss of a boat or ship at sea.

shopping arcades
HN November 1991 lead-in term added
UF galleries

shopping malls
HN April 1990 lead-in term added
UF galleries

shops, specialist
USE **specialty stores**

shops, specialty
USE **specialty stores**

shorers
HN September 1990 scope note added
SN Workers who build or install shores.

shores (landforms)
HN May 1991 descriptor changed, was **shores**
May 1991 alternate term changed, was **shore**
ALT **shore (landform)**

shower baths
USE **shower stalls**

shower rooms
HN March 1991 added
BT *<bath, dressing, and sanitary spaces>* RM.65
ALT **shower room**
SN Use for rooms or areas equipped with several showerheads or shower stalls for use by a number of people at the same time. (RHDEL2)
UF rooms, showers
showers

shower stalls
HN March 1991 lead-in terms added
August 1990 scope note added
SN Use for individual compartments or self-contained units having a single shower and accommodating one person. (RHDEL2)
UF baths, shower
shower baths
showers

showers
HN March 1991 deleted, made lead-in to **shower rooms** and **shower stalls**

showers
USE **shower rooms**
shower stalls

shrines, spirit
USE **spirit houses**

shuffleboard courts
HN September 1990 scope note added
SN Use for areas including one or more long, rectangular, smoothly sur-

faced lanes marked for the game of shuffleboard.

shutting posts
HN April 1991 lead-in term added
April 1991 scope note source changed to DAC
UF gateposts

siblings
HN November 1990 added
BT *<people by family relationship>* HG.8
ALT **sibling**
SN Individuals having a common parent or parents. (WCOL9)
RT **families**

Siboney
USE **Ciboney**

sick
USE **ill**

sick building syndrome
HN March 1991 moved
BT **disease**

sickness
USE **illness**

side altars
HN March 1991 descriptor split, use **side** + **altars**

side gables
HN April 1991 scope note added
SN Use for gables at the sides of buildings, not over the front or rear.

side light
USE **side lighting**

side lighting
HN April 1991 added
BT **directional lighting**
SN Illumination from the side, generally used to enhance modeling.
UF light, side
lighting, side
side light

side shows
HN May 1991 alternate term added
ALT **side show**

siderography
HN October 1991 moved
March 1991 lead-in term **steel engraving** deleted
BT **engraving (printing process)**

sidewalk elevators
HN April 1991 scope note added
SN Use for elevators operating through a sidewalk, especially for the handling of goods or refuse. (W)

sidewalks
HN December 1990 moved
August 1990 scope note added
BT **pedestrian facilities**
SN Use for pedestrian walkways along the sides of roads or streets.

signals, traffic control
USE **traffic signals**

signatories
USE **signers**

signers
HN September 1990 lead-in term added
UF signatories

signing
HN January 1991 added
BT **writing**
ALT **signed**
SN Affixing one's signature to something.

silica (mineral)
HN May 1991 descriptor changed, was
silica

silicate paint
HN August 1991 scope note changed
SN An extremely durable paint, the vehicle of which consists chiefly of water glass, used especially for painting on mortar, sometimes on dry plaster; can be indistinguishable from true fresco. (WEHLTE)

sill courses
HN April 1991 scope note source changed to DAC

sill plates
HN April 1991 scope note changed
SN Horizontal timbers at the bottom of the frame of a wood structure, that rest on the foundation or subfloor. (DAC)

sills
HN April 1991 scope note changed
SN Members forming the lower sides of openings. For the horizontal timbers at the bottom of the frame of a wooden structure, use **sill plates.**

sills, door
USE **doorsills**

silver amalgam
HN February 1991 added
BT **amalgams**
SN Alloy of silver and mercury.

silver mirroring
HN October 1990 moved
BT *<conditions and effects: photography>*

silviculture
HN April 1990 added
BT **forestry**
SN Cultivation and study of forest trees, especially those raised for timber. For the raising and care of trees and shrubs in gardens or for ornamental purposes, use **arboriculture.**

sima rectas
USE **cyma rectas**

sima reversas
USE **cyma reversas**

simas (cornice components)
USE **cymatia**

simas (moldings)
USE **cymas**

simple beams
HN April 1991 scope note changed
April 1991 lead-in terms added
SN Use for beams supported at each end so their ends are free to rotate. (SALHEL)
UF beams, end-supported
beams, simply supported
end-supported beams
simply supported beams

simply supported beams
USE **simple beams**

simulated thatch roofs
USE **false thatched roofs**

Simulationist
HN May 1990 added
BT *<post-1945 fine arts styles and movements>* FL.3712
ALT **Simulationism**

single-hung windows
HN April 1991 scope note changed
SN Windows having one vertically hung movable sash and one fixed sash.

single-story
HN March 1991 moved
BT *<building elevation attributes>*

sinks
HN April 1991 scope note added
SN Use for basins connected with a drain and usually a water supply for washing and drainage. (W)

sinopie
HN January 1991 scope note added
SN Underdrawings for fresco paintings made with the red earth pigment sinopie, which is brushed on the arriccio layer and over which the intonaco is applied before painting.

sisters
HN December 1990 added
BT **siblings**
ALT **sister**
SN Female siblings.

sites and services
HN December 1990 added
BT **development**
SN Use for self-help development practices where individuals, families, or cooperatives are provided with title and improved land on which buildings, usually housing, can be built.
UF services, sites and

sitters
HN February 1991 added
BT **models (people)**
ALT **sitter**

SN People who are the subjects of portraits.

Situationist
HN April 1990 added
BT *<post-1945 fine arts styles and movements>* FL.3712
ALT **Situationism**
UF Internationale Situationiste
Situationist International

Situationist International
USE **Situationist**

size (geometric concept)
HN May 1991 descriptor changed, was
size

size (material)
HN July 1990 descriptor changed, was
size (materials)

size color
USE **distemper paint**

size paint
USE **distemper paint**

skaters
HN December 1990 added
BT *<people by activity>* HG.705
ALT **skater**

skaters, ice
USE **ice skaters**

skating rinks
HN September 1990 scope note added
SN Use for structures containing large, bounded, smoothly surfaced areas for skating.

sketchbooks
HN January 1991 scope note changed
SN Books or pads of blank sheets used or intended for sketching. (AHD)

sketching
HN January 1991 scope note added
January 1991 related term added
SN Working out or recording the chief features of a visual form, usually but not necessarily by drawing.
RT **drawing (image making)**

sketching paper
USE **drawing paper**

skew arches
HN March 1991 scope note changed, DAC added as source
March 1991 lead-in term changed, was **skew arches**
March 1991 descriptor changed, was **oblique arches**
March 1991 alternate term changed, was **oblique arch**
ALT **skew arch**
UF oblique arches

ski jumps
HN September 1990 scope note added
SN Use for steeply inclined, snow-covered courses with a horizontal

take-off at the end from which skiers glide off into the air.

ski-lift stations
HN September 1990 scope note added
SN Use for structures located along ski lifts and designed for loading and unloading skiers, which usually include ski-lift controls and shelter for operators. (PC)

ski lifts
HN September 1990 scope note added
SN Use for conveyances that transport skiers up slopes or mountainsides, consisting typically of a series of seats suspended from an endless cable driven by motors.

skill training centers
USE **training centers**

skirt-roofs
HN November 1991 lead-in term **roofs, skirt** deleted
November 1991 lead-in term changed, was **roofs, pent (skirt roofs)**
November 1991 lead-in term changed, was **roofs, penthouse (skirt roofs)**
April 1991 descriptor changed, was **skirt roofs**
April 1991 alternate term changed, was **skirt roof**
April 1991 lead-in term changed, was **pent roofs (skirt roofs)**
April 1991 lead-in term changed, was **penthouse roofs (skirt roofs)**
ALT **skirt-roof**
UF pent roofs
penthouse roofs
roofs, pent
roofs, penthouse

skittle alleys
HN September 1990 scope note added
SN Use for buildings containing equipment and bowling lanes for the pin game of skittles.

skylights
HN September 1991 scope note changed
SN Openings in a roof, glazed or filled with other transparent or translucent material, serving to admit light to a space below.

slab building (pottery technique)
USE **slab method**

slab construction (pottery technique)
USE **slab method**

slab foundations
HN March 1991 descriptor split, use **slab (ALT of slabs) + foundations**

slab method
HN November 1990 lead-in terms added
UF building, slab (pottery technique)
construction, slab (pottery technique)
method, slab
slab building (pottery technique)
slab construction (pottery technique)

slab systems, waffle concrete
USE **waffle slabs**

slabs (structural elements)
HN March 1991 descriptor changed, was **slabs**
March 1991 alternate term changed, was **slab**
ALT **slab (structural element)**

slabs, one-direction spanning
USE **one-way solid slab systems**

slabs, one-way
USE **one-way beam and slab systems**
one-way solid slab systems

slabs, ribbed
USE **one-way joist systems**

slabs, two-way
USE **two-way beam and slab systems**

slag
HN May 1990 lead-in term added
UF blast-furnace slag

slant elevators
USE **inclined elevators**

slate purple, dark
USE **dark reddish purple**

sleeper walls
HN April 1991 scope note changed
SN Use for any short wall that supports floor joists. (MEANS)

sleet
HN October 1990 moved
BT *<water by form>*

slides (photographs)
HN September 1991 descriptor changed, was **slides**
September 1991 alternate term changed, was **slide**
ALT **slide (photograph)**

sliding doors
HN April 1991 scope note changed
SN Doors that open by sliding sideways.

sliding sash windows
USE **sliding windows**

sliding sashes
USE **sliding windows**

sliding windows
HN April 1991 scope note added
April 1991 lead-in terms added
SN Use for windows that open by means of sashes sliding horizontally.

UF sash windows, sliding
sashes, sliding
sliding sash windows
sliding sashes
windows, sliding sash

slip sills
HN April 1991 scope note changed, PUTNAM added as source

slop sinks
HN April 1991 scope note changed
SN Deep sinks, usually set low, principally used for emptying waste water. (DAC)

sloping roofs
USE **pitched roofs**

sluice gates
HN March 1991 scope note added
SN Barriers used to close sluices.

slum clearance
HN February 1991 scope note added
December 1990 moved
BT **urban renewal**
SN Removing a slum by demolishing it, or altering it by correcting the conditions that caused it. (LOC)

smalt
USE **moderate blue**

smells
USE **odors**

smoke detectors
HN April 1991 scope note added
SN Use for components of fire alarm systems that are activated by the presence of smoke.

smoke detectors, photoelectric
USE **photoelectric smoke detectors**

smoke pipes
USE **flues**

smoking parlors
USE **smoking rooms**

smoking rooms
HN April 1990 lead-in terms added
UF parlors, smoking
smoking parlors

snakewood
HN April 1990 added
BT **hardwood**
UF Brosium aubletti
leopardwood
letterwood

snow
HN October 1990 moved
BT *<water by form>*

snow guards
HN April 1991 scope note changed, PUTNAM added as source

snow loads
  HN January 1991 alternate term added
  ALT snow load

snowstorms
  HN May 1991 alternate term added
  ALT snowstorm

soak-stain technique
  HN July 1990 lead-in terms added
  UF painting, stain
    stain painting
    staining technique (painting technique)
    technique, soak-stain
    technique, staining (painting technique)

soap
  HN March 1991 scope note added
  SN Cleansing and emulsifying agent made by boiling an oil, fat, resin, or wax with an alkali.

social anthropology
  HN September 1991 moved
    May 1991 scope note added
  BT anthropology
  SN Branch of anthropology focusing on the origins, history, and development of human societies and social structure, including in its scope aspects of archaeology, ethnology, and ethnography. (RHDEL2)

social classes
  HN May 1991 moved
  BT social groups

social conflict
  HN January 1991 related term added
  RT revolutions

social discrimination
  USE discrimination

social ecology
  USE human ecology

social groups
  HN June 1991 scope note added
    June 1991 lead-in term added
    June 1991 alternate term added
    June 1991 guide term changed, was
      <social groups> HG.878
    May 1991 moved
  BT <groups of people>
  ALT social group
  SN Groups of people whose members have one or more social characteristics in common. (TSIT)
  UF groups, social

social issues
  HN February 1991 related term added
  RT prostitution

social psychology
  HN September 1991 moved
  BT psychology

social scientists
  HN May 1991 scope note added
    May 1991 lead-in term added
    May 1991 alternate term added
    May 1991 guide term changed, was
      <people in the social sciences>
      HG.250
  ALT social scientist
  SN People who study or work in any of the social sciences.
  UF scientists, social

socialism
  HN May 1991 scope note added
    May 1991 related term added
    May 1991 alternate term added
  ALT socialist
  SN Political and economic ideology advocating collective or governmental ownership and administration of the means of production and distribution of goods. (WCOL9)
  RT socialists

socialists
  HN May 1991 added
  BT <people by ideology or political activity> HG.747
  ALT socialist
  SN People who advocate or practice socialism. (WCOL9)
  RT socialism

sociolinguistics
  HN February 1991 alternate term added
  ALT sociolinguistic

sociology
  HN September 1991 moved
    February 1991 alternate term added
  BT behavioral sciences
  ALT sociological

sociology of knowledge
  HN September 1991 moved
  BT sociology

socles
  HN November 1990 moved
  BT <supporting and resisting elements> RT.59

soda
  USE sodium carbonate

soda ash
  USE sodium carbonate

soda crystals
  USE sodium carbonate

soda fountains
  HN April 1990 added
  BT restaurants
  ALT soda fountain
  SN Use for restaurants with counters at which soda water, ice cream, and light meals are served; may also be used to designate the dispensing equipment or counter itself, especially when found as fixtures in commercial buildings, such as drugstores.
  UF fountains, soda

soda, sal
  USE sodium carbonate

soda, washing
  USE sodium carbonate

sodium carbonate
  HN July 1990 added
  BT alkali
  UF ash, soda
    carbonate, sodium
    crystals, soda
    sal soda
    soda
    soda ash
    soda crystals
    soda, sal
    soda, washing
    washing soda

sodium chloride
  HN July 1990 added
  BT salt
  UF chloride, sodium
    common salt
    salt, common
    salt, table
    table salt

sodium hydroxide
  HN July 1990 lead-in term added
  UF lye

sofa art
  HN April 1990 added
  BT <art genres> BM.229
  SN Art works, especially paintings and prints, designed for popular taste and marketed as home furnishings.
  UF art, sofa

soffit vents
  HN April 1991 descriptor split, use soffit (ALT of soffits) + vents

soffits
  HN April 1991 lead-in term planciers deleted
    April 1991 lead-in term plancier pieces deleted

soft ground
  HN July 1990 added
  BT etching ground
  SN Etching ground containing grease so that it does not harden.
  UF ground, soft

soft-ground etching
  HN October 1991 moved
    October 1991 scope note changed
    July 1990 alternate term soft-ground etched deleted
  BT etching (printing process)
  SN Use for the printing process in which the ground is mixed with a soft substance, such as tallow, allowing the rendering of textured lines and areas

when the plate is etched. Sometimes, paper is placed over the grounded plate and drawn on, to pick up the ground.

Sogdian
HN November 1990 lead-in term changed, was **K'ana-chu**
UF K'ang-chu

solar-assisted heat pumps
HN June 1991 scope note added
SN Use for heat pumps whose operation is at times supplemented by solar collector-storage systems.

solar heating
HN April 1991 scope note added
SN Systems supplying heat and hot water by the capture and conversion of radiant energy from the sun. (W)

solar water heaters
HN June 1991 scope note added
SN Use for water heaters whose primary source of heat energy is the sun.

soldiers
HN November 1990 added
BT **military personnel**
ALT **soldier**
SN Enlisted men or women belonging to an army.

solid-core doors
HN June 1991 scope note changed
SN Flush doors having cores of solid wood or mineral composition. (DAC)

solid newel stairs
HN June 1991 scope note changed
SN Stairs whose tapered treads wind around, and engage in, a solid, central newel. (DAC)

solid slabs, one-way
USE **one-way solid slab systems**

solid vaults
HN March 1991 deleted
BT *<vaults by form: construction>* RT.548

solid waste management
HN April 1991 moved
   April 1991 scope note added
   April 1991 lead-in term **sewage treatment** deleted
BT **waste management**
SN Systematic administration of activities that provide for collection, processing, and disposal of solid wastes, including the recovery of materials and energy. (ENCYES)

solids (geometric)
HN January 1991 alternate term added
ALT **solid (geometric)**

solids (materials)
HN May 1991 descriptor changed, was **solids**
   August 1990 alternate term added
ALT **solid (material)**

solubility
HN January 1991 alternate term added
ALT **soluble**

solutions, antifreeze
USE **antifreeze**

Solutrean
HN November 1990 descriptor changed, was **Solutrian**

Songhai
HN November 1990 lead-in term added
UF Songhay Kingdom

Songhay Kingdom
USE **Songhai**

soot doors
HN June 1991 scope note added
SN Use for doors that provide access for cleaning or repairing flues.

sopraporte
USE **overdoors**

soprapportas
USE **overdoors**

soufflets
USE **daggers (tracery components)**

sound recordings
HN March 1991 related term added
RT **discographies**

sounding boards
HN March 1991 moved
   March 1991 scope note added
BT **acoustic equipment**
SN Structures placed behind or over pulpits, rostrums, or platforms to reflect sound toward the audience. (RHDEL2)

souvenir albums
HN June 1991 deleted, made lead-in to viewbooks

souvenir albums
USE **viewbooks**

sovereigns (rulers)
USE **rulers (people)**

soy oil
USE **soybean oil**

soybean oil
HN October 1991 lead-in term **soyabean oil** deleted
   October 1990 moved
   June 1990 lead-in term added
BT **vegetable oil**
UF soy oil

space frames
HN March 1991 lead-in term added
   March 1991 moved
BT *<trusses by construction>*
UF frame structures, space

space planning
HN March 1991 moved
BT **interior design**

spaces, alternative
USE **alternative spaces**

spandrels
HN August 1991 scope note changed
SN Use for surfaces adjacent to an arch above its springing, also by extension the walls above or below window openings in modern curtain wall construction.

<Spanish Renaissance-Baroque architecture styles> FL.3248
HN May 1991 deleted
BT *<Spanish Renaissance-Baroque styles>*

spanning slabs, one-direction
USE **one-way solid slab systems**

special education
HN October 1990 added
BT *<education by subdiscipline>* KD.128
UF education, special
RT **exceptional persons**

specialist shops
USE **specialty stores**

specialists
HN September 1990 scope note added
SN People who devote themselves to a particular occupation, activity, or branch of knowledge. (WCOL9)

specialty shops
USE **specialty stores**

specialty stores
HN August 1991 lead-in terms added
UF shops, specialist
   shops, specialty
   specialist shops
   specialty shops

spectators
HN February 1991 added
BT *<people by activity>* HG.705
ALT **spectator**
SN Use for those who are present at and observe live events. For those who view exhibitions or individual works of art or architecture, television programs, or motion pictures, use **viewers**.
UF beholders
   viewers (spectators)
RT **audiences**
   viewers

spectators (viewers)
USE **viewers**

spectrometry, infrared
USE **infrared spectroscopy**

spectroscopy
HN April 1990 added
BT *<analysis and testing techniques>* KT.10
SN Means of analyzing a substance from the way it transmits, emits, or responds to various wavelengths in the electromagnetic energy spectrum. (ICPEP)

UF   analysis, spectrum
      spectrum analysis

spectroscopy, infrared
  USE **infrared spectroscopy**

spectroscopy, near-infrared
  USE **near-infrared spectroscopy**

spectrum analysis
  USE **spectroscopy**

speculating
  HN   May 1990 scope note changed,
       RHDEL2 added as source

spermaceti
  HN   December 1990 moved
  BT   **animal wax**

spheres
  HN   July 1991 alternate term added
  ALT **sphere**

spike lavender
  USE **spike oil**

spike oil
  HN   November 1991 lead-in term
       changed, was **spike lavender, oil of**
       July 1990 lead-in terms added
       July 1990 lead-in term changed, was
       oil of spike lavender
  UF   lavender, spike
       oil of spike
       spike lavender
       spike, oil of

spike, oil of
  USE **spike oil**

spiral columns
  HN   August 1991 lead-in term changed,
       was **Salomonicas**
  UF   salomónicas

spiral vaults
  HN   November 1991 lead-in terms added
       September 1991 scope note changed
  SN   Annular vaults with a spiral axis used
       to support, for example, the steps of
       a spiral stair. (RS)
  UF   helical vaults
       vaults, helical

spirals
  HN   May 1990 lead-in term added
  UF   coils (spirals)

spire lights
  HN   March 1991 deleted
  BT   <*windows by location or context*>
       RT.957

spirit dwellings
  USE **spirit houses**

spirit ground
  HN   April 1990 added
  BT   **etching ground**
  SN   Rosin or asphalt dissolved in a dis-
       tilled spirit such as alcohol, which,
       when applied to a printing plate,

dries to leave an acid-resistant ground
for aquatint.
  UF   ground, liquid
       ground, spirit
       liquid ground

spirit houses
  HN   July 1991 added
  BT   <*religious structures*> RK.1082
  ALT **spirit house**
  SN   Use for miniature houses in which
       guardian spirits are invited to live,
       usually set on wooden posts in house
       compounds or adjacent to other
       buildings; common in Thailand.
  UF   dwellings, spirit
       houses, spirit
       shrines, spirit
       spirit dwellings
       spirit shrines
  RT   **animism**

spirit shrines
  USE **spirit houses**

spirit varnish
  HN   July 1990 lead-in terms added
  UF   alcohol-resin varnish
       varnish, alcohol-resin

spit biting
  HN   April 1990 added
  BT   <*biting techniques*>
  SN   The technique of dropping or
       painting acid onto an aquatint
       ground to allow localized and con-
       trolled biting. (CHAMET)
  UF   biting, brush
       biting, spit
       brush biting

splayed arches
  HN   June 1991 lead-in terms added
  UF   arches, fluing
       fluing arches

split-level houses
  HN   November 1990 scope note added
       November 1990 lead-in terms added
  SN   Use for houses in which the floor
       levels of adjacent living areas differ
       by less than a full story.
  UF   levels, split
       split levels

split levels
  USE **split-level houses**

sponsors
  HN   December 1990 added
  BT   <*people by activity*> HG.705
  ALT **sponsor**
  SN   Those who pay for or plan and carry
       out projects or activities, or other-
       wise assume primary responsibility
       for them. For those who support in-
       dividuals, institutions, or causes but
       do not necessarily take primary re-
       sponsibility for them, use **patrons**.
       (WCOL9)
  RT   **patrons**

sports
  HN   February 1991 scope note added
       February 1991 alternate term added
  SN   Athletic activity or games engaged in
       for recreation on the part of the
       participants or spectators.

sports buildings
  HN   September 1990 scope note added
  SN   Designates buildings providing facil-
       ities for athletic events or training
       and, usually, support facilities for
       participants and spectators.

spotlighting
  HN   May 1991 deleted
  BT   <*lighting by form*>

spray painting
  HN   October 1990 moved
  BT   **painting (coating)**

<*spread footing components*>
  HN   August 1991 guide term changed,
       was <*spread foundation compo-
       nents*> RT.170

spread footings
  HN   August 1991 scope note changed
       August 1991 lead-in terms added
       August 1991 descriptor changed, was
       spread foundations
       August 1991 alternate term changed,
       was **spread foundation**
  ALT **spread footing**
  SN   Use for foundations that sustain loads
       by distributing them over a large
       planar surface; may support one or
       more columns, piers, or walls.
  UF   footings, spread
       spread foundations

<*spread footings and spread footing
components*>
  HN   August 1991 guide term changed,
       was <*spread foundations and spread
       foundation components*> RT.165

spread foundations
  USE **spread footings**

springers
  HN   June 1991 scope note changed
       June 1991 lead-in term added
  SN   The lower voussoirs, or bottom stones
       of an arch or vault from which the
       curve of the arch or vault begins.
  UF   springing

springing
  USE **springers**

sprung floors
  HN   April 1991 deleted
  BT   **floors**

spun glass
  USE **fiberglass**

spurs
  HN   November 1990 moved
  BT   **knee braces**

square bay windows
HN April 1991 deleted
BT bay windows

squares (open spaces)
HN May 1991 descriptor changed, was
    squares
    May 1991 alternate term changed,
    was square
ALT square (open space)

squaring (forming)
HN May 1991 descriptor changed, was
    squaring

squaring (transferring technique)
HN July 1990 alternate term added
ALT squared

squash courts
HN September 1990 scope note added
SN Use for four-walled, enclosed courts
    marked for the racket and ball game
    of squash.

squinches
HN August 1991 scope note changed
    April 1991 moved
BT <supporting and resisting elements>
    RT.59
SN Use for arches or corbeled transi-
    tional elements that span the inte-
    rior corners of a square or polygo-
    nal structure serving to support a
    circular or polygonal superstruc-
    ture.

squints
HN June 1991 lead-in term added
UF hagioscopes

Srivijaya (Javanese)
HN May 1991 descriptor changed, was
    Srivijaya

stacco
HN September 1991 moved
BT <transferring techniques> KT.739

stacks, ventilating
USE vent stacks

<stage set components> RT.1278
HN October 1991 deleted
BT <stage sets and stage set components>

stage sets
HN December 1990 descriptor split, use
    stage (ALT of stages) + sets (ar-
    chitectural elements)

<stage sets and stage set components>
    RT.1276
HN October 1991 deleted
BT <theater elements> RT.1264

staged photographs
HN September 1990 added
BT <photographs by picture-taking tech-
    nique> VJ.93
ALT staged photograph
SN Photographs taken of a scene or in-
    stallation fabricated by the photog-

rapher specifically for the purpose of
photographing it.
UF directorial photographs
    fabricated photographs
    photographs, directorial
    photographs, fabricated
    photographs, staged

stages, puppet
USE puppet theaters

stain painting
USE soak-stain technique

staining technique (painting technique)
USE soak-stain technique

stair dormers
HN April 1991 deleted
BT dormers

stair horses
USE strings

stair strings, finish
USE face strings

staircases, flying
USE flying stairs

staircases, water
USE water stairs (landscaped-site ele-
    ments)

<stairs by form>
HN August 1991 related term added
RT water stairs (landscaped-site ele-
    ments)

stairs, angled
USE quarter-turn stairs

stairs, double helix
USE double spiral stairs

stairs, hollow newel
USE open newel stairs

stairs, open well
USE open newel stairs

stairs, three-quarter-turn
USE three-quarter-turn stairs

stairs, water (embarkation elements)
USE water stairs (embarkation elements)

stairs, water (landscaped-site elements)
USE water stairs (landscaped-site ele-
    ments)

stairways, water
USE water stairs (landscaped-site ele-
    ments)

stalks, chimney
USE chimney stacks

stalls (mercantile structures)
USE stands (mercantile structures)

stamping, blind
USE blind stamping

stamps, rubber
USE rubber stamps

stand oil
HN July 1990 lead-in terms added
UF lithographic oil
    oil, lithographic

standardization
HN January 1991 scope note added
    November 1990 moved
    January 1990 alternate term added
BT <organizational functions> KG.138
ALT standardized
SN Establishing or bringing into con-
    formity with standards.

standards
HN January 1991 scope note added
SN Criteria or rules established by offi-
    cial authority, custom, or general
    consent, that serve as examples to be
    followed or as measures for evalua-
    tion or comparative judgment. (W)

standards, light
USE lampposts

stands (mercantile structures)
HN April 1990 lead-in term added
    April 1990 guide term changed, was
    <stands and stalls> RK.144
UF stalls (mercantile structures)

stands (support furniture)
HN May 1991 descriptor changed, was
    stands
    May 1991 alternate term changed,
    was stand
ALT stand (support furniture)

stands, food
USE food stands

stands, pedestal
USE pedestals

starvation
HN April 1991 added
BT <health-related concepts>
SN Condition of suffering severely or
    perishing from malnutrition or hun-
    ger. (RHDEL2)

state colleges
HN September 1990 scope note added
SN Colleges that are financially sup-
    ported by a state government.

state guidebooks
HN March 1991 descriptor split, use state
    (ALT of states) + guidebooks

state maps
HN July 1991 descriptor split, use state
    (ALT of states) + maps

state universities
HN September 1990 scope note added
SN Universities that are financially sup-
    ported by a state government.

statements, artists
USE artists statements

statesmen
HN September 1990 scope note added
SN People who are experienced in the art of government or versed in the administration of government affairs. (RHDEL2)

statically indeterminate structures
HN June 1991 scope note changed
SN Use for structures that cannot be analyzed using principles of equilibrium or equations of statistics because there are more than three unknown reactions on the given structure. (DS)

stations, border
USE **border inspection stations**

stations, border inspection
USE **border inspection stations**

stealing
USE **theft**

steam baths
HN September 1990 scope note added
SN Use for establishments containing special enclosures for cleansing or refreshing oneself in a bath of steam.

steam boilers
HN June 1991 scope note added
SN Use for boilers that supply hot water or steam for space heating, processing, or power. (STEIN)

steam heating
HN June 1991 scope note added
SN Use for heating systems utilizing steam circulated through radiators and pipes. (RHDEL2)

steel engraving
HN March 1991 added
BT **engraving (printing process)**
SN Printmaking process of engraving using plates of steel or steel-faced copper; replaced the use of less durable copper plates in the early 19th century. For the engraving of steel plates for the production of documents such as banknotes, use **siderography**.
UF engraving, steel

steel joists, open web
USE **open web joists**

steel, Cor-Ten (TM)
USE **Cor-Ten steel (TM)**

stellar vaults
HN June 1991 lead-in term added
UF ribbed vaults, star

stencil paper
HN July 1990 added
BT *<paper by function>* MT.1924
SN Strong, thick paper treated with wax or oil and used to make stencils.
UF paper, stencil

stencil printing
USE **stenciling**

stencil work
USE **stenciling**

stenciling
HN July 1990 lead-in terms added
UF printing, stencil
stencil printing
stencil work
work, stencil

step cascades
USE **water stairs (landscaped-site elements)**

step-by-step housing
USE **incremental housing**

stepped arches
HN June 1991 scope note changed
SN Use for arches whose extradoses are stepped to correspond with the courses of masonry units in the wall around the opening. (BCMTC)

stepped gables
USE **corbie gables**

steps
HN June 1991 scope note changed, source DAC deleted

stereochromy
USE **mineral painting**

stereographs, half
USE **half stereographs**

stereographs, one-half
USE **half stereographs**

stereos, half
USE **half stereographs**

stereotomy
HN March 1990 scope note source changed to DAC

stiles (surface components)
HN April 1991 descriptor changed, was **stiles**
April 1991 alternate term changed, was **stile**
ALT **stile (surface component)**

stillingia oil
HN July 1990 added
BT **vegetable oil**
UF oil, stillingia
oil, tallowseed
tallowseed oil

stillrooms
HN August 1990 scope note added
SN Use for certain rooms or spaces in large houses, usually connected to kitchens, where liquors, preserves, and cakes are kept. (W)

stilt houses
HN November 1990 moved
BT *<houses by construction technique>* RK.312

stilted arches
HN June 1991 scope note changed
SN Use for arches sprung from a point above the imposts.

stilted arches, semi-circular
USE **surmounted arches**

stilts
HN June 1991 scope note changed, W added as source

stipple engraving
HN October 1991 moved
August 1991 scope note changed
BT **engraving (printing process)**
SN Printmaking process that achieves tonal areas by directly engraving short flicks or dots, usually in conjunction with engraved or etched lines. For the 15th-century process of making relief-printed engravings with stippled areas, use **dotted manner**.

stock breeders
USE **livestock breeders**

stockbrokers
HN April 1991 lead-in term added
UF brokers, stock

stone, Mankato
USE **Mankato stone**

stonecutters
HN September 1990 lead-in term added
UF stoneworkers

stones, door
USE **doorstones**

stoneworkers
USE **stonecutters**

stop-out
USE **resist**
stopping-out varnish

stop-out varnish
USE **stopping-out varnish**

stopping out
HN April 1990 added
BT **coating**
SN Coating selected areas of a surface to prevent them from being acted upon, as in etching or screen printing.
UF blocking out

stopping-out varnish
HN July 1990 added
BT *<varnish by function>* MT.2471
SN Varnish used for stopping out areas of a printing plate.

UF stop-out
  stop-out varnish
  varnish, stop-out
  varnish, stopping-out

storax
USE **styrax**

storefronts
  HN June 1991 scope note changed
  SN Facades of stores or store buildings fronting a street and usually containing window display spaces. (RHDEL2)

storm doors
  HN June 1991 scope note added
  SN Doors fitted to the outside of the frame of an exterior door to provide additional protection against cold and wind. (MEANS)

storm drains
  HN June 1991 lead-in terms added
  UF drains, storm water
  storm water drains

storm sashes
USE **storm windows**

storm water drains
USE **storm drains**

storm windows
  HN October 1991 lead-in term added
    June 1991 scope note added
    June 1991 lead-in term added
  SN Exterior windows placed over existing windows to provide additional protection against the weather. (MEANS)
  UF sashes, storm
  storm sashes

storms
  HN May 1991 alternate term added
  ALT storm

stormwater systems
  HN June 1991 scope note added
    June 1991 lead-in term **water systems, storm** deleted
    June 1991 descriptor changed, was **storm water systems**
    June 1991 lead-in term changed, was **systems, storm water**
    June 1991 alternate term changed, was **storm water system**
  ALT **stormwater system**
  SN Systems used for conveying rainwater, surface water, condensate, cooling water, or similar liquid wastes, exclusive of sewage or industrial waste, to the storm sewer or other legal place of disposal. (STEIN)
  UF systems, stormwater

strainer arches
USE **straining arches**

straining arches
  HN June 1991 scope note changed
    June 1991 lead-in terms added
  SN Use for arches introduced to resist

the deformation of piers under stress. (ACLAND)
  UF arches, strainer
  strainer arches

strappo
  HN September 1991 moved
  BT <*transferring techniques*> KT.739

stratigraphy
  HN April 1991 added
  BT geology
  SN Study of the origin, composition, distribution, and succession of strata or layers.

street people
USE **homeless persons**

streetwalkers
USE **prostitutes**

stressed-skin construction
USE **stressed-skin structures**

stressed-skin structures
  HN May 1991 lead-in terms added
  UF construction, stressed-skin
  stressed-skin construction

stretchers (furniture components)
  HN January 1991 descriptor changed, was **stretchers**
    January 1991 alternate term changed, was **stretcher**
  ALT **stretcher (furniture component)**

strikes (events)
  HN May 1991 alternate term added
  ALT **strike (event)**

strikes (components)
  HN September 1991 descriptor changed, was **strikes**
    September 1991 alternate term changed, was **strike**
  ALT **strike (component)**

stringcourses
  HN June 1991 scope note source changed to DAC

strings
  HN June 1991 scope note changed
    June 1991 lead-in term added
  SN Inclined boards that support the ends treads and risers of a stair.
  UF stair horses

strings, finish stair
USE **face strings**

strip windows
  HN June 1991 lead-in terms added
  UF ribbon windows
  window band
  windows, ribbon

strips, median
USE **median strips**

strong greenish yellow
  HN April 1990 lead-in terms added
  UF citron yellow
  yellow, citron

strong oil
  HN July 1990 deleted
  BT stand oil

strong yellowish pink
  HN April 1990 lead-in terms added
  UF pink, salmon
  salmon pink

structural anthropology
  HN September 1991 moved
  BT anthropology

structural drawings
  HN April 1991 scope note added
  SN Drawings that pertain specifically to the structural layout of a building.

structural failures
  HN January 1991 alternate term added
  ALT structural failure

structural geology
  HN April 1991 scope note changed
  SN Use for the study of individual geological structures such as anticlines, thrust vaults, and lineations. For the study of larger-scale units of the earth's crust, use tectonics (geology). (BADGLE)

structural systems, lamella
USE **lamella roofs**

structures (single built works)
  HN May 1991 descriptor changed, was **structures**
    May 1991 alternate term changed, was **structure**
  ALT **structure (single built work)**

structures, cable beam
USE **double-cable structures**

structures, cable supported
USE **cable-stayed structures**

structures, cable tent
USE **cable net structures**

structures, guyed
USE **cable-stayed structures**

structures, suspension cable
USE **suspension structures**

stud farms
USE **horse farms**

studbooks
  HN June 1990 lead-in terms added
  UF animal pedigrees
  herd-books
  pedigrees, animal

student competitions
  HN July 1990 added
  BT competitions
  ALT student competition

SN Design competitions available for students, sponsored usually by a school, foundation, or sector of the business community, for which prizes are awarded.
UF competitions, student

student mobility
HN October 1990 moved
BT **demographics**

studies (rooms)
HN August 1990 scope note added
SN Rooms or spaces in domestic contexts used for reading, writing, and study.

studies, behavior-environment
USE **environmental psychology**

studies, environment-behavior
USE **environmental psychology**

studies, ethnic
USE **ethnic studies**

studies, ethnic group
USE **ethnic studies**

studies, people-environment
USE **environmental psychology**

studies, women's
USE **women's studies**

studio ceramics
HN October 1990 added
BT <*object genres*> VB.82
SN Use for 20th-century ceramics that were produced by an individual artist who was responsible for all steps in the design and execution.
UF ceramics, studio
pottery, studio
studio pottery
studioware

studio pottery
USE **studio ceramics**

studios (organizations)
HN September 1990 scope note changed
September 1990 descriptor changed, was studios
September 1990 alternate term changed, was studio
ALT **studio (organization)**
SN Use for groups consisting of a master artist or an architect and his or her assistants or pupils, especially in the 19th and 20th centuries; earlier, use **workshops (organizations)**.

studioware
USE **studio ceramics**

studs (structural components)
HN May 1991 descriptor changed, was studs
May 1991 alternate term changed, was stud
ALT **stud (structural component)**

stuff (pulp)
HN July 1990 added
BT **wood pulp**
SN Prepared paper pulp ready for use. (TYLER)

stumping
HN October 1990 moved
BT **drawing techniques**

stunning
HN November 1990 added
BT <*carving techniques*>
SN Bruising the surface of stone by striking with a blunt tool.

stylebooks
HN June 1991 moved
BT <*books by subject*> VW.522

stylization
HN May 1990 scope note changed, MAYER added as source

styrax
HN July 1990 lead-in term added
July 1990 descriptor changed, was storax
UF storax

styrene-butadiene rubber
HN May 1990 lead-in term changed, was bunas
UF Buna S

subcontinents
HN June 1990 added
BT <*landforms by plate tectonics*> RD.178
ALT **subcontinent**
SN Land masses of great size but smaller than those generally called continents; also large subdivisions of continents having a certain geographical independence.

subcontracting
HN January 1991 scope note added
SN Contracting with a third party to perform all or a specific part of the obligations required in another contract.

subdivision
USE **land subdivision**

subject cataloging
HN May 1990 lead-in term added
UF cataloging, subject

subject searching
HN January 1991 scope note added
SN Querying a file or collection for items about or representing particular topics, people, or things.

Subjective photography
HN May 1990 added
BT <*post-1945 fine arts styles and movements*> FL.3712
UF photography, Subjective

submissions
USE **submittals**

submittals
HN March 1991 scope note added
March 1991 lead-in term added
SN Documents by which a dispute is referred to arbitration pursuant to an agreement between the parties. (OCLD)
UF submissions

subsidences (earth movements)
HN May 1991 alternate term added
ALT **subsidence (earth movement)**

subsidies
HN January 1991 alternate term added
ALT **subsidy**

substance abuse
HN January 1991 added
BT **behavior disorders**
SN The long term or excessive use or misuse of narcotics, alcohol, or other substances. For the state of being physically or psychologically habituated to a substance or practice to such an extent that its cessation causes severe trauma, use **addiction**.
UF abuse of substances
abuse, substance
RT **addiction**
addicts

substructures
HN July 1991 scope note changed
SN Use for the support systems and areas of buildings or other structures located below ground level or at the lower portions of structures when distinguishing these portions from the above ground or upper levels, in which case use **superstructures**. Use **foundations** specifically for those parts of structures, usually below ground, that transmit loads to the supporting earth or rock.

sucus
USE **sap green**

sugar
HN July 1990 added
BT **organic materials**

sugar aquatint
USE **sugar-lift**

sugar-lift
HN March 1991 added
BT **lift-ground**
SN Lift-ground technique in which sugar solution is used.
UF aquatint, sugar
aquatint, sugar-lift
etching, sugar-lift
sugar aquatint
sugar-lift aquatint
sugar-lift etching

sugar-lift aquatint
USE **sugar-lift**

129

sugar-lift etching
USE **sugar-lift**

suicides
HN May 1991 alternate term added
ALT **suicide**

suites (rooms)
HN May 1991 descriptor changed, was
suites
May 1991 alternate term changed,
was **suite**
ALT **suite (room)**

sulfur
HN April 1990 lead-in term added
UF **sulphur**

sulfur dioxide
HN May 1990 lead-in term added
UF **sulphur dioxide**

sulfuric acid
HN May 1990 lead-in term added
UF **sulphuric acid**

sulphur
USE **sulfur**

sulphur dioxide
USE **sulfur dioxide**

sulphuric acid
USE **sulfuric acid**

sumi-e
HN July 1990 descriptor changed, was
sumie

sun-bleached oil
USE **sun-refined oil**

sun-refined oil
HN July 1990 added
BT *<oil by technique>* MT.1995
UF oil, sun-bleached
oil, sun-refined
sun-bleached oil

Sunday schools
HN September 1990 scope note added
SN Use for schools, usually associated
with churches and mainly for children, in which religious instruction
is given on Sundays.

sunflower oil
HN October 1990 moved
BT **vegetable oil**

Sungu
USE **Tetela**

sunk relief
USE **coelanaglyphic relief**
intaglio

superabaci
USE **impost blocks**

superstructures
HN July 1991 scope note changed
SN Use for the upper portions of build-
ings or other structures located above

the foundation and usually above
ground level.

supervising
HN August 1991 scope note changed
January 1991 alternate term added
ALT **supervised**
SN Overseeing activity in an organization; also, the overseeing by the
original artist of the production of
such things as photographic prints.
For the activity of directing the business affairs and human and material
resources of an organization or enterprise, involving primarily the formulation of policy, use **administering.**

supplementary lighting
HN June 1991 moved
June 1991 scope note added
BT *<lighting techniques by distribution>*
SN Lighting technique providing addi-
tional quality and quantity of illu-
mination to supplement the general
lighting system.

supplies, artists
USE **artists materials**

supply, water
USE **water resources**

supports, pedestal
USE **pedestals**

surbased vaults
HN May 1991 deleted
BT *<vaults by form: profile>* RT.559

surface printing
USE **planographic printing**

surmounted arches
HN November 1991 lead-in terms added
June 1991 scope note changed, RS
added as source
UF arches, semi-circular stilted
semi-circular stilted arches
stilted arches, semi-circular

surmounted vaults
HN May 1991 deleted
BT **barrel vaults**

suspended floors
HN April 1990 lead-in terms added
UF cavity floors
floors, cavity

suspension cable structures
USE **suspension structures**

suspension roofs
USE **suspension structures**

suspension structures
HN August 1991 scope note added
August 1991 lead-in terms added
August 1991 lead-in term **sus-
pended structures** deleted
August 1991 lead-in term **struc-
tures, suspended** deleted
SN Designates structural systems in

which the structural elements or the
roofing elements are hung from
cables or in which the roofing is
supported by cables.
UF cable structures, suspension
roofs, suspension
structures, suspension cable
suspension cable structures
suspension roofs

sustainable development
HN May 1990 added
BT **development**
SN Development designed to ensure that
the utilization of resources and the
environment today does not damage
prospects for their use by future
generations.
UF development, sustainable

sweathouses
HN September 1990 scope note added
SN Use for structures heated by steam
produced by pouring water on hot
stones and used by Native Americans for ritual and therapeutic
sweating. (W)

sweatshops
HN April 1990 added
BT **industrial buildings**
ALT **sweatshop**
SN Industrial establishments where employees are underpaid and over-
worked usually under unsanitary or
otherwise barely tolerable conditions.

swimmers
HN December 1990 added
BT *<people by activity>* HG.705
ALT **swimmer**
SN Use for people actively propelling
themselves through the water by
natural means. For people washing
themselves with water, or immersed
in water, use **bathers.**

swimming pools
HN September 1990 scope note added
SN Use for structures containing an artificial body of water and designed
for swimming.

switchboards
HN November 1991 lead-in term
changed, was **switch gear, electric**
June 1990 lead-in term changed, was
electric switch gear
UF electric switchgear
switchgear, electric

switchgear, electric
USE **switchboards**

symbolism
HN January 1991 alternate term added
ALT **symbolic**

symposia
HN May 1991 alternate term added
ALT **symposium**

Synadicum marble
USE **pavonazzetto**

Synasol (TM)
USE **denatured alcohol**

syntax
HN February 1991 alternate term added
ALT syntactic

synthetic wax
HN December 1990 moved
BT *<wax by composition or origin>*

system, Guastavino
USE **Guastavino vaults**

system, Guastavino vault
USE **Guastavino vaults**

systems, burglar alarm
USE **burglar alarms**

systems, cogeneration
USE **cogeneration plants**

systems, electronic security
USE **electronic security systems**

systems, exterior insulation and finish
USE **exterior insulation and finish systems**

systems, incremental
USE **incremental air conditioning**

systems, incremental HVAC
USE **incremental air conditioning**

systems, lighting
USE **lighting**

systems, local
USE **local fire alarm systems**

systems, man-environment
USE **environmental psychology**

systems, one-way concrete joist
USE **one-way joist systems**

systems, one-way floor
USE **one-way beam and slab systems**

systems, pneumatic dispatch
USE **pneumatic tubes**

systems, pneumatic tube
USE **pneumatic tubes**

systems, stormwater
USE **stormwater systems**

systems, waffle concrete slab
USE **waffle slabs**

systems, wind turbine
USE **wind turbines**

T-bars
USE **T-beams**

T-beams
HN June 1991 scope note added
June 1991 lead-in terms added
SN Use for beams composed of a stem and a flange so that their section re-

sembles a T, usually of rolled metal. (MEANS)
UF T-bars
T-shapes
tee bars

T-shapes
USE **T-beams**

Taba Zikamambo
USE **Thabas-zi-ka-Mambo**

table fire screens
USE **candle screens**

table salt
USE **sodium chloride**

tables (support furniture)
HN May 1991 descriptor changed, was tables
May 1991 alternate term changed, was table
ALT table (support furniture)

tables (surface components)
USE **panels (surface components)**

tablets
HN May 1991 scope note added
SN Flat surfaces or slabs bearing or intended to bear inscriptions, or thin, rigid slabs used as writing surfaces.

tablets, wax
USE **wax tablets**

tactile orientation models
USE **braille maps**

taigas
HN July 1991 scope note source changed to ALLAB2

talc (mineral)
HN May 1991 descriptor changed, was talc

tales, fairy
USE **fairy tales**

tallboys (chimney pots)
HN June 1991 scope note source changed to DAC

tallboys (furniture)
HN May 1991 descriptor changed, was tallboys
May 1991 alternate term changed, was tallboy
ALT tallboy (furniture)

tallowseed oil
USE **stillingia oil**

tannic acid
USE **tannin**

tannin
HN November 1990 added
BT **organic compounds**
SN Any of a group of astringent vegetable principles or compounds, chiefly complex glucosides of ca-

techol and pyrogallol, used for their tanning properties. (RHDEL2)
UF acid, tannic
tannic acid

tanning
HN October 1991 moved
BT **leatherworking**

tar paper
HN July 1990 lead-in terms added
UF asphalt prepared roofing
bituminous felt
felt, bituminous
felt, tarred
roofing, asphalt prepared
tarred felt

tarlatan
HN July 1990 added
BT **cotton**
SN Sheer, thin, heavily-sized cotton with an open weave; used for linings and as a wiping cloth in printmaking.

tarred felt
USE **tar paper**

task forces
HN September 1990 lead-in term added
UF groups, working

task lighting
HN June 1991 moved
June 1991 scope note added
BT **local lighting**
SN Use for illumination directed at a specific target area for aiding visual tasks.

taxi stands
HN December 1990 moved
BT **pedestrian facilities**

taxing
HN January 1991 scope note added
SN Imposition by a public authority of compulsory contributions to raise revenue. (W)

taxiway lights
HN May 1990 added
BT **aeronautical ground lights**
ALT taxiway light
SN Aeronautical ground lights provided to indicate the route to be followed by taxiing aircrafts. (IESREF)
UF lights, taxiway

teachers colleges
HN September 1990 scope note added
September 1990 lead-in terms added
SN Use for four-year colleges offering courses for the training of primary and secondary school teachers and granting bachelor's degrees and often advanced degrees.
UF normal schools
schools, normal

teaching
- HN April 1991 moved
  April 1991 lead-in term **educating** deleted
  April 1991 lead-in term changed, was **instruction**
  February 1991 scope note added
  December 1990 lead-in term **training** deleted
- BT **educating**
- SN Directly instructing others in knowledge, attitudes, or skills. For the acquiring or imparting of specific skills relating to particular functions or activities through instruction or practice, use **training**.
- UF instructing

technical illustration
- HN May 1991 scope note added
- SN The activity of making technical illustrations.

technical reports
- HN September 1991 scope note added
- SN Reports giving details and results of a specific investigation of a scientific or technical problem. (ALAG)

technical writing
- HN January 1991 scope note added
- SN Writing reports, proposals, or other documentation, usually highly specialized or concerned with practical applications, used for scientific, engineering, business, or other technical purposes. (ERIC9)

technique
- HN May 1990 scope note changed, W added as source

technique, drip
- USE **drip painting**

technique, mixed
- USE **mixed technique**

technique, soak-stain
- USE **soak-stain technique**

technique, staining (painting technique)
- USE **soak-stain technique**

technique, tempera
- USE **tempera painting**

technique, wash
- USE **wash technique**

technique, wet-into-wet
- USE **mixed technique**

technology
- HN January 1991 alternate term added
- ALT **technological**

<technology-related functions>
- HN November 1990 added
- BT <functions by general context> KG.2

tectonics (architectural theory)
- HN May 1991 descriptor changed, was **tectonics**

tee bars
- USE **T-beams**

teen-age
- USE **adolescence**

teenagers
- USE **adolescents**

television antenna systems
- HN July 1991 scope note added
- SN Systems which include equipment that supplies a television signal to a building or complex.

television stations
- HN April 1990 scope note added
- SN Broadcasting stations for sending and receiving television programming transmissions; for rooms and spaces designed for the origination or recording of television programs, use **television studios**.

tempera
- HN November 1991 lead-in term added
  July 1990 lead-in term added
- UF paint, tempera
  tempera paint

tempera paint
- USE **tempera**

tempera painting
- HN April 1990 added
- BT <painting techniques by medium> KT.239
- UF painting, tempera
  technique, tempera
  tempera technique

tempera technique
- USE **tempera painting**

tempera, egg-and-oil
- USE **egg-oil tempera**

tempera, egg-oil
- USE **egg-oil tempera**

temperature detectors
- HN July 1991 scope note added
  July 1991 lead-in terms added
- SN Fire detectors that sense the presence of heat sufficient to indicate the presence of an openly burning fire. (MSR7)
- UF detectors, heat-actuated
  detectors, heat-sensing
  detectors, thermal
  detectors, thermostatic
  heat-actuated detectors
  heat-sensing detectors
  thermal detectors
  thermostatic detectors

tempering
- HN May 1991 moved
- BT <temperature related processes> KT.726

temporary housing
- HN February 1991 related term added
- RT **ECHO houses**

Tena
- USE **Ingalik**

tenancy, joint
- USE **joint occupancy**

tennis clubs
- HN November 1991 moved
- BT <club complexes>

tennis courts
- HN September 1990 scope note added
- SN Courts marked and equipped for the game of tennis.

tensegrity structures
- HN March 1991 moved
- BT **space frames**

tensile structures
- HN July 1991 scope note added
- SN Use for structures under tensile loads, such as cable or membrane structures.

tent structures
- HN August 1991 scope note added
- SN Use for membrane structures in which fabric is stretched across or supported on masts or poles, with or without the aid of guys.

tent structures, cable
- USE **cable net structures**

tents, cable-supported
- USE **cable net structures**

Teotihuacán II
- USE **Miccaotli**

Teotihuacán IIIa
- USE **Xolalpan**

Teotihuacán IV
- USE **Metepec**

Teotihuán II
- USE **Miccaotli**

Tepalcingo
- HN June 1991 moved
- BT <Colonial Latin American architecture styles> FL.1710

Tepe Hissar
- USE **Hissar**

terminally ill
- HN May 1991 moved
- BT **ill**

terminals, heating
- USE **heat-distributing units**

terminating
- HN January 1991 added
- BT <organizational functions> KG.138
- ALT **terminated**
- SN Concluding or discontinuing an activity, program, or job position. For the act of dismissing an employee, use **firing**.

termination (employees)
USE firing (managing)

terra cotta
USE terracotta

terracotta
HN May 1991 lead-in term added
UF terra cotta

terre de pipe
USE pipe clay

terre de pipe ware
USE pipe clay

terrepleine
USE terrepleins

terrepleins
HN July 1991 lead-in term added
UF terrepleine

Territorial Style
HN April 1990 added
BT *<modern North American architecture styles and movements>* FL.1730

Tetela
HN August 1990 lead-in term added
UF Sungu

textiles
HN October 1990 alternate term added
ALT textile

Thabas-zi-ka-Mambo
HN November 1990 lead-in term added
UF Taba Zikamambo

Thalo blue (TM)
USE phthalocyanine blue

thatch roofs, simulated
USE false thatched roofs

theater
HN April 1990 scope note changed, PG added as source

theater design
HN March 1991 moved
BT design

theaters
HN September 1990 scope note added
SN Designates buildings having a stage or projection screen for the presentation of dramatic performances and providing seating areas for spectators.

theaters, marionette
USE puppet theaters

theft
HN January 1990 scope note added
January 1990 lead-in term added
SN The wrongful taking of property with the intention of permanently depriving the rightful owner of it.
UF stealing

theme
HN July 1991 added
BT *<historical, theoretical and critical concepts>* BM.285
SN An underlying intent or meaning in a work of visual or literary art; also a motif, subject, or idea repeated in a number of artistic works.

theocracy
HN January 1991 alternate term added
ALT theocratic

<theological schools> RK.819
HN May 1991 deleted
BT *<schools by subject>* RK.801

theological seminaries
HN May 1991 moved
May 1991 scope note added
BT *<schools by subject>* RK.801
SN Schools providing education in, for example, theology and religious history, primarily, but not exclusively, to prepare students for jobs as priests, ministers, or church workers; usually sponsored or controlled by a church or other religious organization. For schools devoted especially to the training of rabbis, use **rabbinical seminaries.**

theology
HN February 1991 alternate term added
ALT theological

theosophy
HN January 1991 alternate term added
ALT theosophical

therapists
HN January 1991 moved
BT *<people in health and medicine>* HG.380

therapists, occupational
USE occupational therapists

therapy, occupational
USE occupational therapy

thermal bridges
HN October 1990 moved
BT *<conditions and effects: architecture>*

thermal detectors
USE temperature detectors

thermal insulation
HN June 1991 moved
BT *<insulation by function>*

thermal windows
USE Diocletian windows

thermoluminescence dating
HN March 1990 lead-in term added
UF TL dating

thermoplastic polyester
HN May 1990 lead-in term added
UF PES-tp

thermostatic detectors
USE temperature detectors

thieves
HN April 1991 lead-in term added
UF robbers

thin oil
HN July 1990 deleted
BT stand oil

thin shells
USE shell structures

Thiokol (TM)
USE polysulfide elastomer

Thonga
HN June 1990 lead-in terms added
UF Hlengwe
Ronga
Shangana

three-centered arches
HN July 1991 scope note changed
July 1991 lead-in terms added
SN Arches struck from three centers in which a large central arch is continued to each side by two smaller circles, so that the arch resembles a semi-ellipse.
UF arches, basket
arches, basket handle
basket arches
basket handle arches

three-deckers (houses)
HN May 1991 descriptor changed, was three-deckers
May 1991 alternate term changed, was three-decker
ALT three-decker (house)

three-deckers (pulpits)
HN March 1991 moved
BT pulpits

three-hinged arches
HN July 1991 lead-in term changed, was three pinned arches
UF three-pinned arches

three-pinned arches
USE three-hinged arches

three-quarter-turn stairs
HN July 1991 descriptor changed, was three-quarter turn stairs
July 1991 lead-in term changed, was stairs, three-quarter turn
July 1991 alternate term changed, was three-quarter turn stair
ALT three-quarter-turn stair
UF stairs, three-quarter-turn

three-story
HN March 1991 moved
BT *<building elevation attributes>*

threshold combs
HN May 1991 deleted
BT *<horizontal and diagonal conveying system components>* RT.1325

threshold lights
HN   May 1990 added
BT   **runway lights**
ALT   **threshold light**
SN   Runway lights placed to indicate the longitudinal limits of that portion of a runway, channel, or landing path usable for landing. (IESREF)
UF   lights, threshold

threshold plates
HN   May 1991 deleted
BT   *<horizontal and diagonal conveying system components>* RT.1325

thresholds
HN   May 1991 moved
       May 1991 scope note changed
BT   *<doorway components>* RT.833
SN   Strips fastened to the floor beneath a door, usually required to cover the joint when two types of floor material meet; may provide weather protection on external doors; for the lower sides and bottom of doorways, use **doorsills**. (DAC)

through trusses
HN   March 1991 moved
       March 1991 scope note changed
       March 1991 lead-in term **deck trusses** deleted
BT   *<trusses by location or context>* RT.377
SN   Bridge trusses supporting loads on their lower chords and having lateral bracing between their top chords.

throwing (pottery technique)
HN   November 1990 lead-in term added
UF   wheel-throwing

thumbnail sketches
HN   April 1991 scope note added
SN   Small, brief, concise drawings. (W)

thunderstorms
HN   May 1991 alternate term added
ALT   **thunderstorm**

tickets
HN   August 1991 moved to hierarchy under development

Ticomán
HN   November 1990 lead-in term added
UF   Cuilcuilco-Ticomán

tidal waves
HN   May 1991 alternate term added
ALT   **tidal wave**

ties, angle
USE   **knee braces**

ties, dragging
USE   **dragon beams**

timbrel vaults
HN   May 1990 scope note changed
       May 1990 lead-in terms added
SN   Thin vaults of one or more layers of terracotta tiles laid flat edge to edge

and deriving their rigidity from cohesion and curvature rather than from massiveness or compression; can be erected without centering.
UF   Catalan vaults
       vaults, Catalan

time zone charts
USE   **time zone maps**

time zone maps
HN   April 1990 lead-in terms added
UF   charts, time zone
       time zone charts

timesharing (real estate)
HN   May 1990 added
BT   *<legal concepts>* BM.442
SN   Property ownership arrangement in which persons or groups of persons share ownership or rental, usually of vacation housing, and each owner holds title for a specified time each year.

tinsel
HN   July 1990 added
BT   **trimmings**

tintype
HN   February 1991 moved
BT   **wet collodion process**

TL dating
USE   **thermoluminescence dating**

Tlakluit
USE   **Wishram**

tobacco seed oil
HN   October 1990 moved
BT   **vegetable oil**

toboggan runs
HN   September 1990 scope note added
SN   Snow- or ice-covered inclined courses used for toboggan sledding.

toilet compartments
HN   August 1990 scope note added
       August 1990 lead-in terms added
       August 1990 lead-in term **toilet partitions** deleted
SN   Use for enclosures erected around toilets for privacy. (MEANS)
UF   compartments, WC
       cubicles, toilet
       enclosures, toilet
       toilet cubicles
       toilet enclosures
       WC compartments

toilet cubicles
USE   **toilet compartments**

toilet enclosures
USE   **toilet compartments**

toilets
HN   July 1991 lead-in term added
UF   W.C.s

toilets, chemical
USE   **chemical toilets**

tomb gifts
USE   **grave goods**

tombstone lights
HN   May 1991 deleted
BT   *<windows by form>* RT.907

toning (painting)
HN   September 1991 alternate term changed, was **toned**
       May 1991 descriptor changed, was toning
ALT   **toned (painting)**

Too-an-hooch
USE   **Twana**

top light
USE   **top lighting**

top lighting
HN   April 1991 added
BT   **directional lighting**
SN   Illumination of a subject from directly above; used to produce highlights.
UF   light, top
       lighting, top
       top light

toppings out
HN   May 1991 alternate term added
ALT   **topping out**

torchères (stands)
HN   August 1991 descriptor changed, was torchères
       August 1991 alternate term changed, was torchère
ALT   **torchère (stand)**

torchis
HN   February 1991 moved
BT   **clay products**

torinoko
HN   July 1990 added
BT   **handmade paper**
SN   Handmade oriental paper made with 20% kozo.

tornadoes
HN   May 1991 alternate term added
ALT   **tornado**

toruses
HN   April 1991 scope note changed
SN   Bold projecting moldings, convex in shape, generally forming the lowest member of a base of a column over the plinth. (DAC)

totalitarianism
HN   January 1991 alternate term added
ALT   **totalitarian**

Totolapan
HN   November 1990 added
BT   **Tzotzil**

tournaments
HN   May 1991 alternate term added
ALT   **tournament**

tours
HN May 1991 alternate term added
ALT tour

tower houses
HN June 1990 added
BT <houses by form: massing or shape> RK.244
ALT tower house
SN Use for distinctly vertical dwellings, built for defensive purposes, usually of stone and with at least three to four stories.
UF houses, tower
peel towers
peels
towers, peel

towers (single built works)
HN May 1991 descriptor changed, was towers
May 1991 alternate term changed, was tower
ALT tower (single built work)

towers, peel
USE tower houses

town halls
HN September 1990 scope note added
SN Use for the principal public administration buildings of towns and villages housing offices for transaction of government business and places for public assembly.

Town lattice trusses
HN March 1991 moved
March 1991 scope note changed
BT <trusses by form> RT.357
SN Use for trusses of closely spaced intersecting diagonal members, usually of wood, following a design patented by Ithiel Town in 1820.

town meetings
HN May 1991 alternate term added
ALT town meeting

township maps
HN July 1991 descriptor split, use township (ALT of townships) + maps

tracings
HN April 1991 scope note added
SN Images made by tracing.

traction elevators
HN July 1991 lead-in terms added
UF machines, traction
traction machines

traction machines
USE traction elevators

trade
HN January 1991 scope note changed
November 1990 moved
BT business
SN Use for the activity of buying, selling, or bartering commodities. (W)

trade centers, world
USE world trade centers

trade shows
HN May 1991 alternate term added
ALT trade show

trade, art
USE art market

trading cards
HN May 1991 added
BT cards
ALT trading card
SN Cards depicting professional athletes, cartoon figures or the like, and that are collected and traded.
UF cards, trading

traffic circles
HN August 1990 lead-in terms added
August 1990 lead-in term turning circles deleted
UF intersections, rotary
rotary intersections

traffic control signals
USE traffic signals

traffic loads
HN January 1991 alternate term added
ALT traffic load

traffic signals
HN August 1990 lead-in terms added
UF control signals, traffic
signals, traffic control
traffic control signals

trailers (mobile homes)
USE mobile homes

training
HN December 1990 added
BT educating
SN Acquiring or imparting specific skills relating to particular functions or activities through instruction or practice. For directly instructing others in knowledge, attitudes, or skills, use teaching. (ERIC12)
UF instructing

training centers
HN May 1990 added
BT <single built works by function> RK.39
ALT training center
SN Use for buildings, often containing educational, research, and recreational facilities, erected by corporations specifically for the training of corporate personnel.
UF centers, job training
centers, skill training
centers, training
job training centers
skill training centers

training schools, military
USE military academies

training, job
USE vocational training

training, occupational
USE vocational training

training, vocational
USE vocational training

transepts
HN August 1990 scope note changed, source W deleted

transfer lithography
HN October 1991 moved
July 1990 scope note changed
BT lithography
SN Type of lithography in which the image is created on another surface and then transferred to the stone or plate for printing. (GASCO)

transfer printing
HN October 1990 moved
BT printing

transformers
HN July 1991 scope note added
SN Electric devices for introducing mutual coupling between circuits, generally used to convert a power supply at one voltage to another voltage.

transient labor
USE migrant workers

transient workers
USE migrant workers

Transoxianan
USE Central Asian

transparent base
HN July 1990 added
BT extenders
SN In printmaking, a substance used to modify ink by increasing its transparency and workability.
UF base, transparent

transparent watercolor
USE aquarelle

transverse arches
HN October 1991 scope note changed
SN Use for arches which separate the bays of vaults, particularly in a groin- or barrel-vaulted space; in a ribbed vault context, use transverse ribs; for arches across a nave or hall that support walls rather than vaults, use diaphragm arches.

transverse ribs
HN October 1991 scope note changed
SN Ribs which span at right angles to the longitudinal axis of the space being spanned, dividing it into bays or compartments; for arches separating the bays of vaults, particularly in a groin- or barrel-vaulted space, use transverse arches. (DAC)

transverse ridge ribs
HN May 1991 descriptor split, use transverse + ridge ribs

trapeziums
HN July 1991 alternate term added
ALT trapezium

trapezoids
HN July 1991 alternate term added
ALT trapezoid

trash
USE rubbish

travel trailers
HN January 1991 related term added
RT mobile homes

travelers' checks
HN July 1991 moved to hierarchy under development

traveling exhibitions
HN May 1991 alternate term added
ALT traveling exhibition

treatises
HN April 1990 scope note changed, RHDEL2 added as source

treatment, sewage
USE sewage treatment

trestles (furniture components)
HN May 1991 descriptor changed, was trestles
May 1991 alternate term changed, was trestle
ALT trestle (furniture component)

trials
HN May 1991 alternate term added
ALT trial

triangles (polygons)
HN July 1991 alternate term added
May 1991 descriptor changed, was triangles
ALT triangle (polygon)

tribes
HN May 1991 moved
BT <kinship groups> HG.879

triclinia (rooms)
HN May 1991 descriptor changed, was triclinia
May 1991 alternate term changed, was triclinium
ALT triclinium (room)

trim
USE trimmings

trim, cap
USE cap moldings

trimmings
HN July 1990 added
BT <materials by function> MT.2291
UF trim

tripods (camera accessories)
HN May 1991 descriptor changed, was tripods
May 1991 alternate term changed, was tripod
ALT tripod (camera accessory)

troughs, eaves
USE eaves gutters

trumeaux
HN July 1991 scope note changed
SN Use for the central uprights placed in the center of large doorways to support the lintel. (A-Z)

trunnels
USE guttae

trussed rafter roofs
HN July 1991 scope note added
SN Roof systems in which the cross framing members are some form of light wood truss. (MEANS)

trussed rafters
HN May 1991 scope note changed
March 1991 moved
BT <trusses by location or context> RT.377
SN Designates light, wood, roof trusses, usually prefabricated and often used in residential construction.

<trusses by construction>
HN March 1991 added
BT trusses

tsun
HN April 1990 added
BT brushwork
SN Type of brush strokes used in Chinese painting to indicate wrinkles, markings, and modeling on mountains, rocks, trees, and stones. (DCJA)

tube-in-tube construction
USE tube structures

tube structures
HN May 1991 scope note changed
May 1991 lead-in terms added
SN Use for rigid frame structures with closely spaced exterior columns rigidly connected to spandrel beams to form a tubelike exterior framework that carries all lateral loads, as in the World Trade Center towers, New York City.
UF construction, tube-in-tube
tube-in-tube construction

tung oil
HN October 1990 moved
BT vegetable oil

turbine systems, wind
USE wind turbines

turbines, wind
USE wind turbines

Turkish
HN June 1991 added
BT <West Asian>

Turkish baths
HN September 1990 scope note added
SN Use for buildings in which bathers pass through a succession of steam rooms of increasing temperature followed by spaces for rubdowns and massages. (W)

Turkoman of the Black Sheep
USE Karakoyunlu

turpentine
HN July 1990 lead-in terms added
UF oil, turpentine
turpentine oil

turpentine oil
USE turpentine

turret steps
HN July 1991 alternate term added
July 1991 scope note source changed to DAC
ALT turret step

turrets (towers)
HN May 1991 descriptor changed, was turrets
May 1991 alternate term changed, was turret
ALT turret (tower)

Tuscan order
HN August 1991 scope note added
SN Use for the architectural order characterized by unfluted columns, torus bases, unadorned cushion capitals, and plain friezes.

Tuscarora (Southeastern Native American)
HN May 1991 descriptor changed, was Tuscarora

tusche
HN December 1990 lead-in terms added
November 1990 moved
BT <coatings by form> MT.2492
UF litho tusche
lithographic tusche
tusche, litho

tusche, litho
USE tusche

Twana
HN November 1990 lead-in term changed, was Too-an-hooch Indians
UF Too-an-hooch

tweed
HN June 1991 moved
April 1991 scope note source changed to EOT2
BT <cloth by composition or origin> MT.1845

twin-lights
USE coupled windows

two-centered arches
HN July 1991 scope note source changed to DAC

two-lights
USE coupled windows

two-story
HN March 1991 moved
BT *<building elevation attributes>*

two-way beam and slab systems
HN August 1991 scope note changed
August 1991 lead-in terms added
August 1991 lead-in term **flat slab and beam systems** deleted
August 1991 lead-in term **beam systems, flat slab and** deleted
August 1991 lead-in term **systems, flat slab and beam** deleted
SN Use for two-way, flat concrete slabs supported by beams spanning between columns in both directions; the slab and beams are poured to be monolithic.
UF beam-and-slab floor constructions
beam-and-slab floors
constructions, beam-and-slab floor
floor constructions, beam-and-slab
floors, beam-and-slab
slabs, two-way
two-way slabs

two-way slabs
USE **two-way beam and slab systems**

tympana
HN July 1991 scope note source changed to DAC

typewriter paper
HN July 1990 added
BT *<paper by function>* MT.1924
UF paper, typewriter
typing paper

typewriters
HN January 1991 added
BT *<drafting, drawing and writing equipment by specific type>* TB.234
ALT **typewriter**
SN Machines for writing in characters like those produced by printers' types, by which steel dies strike a paper through an inked ribbon. (W)

typhoons
HN May 1991 alternate term added
ALT **typhoon**

typicons
HN January 1991 added
BT **religious books**
ALT **typicon**
SN Books containing rules and rubrics for the religious services of the Eastern Church year.

typing paper
USE **typewriter paper**

typographers
HN December 1990 moved
BT **graphic designers**

Tzotzil
HN November 1990 lead-in term added
November 1990 lead-in term changed, was **Zatzil**
UF Chamula
Zotzil

Tzutujil
HN November 1990 lead-in term changed, was **Zutujil**
UF Zutuhil

Uchi
USE **Yuchi**

ultimate-strength design
USE **plastic design**

Ultrabaroque
HN June 1991 moved
BT *<Colonial Latin American architecture styles>* FL.1710

unbleached beeswax
HN December 1990 moved
BT **beeswax**

under-flashing
USE **base flashing**

underbiting
HN April 1990 added
BT *<biting techniques>*
ALT **underbitten**
SN Insufficient biting of a printing plate.

underlayment
HN July 1991 scope note changed, DAC added as source

underpainting
HN October 1990 moved to hierarchy under development

underpitch vaults
HN September 1991 scope note changed
SN Groined vaults formed by the penetration of two vaults of unequal size springing from the same level. (DAC)

undertakings, joint
USE **joint ventures**

uniform loads
HN January 1991 alternate term added
ALT **uniform load**

uninked embossing
USE **blind embossing**

unions, art
USE **art unions**

unit air conditioning
HN May 1991 deleted
BT **air conditioning**

units, dwelling
USE **apartments**

units, ECHO
USE **ECHO houses**

units, living
USE **apartments**

universities
HN September 1990 scope note added
SN Use for buildings or groups of buildings that house degree-granting institutions which may typically include liberal arts undergraduate colleges, graduate schools, and undergraduate or graduate professional schools. (ERIC9)

unskilled labor
USE **laborers**

unskilled workers
USE **laborers**

upfeed systems
HN May 1991 scope note added
SN Use for water distribution systems in which water is forced upward by pumps or pressure within a main.

upper class
HN May 1991 moved
May 1991 lead-in term added
May 1991 alternate term **upper class** deleted
May 1991 descriptor changed, was **upper classes**
BT **social classes**
UF class, upper

urban blight
HN April 1991 scope note added
April 1991 lead-in term added
October 1990 moved
BT **social issues**
SN Use for the condition of urban areas characterized by general deterioration in the quality of existing buildings and infrastructural systems, often caused by adverse economic, environmental, or zoning forces.
UF urban decay

urban decay
HN April 1991 deleted, made lead-in to **urban blight**

urban decay
USE **urban blight**

urban design
HN February 1991 added
BT **social sciences**
SN Use for the field of study that falls between and overlaps architecture and planning, and whose concern is the specific design and contextual integration of city buildings and spaces; includes expertise in, for example, landscape architecture, urban sociology, environmental psychology, and law.
UF design, urban

urban fringes
HN May 1990 lead-in term added
UF peripheries

urban geography
USE **human geography**

urban renewal
HN January 1991 scope note added
SN Activity of clearing, rebuilding, restoring, or refurbishing urban areas.

urban sociology
HN September 1991 moved
BT **sociology**

urban to rural migration
USE **urban-rural migration**

urban universities
HN September 1990 scope note added
SN Universities located in and serving urban communities, although not necessarily maintained by municipalities. (ERIC9)

urban villages
HN May 1990 added
BT *<settlements by planning concept>* RD.80
ALT **urban village**
SN Mixed-use communities designed to combine residential sections in close proximity to employment, retail, and entertainment facilities linked by pedestrian-oriented thoroughfares; often located in suburban contexts.
UF **villages, urban**

urban-rural migration
HN April 1991 moved
January 1991 scope note added
January 1991 lead-in term added
BT **internal migration**
SN Migration within a country or region from towns or cities to rural areas.
UF **urban to rural migration**

urbanization
HN January 1991 scope note added
January 1991 alternate term added
ALT **urbanized**
SN Causing to become densely populated and built up like towns and cities.

urethane
USE **polyurethane**

Usonian houses
HN January 1991 added
BT *<houses by construction technique>* RK.312
ALT **Usonian house**
SN Designates a group of Frank Lloyd Wright's small, single-family houses constructed during the late 1930s and early 1940s and generally characterized by low cost, natural materials, open planning, and a close relationship between the building and the site and climate.
UF **houses, Usonian**
RT **affordable housing**
architect-designed houses

Uthman II
USE **Osman II**

utility poles
HN August 1990 scope note added
SN Use for outdoor poles installed by utility companies to support tele-

phone, electric, or other cables. (MEANS)

vacations
HN June 1991 added
BT *<leisure events>*
ALT **vacation**
SN Periods of time devoted to rest, relaxation, or recreation. (ERIC12)

Vaisali
HN November 1990 lead-in term added
November 1990 descriptor changed, was **Vaisali (Nepalese)**
UF **Vasali**

valance lighting
HN April 1991 scope note added
SN Lighting arrangements with light sources shielded by a panel parallel to the wall and set at the top of windows; light may be directed upward or downward.

Valenciennes lace
HN April 1991 scope note source changed to EOT2

Valenge
USE **Chopi**

valla
HN May 1991 deleted
BT **ramparts**

valley gutters
HN July 1991 scope note added
SN Use for exposed, open gutters in the valleys of roofs. (MEANS)

valleys (landforms)
HN May 1991 descriptor changed, was **valleys**
May 1991 alternate term changed, was **valley**
ALT **valley (landform)**

value (economic concept)
HN May 1991 descriptor changed, was **value**

vandalism
HN January 1991 scope note added
SN Willful destruction of or damage to property belonging to another or to the public. (WCOL9)

variety theaters
HN September 1990 scope note added
SN Use for theaters devoted primarily to the presentation of such performing art forms as pantomime, puppetry, or shadow shows; popular in France and Italy during the late 19th century. (TOCCAB)

varnish, alcohol-resin
USE **spirit varnish**

varnish, stop-out
USE **stopping-out varnish**

varnish, stopping-out
USE **stopping-out varnish**

Varnolene (TM)
USE **mineral spirits**

Vasali
USE **Vaisali**

vault system, Guastavino
USE **Guastavino vaults**

vaults (structural elements)
HN May 1991 descriptor changed, was **vaults**
May 1991 alternate term changed, was **vault**
ALT **vault (structural element)**

vaults, Catalan
USE **timbrel vaults**

vaults, helical
USE **spiral vaults**

vaults, ribbed
USE **ribbed vaults**

vaults, wagon
USE **barrel vaults**

VDU's
USE **monitors (data processing equipment)**

vegetable oil
HN July 1990 scope note added
SN Oil obtained from plants. (W)

vegetable wax
HN December 1990 moved
BT *<wax by composition or origin>*

velum
HN June 1991 moved
BT *<cloth by composition or origin>* MT.1845

veneer
HN June 1990 alternate term added
ALT **veneers**

vent stacks
HN July 1991 lead-in terms added
UF **stacks, ventilating**
ventilating stacks

ventilating stacks
USE **vent stacks**

ventilators, hopper
USE **hopper windows**

verism
HN October 1990 alternate term added
ALT **verist**

<vertical roof frame components>
HN December 1990 guide term changed, was *<roof posts>* RT.510

very pale blue
HN April 1990 lead-in terms added
UF **blue, dull**
dull blue

very pale purple
HN April 1990 lead-in terms added
UF mauve, pale
 pale mauve

very pale purplish blue
HN April 1990 lead-in terms added
UF blue, dull
 dull blue

veterans
HN May 1991 added
BT <*people by state or condition*> HG.775
ALT veteran
SN People of long experience in some activity; with reference to military personnel, use for those who have served in war or who have retired from membership in the armed forces. (WCOL9)
RT **military personnel**

veterinary colleges
HN September 1990 scope note added
SN Colleges devoted to teaching veterinary medicine and to training veterinarians.

vice presidents
HN September 1990 scope note added
SN Officers ranking below the office of president in a government or organization, and able to act as president in case of that officer's absence or disability. (W)

vices
USE **vises**

video arcades
HN September 1990 scope note added
SN Amusement arcades that contain predominantly video games.

video art
HN October 1991 moved to hierarchy under development

videocassettes
HN March 1990 alternate term changed, was video cassette
ALT **videocassette**

Vierendeel trusses
HN March 1991 moved
BT <*trusses by form*> RT.357

view albums
USE **viewbooks**

viewbooks
HN June 1991 lead-in term added
 May 1991 moved
 May 1991 scope note changed
 May 1991 lead-in terms added
 May 1991 descriptor changed, was view albums
 May 1991 scope note changed, source HCOP deleted
 May 1991 alternate term changed, was view album
BT <*books by form or function*> VW.483
ALT **viewbook**

SN Commercially published groups of photographs of one place, event, or activity, sometimes spiral bound or accordion folded.
UF albums, souvenir
 souvenir albums
 view albums

viewers
HN February 1991 added
BT <*people by activity*> HG.705
ALT **viewer**
SN Use for those who view exhibitions or individual works of art or architecture, television programs, or motion pictures. For those who are present at and observe live events, use **spectators.**
UF beholders
 observers
 spectators (viewers)
RT **audiences**
 spectators

viewers (spectators)
USE **spectators**

villages, golf course
USE **golf course communities**

villages, urban
USE **urban villages**

villes neuves
USE **new towns**

vintage prints
HN September 1991 scope note changed
SN Photographic prints made by the original photographer or soon after the picture was taken, that is, of the same historical vintage as the original. For prints made much later from the same negative, use **later prints.**

vinyl paint
HN July 1990 added
BT <*synthetic resin paint*> MT.2530
UF paint, vinyl

Vinylite (TM)
HN July 1990 added
BT **polyvinyl acetate**

violence
HN May 1991 added
BT **social issues**
SN The use of physical force so as to kill, injure, damage, or abuse. (WCOL9)

violet, bright
USE **light violet**

violet, dull bluish
USE **moderate violet**

violet, Nuernberg
USE **manganese violet**

virgins
HN December 1990 added
BT <*people by state or condition*> HG.775
ALT **virgin**

SN People who have not had sexual intercourse; also, chaste, pious women accorded a special place in the Christian community, especially in the early church. (W)

vises
HN July 1990 lead-in term added
UF vices

visionary architecture
HN September 1991 scope note changed
SN Use for designs that are rhetorical, reflecting a theoretical or speculative architectural position on social or political issues, often considered ahead of their time, and usually not intended to be carried out; often applied, but not necessarily restricted, to designs by certain French architects of the late 18th and early 19th centuries.

visual perception
HN May 1991 added
BT **perception**
SN The process of receiving and interpreting sensory impressions attained by sight.
UF perception, visual

visual poetry
HN July 1991 added
BT **poetry**
SN Use for works that employ words but that are designed also to have a visual impact.
UF art, word
 poetry, shaped
 poetry, visual
 shaped poetry
 word art

vocational guidance
HN May 1990 lead-in terms added
UF guidance, career
 guidance, occupational

vocational schools
HN September 1990 scope note added
SN Schools offering instruction in one or more skilled or semiskilled trades or occupations. (RHDEL2)

vocational training
HN December 1990 added
BT **training**
SN Use to denote activities aimed at providing the skills and knowledge required for employment in a particular occupation and which may be prepared and conducted by undertakings, by educational institutions, or by both in cooperation. (UNESCO)
UF job training
 occupational training
 training, job
 training, occupational
 training, vocational

volleyball courts
HN September 1990 scope note added
SN Courts marked and equipped for the team sport of volleyball.

voters
HN January 1991 added
BT *<people by activity>* HG.705
ALT voter
SN Citizens of a community or members of another group who vote in the group's elections and on other occasions of decision making.
RT voting

voting
HN January 1991 added
BT *<communication functions>* KG.32
ALT voted
SN Expressing opinion or choice in a matter by some specific means, such as casting a ballot or raising a hand, among a group of other voters.
RT citizen participation
voters

voyages
USE **journeys**

W.C.s
USE **toilets**

Wabende
USE **Bende (Kenya)**

waffle concrete slab systems
USE **waffle slabs**

waffle floors
USE **waffle slabs**

waffle slabs
HN May 1991 lead-in terms added
UF concrete slab systems, waffle
floors, waffle
slab systems, waffle concrete
systems, waffle concrete slab
waffle concrete slab systems
waffle floors

Wagogo
USE **Gogo**

waiting rooms
HN August 1990 scope note added
SN Rooms furnished for the use of persons waiting, as in railroad stations or medical offices.

wakes
HN May 1991 alternate term added
ALT wake

wall painting
USE **mural painting**

wall plates (structural element components)
HN May 1991 descriptor changed, was **wall plates**
May 1991 alternate term changed, was **wall plate**
ALT **wall plate (structural element component)**

walling wax
USE **bordering wax**

walls, flue
USE **hot walls**

walls, hot
USE **hot walls**

walnut oil
HN October 1990 moved
BT **vegetable oil**

Wamatengo
USE **Matengo**

Wanka
USE **Huari**

wardrobes (case furniture)
HN May 1991 descriptor changed, was **wardrobes**
May 1991 alternate term changed, was **wardrobe**
ALT **wardrobe (case furniture)**

wards
USE **baileys**
hospital wards

ware, marbled
USE **marbled ware**

warehouses
HN February 1991 related term added
May 1990 scope note added
SN Structures designed or used for the storage of commodities or merchandise.
RT **distribution centers**

warfare
USE **wars**

warfare, guerrilla
USE **guerrilla warfare**

Warouwen
USE **Warrau**

Warrau
HN December 1990 lead-in terms added
UF Guarao
Warouwen

Warren trusses
HN March 1991 moved
March 1991 scope note changed
BT *<trusses by construction>*
SN Trusses with parallel chords between which the braces and ties are set at the same angle so as to form a series of isoceles triangles, the diagonals of which are alternately placed either in tension or compression. (RS)

wars
HN January 1991 lead-in term added
January 1991 scope note added
January 1991 alternate term added
November 1990 moved
January 1990 descriptor changed, was **war**
BT **armed conflicts**

ALT war
SN Open and declared hostile armed conflict between nations or parties within a nation.

UF warfare

wars, atomic
USE **nuclear wars**

wars, guerrilla
USE **guerrilla warfare**

wars, nuclear
USE **nuclear wars**

wash (technique)
USE **wash technique**

wash technique
HN June 1990 added
BT *<painting techniques by application method>* KT.220
SN The application of a broad thin film of highly diluted pigment.
UF technique, wash
wash (technique)

wash, flat
USE **flat wash**

washerwomen
USE **laundresses**

washes, car
USE **car washes**

washing soda
USE **sodium carbonate**

waste disposal
HN April 1991 moved
April 1991 scope note added
BT **waste management**
SN Discarding or throwing away unneeded or excess material including equipment, products, or materials in any form including oils, chemicals, gases, or liquids. (ERIC12)

waste handling
USE **waste management**

waste management
HN April 1991 added
BT **environmental protection**
SN Collecting, processing, recycling, and disposing of discarded or excess equipment, products, or material in any form, including solids, oils, chemicals, liquids, and gases.
UF handling, waste
management, waste
waste handling

waste stacks
HN June 1991 scope note changed
SN Vertical stacks that discharge waste from units other than toilets or urinals, such as sinks or bathtubs.

water-base paint
HN July 1990 added
BT *<paint by composition or origin>*
    MT.2510
UF paint, water-base

<water by form>
HN October 1990 guide term changed,
    was *<water by state>* MT.323

water chains
HN July 1991 added
BT water features
ALT water chain
SN Use for a series of intertwined or
    chained pools channeling falling
    water down stepped inclines; often
    elaborately sculpted, especially as
    found in Italian, 16th-century for-
    mal gardens.
UF cascades, chain
    cascades, cordonata
    catane d'acqua
    chain cascades
    chains, water
    cordonata cascades
    cordonate
RT formal gardens

water features
HN May 1990 added
BT *<landscaped-site elements>* RM.449
ALT water feature
SN Designates passive reflective or dy-
    namic elements in the cultural land-
    scape that incorporate water as the
    primary design feature; for natu-
    rally occurring areas of water use the
    terms under **bodies of water.**
UF features, water

water fun parks
USE **waterparks**

water-glass painting
USE **mineral painting**

water mains
HN August 1990 scope note added
SN Designates the primary supply pipes
    in a system providing water for pub-
    lic or community use. (DAC)

water pattern
USE **guilloche**

water quality management
HN April 1991 related term added
RT sewage treatment

water ramps
USE **water stairs (landscaped-site ele-
    ments)**

water resources
HN February 1991 added
BT natural resources
SN Natural sources of water, such as
    lakes, rivers, and ground water,
    available for use.

UF resources, water
    supply, water
    water supply

water slides
HN July 1991 related term added
    September 1990 scope note added
SN Descending troughs partially filled
    with constantly moving water
    through which people may ride or
    slide, usually down to a pool of water
    at the end.
RT waterparks

water staircases
USE **water stairs (landscaped-site ele-
    ments)**

water stairs (embarkation elements)
HN August 1991 descriptor changed, was
    water stairs
    August 1991 lead-in term changed,
    was stairs, water
    August 1991 alternate term changed,
    was water stair
ALT **water stair (embarkation element)**
UF stairs, water (embarkation elements)

water stairs (landscaped-site elements)
HN August 1991 added
BT water features
ALT **water stair (landscaped-site ele-
    ment)**
SN Use for landscape features that have
    water cascading or spilling down a
    stepped incline, usually in con-
    trolled channels; found in Islamic
    and 16th-century and later Italian
    formal gardens.
UF cascades, step
    ramps, water
    staircases, water
    stairs, water (landscaped-site ele-
    ments)
    stairways, water
    step cascades
    water ramps
    water staircases
    water stairways
RT *<stairs by form>*

water stairways
USE **water stairs (landscaped-site ele-
    ments)**

water supply
USE **water resources**

water tables
HN May 1991 moved
    May 1991 scope note changed
BT courses
SN Use for courses of stone projecting
    beyond the face of a wall to guide
    water away from the face of the wall.
    (RS)

watercolor paper, Arches
USE **Arches paper**

watercolor, transparent
USE **aquarelle**

waterleaf
HN July 1990 added
BT *<paper by composition or origin>*
    MT.1983
SN Paper without sizing. (COMPRI)
UF paper, waterleaf
    waterleaf paper

waterleaf paper
USE **waterleaf**

waterless toilets
USE **chemical toilets**

waterparks
HN July 1991 added
BT theme parks
ALT waterpark
SN Aquatic recreation facilities with at-
    tractions based on fast-moving, rather
    than static, water.
UF fun parks, water
    parks, water fun
    water fun parks
RT water slides

<wax by composition or origin>
HN December 1990 added
BT wax

<wax by form or function>
HN December 1990 added
BT wax

wax engraving
USE **cerography**

wax paint
USE **encaustic paint**

wax paper
USE **waxed paper**

wax tablets
HN May 1991 added
BT tablets
ALT wax tablet
SN Tablets made for writing, usually of
    wood or bone, covered with wax
    which was written on with a stylus;
    used especially in ancient Rome and
    during the Middle Ages.
UF tablets, wax
RT paleography

wax, bordering
USE **bordering wax**

wax, walling
USE **bordering wax**

waxed paper
HN January 1991 added
BT *<paper by form>* MT.1903
SN Paper treated with a coating of wax.
UF paper, wax
    paper, waxed
    wax paper

WC compartments
USE **toilet compartments**

weather maps
HN March 1991 lead-in terms added
UF maps, meteorological
    meteorological maps

wedding invitations
HN May 1991 descriptor split, use wedding (ALT of weddings) + invitations

weddings
HN May 1991 alternate term added
ALT wedding

welded wire fabric
HN April 1991 added
BT building materials
SN Designates heavy metal wire welded together in a grid pattern and used as reinforcing in concrete slabs.
UF fabric reinforcement, wire
    fabric, welded wire
    mesh reinforcement
    mesh, welded wire
    reinforcement, mesh
    reinforcement, wire fabric
    welded wire mesh
    wire fabric reinforcement
    wire fabric, welded
    wire mesh, welded

welded wire mesh
USE welded wire fabric

welding, heliarc
USE shielded metal arc welding

Wenatchi
HN December 1990 lead-in term added
UF Pisquow

<West Asian>
HN June 1991 added
BT Asian

Western Arctic Inuit
HN December 1990 lead-in term added
UF Mackenzie Eskimo

Western Caroline
USE Palau

western framing
USE platform frames

wet-into-wet technique
USE mixed technique

Whatman paper
USE wove paper

wheel tracery
HN May 1991 deleted
BT bar tracery

wheel-engraving
HN October 1990 moved
BT engraving (incising)

wheel-throwing
USE throwing (pottery technique)

Whipple trusses
HN March 1991 moved
    March 1991 scope note changed, DAC added as source
BT Pratt trusses

white line engraving
HN October 1991 moved
    October 1991 scope note changed
    July 1990 lead-in term added
    July 1990 descriptor changed, was **white line process**
BT *<relief printing processes>*
SN Use for relief printing processes in which the nonprinting engraved lines form a white image on a black background. Most often used in reference to wood engraving and the dotted manner. (MAYER)
UF white line process

white line process
USE white line engraving

white, enamel
USE blanc fixe

white, flying
USE fei po

whitewash
HN August 1991 moved
BT distemper paint

whiting
HN November 1990 moved
    November 1990 scope note changed
    November 1990 lead-in term added
BT chalk
SN Chalk that has been ground and washed for use in paints, inks, and putty. (MH12)
UF English white

whole plate
HN February 1991 lead-in term added
UF full plate

wica
USE witchcraft

wind braces
HN November 1990 moved
BT knee braces

wind loads
HN January 1991 alternate term added
ALT wind load

wind power plants
HN February 1991 related term added
RT wind turbines

wind turbine systems
USE wind turbines

wind turbines
HN February 1991 added
BT turbines
ALT wind turbine
SN Use for turbines, typically with three or fewer blades, powered by the wind.

UF systems, wind turbine
    turbine systems, wind
    turbines, wind
    wind turbine systems
RT wind power plants

windbreaks
HN August 1990 scope note added
SN Fences, walls, or dense plantings of trees provided, usually in open areas, as protection against wind.

window band
USE strip windows

windows, bull's eye
USE oculi

windows, dormer
USE dormers

windows, eyebrow
USE eyebrow dormers

windows, hospital
USE hopper windows

windows, judas
USE peepholes

windows, ribbon
USE strip windows

windows, Serlian
USE Palladian windows

windows, sliding sash
USE sliding windows

windows, thermal
USE Diocletian windows

windstorms
HN May 1991 alternate term added
ALT windstorm

wine making
HN January 1991 added
BT *<food and beverage making processes and techniques>*
UF enology

wings (furniture components)
HN March 1991 lead-in term changed, was **lugs**
UF lugs (furniture components)

wings, domestic
USE apartments

wings, private
USE apartments

wings, residential
USE apartments

wire fabric reinforcement
USE welded wire fabric

wire fabric, welded
USE welded wire fabric

wire mesh, welded
USE welded wire fabric

wiredrawing dies
USE **drawplates**

Wishram
HN   December 1990 lead-in term added
UF   Tlakluit

witchcraft
HN   April 1991 added
BT   **occult sciences**
SN   Study and exercise of supernatural powers by means of magic, psychic powers, and communication with good or evil spirits.
UF   wica

withdrawing chambers
USE   **drawing rooms**

withdrawing rooms
USE   **drawing rooms**

women
HN   January 1991 related term added
        September 1990 lead-in terms added
UF   females, human
        human females
RT   **female**

women's shelters
USE   **crisis shelters**

women's shelters, battered
USE   **crisis shelters**

women's studies
HN   July 1991 added
BT   **social sciences**
SN   Subject area encompassing the history and contemporary social, political, and cultural situation of women. (ERIC12)
UF   studies, women's

wood bricks
USE   **nailing blocks**

wood-carvers
HN   May 1991 scope note added
SN   People who carve objects or ornament in wood; for those who make woodcut blocks or prints from them, use **woodcutters**.

wood cellulose fiber
USE   **excelsior**

wood engravers
HN   May 1991 scope note added
SN   People who engage in making wood engravings.

wood engraving
HN   October 1991 moved
        October 1991 scope note changed
BT   <*relief printing processes*>
SN   A relief process in which the design is cut into and printed from the grain end of a wood block; distinct from **woodcut**, which is a relief process using the plank side of a wood block.

wood fiber
USE   **excelsior**

wood inlay
USE   **marquetry**

wood-pulp
USE   **wood pulp**

wood pulp
HN   July 1990 descriptor changed, was wood-pulp
        July 1990 lead-in term changed, was wood pulp
UF   wood-pulp

wood pulp paper
HN   July 1990 lead-in terms added
UF   paper, pulp
        pulp paper

wood pulp, chemical
USE   **chemical pulp**

wood pulp, mechanical
USE   **mechanical wood pulp**

wood wool
USE   **excelsior**

wood, cocos
USE   **granadilla**

wood, ground
USE   **mechanical wood pulp**

wood, plastic
USE   **Plastic Wood (TM)**

woodcut
HN   November 1991 lead-in term **woodcut process** deleted
        October 1991 lead-in term **printing, woodcut** deleted
        October 1991 moved
        October 1991 scope note changed
        October 1990 lead-in term **printing, wood-block** deleted
        October 1990 lead-in term changed, was **woodcut printing**
        October 1990 descriptor changed, was **wood-block printing**
BT   <*relief printing processes*>
SN   A relief process in which the design is cut into and printed from the plank side of a wood block; distinct from **wood engraving**, which is a relief process using the grain end of a wood block.
UF   woodcutting

woodcutters
HN   May 1991 scope note changed
SN   Use for people who make woodcut blocks or the prints from them; for those who cut trees for lumber, use **loggers**; for those who carve objects or ornament in wood, use **woodcarvers**.

woodcutters (loggers)
USE   **loggers**

woodcutting
USE   **woodcut**

wool, wood
USE   **excelsior**

word art
USE   **visual poetry**

work prints
HN   January 1991 added
BT   **photographic prints**
ALT   **work print**
SN   Use for photographic prints made for examination and reference, such as those done before an edition is produced.
UF   prints, work

work safety
USE   **occupational safety**

work, boasted
USE   **boasted work**

work, drill
USE   **drillwork**

work, stencil
USE   **stenciling**

workers, transient
USE   **migrant workers**

workers, unskilled
USE   **laborers**

working class
HN   May 1991 moved
        September 1990 scope note added
BT   **social classes**
SN   Class of persons employed for wages, usually at manual labor. (W)

works, gunpowder
USE   **powder mills**

works, intermedia
USE   **intermedia**

workshops (organizations)
HN   September 1990 scope note changed
        September 1990 descriptor changed, was **workshops**
        September 1990 alternate term changed, was **workshop**
ALT   **workshop (organization)**
SN   Use for groups of artists or craftsmen collaborating to produce works, often under a master's name. In the 19th and 20th centuries (when a master artist takes on pupils rather than apprentices), use **studios (organizations)**.

workshops (seminars)
HN   May 1991 alternate term added
ALT   **workshop (seminar)**

workshops (work spaces)
HN   August 1990 scope note changed
SN   Use for rooms set aside for specific work to be done, especially crafts or light machine work.

world trade centers
HN July 1990 added
BT commercial buildings
ALT world trade center
SN Use for mixed-use buildings or groups of buildings providing facilities for public and private organizations involved in international trade.
UF centers, world trade
trade centers, world

world's fairs
HN May 1991 alternate term added
ALT world's fair

worldwide approach
USE globalism

wove paper
HN May 1991 scope note changed
May 1991 related term added
July 1990 lead-in terms added
SN Paper produced with a woven or even appearance in transmitted light; distinguished from laid paper, which shows a pattern of thick and thin lines.
UF paper, Whatman
Whatman paper
RT laid paper

writing, picture
USE pattern poetry

X factor
USE barrier-free design

Xianfeng
HN December 1990 lead-in term changed, was Hsien-feng
UF Hsien-fêng

Xicaque
USE Jicaque

Xolalpan
HN December 1990 lead-in term changed, was Teotihuacan IIIa
UF Teotihuacán IIIa

Xuande
HN December 1990 lead-in term changed, was Hsuan-te
UF Hsüan-tê

Xuantong
HN December 1990 lead-in term changed, was Hsuan-t'ung
UF Hsüan-t'ung

yacht clubs
HN November 1991 moved
BT boat clubs

Yahgan
HN December 1990 lead-in term changed, was Yamana
UF Yámana

Yámana
USE Yahgan

yellow oxide
USE Mars yellow

yellow, canary
USE light greenish yellow

yellow, citron
USE strong greenish yellow

yeshivas
HN August 1991 scope note changed
May 1991 moved
May 1991 alternate term added
BT <schools by subject> RK.801
ALT yeshiva
SN Use either for Hebrew-English day schools providing both secular and religious instruction, usually operated under Orthodox Jewish auspices, or for schools providing training in Talmudic law and which may ordain rabbis. For educational facilities specifically devoted to the training of rabbis, use rabbinical seminaries. For day schools operated under Reform or Conservative Jewish auspices, use Hebrew schools.

Yin
USE Shang

young people
USE youth

young persons
USE youth

youth
HN September 1990 lead-in terms added
UF young people
young persons

Yuchi
HN December 1990 lead-in term added
UF Uchi

Zangid
USE Zengid

Zaramo
HN June 1990 lead-in term added
UF Dzalamo

Zengid
HN January 1991 lead-in term added
UF Zangid

Zenitist
HN May 1991 added
BT <modern Yugoslav styles and movements>
ALT Zenitism

Zhengzhou
HN November 1991 lead-in term changed, was Cheng chou
January 1991 lead-in term changed, was Cheng chow
UF Chêng chou
Chengchow

Zhou
HN January 1991 lead-in term added
UF Chou

zigzags
HN April 1991 lead-in terms added
UF bands, chevroned
chevroned bands

zincography
HN October 1991 moved
April 1991 scope note changed
BT <printing processes>
SN May be used generally for processes of preparing a printing surface on a zinc plate, either for lithography or etched for letterpress printing. When possible, use two expressions: the specific process term, such as lithography, and zinc plus printing plates.

zip code maps
HN March 1991 moved
BT <maps by subject> VW.178

zones, heritage
USE historic districts

zoning, incentive
USE incentive zoning

Zonist
HN April 1991 moved
BT <modern Polish fine arts styles and movements> FL.3409

zoological illustration
HN May 1991 descriptor split, use zoological (ALT of zoology) + illustration

zoological illustrations
HN May 1991 descriptor split, use zoological (ALT of zoology) + illustrations

zoology
HN February 1991 alternate term added
ALT zoological

Zotzil
USE Tzotzil

Zutuhil
USE Tzutujil

Changed Terms

This section provides an alphabetical list of the original terms that were changed as well as the new terms that replaced them. It is subdivided under descriptors, guide terms and lead-in terms.

The change refers to either a change in the form of the original term or the replacement of the old term by a new one.

Descriptors

ORIGINAL TERM	CHANGED TERM
abaci	abaci (capital components)
Abbasid (dynasty)	Abbasid
acid-biting	biting
aerial perspective	atmospheric perspective
aged	elderly
amber	amber (fossil resin)
annuals	annuals (publications)
Archaic	Archaic (Greek)
Auto-destructive	Destructive Art
axes	axes (tools)
backs	backs (furniture components)
Bamana	Bambara
banquettes	banquettes (benches)
baptism	baptisms
bars	bars (commercial buildings)
bays	bays (bodies of water)
bellcotes	bell cotes
berths	berths (waterfront spaces)
bidets	bidets (plumbing fixtures)
birth	births
bits	bits (tool components)
bleeding	bleeding (seeping)
bolts	bolts (fasteners)
braces	braces (supporting elements)
brackets	brackets (structural elements)
brass	brass (alloy)
briefs	briefs (legal documents)
burnishing	burnishing (polishing)
cabinets	cabinets (case furniture)
canephores	canephorae
canterburies	canterburies (storage furniture)
cantilevered footings	cantilever footings
cantons	cantons (administrative bodies)
Carpenter's Gothic	Carpenter Gothic
caulicoles	cauliculi
channel beams	channels (rolled sections)
channels	channels (water body components)
chiffoniers	chiffoniers (chests of drawers)
circulation	circulation (collections management)
circumcision	circumcisions
circuses	circuses (performances)
civil war	civil wars
clove oil	oil of cloves

ORIGINAL TERM	CHANGED TERM
coiffeuses	coiffeuses (tables)
communion	communions
compensation	compensation (economic concept)
conductors	conductors (materials)
conductors (music)	conductors (musicians)
conductors (piping)	downspouts
confirmation	confirmations
consecration	consecrations
coping	copings
Coptic	Coptic (Christian sect)
cork	cork (bark)
coronas	coronas (cornice components)
costumers	costumers (furniture)
couching	couching (embroidery)
counter flashing	counterflashing
crescents	crescents (shapes)
crow-stepped gables	corbie gables
crowsteps	corbiesteps
curing (leather)	curing
curtain walls	curtain walls (nonbearing walls)
cutch-grass	couch grass
cylinders	cylinders (solids)
davenports	davenports (sofas)
death	deaths
deconsecration	deconsecrations
dedications	dedications (documents)
dikka	dikkas
directors	directors (administrators)
dispensaries	dispensaries (health facilities)
door jambs	doorjambs
dormitories	dormitories (buildings)
double-printing	double printing
draftsmen	draftsmen (artists)
drawing	drawing (image making)
dressers	dressers (cupboards)
duchesses	duchesses (chaise longues)
dumbwaiters	dumbwaiters (conveying systems)
Dutch arches	French arches
Dông-Son	Dông-Son (Indonesian)
Early Andra	Early Andhra
Early Dynastic	Early Dynastic (Mesopotamian)
earthworks	earthworks (engineering works)
eaves fascias	fascia boards

ORIGINAL TERM	CHANGED TERM
educational societies	educational associations
elevations	elevations (drawings)
emblems	emblems (symbols)
engraving (printmaking)	engraving (printing process)
engraving (surface decorating)	engraving (incising)
episcaenia	espiscenia
escarpments	scraps
etching (printmaking)	etching (printing process)
etching (surface decoration)	etching (corroding)
ethics	ethics (concept)
exedrae	exedrae (interior spaces)
false windows	blind windows
files	files (documents)
film	film (material)
fire towers	fire towers (watchtowers)
firing	firing (managing)
flashing	flashing (building components)
flats	flats (apartments)
fleches	flèches
flowing tracery	curvilinear tracery
forms	forms (documents)
foundations	foundations (structural elements)
founders	founders (originators)
frieze band windows	frieze-band windows
functions	functions (activities)
gabled dormers	gable dormers
galleries	galleries (rooms)
Garwhal	Garhwal
Geokysur	Geoksyur
glazing	glazing (coating)
glycerine process	glycerin process
gorges	gorges (landforms)
grinders	grinders (tools)
groins	groins (vault components)
guerilla warfare	guerrilla warfare
gutters (storm water systems)	gutters (building drainage components)
headers	headers (masonry units)
hinge stiles	hanging stiles
hoods (roofs)	hoods (enclosing structures)
hooks (hardware)	hooks
hotels	hotels (public accommodations)
hôtels	hôtels (town houses)
initials	initials (abbreviations)

ORIGINAL TERM	CHANGED TERM
jetties	jetties (erosion protection works)
Jin	Jin (Golden Tartars)
keys	keys (hardware)
label moldings	labels (moldings)
labels	labels (documentary artifacts)
lac	lac (resin)
lake pigment	lakes (pigments)
lakes	lakes (bodies of water)
lally columns	Lally columns (TM)
lamella structures	lamella roofs
landings	landings (stair components)
lanes	lanes (roads)
laurel	laurel (wood)
leaves	leaves (plant materials)
Lettrism	Lettrist
liberal arts	liberal arts (cross-disciplinary studies)
libraries	libraries (buildings)
lich-gates	lich gates
lifting	lifting (transporting)
lightwells	light wells
linocut	linoleum-block printing
literature	literature (humanities)
loadbearing walls	bearing walls
louvers	louvers (built works components)
maize oil	corn oil
markets	markets (buildings)
maroger medium	Maroger medium
mass	mass (physical sciences concept)
matting	matting (supporting)
meanders	meanders (water body components)
mechanical drawings	mechanical drawings (tool-aided drawings)
mechanically operated doors	automatic doors
median	median (statistics)
medians	median strips
Memeh	Mehmeh
mental illness	mental disorders
meshrebeeyeh	meshrebeeyehs
mica	mica (mineral)
monitors	monitors (data processing equipment)
mounts	mounts (hardware)
Muscovite	Muscovite (style)
mutes	mutes (physically handicapped)

ORIGINAL TERM	CHANGED TERM
nature preserves	nature reserves
necking	neckings
Neo-Grec	Néo-Grec
nuclear war	nuclear wars
oblique arches	skew arches
observation car elevators	observation elevators
olive	olive (hardwood)
openings	openings (architectural elements)
Pacific	Oceanic
painting	painting (image making)
Paleo-Indian	Paleo-Indian (Pre-Columbian North American)
panels	panels (surface components)
parishes	parishes (religious districts)
parodoses	parodoi
paste	paste (adhesive)
pastels	pastels (works)
pastels (crayons)	pastels (chalk)
pavilions	pavilions (garden structures)
Pennsylvania Dutch	Pennsylvania German
pensions	pensions (compensation)
photoelectric detectors	photoelectric smoke detectors
piers	piers (supporting elements)
pietra dure	pietre dure
pits	pits (earthworks)
pivoting windows	pivoted windows
plain-sawed lumber	plain sawed lumber
planes	planes (tools)
plans	plans (drawings)
plastic wood	Plastic Wood (TM)
pointing	pointing (filling)
pointing (sculpture)	pointing (transferring technique)
Polish	Polish (European region)
presentation drawings	presentation drawings (proposals)
printers	printers (output devices)
profiles	profiles (orthographic drawings)
pumice	pumice (lava)
punchwork	punchwork (metalwork)
pyramids	pyramids (tombs)
quotations	quotations (texts)
racks	racks (support furniture)
Rashtrakuta	Rashtrakutan
red ocher	red ocher (pigment)

ORIGINAL TERM	CHANGED TERM
red polished ware	red-polished ware (Cypriote)
red-polished ware	red-polished ware (Egyptian)
registering	registration (transferring technique)
registrars	registrars (museology)
restoration	restoration (process)
revolution	revolutions
ridges	ridges (roof components)
risers	risers (step components)
rolling-up	rolling up
rotundas	rotundas (interior spaces)
sale catalogs	sales catalogs
Santa Maria	Santa Maria (period)
scarifiers	scarifiers (masonry and plastering tools)
schedules	schedules (timetables)
schedules (contract documents)	schedules (architectural records)
scrapers	scrapers (finishing tools)
scrolls	scrolls (documents)
secretaries	secretaries (furniture)
serigraphy	screen printing
serpentine	serpentine (shape)
Settchuyo	Setchuyo
sewers	sewers (drainage structures)
shores	shores (landforms)
silica	silica (mineral)
size	size (geometric concept)
size (materials)	size (material)
skirt roofs	skirt-roofs
slabs	slabs (structural elements)
slant elevators	inclined elevators
slides	slides (photographs)
solids	solids (materials)
Solutrian	Solutrean
spread foundations	spread footings
squares	squares (open spaces)
squaring	squaring (forming)
Srivijaya	Srivijaya (Javanese)
stands	stands (support furniture)
stiles	stiles (surface components)
storax	styrax
storm water systems	stormwater systems
stretchers	stretchers (furniture components)
strikes	strikes (components)
structures	structures (single built works)

ORIGINAL TERM	CHANGED TERM
studios	studios (organizations)
studs	studs (structural components)
suites	suites (rooms)
sumie	sumi-e
tables	tables (support furniture)
talc	talc (mineral)
tallboys	tallboys (furniture)
tectonics	tectonics (architectural theory)
teenagers	adolescents
three-deckers	three-deckers (houses)
three-quarter turn stairs	three-quarter-turn stairs
toning	toning (painting)
torchères	torchères (stands)
towers	towers (single built works)
trestles	trestles (furniture components)
triangles	triangles (polygons)
triclinia	triclinia (rooms)
tripods	tripods (camera accessories)
turrets	turrets (towers)
Tuscarora	Tuscarora (Southeastern Native American)
upper classes	upper class
urban geography	human geography
Vaisali (Nepalese)	Vaisali
valleys	valleys (landforms)
value	value (economic concept)
vaults	vaults (structural elements)
view albums	viewbooks
wall plates	wall plates (structural element components)
war	wars
wardrobes	wardrobes (case furniture)
water stairs	water stairs (embarkation elements)
waterless toilets	chemical toilets
white line process	white line engraving
wood-block printing	woodcut
wood-pulp	wood pulp
workshops	workshops (organizations)
'Izz-ad-Din Qilich Arslan III	Izz-al-Din Qilich Arslan III

Guide Terms

ORIGINAL TERM	CHANGED TERM
\<environmental sciences concepts\>	\<environmental concepts\>
\<building plan attributes: number of stories\>	\<building elevation attributes\>
\<modern American styles and movements\>	\<modern American styles and periods\>
\<social groups\>	social groups
\<people in the social sciences\>	social scientists
\<protective processes\>	\<protective processes and techniques\>
\<inorganic materials\>	inorganic materials
\<water by state\>	\<water by form\>
\<stands and stalls\>	stands (mercantile structures)
\<lighting by light source\>	\<lighting by method of illumination\>
\<spread foundation components\>	\<spread footing components\>
\<spread foundations and spread foundation components\>	\<spread footings and spread footing components\>
\<roof beams\>	\<horizontal roof frame components\>
\<roof posts\>	\<vertical roof frame components\>

Lead-in Terms

ORIGINAL TERM	CHANGED TERM
Abies Fraseri	Abies fraseri
acra red	Acra red (TM)
adolescents	teenagers
andaman marblewood	Andaman marblewood
Andra, Early	Andhra, Early
angle stairs	angled stairs
anime	animé
anti-freeze solutions	antifreeze solutions
atmospheric perspective	aerial perspective
automatic doors	mechanically operated doors
bearing walls	loadbearing walls
beaverboard	Beaverboard (TM)
blind windows	false windows
block-printing, linoleum	printing, linoleum-block
blue, Thalo	blue, Thalo (TM)
books, receipt	books, receipt (cookbooks)
bright mauve	bright violet
bull's-eye windows	bull's eye windows
bunas	Buna S
busducts	bus ducts
Californian, Middle period	Californian Middle period
canary	canary yellow
cantoriae	cantorias

ORIGINAL TERM	CHANGED TERM
Carancahua Indians	Carancahua
catalogs, sale	catalogs, sales
Catoquina Indians	Catoquina
cellosolve	Cellosolve (TM)
Chêng chou	Chêng chou
Cheng chow	Chengchow
China-clay	China clay
cocus wood	cocuswood
coffering (ceiling components)	coffering
conges	congés
corbiestepped gables	corbiestep gables
corbiesteps	crowsteps
corn oil	maize oil
cross-springers	cross springers
cul-de-fours	cul de fours
curvilinear tracery	flowing tracery
dormers, gabled	dormers, gable
drawings, mechanical	drawings, mechanical (tool-aided drawings)
drawings, presentation	drawings, presentation (proposals)
edge planes, piano maker's	edge planes, pianomaker's
email en bosse ronde	émail en ronde bosse
fascia boards	eaves fascias
ferrite	Ferrite (TM)
ferrox	Ferrox (TM)
French arches	Dutch arches
gables, corbiestepped	gables, corbiestep
gables, crow-stepped	gables, crowstepped
gables, step	gables, stepped
gate posts	gateposts
grayish lilac	gray lilac
guglias (finials)	guglias
guglias (pinnacles)	guglias
hanging stiles	hinge stiles
hinge posts	hinging posts
horses (stair components)	roughstrings
Hsien-fêng	Hsien-fêng
Hsuan-t'ung	Hsüan-t'ung
Hsuan-te	Hsüan-tê
inclined elevators	slant elevators
instruction	instructing
Judas holes	judas-holes
K'ana-chu	K'ang-chu

ORIGINAL TERM	CHANGED TERM
Kuang-hsu	Kuang-hsü
lamella roofs	lamella structures
lemon	lemon (color)
lilac, grayish	lilac, gray
linoleum cut	linocutting
lugs	lugs (furniture components)
lunense macchiato	Luniense marble
marble, Synnadicum	marble, Synadicum
mauve, bright	violet, bright
Maxia jia	Maxiajia
mushrebiyeh	mushrebiyehs
Na-ga	Nan-ga
nature reserves	nature preserves
Nürnburg violet	Nuernberg violet
observation elevators	observation car elevators
Oceanic	Oceanian
oil of cloves	clove oil
oil of spike lavender	oil of spike
Pennsylvania German	Pennsylvania Dutch
pent roofs (skirt roofs)	pent roofs
penthouse roofs (shed roofs)	penthouse roofs
penthouse roofs (skirt roofs)	penthouse roofs
phthalocyaninblau	Phthalocyaninblau
piano maker's edge planes	pianomaker's edge planes
Pit River Indians	Pit River
planes, piano maker's edge	planes, pianomaker's edge
printing, wood-block	printing, wood block
receipt books	receipt books (cookbooks)
red, acra	red, Acra (TM)
registration	registration (information handling)
roof trees	rooftrees
roofs, pent (skirt roofs)	roofs, pent
roofs, penthouse (shed roofs)	roofs, penthouse
roofs, penthouse (skirt roofs)	roofs, penthouse
rose violet	rose lilac
rough strings	roughstrings
Salomonicas	salomónicas
sash-bars	sash bars
Satvahana	Satavahana
serliana	Serliana
sheetrock	Sheetrock (TM)
skew arches	oblique arches

ORIGINAL TERM	CHANGED TERM
societies, educational	associations, educational
sovereigns	sovereigns (rulers)
spike lavender, oil of	spike, oil of
stairs, angle	stairs, angled
stairs, three-quarter turn	stairs, three-quarter-turn
stairs, water	stairs, water (embarkation elements)
step gables	stepped gables
switch gear, electric	switchgear, electric
synasol	Synasol (TM)
Synnadicum marble	Synadicum marble
systems, storm water	systems, stormwater
tables (panels)	tables (surface components)
Tena	Ten'a
Teotihuacan II	Teotihuacán II
Teotihuacan IIIa	Teotihuacán IIIa
Teotihuacan IV	Teotihuaán IV
Thalo blue	Thalo blue (TM)
thiokol	Thiokol (TM)
three pinned arches	three-pinned arches
Too-an-hooch Indians	Too-an-hooch
Transoxiana	Transoxianan
varnolene	Varnolene (TM)
violet, Nürnburg	violet, Nuernberg
violet, rose	lilac, rose
warfare, guerilla	warfare, guerrilla
water-pattern	water pattern
windows, bull's-eye	windows, bull's eye
windows, Judas	windows, judas
wood pulp	wood-pulp
wood, cocus	wood, cocos
woodcut printing	woodcutting
Yamana	Yámana
Zatzil	Zotzil
Zutujil	Zutuhil

Summary of Term Changes

This section is intended to give an overview of the changes in this supplement and, therefore, does not provide detailed information. The *Alphabetical Listing of Term Changes* gives the details of each change and its location in the 1990 edition.

The *Summary of Term Changes* section contains descriptors, guide terms, and lead-in terms grouped according to the categories of change. These categories are: New Terms, Deleted Terms, Moved Terms, and Split Terms. They are further subdivided by the type of term: descriptors, guide terms, and lead-in terms. The terms are arranged alphabetically under their respective headings.

Descriptors, guide terms, and lead-in terms that have a change to the form of the term or have been replaced by another term are found in the *Changed Terms* section.

NEW TERMS

Descriptors

à la poupée
abrash
absorbency
accent lighting
Acolapissa
acrylic painting
addiction
addicts
adolescence
adulthood
Advent
aeronautical ground lights
alcoholics
alcoholism
aldanite
allées
alternative publications
alternative spaces
alum
aluminum paper
alumni centers
amalgams
ambassadors
amending
ammonium chloride
Amstel
animal glue
antebellum
antiphonaries
approach lights
appropriation (critical concept)
arboriculture
arboriculturists
arcanists
Arches paper
architectural terracotta
armed conflicts
art for art's sake
art glass
art photography
art pottery
art unions
artists' colors
artists' statements
associationism
audiences
aviation
bachelors (academics)
backlighting
bake ovens
baked enamel

barbers
base lighting
bathers
batiste
battles
beggars
behavior disorders
behavioral sciences
Belgian linen
blanket insulation
bleeding (printing technique)
blind embossing
blind stamping
bloom
boardwalks
boasted work
border inspection stations
bordering wax
bosses
Botticino marble
boundary lights
bousillage
brackets (finish hardware)
British Colonial
Broad Manner
bronze paint
bronze powder
brothers
building directories
burglar alarms
burglary
cadavres exquis
cameo glass
candle screens
captions
car washes
Carborundum (TM)
card games
CD-ROMs
cellae
censors
centennials
centering
channel lights
chemical pulp
Chicago School
childhood
Chilkat
China paper
chops
cider mills
coelanaglyphic relief

cogeneration plants
cohousing (TM)
cold-pressed paper
color lithography
columnar screens
community design centers
community schools
conservation board
conservation scientists
construction paper
convicts
copper engraving
copy prints
copyediting
copyeditors
Cor-Ten steel (TM)
corrugated board
corrugated paper
costume
cotton fiber
countermarks
countermines
course lights
crayon manner
creeping bite
Creole
crepe
crevé
crisis shelters
crosslighting
decorative lighting
development
diffuse reflectance
diffuse reflection
disasters
distribution centers
diversifying
dotted manner
doweling
drillwork
drug abuse
drug addiction
drug addicts
dry rot
easel painting
Eccentric Abstraction
ECHO houses
Ecuadorian
educating
egg crate louvers
egg-oil tempera
electronic security systems

New Terms

emancipation
emigrants
encarnacione
encaustic paint
environmental psychology
equestrians
estofado
etch
etching ground
ethnic studies
exposure
exterior insulation and finish systems
faculty housing
fairy tales
fancy dress balls
farming
fast-track method
fei po
female
ferric chloride
fetishes
fiber optics
fiberglass
fibrous composites
fill light
filmographies
Fine Manner
flammability
flat wash
folium
Fome-Cor (TM)
food stands
Formist
foul biting
galleting
garbage
gasenshi
geosynthetics
geotextiles
glair
glassine
glitter
globalism
glycerin
gold ruby glass
golf course communities
granges (fraternal buildings)
graphite paper
grave goods
green design
greenways
habitat

half stereographs
hard ground
hard light
hatchments
health clubs
heaven
heiaus
heliotype
heliotypes
hell
herbals
hewing
hinging
historic landscapes
historic structure reports
holism
home offices
horse farms
hosho
hot walls
hot-pressed paper
housebarns
human ecology
ice skaters
ill
illness
illusion
imperfection
in register
incentive zoning
Inconel (TM)
incremental housing
industrial paint
infancy
infants
influencing
informing
infrared spectroscopy
initialing
inlets
inmates
installations (exhibitions)
intaglio
intermedia
invited competitions
irons (tools)
Israeli
istoria
jockeys
kakemono
Kasama
Kauma

ketubahs
key light
keys (documents)
landing direction indicators
later prints
laundresses
lazy lines
letterpress printing
lignin
limited competitions
linters
literature (writings)
lithographic ink
lithotine
lotteries
lovers
madrona
magi
mahallas
maisons de plaisance
male
man-made disasters
Mankato stone
marbled ware
martyrs
masa
masques
mechanical wood pulp
media rooms
melting
menologions
mental health
mental retardation
mentally ill
mentally retarded
metallic paint
metallic paper
Mexican American
mezzo rilievo
middle age
millstones
mineral painting
mixed technique
mobile homes
montage
Monterey Style
Moorish Revival
moriki
Mormonism
mounting board
mourners
mulberry paper

NEW TERMS

mural painting
nailing blocks
naive artists
Napoleon gray marble
narratives
natural disasters
Nature
Naugahyde (TM)
near-infrared spectroscopy
neon
New Deal
New Year cards
nogging
nogging pieces
novelists
nudes
obstruction lights
occupational safety
occupational therapists
occupational therapy
odors
officers
offset lithography
offsets
oil of cedar
oil of lemon
oil painting
old age
open biting
open competitions
optical fibers
ornamentists
ostraka
out of register
outline lighting
over life-size
overbiting
panel painting
papers
papyrology
parables
parabolic louvers
parade grounds
paraffin oil
parolees
parterres
pastel paper
pâte-sur-pâte
patients
pattern poetry
pedestrian facilities
pendants (companion pieces)

perfection
perforating
perrons
petitioning
pharmacists
pharmacologists
phosphoric acid
phosphorus
photographic postcards
photoluminescence
photosculpture
pipe clay
plastic cement
plastisol
plate marks
poor
porcelain enamel
portfolios (groups of works)
poster board
potash
poteaux sur solle construction
pounce
powder mills
pregnancy
press boxes
pressboard
preventing
primitive hut
printing ink
printing plates
Proconnesian marble
producers
promoting
prophets
prostitutes
prostitution
proverbs
punchwork (carving technique)
quality
radiant barriers
receipting
recycling
reflectance
reflecting pools
reflection
refuse
regalia
regions
relative humidity
relief etching
remarques
republics

resistance movements
retroussage
revising
Rhythmist
rilievo schiacciato
risk management
robotics
rock art
romances
rosin ground
royalty
rubber stamps
rubberized cloth
rubbing
rubbing ink
rubbish
runway lights
sacramentaries
sails
salt
Santa Fe Style
satellite home antennas
sequins
sets (architectural elements)
settlement houses
sewage treatment
sheets (papers)
shipwrecks
shower rooms
siblings
side lighting
signing
silver amalgam
silviculture
Simulationist
sisters
sites and services
sitters
Situationist
skaters
snakewood
socialists
soda fountains
sodium carbonate
sodium chloride
sofa art
soft ground
soldiers
special education
spectators
spectroscopy
spirit ground

NEW TERMS

spirit houses
spit biting
sponsors
staged photographs
starvation
steel engraving
stencil paper
stillingia oil
stopping out
stopping-out varnish
stratigraphy
student competitions
studio ceramics
stuff (pulp)
stunning
subcontinents
Subjective photography
substance abuse
sugar
sugar-lift
sun-refined oil
sustainable development
sweatshops
swimmers
tannin
tarlatan
taxiway lights
tempera painting
terminating
Territorial Style
theme
threshold lights
timesharing (real estate)
tinsel
top lighting
torinoko
Totolapan
tower houses
trading cards
training
training centers
transparent base
trimmings
ts'un
Turkish
typewriter paper
typewriters
typicons
underbiting
urban design
urban villages
Usonian houses

vacations
veterans
viewers
vinyl paint
Vinylite (TM)
violence
virgins
visual perception
visual poetry
vocational training
voters
voting
wash technique
waste management
water chains
water features
water resources
water stairs (landscaped-site
  elements)
water-base paint
waterleaf
waterparks
wax tablets
waxed paper
welded wire fabric
wind turbines
wine making
witchcraft
women's studies
work prints
world trade centers
Zenitist

Guide Terms

<aeronautical site elements>
<agricultural functions>
<architrave components>
<architraves and architrave
  components>
<bases: furniture components>
<behavior and mental disorders>
<biting techniques>
<business and related functions>
<business-related functions>
<carving and carving techniques>
<carving techniques>
<club complexes>
<conditions and effects: architecture>
<conditions and effects: photography>
<conditions and effects: printing and
  printmaking>
<conditions and effects: textiles>

<developmental concepts>
<education by subject>
<food and beverage making processes and
  techniques>
<grinding and milling equipment
  components>
<groups of people by activity>
<groups of people by state or condition>
<groups of people>
<health and related concepts>
<health-related concepts>
<hearth components>
<hearths and hearth components>
<ink by composition or origin>
<ink by function>
<ink by property>
<insulation by form>
<insulation by function>
<intaglio printing processes>
<leisure events>
<life stages>
<lighting techniques by direction>
<lighting techniques by distribution>
<lighting techniques>
<matrix preparation techniques>
<modern Dutch decorative arts styles and
  movements>
<modern Dutch pottery styles>
<modern North American periods>
<modern Polish decorative arts styles and
  movements>
<modern Polish styles and movements>
<modern Yugoslav styles and
  movements>
<planographic printing processes>
<plastics by function>
<political events>
<pottery glazing techniques>
<printing and printing processes and
  techniques>
<printing processes>
<printing techniques>
<relief printing processes>
<religious seasons>
<rooflike enclosing structures>
<security system components>
<security systems and security system
  components>
<technology-related functions>
<trusses by construction>
<wax by composition or origin>

NEW TERMS

<wax by form or function>
<West Asian>

Lead-in Terms

100% cotton rag board
à trois crayons (printmaking)
Abstraction, Eccentric
abuse of substances
abuse, drug
abuse, substance
acanthus leaf
accent light
accessibility
achievements, funereal
achromatic colors
acid precipitation
acid, orthophosphoric
acid, phosphoric
acid, tannic
acid-biting
Acryloid (TM)
addiction, drug
addiction, narcotic
addicts, dope
addicts, drug
addicts, narcotic
additive, antistatic
advancement
adventures, joint
aerodrome obstruction lights
agalmatolite
age, middle
age, old
aged
agents, business
Ahmad III
Ahmet III
Aja
alarms, burglar
albums, souvenir
alcohol dependency
alcohol-resin varnish
allover backing
allover mounting
alloys, mercury
altar cavities
alternative press publications
alto rilievo
alum, potash
amboyna
Ambuun
American, Mexican

ammoniac, sal
Amstel porcelain
Amul ware
Anachronism (Pittura Colta)
analysis, spectrum
Analytic Cubist
angle braces
angle sections
angle ties
animal pedigrees
annulated shafts
antennas, dish
antennas, satellite
antennas, satellite home
anthro-geography
anti semitism
anti-semitism
antiphonals
antistatic additive
apothecaries (people)
applied columns
approach, global
approach, worldwide
approach-light beacons
appropriated imagery
appropriated images
appropriationism
apron pieces
Aqua-Tec (TM)
aquatint, sugar
aquatint, sugar-lift
Arbutus menziesii
arcades, intersecting
arch bands
Arches watercolor paper
arches, basket
arches, basket handle
arches, blunt
arches, broken
arches, false
arches, fluing
arches, Palladian
arches, semi-circular stilted
arches, Serlian
arches, strainer
architects, garden
architectural fantasies
architectural psychology
architecture, bizarre
architecture, library
archive buildings
aromas

arrangers, flower
art materials
art trade
art, rock
art, sofa
art, word
artists' supplies
artists, naive
ash, pearl
ash, soda
asphalt prepared roofing
assembling (sculpture technique)
assistance
association of ideas
asylums (psychiatric hospitals)
atlases, fire insurance
atmospheric humidity
atomic wars
attorney, letters of
auto washes
Auto-destructive
automatic data processing
axonometrics
B-ES
babies
Babwendi
baby pink
babyhood
backing
backlight
bail handles
bakers' ovens
baking ovens
balls, fancy
balls, fancy dress
Bamana
banana oil
bandleaders
bands, arch
bands, chevroned
Bangombe
Bangongo
Banmana
Barba
barite
barns, cider
barriers, radiant
bars, sash
base light
base, transparent
basket arches
basket handle arches

162

NEW TERMS

baths, shower
battered women's shelters
batts
beacons, approach-light
beam and slab systems, one-way
beam-and-girder constructions
beam-and-slab floor constructions
beam-and-slab floors
beam-and-slab floors
beams, end-supported
beams, simply supported
Beaverboard (TM)
beehive ovens (bake ovens)
behavior, environment and
behavior-environment studies
beholders
beholders
bells, door
Betjek
bicycle-wheel roofs
bigotry
binder moldings
bistre
bistre brown
bistros
bite, creeping
bite, deep
biting in
biting, brush
biting, false
biting, foul
biting, open
biting, spit
bituminous felt
bizarre architecture
black-and-gold marble
black manner
blankets (insulation)
blast-furnace slag
bled-to-the edge
blind doors
blind intaglio
blind-stamping
blocked columns
blocking in
blocking out
blocks, fixing
blocks, nailing
blue, Della Robbia
blue, dull
blue, dull
blue, dull

blue-green
bluish violet, dull
blunt arches
board, 100% cotton rag
board, chemical wood pulp
board, conservation
board, corrugated
board, foamcore
board, mounting
board, poster
body color
Bongu
border posts
border stations
boulle
boxes, press
braces, angle
brazing
breeders, livestock
breeders, stock
bricks, wood
bridging joists
broken arches
brokers, real estate
brokers, stock
Brosium aubletti
brown, bistre
brown, mummy
brush biting
building design, green
building machinery
building services
building, fast
building, slab (pottery technique)
buildings, archive
buildings, library
buildings, school
Bunyoro
burglar alarm systems
burial gifts
business agents
byre-houses
cabin, rustic
cabinet-sized photographs
cabinets (photographs)
cable-beam structures
cable roofs
cable structures, suspension
cable-supported cantilever roofs
cable-supported roofs, double-layer
cable-supported structures
cable-supported tents

cable tent structures
Cadioéo
calamities
calamities, natural
call girls
camaieu
Canadian Eskimo
canary yellow
candle guards
candles, gauze
cantilever roofs, cable-supported
cantors, Jewish
canvas, glass
cap trim
capitals, cube
capitals, proto-Ionic
capitals, pseudo-Ionic
captains, ship
carbon ink
carbonate, sodium
cardboard, corrugated
cards, trading
Caribbean pine
carmine, dark
Carpenteresque
Carrack porcelain
carthamin
caryophil oil
cascades, chain
cascades, cordonata
cascades, step
casements
casements, hopper
cast products
cataclysms
Catalan vaults
cataloging, subject
catane d'acqua
catastrophes
catches, eaves
cavities, altar
cavity floors
cavo relievo
CDCs
cedar, oil of
cedarwood oil
celebrations, centennial
cellular frames
cellulose fiber
cellulose fiber, wood
Celotex (TM)
cement (adhesive)

163

NEW TERMS

cement, plastic
centenaries
centennial celebrations
centers, alumni
centers, community design
centers, crisis
centers, distribution
centers, fitness
centers, job training
centers, physical fitness
centers, skill training
centers, training
centers, world trade
ceramics, studio
Ch'êng-hua
chain cascades
chains, water
chalcography
chalcography
chalk engraving
chalk manner
chalk method
chambers, drawing
chambers, withdrawing
Chamula
channel beams
chapter rooms
charging
charts, time zone
checkpoints
cheeks, door
chemical closets
chemical wood pulp
chemical wood pulp board
chevroned bands
Chicano
childbirths
childhood, early
chill
chimes, door
chimney pieces
chimney stalks
Chinese paper
Chinese white
chloride, ammonium
chloride, ferric
chloride, iron
chloride, sodium
chop marks (printers' marks)
Chou
CHP generating plants
cider barns

cider houses
citron yellow
civil liberties
clamshell grabs
class, upper
clay, pipe
clerks
clichés-glace
climate control, indoor
closets, chemical
cloth, rubberized
cloud pattern
cloverleaf interchanges
cloves, oil of
clubs, health
clustered piers
coating, roller
cocoawood
cocos wood
cocuswood
coefficient of reflection
coefficient, reflection
cogeneration facilities
cogeneration systems
coil building
coils (spirals)
collagraphy
colleges, military
Colonial, British
colonizing
color, body
color, encaustic
color, scenic
color, size
colors, achromatic
colors, artists'
colour, reflected
column screens
columned screens
columns (TM), Lally
columns, applied
columns, blocked
columns, knotted
columns, paired
combined cycle power plants
combined heat and power generating
    plants
common joists
common salt
communication
communities, golf course
compact disks read-only memory

companion pieces
compartments, WC
competitions, invited
competitions, limited
competitions, open
competitions, student
composites, fibrous
composites, fibrous reinforced
composites, filament reinforced
computerization
concave relief
conches (semidomes)
concrete joist systems, one-way
concrete slab systems, waffle
concrete, plastic
concrete, porous
conductors (downspouts)
Congregationalist
construction machinery
construction, fast-track
construction, incremental self-help
construction, metal pan
construction, one-way joist
construction, phased
construction, platform frame
construction, poteaux sur solle
construction, slab (pottery
    technique)
construction, stressed-skin
construction, tube-in-tube
constructions, beam-and-girder
constructions, beam-and-slab floor
constructions, beam-and-slab floor
constructions, one-way
control signals, traffic
convection heaters
copies (photographic prints)
Copper Eskimo
copperplate engraving
copy photographs
copy photoprints
copyprints
copyreading
corbel rings
corbiestep gables
cordonata cascades
cordonate
corpses, exquisite
corrugated cardboard
corrugated paperboard
cottages, elder
cotton (fiber)

NEW TERMS

cotton linters
cotton rag board, 100%
countermine galleries
counterstamps
crayon engraving
crayon method
crescent moons
crewel embroidery
criblé
crimson madder
crisis centers
crossings, railroad
crosslight
crow gables
crowns (spires)
crowstepped gables
CRT's
cruciform-plan
cruciform-plan
crushed relief
crystals, soda
cube capitals
cubicles, toilet
Cuilcuilco-Ticomán
cul de fours
culture, mass
cupolas (domes)
curvature
customs posts
cutch-grass
Cyzican marble
dark carmine
dark purplish gray
dark slate purple
decorative motifs
deep bite
deep etch
deep relief
deficiency, mental
Della Robbia blue
demi-relief
departments, maternity
dependency, alcohol
dependency, drug
dependency, narcotics
depiction
design centers, community
design, green
design, urban
designers, floral
detectors, heat-actuated
detectors, heat-sensing

detectors, photoelectric smoke
detectors, thermal
detectors, thermostatic
development, linear
development, sustainable
direct lighting system
direction indicators, landing
directorial photographs
directories, building
disadvantaged, economically
disasters, man-made
disasters, natural
diseases
diseases, mental
dish antennas
dishes (satellite antennas)
dishes, satellite
dismissal
disorder, mental
disorders, behavior
disorders, mental
dispatch systems, pneumatic
distribution equipment, heat
distribution, downfeed
doctors, medical
documents, base bid
dolly method
domestic wings
door bells
door cheeks
door chimes
door heads
door jambs
door posts
door sills
door stones
doors, blind
dope addicts
dormer windows
dormers, gable
dormers, gable-roof
dormers, hipped-roof
double helix stairs
double-layer cable-supported roofs
double run
down pipes
drafting paper
dragging ties
drains, storm water
drama, sacred
drawing chambers
drawings of record

drawings, planometric
driers
drill work
drilling (sculpture technique)
drip and pour technique
drive-ins
drug dependence
druggists
Duco (TM)
dull blue
dull blue
dull blue
dull bluish violet
dust ground
dwelling units
dwellings, ECHO
dwellings, spirit
Dynastic, Early (Mesopotamian)
Dzalamo
early childhood
earth wax
Eastern Luba
eaves catches
eaves laths
eaves troughs
ECHO dwellings
ECHO homes
ECHO units
ecological psychology
ecology, human
ecology, social
economically disadvantaged
education, special
egg-and-oil tempera
egg-oil paint
EIF systems
EIFS
Einfühling
Elder Cottage Housing Opportunity
    units
elder cottages
electric files
electric light
electricity supply, emergency
elevators, hydroelectric
elevators, observation
emblem poems
embossing, blind
embossing, uninked
emergency electricity supply
emigrating
emulsion, egg/oil

New Terms

en camaieu
enamel white
enamel, baked
encarnado
encaustic color
enclosures, toilet
end-supported beams
engine houses
English white
engraving, chalk
engraving, copper
engraving, copperplate
engraving, crayon
engraving, steel
enology
entablatures, friezeless
environment and behavior
environment-behavior studies
Erh-li-kang
escarpments (fortification elements)
escarps
Eskimo, Canadian
Eskimo, Copper
etch, deep
etch, gum
etch, lithographic
etch, open
etching (biting)
etching, relief
etching, sugar-lift
ethnic group studies
evolutionary housing
exposing
exquisite corpses
eyebrow windows
fabric reinforcement, wire
fabric, rubberized
fabric, welded wire
fabricated photographs
facilities, cogeneration
facilities, pedestrian
factor, reflection
factories, gunpowder
falchions
false arches
false biting
family quarters, private
Famosa marble
fancy balls
farms, horse
farms, stud
fascias (eave components)

fast building
fast-track construction
features, water
fei pai
felt-tip markers
felt, bituminous
felt, tarred
females, human
Ferrite (TM)
Ferrox (TM)
fiber reinforced composites
fiber, cellulose
fiber, cotton
fiber, wood
Fiberglas (TM)
fibers, optical
fibrous glass
fiction, romance
filament reinforced composites
files, electric
fill
filletsters
film museums
finish stair strings
finish systems, exterior insulation and
fire detectors, ionization
fire detectors, photoelectric
fire stations, manual
fiscal records
fitness centers
fixing blocks
Flandreau
flats, granny
flawlessness
floor constructions, beam-and-slab
floor systems, one-way
floors, beam-and-slab
floors, beam-and-slab
floors, cavity
floors, pan
floors, raised
floors, waffle
flower arrangers
flue walls
fluing arches
fluorescent light
flyers
flying staircases
flying white
foamcore board
footings, spread
foundations, mat

founding fathers
foundresses
fountains, soda
frame construction, platform
frame structures, space
frame windows, double
frames, cellular
framing, platform
framing, western
Freons (TM)
frets, labyrinth
friezeless entablatures
frontal depiction
fuchsia purple
fuelwood
full plate
fun parks, water
funeral gifts
funereal achievements
gable-roof dormers
gables, corbiestep
gables, crow
gables, crowstepped
gables, stepped
gaged brick
gallerias
gallerias
galleries, countermine
galleries, organ
gambrels
games, card
garden architects
garreting
gasen
gasenshi echizen
gateposts
gates, lich
gauffrage
gauze candles
geisons
gender
gender identity
gender role
general illumination
general lighting system
generating plants, CHP
geniuses
geography, human
Gere
gestation
gifts, burial
gifts, funeral

166

gifts, grave
gifts, tomb
glass canvas
glass fiber
glass paste
glass, art
glass, cameo
glass, fiber
glass, gold ruby
glass, spun
glassoid
global approach
glue, animal
glycerin development
glycerol
glyptic art
goat's heads
Golden Tartars
goldrubinglas
golf communities
golf course villages
goods, grave
Gothic, Carpenter
Gothic, High Victorian
Gothick
grange halls
granny flats
grave gifts
gravure
gray marble, Napoleon
gray, dark purplish
gray, light purplish
gray, olive
grayish green
green building design
green, grayish
green, light lime
grey dawn
grievers
grindstones (millstones)
ground (etching)
ground lights, aeronautical
ground wood
ground, dust
ground, hard
ground, liquid
ground, resin
ground, rosin
ground, spirit
grounds, parade
groundwood pulp
groups, ethnic

groups, minority
groups, social
groups, working
growth ring dating
Guarao
guards, candle
Guastavino system
Guastavino vault system
guerrilla wars
guidance, career
guidance, occupational
guides, light
gum arabic etch
gum etch
gunpowder factories
gunpowder mills
gunpowder works
guyed structures
habit, narcotic
hagioscopes
half-relief
half rounds
half stereos
halite
halls, grange
halls, pillared
handles, bail
handling, waste
hawkers
heads, door
health departments
health, mental
heat-actuated detectors
heat distribution equipment
heat-sensing detectors
heaters, convection
heating terminals
heliarc welding
helical vaults
heliotypgraphy
herd-books
heritage zones
heroic
hip jack rafters
hipped-roof dormers
historia
Hlengwe
hollow newel stairs
hollow relief
home antennas, satellite
home offices (corporate
  headquarters)

homes, ECHO
hookers
hopper casements
hopper ventilators
horseback riders
hospital lights
hospital windows
houses, cider
houses, ECHO
houses, long
houses, long (housebarns)
houses, mixed
houses, neighborhood
houses, settlement
houses, spirit
houses, tower
houses, Usonian
housing, evolutionary
housing, faculty
housing, incremental
housing, step-by-step
HSRs
human females
human males
Humbu
humidity, atmospheric
humidity, relative
hut, primitive
HVAC systems, incremental
hydrants
hydroelectric elevators
Hyper-Mannerism
hyperthyra
hyperthyra
hypostyle rooms
hypostyles
identity, gender
identity, sex
ill health
illumination (illustration)
illumination, general
immigrating
impoverished people
incised relief
incremental construction
incremental HVAC systems
incremental self-help construction
indexes, KWAC
indexes, KWIC
indexes, KWOC
indexes, KWOT
India paper

NEW TERMS

India proof paper
indicators, landing direction
industrial safety
inflatable structures
information processing
infrared spectrometry
ink, lithographic
ink, printer's
ink, printing
ink, rubbing
inkless intaglio
inlay, wood
inspection stations, border
instructing
insulation and finish systems,
  exterior
insulation, blanket
insulation, roll
intaglio, blind
intaglio, inkless
inter-media works
interchanges, cloverleaf
intermedia works
intermedial works
Internationale Situationiste
intersecting arcades
intersections, rotary
invited contests
ionization fire detectors
ionization particle detectors
IR
iron chloride
iron perchloride
iron, perchloride of
irons, marking
isometrics
Italianist
jack rafters, hip
Jewish cantors
job training
job training centers
joiner saws
joint adventures
joint tenancy
joint undertakings
joist construction, one-way
joist systems, one-way
joists, bridging
joists, common
joists, open web steel
Ju-chên
judases

Kara-Kuyunli
Kawende
Kellogg's oak
ketubot
key lighting
khivi
Kitara
knees (braces)
Koko
kozo paper
Krapplack
Kwagiutl
Kweli
Kwiri
l'art pour l'art
labor, unskilled
labyrinth frets
ladders, scaling
laid down
lamella structural systems
lancets
landscapes, historic
lantern screens
laque de garance
Late Hittite
lavender, spike
laymen
leader pipes
leaders (downspouts)
leaf, acanthus
legends (captions)
legends (keys)
lemon, oil of
lemongrass oil
leopardwood
letters of attorney
letterwood
levels, split
liberties, civil
library architecture
library buildings
life-size, over
lift-etching
light guides
light lime green
light purplish gray
light red
light standards
light, accent
light, base
light, electric
light, fill

light, fluorescent
light, hard
light, key
light, side
light, top
lighting system, direct
lighting system, general
lighting systems
lighting, accent
lighting, base
lighting, decorative
lighting, key
lighting, outline
lighting, rim
lighting, side
lighting, top
lights, aeronautical ground
lights, approach
lights, boundary
lights, channel
lights, course
lights, hospital
lights, obstruction
lights, runway
lights, taxiway
lights, threshold
lime green, light
linear development
linen, Belgian
lines, lazy
lines, plate
linocut
linocutting
liquid ground
Liquitex (TM)
literature, romance
litho tusche
lithographic etch
lithographic oil
lithographic tusche
lithographic varnish
lithography, color
lithography, offset
living quarters
living units
loads, seismic
local systems
London brick
long houses (housebarns)
loops
loops
louvers, parabolic

New Terms

low income people
low income persons
lych gates
lye
M-ES
Macgilp
machines, traction
Mackenzie Eskimo
Madinka
magilp
magna
maisonettes
males, human
man-environment systems
management, risk
management, waste
Manchu
manière anglaise
manière criblée
manière noire
manner, black
Manner, Broad
manner, chalk
manner, crayon
manner, dotted
Manner, Fine
manual fire stations
manumission
maps, meteorological
marble, black-and-gold
marble, Botticino
marble, Cyzican
marble, Famosa
marble, Napoleon gray
marble, Proconnesian
mariners
marionette theaters
markers, felt-tip
marking irons
marks, chop (printers' marks)
marks, plate
mashrabiyahs
Maskoki
masks (performances)
mass culture
mat foundations
materials, mixed
maternity departments
matter, organic
mauve, pale
McGuilp
MDs

mechanical pulp
media, mixed
medical doctors
medium relief
medium, Maroger
mediums, mixed
megass
mendicants
mental deficiency
mental diseases
mental illness
mental pathology
mental retardation facilities
mercury alloys
mesh reinforcement
mesh, welded wire
metal pan construction
meteorological maps
method, chalk
method, crayon
method, dolly
method, fast-track
method, mixed (painting)
method, slab
mezzo relievo
middle relief
midlife
military colleges
military servicemen
military training schools
mills, cider
mills, gunpowder
mills, powder
minority groups
miscellanies
misregistration
mixed houses
mixed materials
mixed mediums
mixed method (painting)
mixed method (printmaking)
moldings, binder
moldings, ogee
moldings, rake
mollahs
moons, crescent
Moqui
Mormon Church
motifs, decorative
motion-picture museums
movements, resistance
mukarnas

mulberry, paper
mummy brown
museums, film
museums, motion-picture
Musquakie
mutilating
Nanai
narcotic addicts
narcotic dependence
narcotic habit
narcotics addiction
natural calamities
neighborhood houses
New Image
Nieuwe Beelding
Nishga
nobles (nobility)
nogs
nogs
nonloadbearing walls
normal schools
nuclear warfare
Nyangi
observation car elevators
observers
occupational training
Oceanian
officers, police
offices, home
offices, home (corporate
  headquarters)
ogee moldings
oil of spike
oil, caryophil
oil, cedarwood
oil, lemongrass
oil, lithographic
oil, paraffin
oil, rapeseed
oil, stillingia
oil, sun-bleached
oil, sun-refined
oil, tallowseed
oil, turpentine
older adults
olive gray
one-direction spanning slabs
one-half stereographs
one-way concrete joist systems
one-way constructions
one-way floor systems
one-way joist construction

NEW TERMS

one-way joist floors
one-way slabs
one-way slabs
one-way solid slabs
one-way systems
open etch
open form
open pediments
open web steel joists
open well stairs
optical refinement
optics, fiber
organ galleries
organic matter
ornamentalists
orthophosphoric acid
outlets, power
ovens, bake
ovens, baking
ovens, beehive (bake ovens)
PA systems
pacific madrone
paint, bronze
paint, egg-oil
paint, encaustic
paint, industrial
paint, metallic
paint, plastic
paint, size
paint, tempera
paint, vinyl
paint, water-base
paint, wax
painting, acrylic
painting, easel
painting, mineral
painting, mural
painting, oil
painting, panel
painting, polymer
painting, stain
painting, tempera
painting, water-glass
paintng, wall
paired columns
pale mauve
Palladian arches
pan floors
panel heating, radiant
panels (door components)
paper mulberry
paper, aluminum

paper, Arches
paper, China
paper, cold-pressed
paper, construction
paper, corrugated
paper, drafting
paper, graphite
paper, hot-pressed
paper, India
paper, kozo
paper, metallic
paper, mulberry
paper, pastel
paper, pulp
paper, sketching
paper, stencil
paper, typewriter
paper, waterleaf
paper, wax
paper, waxed
paper, Whatman
paperboard, corrugated
paramours
parks, water fun
parlors, smoking
participation, public
particle detectors, ionization
pâte-de-verre
pathology, mental
pattern, cloud
pearl ash
pedestal stands
pedestal supports
pedigrees, animal
pediments, open
peel towers
peels
people-environment studies
people-movers
people-movers
people, homeless
people, impoverished
people, low income
people, street
perception, visual
perchloride of iron
perchloride, iron
peripheries
persons, low income
PES-tp
petrolatum
pharmaceutics

phased construction
photoelectric detectors
photoelectric fire detectors
photographers, press
photographs, copy
photographs, directorial
photographs, fabricated
photographs, staged
photography, Subjective
photoprints, copy
physical fitness centers
picture writing
pieces, apron
pieces, chimney
pieces, nogging
piers, clustered
pilework
pillared halls
pillars
pink, baby
pink, salmon
pipes, down
pipes, leader
pipes, rainwater
pipes, smoke
Pisquow
planned towns
planography
planometric drawings
planometric projections
planters
plants, CHP generating
plants, cogeneration
plants, combined cycle power
plants, combined heat and power
    generating
plants, heating
plastic concrete
plastic paint
plate lines
plates (printing equipment)
plates, engraving
platform frame construction
platform framing
pneumatic dispatch systems
poems, emblem
poetry, pattern
poetry, shaped
poetry, shaped
poetry, visual
pointed arches, segmental
polymer painting

170

NEW TERMS

NEW TERMS

roofs, sloping
roofs, suspension
rooms, chapter
rooms, hypostyle
rooms, media
rooms, showers
rooms, withdrawing
ropework (cable moldings)
rose
rose madder
rosemary
rot, dry
rotary intersections
rubberized fabric
Rubia
rubinglas
ruby glass, gold
rural to urban migration
rustic cabin
sacred drama
safety, industrial
safety, occupational
safety, work
saffron yellow
sailors
sal ammoniac
sal soda
salmon pink
salt, common
salt, table
salted silver print process
salted silver prints
sash bars
sash windows, sliding
sashes, sliding
sashes, storm
satellite antennas
satellite dishes
saws, joiner
scaling ladders
scenery
scenery
scenic color
scents
school buildings
school principals
schools, community
schools, military training
schools, normal
sciences, behavioral
scientists, conservation
scientists, social

scores, music
screen process
screens, candle
screens, columnar
screens, lantern
sections, angle
security systems, electronic
segmental pointed arches
seismic loads
self-help construction, incremental
semi-circular stilted arches
semi-metopes
serigraphy
Serlian arches
Serlian windows
service, building
servicemen
services, sites and
settings
settlements (welfare buildings)
sex identity
shafts, annulated
Shang-Yin
Shangana
shaped poetry
shaped poetry
sheepherders
shelters, battered women's
shelters, crisis
shelters, women's
ship captains
shops, specialist
shops, specialty
shower baths
showers
showers
shrines, spirit
Siboney
sick
sickness
side light
signals, traffic control
signatories
sills, door
sima rectas
sima reversas
simas (cornice components)
simas (moldings)
simply supported beams
simulated thatch roofs
Situationist International
size color

size paint
skaters, ice
sketching paper
skill training centers
slab building (pottery technique)
slab construction (pottery technique)
slab systems, waffle concrete
slabs, one-direction spanning
slabs, one-way
slabs, one-way
slabs, ribbed
slabs, two-way
slate purple, dark
sliding sash windows
sliding sashes
sloping roofs
smalt
smells
smoke detectors, photoelectric
smoke pipes
smoking parlors
social discrimination
social ecology
soda
soda ash
soda crystals
soda, sal
soda, washing
solid slabs, one-way
Songhay Kingdom
sopraporte
soprapportas
soufflets
souvenir albums
soy oil
spaces, alternative
spanning slabs, one-direction
specialist shops
specialty shops
spectators (viewers)
spectrometry, infrared
spectroscopy, infrared
spectroscopy, near-infrared
spectrum analysis
spike lavender
spike, oil of
spirit dwellings
spirit shrines
split levels
spread foundations
springing
spun glass

NEW TERMS

stacks, ventilating
stages, puppet
stain painting
staining technique (painting technique)
stair horses
stair strings, finish
staircases, flying
staircases, water
stairs, double helix
stairs, hollow newel
stairs, open well
stairs, water (landscaped-site elements)
stairways, water
stalks, chimney
stalls (mercantile structures)
stamping, blind
stamps, rubber
standards, light
stands, food
stands, pedestal
statements, artists'
stations, border
stations, border inspection
stealing
steel joists, open web
steel, Cor-Ten (TM)
stencil printing
stencil work
step-by-step housing
step cascades
stepped gables
stereochromy
stereographs, half
stereographs, one-half
stereos, half
stilted arches, semi-circular
stock breeders
stone, Mankato
stones, door
stoneworkers
stop-out
stop-out
stop-out varnish
storax
storm sashes
storm water drains
strainer arches
street people
streetwalkers
stressed-skin construction

strings, finish stair
strips, median
structural systems, lamella
structures, cable beam
structures, cable supported
structures, cable tent
structures, guyed
structures, suspension cable
stud farms
studies, behavior-environment
studies, environment-behavior
studies, ethnic
studies, ethnic group
studies, people-environment
studies, women's
studio pottery
studioware
subdivision
submissions
sucus
sugar aquatint
sugar-lift aquatint
sugar-lift etching
sulphur
sulphur dioxide
sulphuric acid
sun-bleached oil
Sungu
sunk relief
sunk relief
superabaci
supplies, artists'
supply, water
supports, pedestal
surface printing
suspension cable structures
suspension roofs
system, Guastavino
system, Guastavino vault
systems, burglar alarm
systems, cogeneration
systems, electronic security
systems, exterior insulation and finish
systems, incremental
systems, incremental HVAC
systems, lighting
systems, local
systems, man-environment
systems, one-way concrete joist
systems, one-way floor
systems, pneumatic dispatch
systems, pneumatic tube

systems, waffle concrete slab
systems, wind turbine
T-bars
T-shapes
Taba Zikamambo
table fire screens
table salt
tablets, wax
tactile orientation models
tales, fairy
tallowseed oil
tannic acid
tarred felt
technique, drip
technique, mixed
technique, soak-stain
technique, staining (painting technique)
technique, tempera
technique, wash
technique, wet-into-wet
tee bars
teen-age
tempera paint
tempera technique
tempera, egg-and-oil
tempera, egg-oil
tenancy, joint
tent structures, cable
tents, cable-supported
Teotihuacán II
Teotihuán II
Tepe Hissar
terminals, heating
termination (employees)
terra cotta
terre de pipe
terre de pipe ware
terrepleine
thatch roofs, simulated
theaters, marionette
therapists, occupational
therapy, occupational
thermal detectors
thermal windows
thermostatic detectors
thin shells
ties, angle
ties, dragging
time zone charts
TL dating
Tlakluit

173

NEW TERMS

toilet cubicles
toilet enclosures
toilets, chemical
tomb gifts
top light
towers, peel
traction machines
trade centers, world
trade, art
traffic control signals
trailers (mobile homes)
training schools, military
training, job
training, occupational
training, vocational
transient labor
transient workers
transparent watercolor
trash
treatment, sewage
trim
trim, cap
troughs, eaves
trunnels
tube-in-tube construction
turbine systems, wind
turbines, wind
Turkoman of the Black Sheep
turpentine oil
tusche, litho
twin-lights
two-lights
two-way slabs
typing paper
Uchi
ultimate-strength design
under-flashing
undertakings, joint
uninked embossing
unions, art
units, dwelling
units, ECHO
units, living
unskilled labor
unskilled workers
urban decay
urban geography
urban to rural migration
urethane
Uthman II
Valenge
varnish, alcohol-resin

varnish, stop-out
varnish, stopping-out
Vasali
vault system, Guastavino
vaults, Catalan
vaults, helical
vaults, ribbed
vaults, wagon
VDU's
ventilating stacks
ventilators, hopper
vices
view albums
viewers (spectators)
villages, golf course
villages, urban
villes neuves
violet, dull bluish
voyages
W.C.s
Wabende
waffle concrete slab systems
waffle floors
Wagogo
wall painting
walling wax
walls, flue
walls, hot
Wamatengo
Wanka
wards
wards
ware, marbled
warfare
warfare, guerrilla
Warouwen
wars, atomic
wars, guerrilla
wars, nuclear
wash (technique)
wash, flat
washerwomen
washes, car
washing soda
waste handling
water fun parks
water-glass painting
water ramps
water staircases
water stairways
water supply
watercolor paper, Arches

watercolor, transparent
waterleaf paper
waterless toilets
wax engraving
wax paint
wax paper
wax, bordering
wax, walling
WC compartments
welded wire mesh
welding, heliarc
Western Caroline
western framing
wet-into-wet technique
Whatman paper
wheel-throwing
white line process
white, enamel
white, flying
wica
wind turbine systems
window band
windows, dormer
windows, eyebrow
windows, hospital
windows, ribbon
windows, Serlian
windows, sliding sash
windows, thermal
wings, domestic
wings, private
wings, residential
wire fabric reinforcement
wire fabric, welded
wire mesh, welded
wiredrawing dies
withdrawing chambers
withdrawing rooms
women's shelters
women's shelters, battered
wood block printing
wood bricks
wood cellulose fiber
wood fiber
wood inlay
wood pulp, chemical
wood pulp, mechanical
wood wool
wood, cocos
wood, ground
wood, plastic
woodcutters (loggers)

NEW TERMS

wool, wood
word art
work safety
work, boasted
work, drill
work, stencil
workers, transient
workers, unskilled

works, gunpowder
works, intermedia
worldwide approach
writing, picture
X factor
Xicaque
yellow oxide
yellow, canary

yellow, citron
Yin
young people
young persons
Zangid
zones, heritage
zoning, incentive
Zotzil

DELETED TERMS

Descriptors

African Americans
angle braces
animal fiber
appareilles
art trade
artisans' marks
asarota
bank drafts
Basal Neolithic
bases (furniture components)
battened columns
binding joists
blocked columns
blunt arches
body color
Bolidist
bowl capitals
broken arches
bundle piers
camaieu
canted walls
cave drawings
chalice capitals
chaptrels
chrismatories
cirage
columnae caelatae
common joists
Conté crayons (TM)
correspondence art
curved dormers
dental sinks
domestic stylebooks
driving machines
festoon lighting
film formers
film-stencil method
floor to ceiling windows
grade-level elevators
granges
graphite (black pigment)
heel stones
hollow newel stairs
hooks
hydroelectric elevators
hyperthyra
intermission alarm systems
Islamic Revival
jamba oil
jib-headed windows
journals (bookkeeping records)

land art
Latinos
letters of introduction
linear development
marriage applications
Mexican Americans
Mizui-e
mud
Mudejar Revival
national guidebooks
open well stairs
opus tesselatum
pedestals (furniture)
people-movers
personnel evaluations
planar trusses
porous concrete
postal code maps
ravison oil
raw linseed oil
revales
ribbed arches
rigid arches
roll insulation
rosin-sized paper
secret doors
shaped dormers
showers
solid vaults
souvenir albums
spire lights
spotlighting
sprung floors
square bay windows
stair dormers
strong oil
surbased vaults
surmounted vaults
thin oil
threshold combs
threshold plates
tombstone lights
unit air conditioning
urban decay
valla
wheel tracery

Guide Terms

<art genres by medium>
<development concepts>
<drawings by location or context>
<lighting by form>

<painting techniques by tool>
<pavements by property>
<pavements by technique>
<photographic reversal effects>
<printmaking and printmaking
  techniques>
<pulpit components>
<pulpits and pulpit components>
<sculpture and sculpture techniques>
<Spanish Renaissance-Baroque
  architecture styles>
<stage set components>
<stage sets and stage set components>
<theological schools>

Lead-in Terms

abamuri
Abdül hamit II
accent lighting
aleois
animal glue
aquatint, sugar-lift
arches, cloistered
ash dumps
Atacaman
Bajuni
balconnettes
barrel vaults, transverse
beam systems, flat slab and
belection moldings
Berezovo phase
blanket insulation
block printing, relief
casings
catladders
catsup gables
chancel enclosures
chimney pieces
China clay
cloistered arches
cloistered vaults
columns, rusticated
conservation scientists
conservation technicians
contracting out
convicts
cortiles
cunes
deck trusses
decorative lighting
design, urban
dripping

DELETED TERMS

duckboards
eave troughs
echauguettes
educating
enacting
English white
flat slab and beam systems
flooring systems, raised
flyers (steps)
fores
gables, catsup
galician earth wax
handkerchief vaults
hatchways
health clubs
heat insulation windows
incremental air conditioning systems
indigo blue
lime white
linoleum block-printing
mentally retarded
mobility
moldings, belection
moldings, label
moldings, ogee
moldings, talon
Naga School
offset lithography
ogee moldings
one-direction spanning slabs
outline lighting

owners
panes, window
passive solar heating systems
pendent posts
pent roofs (shed roofs)
peridromes
photographic postcards
pillars (foundation components)
pipe clay
plancier pieces
planciers
polymers
postis
posts, gate
posts, hinge
power systems, standby
preserving
printing, woodcut
producers
pump houses
raised flooring systems
relief block printing
roofs, skirt
rusticated columns
scimatia
segment arches
select bibliographies
sequential photography
serial photography
sewage treatment
simas

slabs, solid
slate color
smalt blue
solid slabs
soyabean oil
spanning slabs, one-direction
standby power systems
state and environment
steel engraving
strings, rough
structures, suspended
sugar-lift aquatint
surface printing
suspended structures
systems, flat slab and beam
systems, incremental air conditioning
talon moldings
Tenjiku yo
Tenjiku-yo
toilet partitions
training
transverse barrel vaults
turning circles
urban design
vaults, cloistered
vaults, transverse barrel
water systems
water systems, storm
white bole
window panes
woodcut process

MOVED TERMS

Descriptors

abat-jours
academicism
acoustical insulation
advertising design
Ahmadnagar
ailerons
air art
airbrushing
almond oil
Altoperuvian
ambos
ambrotype
anastatic printing
animal wax
annealing
annulets
anthropology
anthropometry
appliqué
aquatint
architectural centers
architectural design
architectural education
architraves
Arequipa
aristocracy
art appreciation
art education
art market
Asiatic bases
assemblage
atramentum
Attic bases
Aurangabad
back hearths
baldachins
balks
bas-relief
batt insulation
bed moldings
beeswax
bents
Bijapur
biting
black carbon ink
black oil
bleached beeswax
blind windows
blizzards
block printing
boat clubs

bodied oil
boiled oil
bonds (financial records)
bone glue
bourgeoisie
bowstring trusses
box frames
braced frames
builders' guides
burning in (painting)
Burr arch trusses
bus stops
business
caissons
calcimine
camber arches
camouflage
candelilla wax
candlenut oil
canopies
canterburies (storage furniture)
cantilever footings
carnauba wax
carving
cascades
casemates
castings
castor oil
cave art
ceiling joists
ceresin
certified checks
chair lifts
Chavín horizon
checks
Chinese ink
Chinese insect wax
Chinese silk
chromolithography
cinctures
civil wars
cladding
clans
clearinghouses
collagraph printing
collar beams
colonization
color printing
color separation
colored ink
compact disks
computer-aided design

computer art
concrete poetry
conservators
copy art
copyists
corbel vaults
corner boards
costume design
cottonseed oil
country clubs
county government records
cowls
crayon enlargements
crescent trusses
criticism
crockets
crosswalks
croton oil
crucks
curcas oil
curing
currying
Cuzco
damp courses
Daulatabad
daybooks
Deccani
decentralization
deep etching
defacement
demographic anthropology
design
diamond-point engraving
die stamping
direct carving
direct lighting
directional lighting
discographies
disease
distemper paint
door bucks
doorsills
doorstones
double-cable structures
double printing
dragon ties
drop arches
drypoint
educational associations
elderly
elections
electrical insulation

MOVED TERMS

emigration
engraving (incising)
engraving (printing process)
environmental art
estipites
etching (corroding)
etching (printing process)
ethnic groups
ethnography
ethnology
ethnopsychology
expatriation
facility management
false doors
false fronts
families
fan Fink trusses
fascias
fashion design
fenestellas
fill insulation
finance
finger painting
Fink trusses
fish glue
fish oil
flexible insulation
flexible pavements
floodlighting
foils
follies
French doors
front hearths
ganosis
general diffuse lighting
general lighting
gentrification
glazing (coating)
glyptics
Golconda
graphic design
Greco-Roman
griffes
grillages
grinding wheels
grindstones
grisaille
guerrilla warfare
hail
hammer-beam trusses
Hanukkah
Harlem Renaissance

health
hearths
hearthstones
hempseed oil
Herreran
hide glue
high relief
historical sociology
hoods (enclosing structures)
Howe trusses
Hyderabad
hypocausts
iconostases
immigration
inclined elevators
India ink
indirect lighting
industrial design
industrialization
infill
initials (abbreviations)
insanity
insect wax
intaglio printing
interior decoration
interior design
internal migration
invisible ink
iron gall ink
isinglass
jack trusses
Japan wax
Japanese ink
Japanese tung oil
kangs
kapok oil
kernel oil
king-post trusses
knee braces
labor mobility
land reform
lanolin
laser art
Latin American
laying in
Lent
letters of credit
life drawings
lift-ground
light art
line engraving
linoleum-block printing

linseed oil
lithography
local lighting
longhouses
loop windows
lunettes
madrasas
marbling
marquees
mass production
material culture
matting (supporting)
media
mental disorders
meshrebeeyehs
mezzotint
microcrystalline wax
middle class
migration
mineral wax
minorities
mixed media
modular coordination
money orders
monotype
montan wax
municipal finance
municipal government records
museum board
mustard oil
mutilation
naoi
nature printing
negotiable instruments
nobility
nuclear wars
offset printing
oiticica oil
olive oil
on-dols
open newel stairs
ovens
overprinting
oxidative-reductive deterioration
ozokerite
paleoanthropology
paraffin
Parker trusses
participatory design
pastels (chalk)
pattern books
peanut oil

MOVED TERMS

peasantry
pentimenti
performance art
perilla oil
philosophical anthropology
phrenology
physical anthropology
physiognomy
planographic printing
plate warmers (furniture)
play schools
plinths
Poblano
pointing (transferring technique)
polo clubs
pony trusses
poppy-seed oil
poster color
potato printing
Pratt trusses
priming
printing
printmaking
proletariat
promissory notes
protecting
Provincial Highland
psychoanalysis
psychohistory
psychology
public officers
Puebla
pulpits
punic wax
puppet theaters
pyrography
quality control
queen-post trusses
Quito
rabbinical seminaries
rain
Ramadan
rape oil
reflective insulation
refuse disposal
registration (transferring technique)
relief
relief printing
rent control
resettlement
residential mobility
retreats

revolutions
rice oil
riding clubs
rigid insulation
rigid pavements
roadside improvement
roller painting
Roman sepia
rowlock arches
rural sociology
rural-urban migration
Sabattier effect
safflower oil
sally ports
sanding wheels
scissors trusses
screen printing
sculpture
sculpture techniques
security systems
sepia
sewage disposal
sick building syndrome
siderography
sidewalks
silver mirroring
single-story
sleet
slum clearance
snow
social anthropology
social classes
social psychology
sociology
sociology of knowledge
socles
soft-ground etching
solid waste management
sounding boards
soybean oil
space frames
space planning
spermaceti
spray painting
spurs
squinches
stacco
standardization
stilt houses
stipple engraving
stock certificates
strappo

structural anthropology
student mobility
stumping
stylebooks
sunflower oil
supplementary lighting
synthetic wax
tanning
task lighting
taxi stands
teaching
tempering
tennis clubs
tensegrity structures
Tepalcingo
terminally ill
theater design
theological seminaries
therapists
thermal bridges
thermal insulation
three-deckers (pulpits)
three-story
thresholds
through trusses
tickets
tintype
tobacco seed oil
torchis
Town lattice trusses
trade
transfer lithography
transfer printing
travelers' checks
tribes
trussed rafters
tung oil
tusche
tweed
two-story
typographers
Ultrabaroque
unbleached beeswax
underpainting
upper class
urban blight
urban-rural migration
urban sociology
vegetable wax
velum
video art
Vierendeel trusses

MOVED TERMS

viewbooks
walnut oil
Warren trusses
wars
waste disposal
water tables
wheel-engraving
Whipple trusses
white line engraving
whitewash
whiting
wind braces

wood engraving
woodcut
working class
yacht clubs
yeshivas
zincography
zip code maps
Zonist

Guide Terms

<base components>
<bases and base components>

<building elevation attributes>
<Colonial Latin American architecture styles>
<Colonial Latin American fine arts styles>
<Colonial Latin American styles>
<kinship groups>
<modern Polish fine arts styles and movements>
<psychology and related disciplines>
<psychology-related disciplines>

SPLIT TERMS

Descriptors

aeronautical schools
anatomical illustration
anatomical illustrations
anatomical models
anatomical studies
angle columns
archaeological illustration
architectural firms
architectural schools
art schools
biological illustration
biological illustrations
book illustration
book illustrations
botanical illustration
botanical illustrations
bottom rails
brass rubbing
bridge trusses
camber windows
carborundum paper
carborundum stones
city maps

city plans
climatic charts
collar beam roofs
communion records
concentric arches
convex conoidal vaults
county directories
county maps
design books
drawing books
elevator doors
engineering schools
floor joists
galletted joints
hotel registers
language schools
law schools
local government records
longitudinal ridge ribs
medical illustration
medical illustrations
newspaper illustration
newspaper illustrations
nursing schools

office automation
ornament drawings
painting books
parish maps
periodical illustration
periodical illustrations
perpendicular tracery
printmaking techniques
roof trusses
rustic arches
Rustic order
side altars
slab foundations
soffit vents
stage sets
state guidebooks
state maps
township maps
transverse ridge ribs
wedding invitations
zoological illustration
zoological illustrations

*Art &
Architecture
Thesaurus*

SUPPLEMENT 1

PART III:
Hierarchy
Changes

Hierarchy Changes

The *Hierarchy Changes* section contains segments of hierarchies that have been substantially restructured. Changes to individual terms within the restructured sections appear in the *Summary of Term Changes* and the *Alphabetical Listing of Term Changes*.

The restructured section may include terms that were not changed as well as those that were.

The first line of each segment is the broader term, along with its hierarchy code and line number. This identifies the location of the restructured section in relation to the 1990 edition. The ellipsis represents unchanged portions of the hierarchy.

ASSOCIATED CONCEPTS (BM)

BM.568   *<psychological concepts>*

.

.

.

<behavior and mental disorders>
behavior disorders
  substance abuse
    drug abuse
  mental disorders
    insanity

.

.

.

BM.715   *<biological concepts>*

.

.

.

habitat
<health and related concepts>
  health
    mental health
  <health-related concepts>
    <developmental concepts>
      mental retardation
    disease
      addiction
        alcoholism
          drug addiction
      sick building syndrome
    illness
    starvation

.

.

.

<life stages>
  childhood
    infancy
  adolescence
  adulthood
    middle age
    old age
pregnancy

.

.

.

sex
  female
  male

STYLES AND PERIODS (FL)

FL.2771   *<Egyptian periods>*
         <Egyptian Paleolithic periods>
         Predynastic (Egyptian)
         Early Dynastic (Egyptian)
         Old Kingdom
         .
         .
         .

PEOPLE AND ORGANIZATIONS (HG)

HG.1   people
         .
         .
         .

         <groups of people>
           ethnic groups
           minorities
           social groups
             <kinship groups>
               clans
               families
               tribes
             social classes
               middle class
                 bourgeoisie
               peasantry
               upper class
                 aristocracy
                   nobility
                     royalty
               working class
                 proletariat
         <groups of people by activity>
           audiences
         <groups of people by state or condition>
           ill
             terminally ill
           poor

FUNCTIONS (KG)

KG.2   *<functions by general context>*
.
.
.

development
  beautification
    urban beautification
  civic improvement
    roadside improvement
  community development
    rural development
    urban development
      urban renewal
        gentrification
        slum clearance
  economic development
    industrialization
    real estate development
      infill
      land subdivision
      linkage
      ribbon development
  sites and services
  sustainable development
  urbanization
    suburban growth
.
.
.

KG.110   maintaining
.
.
.

environmental protection
  waste management
    recycling
    sewage treatment
    solid waste management
    waste disposal
.
.
.

preventing
.
.
.

relocating
    resettlement

EVENTS (KM)

KM.1   events
              armed conflicts
                 battles
                 wars
                    civil wars
                    guerrilla warfare
                    nuclear wars
                 .
                 .
                 .

                 <religious seasons>
                    Advent
                    Hanukkah
                    Lent
                    Ramadan
                 .
                 .
                 .

PROCESSES AND TECHNIQUES (KT)

KT.5   *<processes and techniques by specific type>*
                 .
                 .
                 .

                 <lighting techniques>
                    <lighting techniques by direction>
                    directional lighting
                      back lighting
                      crosslighting
                      side lighting
                      top lighting
                    general diffuse lighting
                    <lighting techniques by distribution>
                    direct lighting
                    floodlighting
                    general lighting
                      base lighting
                    hard light
                    indirect lighting
                    local lighting
                      accent lighting
                      task lighting
                    supplementary lighting
                      fill light
                 .
                 .
                 .

KT.171　　*<image-making processes and techniques>*
　　　　　animation
　　　　　　·
　　　　　　·
　　　　　　·

　　　　　<printing and printing processes and techniques>
　　　　　printing
　　　　　　intaglio printing
　　　　　　planographic printing
　　　　　　relief printing
　　　　　　screen printing
　　　　　　transfer printing
　　　　　<printing processes>
　　　　　　collagraph printing
　　　　　　color printing
　　　　　　nature printing
　　　　　　zincography
　　　　　　<intaglio printing processes>
　　　　　　　crayon manner
　　　　　　　engraving (printing process)
　　　　　　　　copper engraving
　　　　　　　　drypoint
　　　　　　　　line engraving
　　　　　　　　mezzotint
　　　　　　　　siderography
　　　　　　　　steel engraving
　　　　　　　　stipple engraving
　　　　　　　etching (printing process)
　　　　　　　　aquatint
　　　　　　　　　lift-ground
　　　　　　　　　　sugar-lift
　　　　　　　　soft-ground etching
　　　　　　<planographic printing processes>
　　　　　　　lithography
　　　　　　　　color lithography
　　　　　　　　　chromolithography
　　　　　　　　offset lithography
　　　　　　　　transfer lithography
　　　　　　　monotype
　　　　　　　offset printing
　　　　　　<relief printing processes>
　　　　　　　block printing
　　　　　　　dotted manner
　　　　　　　letterpress printing
　　　　　　　linoleum-block printing
　　　　　　　potato printing
　　　　　　　relief etching
　　　　　　　　anastatic printing
　　　　　　　white line engraving
　　　　　　　wood engraving
　　　　　　　woodcut

<printing techniques>
    bleeding (printing technique)
    color separation
    double printing
    overprinting
    <matrix preparation techniques>
        à la poupée
        <biting techniques>
            creeping bite
            deep etching
            open biting
            overbiting
            spit biting
            underbiting
        retroussage
printmaking
.
.
.

writing

KT.735   *<transferring and transferring techniques>*
    transferring
      rubbing
      stacco
      stenciling
        pochoir
      strappo
      tracing
    <transferring techniques>
    decalcomania
    frottage
    pointing (transferring technique)
    pouncing
      spolvero
    pricking
    registration (transferring technique)
    squaring (transferring technique)

KT.885   *<conditions and effects>*

        ·

        ·

        ·

      damage
        defacement

        ·

        ·

        ·

      <surface changing conditions and effects>
        bloom
      <conditions and effects: architecture>
        dry rot
        thermal bridges
      <conditions and effects: photography>
        oxidative-reductive deterioration
        Sabbattier effect
        silver mirroring
      <conditions and effects: printing and printmaking>
        crevé
        foul biting
        in register
        offsets
        out of register
        plate marks
      <conditions and effects: textiles>
        abrash
        lazy lines

MATERIALS (MT)

MT.2402   **insulation**
      <insulation by form>
        batt insulation
        flexible insulation
          blanket insulation
          fill insulation
        rigid insulation
      <insulation by function>
        acoustical insulation
        electrical insulation
        thermal insulation
          reflective insulation

MT.2495   ink

           <ink by composition or origin>
               atramentum
               black carbon ink
               Chinese ink
               India ink
               iron gall ink
               Japanese ink
               sepia
                   Roman sepia
            <ink by function>
               lithographic ink
               printing ink
               rubbing ink
            <ink by property>
               colored ink
               invisible ink

BUILT COMPLEXES AND DISTRICTS (RG)

RG.151   recreation areas
           .
           .
           .

           <club complexes>
               boat clubs
                   yacht clubs
               country clubs
               polo clubs
               riding clubs
               tennis clubs
           .
           .
           .

BUILT WORKS COMPONENTS (RT)

RT.112   *<column components>*
           <bases and base components>
               Asiatic bases
               Attic bases
               <base components>
                   griffes
           .
           .
           .

RT.356   **trusses**
                 <trusses by form>
                      bowstring trusses
                      Burr arch trusses
                      crescent trusses
                      Fink trusses
                           fan Fink trusses
                      hammer-beam trusses
                      king-post trusses
                      queen-post trusses
                      scissors trusses
                      Town lattice trusses
                      Vierendeel trusses
                 <trusses by location or context>
                      jack trusses
                      pony trusses
                      through trusses
                      trussed rafters
                 <trusses by construction>
                      Howe trusses
                      Pratt trusses
                           Parker trusses
                           Whipple trusses
                      space frames
                           tensegrity structures
                      Warren trusses

RT.833   *<doorway components>*
                 .
                 .
                 .

                 door bucks
                 <doorframes and doorframe components>
                      doorframes
                      <doorframe components>
                           door jams
                           doorheads
                 .
                 .
                 .

                 doorsills
                 doorstones
                 .
                 .
                 .

                 thresholds
                 .
                 .
                 .

RT.1151   *<fireplace components>*

               .

               .

               .

               <hearths and hearth components>
                  hearths
                     hearthstones
                   <hearth components>
                  back hearths
                  front hearths

               .

               .

               .

RT.1352   **lighting**
               <lighting by function>
                  architectural lighting
                     decorative lighting
                     outline lighting
                  emergency lighting
               <lighting by location or context>
                  exterior lighting
                  interior lighting
                     cornice lighting
                     cove lighting
                     valance lighting
                  stage lighting
               <lighting by method of illumination>
                  electric lighting
                  fluorescent lighting
                  gas-lighting

Art & Architecture Thesaurus

Supplement 1

PART IV:
Sources

Sources

Any new bibliographic sources that have been used as references for the changes listed in this supplement are recorded alphabetically by source code.

6000YR Norbert Schoenauer. *6000 Years of Housing*. 3 vols. New York: Garland STPM Press, 1981.

AAA Jean Lipman. *Art About Art*. New York: E.P. Dutton & Co., 1978.

AAIT65 Rudolf Wittkower. *Art and Architecture in Italy, 1600-1750*. 2d ed. Harmondsworth, England: Penguin Books, 1965.

AAIT73 Rudolf Wittkower: *Art and Architecture in Italy, 1600-1750*. 3d rev. ed. Harmondsworth, England: Penguin Books, 1982.

AARP American Association of Retired Persons. Miscellaneous publications. Washington, D.C.

ACI American Concrete Association. *Cement and Concrete Thesaurus*. Detroit: American Concrete Association and Portland Cement Association, 1970.

ADAIR William Adair. *The Frame in America, 1700-1900*. Washington, D.C.: American Institute of Architects Foundation, 1983.

ADPB Wesley W. Pasko. ed. *American Dictionary of Printing and Bookmaking: Containing a History of These Arts in Europe and America, with Definitions of Technical Terms and Biographical Sketches*. New York: Howard Lockwood & Co., 1894.

AGS1 Charles G. Ramsey and Harold R. Sleeper. *Architectural Graphic Standards*. Facsimile edition of the first edition published in 1932. New York: John Wiley & Sons, 1990.

AHFORT John W. Henderson et al. *Area Handbook for Thailand*. 3rd rev. ed. Washington, D.C.: Government Printing Office, 1971.

AHHHE Amos H. Hawley. *Human Ecology: A Theoretical Essay*. Chicago: University of Chicago Press, 1986.

AIM David Bomford, Jill Dunkerton, Dillian Gordon and Ashok Roy. *Italian Painting Before 1400*. Art in the Making, no. 2. London: National Gallery, 1989.

AINA *Art in America*. New York: Brant Art Publications, 1913-.

AIRMAN Central Treaty Organization. *Airport Management*. Ankara, Turkey: Central Treaty Organization, 1974.

AIRPRT John W. Wood. *Airports: Some Elements of Design and Future Development*. New York: Coward-McCann, 1940.

ALC Abbott L. Cummings, comp. *Bed Hangings: A Treatise on Fabrics and Styles in the Curtaining of Beds, 1650-1850*. Boston: Society for the Preservation of New England Antiquities, 1961.

ALLAB3 Michael Allaby. *Dictionary of the Environment.* 3d ed. New York: New York University Press, 1989.

ALSPAC Lynne Warren. *Alternative Spaces: A History in Chicago.* Chicago: Museum of Contemporary Art, 1984.

ALTPUB Cathy S. Whitaker, ed. *Alternative Publications: A Guide to Directories, Indexes, Bibliographies, and Other Sources.* Jefferson, N.C.: McFarland, 1990.

AMBASZ Emilio Ambasz, ed. *Italy: The New Domestic Landscape.* New York: Museum of Modern Art, 1972.

AMFOPA Abby Aldrich Rockefeller Folk Art Center. *American Folk Paintings: Paintings and Drawings Other than Portraits from the Abby Aldrich Rockefeller Folk Art Center.* The Abby Aldrich Rockefeller Folk Art Center Series, no. 2. Boston: Little, Brown & Co. in association with the Colonial Williamsburg Foundation, 1988.

AMINI Majid Amini. *Oriental Rugs: Care and Repair.* New York: Van Nostrand Reinhold, 1981.

AMSTUD University of Minnesota. University Art Museum. *American Studio Ceramics, 1920-1950.* Minneapolis: University Art Museum, University of Minnesota, 1988.

AN *Artnews.* New York: Artnews Associates, 1923-.

ANATI Emmanuel Anati. *Evolution and Style in Camunian Rock Art: An Inquiry into the Formation of European Civilization.* Brescia, Italy: Edizione Del Centro, 1976.

AOPOS Leone B. Alberti. *On Painting and on Sculpture: The Latin Texts of de Pictura and de Statua.* Edited and translated by Cecil Grayson. London: Phaidon Press, 1972.

APOTM Marion J. Nelson. *Art Pottery of the Midwest.* Minneapolis: University Art Museum, University of Minnesota, 1988.

APUS Paul Evans. *Art Pottery of the United States: An Encyclopedia of Producers and Their Marks.* New York: Charles Scribner's Sons, 1974.

APUS2 Paul Evans. *Art Pottery of the United States: An Encyclopedia of Producers and their Marks.* 2d rev. ed. New York: Feingold & Lewis Publishing, 1987.

AQM University Products, Inc. *Archival Quality Materials: For Conservation, Restoration, and Preservation, 1990/91.* Holyoke, Mass.: University Products, Inc., 1990.

AQUATC Anthony Wylson. *Aquatecture: Architecture and Water.* London: Architectural Press, 1986.

ARCFOR *The Architectural Forum.* New York: Time Inc., 1892-1974.

ARROM William L. MacDonald. *The Architecture of the Roman Empire.* rev. ed. 2 vols. New Haven, Conn.: Yale University Press, 1986.

ARTWD2 Jeanne Siegel, ed. *Artwords 2: Discourse on the Early Eighties.* Ann Arbor, Mich.: UMI Research Press, 1988.

ARTWDS Jeanne Siegel, ed. *Artwords: Discourse on the Sixties and Seventies.* Ann Arbor, Mich.: UMI Research Press, 1985.

ASPAL R. Reed. *Ancient Skins, Parchments and Leathers.* New York: Seminar Press, 1979.

ASPOP John A. Walker. *Art Since Pop.* London: Thames & Hudson, 1975.

ASTMDF American Society for Testing and Materials. Committee on Terminology. *Compilation of ASTM Standard Definitions*. 6th ed. Philadelphia: American Society for Testing and Materials, 1986.

ATGAS Zahira Veliz, ed. *Artists' Techniques in Golden Age Spain: Six Treatises in Translation*. New York: Cambridge University Press, 1986.

AVIATN Gardener B. Manly. *Aviation: From the Ground Up*. Chicago: Frederick J. Drake & Co., 1940.

AWP Wendon Blake. *Acrylic Watercolor Painting*. Edited by Heather Meredith. New York: Watson-Guptill Publications, 1970.

B&H10 Charles B. Breed and George L. Hosmer. *The Principles and Practice of Surveying*. Vol. 1, *Elementary Surveying*. 10th ed. Revised by Alexander J. Bone. New York: John Wiley & Sons, 1970.

BACOT Parrott Bacot. *Nineteenth Century Lighting: Candle-Powered Devices, 1783-1883*. West Chester, Pa.: Schiffer Publishing, 1987.

BAQ *The International Review of African American Art*. Santa Monica, Calif.: Museum of African American Art, 1976-.

BATCOB Matt T. Roberts and Don Etherington. *Bookbinding and the Conservation of Books: A Dictionary of Descriptive Terminology*. Washington, D.C.: Library of Congress. 1982.

BELTR Antonio Beltran. *Rock Art of the Spanish Levant*. Translated by Margaret Brown. New York: Cambridge University Press, 1982.

BERDMV Maurice W. Beresford and John G. Hurst, eds. *Deserted Medieval Villages*. London: Lutterworth Press, 1971.

BHA Bibliography of the History of Art. "BHA Subject Headings: English." Document prepared for internal distribution. 1991.

BHAKIM Besim S. Hakim. *Arabic-Islamic Cities: Building and Planning Principles*. 2d ed. New York: Kegan Paul International, 1988.

BICKF John Bickford. *New Media in Printmaking*. New York: Watson-Guptill Publications, 1976.

BIEGEL J.I. Biegeleisen. *Screen Printing: A Contemporary Guide to the Technique of Screen Printing for Artists, Designers, and Craftsmen*. New York: Watson-Guptill Publications, 1971.

BLDINC *Building in China*. Beijing: China Building Technology Development Centre, 1985-.

BLDR *Builder*. Washington, D.C.: National Association of Home Builders, 1978-.

BOHN Willard Bohn. *The Aesthetics of Visual Poetry, 1914-1928*. New York: Cambridge University Press, 1986.

BOND Francis Bond. *Gothic Architecture in England: An Analysis of the Origin and Development of English Church Architecture from the Norman Conquest to the Dissolution of the Monasteries*. London: B.T. Batsford, 1905.

BONY Jean Bony. *French Gothic Architecture of the Twelfth and Thirteenth Centuries*. California Studies of the History of Art Series. Berkeley: University of California Press, 1983.

BOROE Ignace Schlosser. *The Book of Rugs: Oriental and European*. New York: Bonanza Books, 1963.

BRETON Andre Breton. *What is Surrealism?: Selected Writings*. Edited by Franklin Rosemont. New York: Monad, 1978.

BRFRCO Brooklyn Furniture Co. *Furniture, Carpets, and Furnishings*. Furniture catalog. Brooklyn, N.Y.: Brooklyn Furniture Co., 1887.

BRITCH Seymour Britchky. *The Restaurants of New York*. New York: Simon & Schuster, 1988.

BRSCR Michelle P. Brown. *A Guide to Western Historical Scripts: From Antiquity to 1600*. Toronto: University of Toronto Press, 1990.

BUFFA Poul ter Hofstede, ed. *Fotografia Buffa: Staged Photography in the Netherlands*. Groningen: Groninger Museum, 1986.

BUNNMW Peter C. Bunnell. *Minor White, the Eye that Shapes*. With Maria B. Pellerano and Joseph B. Rauch. Princeton, N.J.: Art Museum, Princeton University, 1989.

C101M Richard Cummings. *One Hundred and One Masks*. New York: David McKay Co., 1968.

CANAVW Charles A. Amsden. *Navaho Weaving: Its Technic and History*. Reprint. Salt Lake City, Utah: Peregrine Smith, 1975.

CASPAL John Caspall. *Making Fire and Light in the Home Pre-1820*. Suffolk, England: Antique Collectors' Club, 1987.

CEBT Henry J. Cowan, ed. *Encyclopedia of Building Technology*. Englewood Cliffs, N.J.: Prentice Hall, 1988.

CELLIS Charles Grant Ellis. *Early Caucasian Rugs*. Washington, D.C.: Textile Museum, 1975.

CHAES Carl Hernmarck. *The Art of the European Silversmith, 1430-1830*. 2 vols. New York: Sotheby Parke Bernet, 1977.

CHAMBD Peter M.B. Walker, ed. *Chambers Science and Technology Dictionary*. Edinburgh: Chambers. Cambridge: Cambridge University Press, 1988.

CHAMET Walt Chamberlain. *Thames and Hudson Manual of Etching and Engraving*. London: Thames & Hudson, 1978.

CHARET Charrette Corporation. *1987 Charrette Catalog*. Architects' supply catalog. Woburn, Mass.: Charrette Corp., 1987.

CHIGO *The Chicago Manual of Style*. 13th ed., rev. and exp. Chicago: University of Chicago Press, 1982.

CLAPP Ann F. Clapp. *Curatorial Care of Works of Art on Paper: Basic Procedures for Paper Preservation*. New York: Lyons & Burford, 1987.

CLARK Garth Clark. *American Ceramics: 1876 to the Present*. New York: Abbeville Press, 1987.

COGC John Fitchen. *Construction of Gothic Cathedrals*. Oxford: Oxford University Press, 1961.

COHOUS Kathryn McCamant and Charles Durrett. *Cohousing: A Contemporary Approach to Housing Ourselves*. Berkeley, Calif.: Habitat Press, 1988.

COLGAD Mary F. Gaston. *Collector's Guide to Art Deco*. Paducah, Ky.: Collector Books, 1989.

COLGDP William B. Welling. *Collector's Guide to Nineteenth Century Photographs*. New York: Macmillan Publishing Co., 1976.

COLGMM Anthony Slide. *Collector's Guide to Movie Memorabilia, with Prices*. Des Moines, Iowa: Wallace-Homestead Book Co., 1983.

COMPRI John Ross, Clare Romano and Tim Ross. *The Complete Printmaker*. rev. and exp. Edited and produced by Roundtable Press. New York: Free Press, 1990.

COMPS Paul D. Spreiregen. *Design Competitions*. New York: McGraw-Hill Book Co., 1979.

CONPW W.G. Constable. *The Painter's Workshop*. Oxford: Oxford University Press, 1954.

COPAD Margaret Holben Ellis. *The Care of Prints and Drawings*. Nashville, Tenn.: AASLH Press, 1987.

CPE Maurice Rickards. *Collecting Printed Ephemera*. New York: Abbeville Press, 1988.

CPGERN Helmut Gernsheim. *Creative Photography: Aesthetic Trends 1839-1960*. New York: Bonanza Books, 1962.

CPL918 Philippe H. Bovy. *Pedestrian Planning and Design: A Bibliography*. Council of Planning Librarians Exchange Bibliography, no. 918. Monticello, Ill.: Council of Planning Librarians, 1975.

CREAT2 Marcia Tiede. *Create: A Procedure Manual for Cataloging Photographs*. 3d ed. Tucson: Center for Creative Photography, University of Arizona, 1991.

CRUMBUL *CRM Bulletin*. Washington, D.C.: Cultural Resources, National Park Service, United States Department of the Interior, 1978-.

CRSREF Walker Art Center. *Cross-References: Sculpture into Photography; James Casebere, Bruce Charlesworth, Bernard Faucon, Ron O'Donnell, Sandy Skoglund, Boyd Webb*. Minneapolis, Minn.: Walker Art Center, 1987.

CWMLU Walt Crawford. *MARC for Library Use: Understanding the USMARC Formats*. Professional Librarian Series. White Plains, N.Y.: Knowledge Industries Publications, 1984.

DANDB Donald Watson. *Designing and Building a Solar House: Your Place in the Sun*. rev. ed. Pownal, Vt.: Garden Way Publishing, 1985.

DARBEE Herbert C. Darbee. *A Glossary of Old Lamps and Lighting Devices*. American Association for State and Local History, Technical Leaflet 30. Nashville, Tenn.: AASLH Press, 1974.

DCJA Hugo Munsterberg. *Dictionary of Chinese and Japanese Art*. New York: Hacker Art Books, 1981.

DDA2 John Fleming and Hugh Honour. *The Penguin Dictionary of Decorative Arts*. rev. ed. New York: Viking Press, 1989.

DENNY Walter B. Denny. *Oriental Rugs*. Smithsonian Illustrated Library of Antiques. New York: Cooper-Hewitt Museum, 1979.

DHI Philip P. Wiener, ed. *Dictionary of the History of Ideas*. 4 vols. New York: Charles Scribner's Sons, 1973.

DIALOG DIALOG Information Services, Inc. Palo Alto, California.

DICBIB John L. McKenzie. *Dictionary of the Bible*. New York: Macmillan Publishing Co., 1965.

DIGBY G.H.S. Bushnell and Adrian Digby. *Ancient American Pottery*. London: Faber & Faber, 1955.

DIRMSC Dona Meilach and Don Seiden. *Direct Metal Sculpture: Creative Techniques and Appreciation.* New York: Crown Publishers, 1966.

DJROP Doreen Jensen and Polly Sargent. *Robes of Power: Totem Poles on Cloth.* Museum Note no. 17. Vancouver: University of British Columbia Press in association with the University of British Columbia Museum of Anthropology, 1986.

DOERN Max Doerner. *The Materials of the Artist and Their Use in Painting, with Notes on the Techniques of the Old Masters.* Translated by Eugen Neuhaus. New York: Harcourt, Brace & Co., 1934.

DOFMG George W. Johnson. *Dictionary of Modern Gardening.* Edited by David Landreth. Philadelphia: Lea & Blanchard, 1847.

DOH Stephen Friar, ed. *A Dictionary of Heraldry.* New York: Harmony Books, 1987.

DOINDP Pete Daniel. *Official Images: New Deal Photography.* Washington, D.C.: Smithsonian Institution Press, 1987.

DUCRET S. Ducret. *German Porcelain and Faience.* Translated by Diana Imber. New York: Universe Books, 1962.

DUFFY Christopher Duffy. *Fire and Stone: The Science of Fortress Warfare, 1660-1860.* Newton Abbot, England: David & Charles, 1975.

DVOXF K.J. Allison, M.W. Beresford and J.G. Hurst. *The Deserted Villages of Oxfordshire.* Department of English Local History, Occasional Papers, no. 17. Leicester, England: University Press, 1966.

EAMILL Martha Zimiles and Murray Zimiles. *Early American Mills.* New York: Clarkson N. Potter, 1973.

EANDE George R. Strakosch. *Vertical Transportation: Elevators and Escalators.* 2d ed. New York: John Wiley & Sons, 1983.

EILAND Murray L. Eiland. *Oriental Rugs: A Comprehensive Guide.* rev. and exp. Boston: New York Graphic Society, 1976.

EIP Charles Seymour, Jr. *Early Italian Paintings in the Yale University Art Gallery.* New Haven, Conn.: Yale University Press, 1970.

ELLIS Charles Grant Ellis. *Oriental Carpets in the Philadelphia Museum of Art.* Philadelphia: Philadelphia Museum of Art, 1988.

ELSPAS Margy L. Elspass. *Illustrated Dictionary of Art Terms.* London: B.T. Batsford, 1984.

ENCMIN Willard L. Roberts, Geroge R. Rapp, Jr. and Julius Weber. *Encyclopedia of Minerals.* New York: Van Nostrand Reinhold, 1974.

ENCPHI Paul Edwards, ed. *The Encyclopedia of Philosophy.* Reprint. New York: Macmillan Publishing Co., 1972.

ENCR+E James Hastings, ed. *Encyclopaedia of Religion and Ethics.* 13 vols. Edinburgh: T & T Clark. New York: Charles Scribner's Sons, 1908.

ENCSPC George L. Clark, ed. *The Encyclopedia of Spectroscopy.* New York: Reinhold Publishing Corp., 1960.

ENCYBF Glenn G. Munn. *Encyclopedia of Banking and Finance.* 8th ed. Revised and expanded by Ferdinand L. Garcia. Boston: Bankers Publishing Co., 1983.

ENCYES Sybil P. Parker, ed. *McGraw-Hill Encyclopedia of Environmental Science.* 2d ed. New York: McGraw-Hill Book Co., 1980.

ENCYHE Asa S. Knowles, ed. *The International Encyclopedia of Higher Education*. 10 vols. San Francisco: Jossey-Bass Publishers, 1977.

ENOFGL Phoebe Phillips. *The Encyclopedia of Glass*. New York: Crown Publishers, 1981.

EPD Larry Klein. *Exhibits: Planning and Design*. New York: Madison Square Press, 1986.

EPP Elisabeth Cameron. *Encyclopedia of Pottery and Porcelain, 1800-1960*. New York: Facts on File Publications, 1986.

ERIC12 James E. Houston, ed. *Thesaurus of Eric Descriptors*. 12th ed. Phoenix, Ariz.: Oryx Press, 1990.

FADS Alfred H. Barr, Jr., ed. *Fantastic Art, Dada, Surrealism*. New York: Museum of Modern Art, 1936.

FAUXPT Isabel O'Neil. *The Art of the Painted Finish for Furniture and Decoration: Antiquing, Lacquering, Gilding, and the Great Impersonators*. New York: William Morrow & Co., 1971.

FCAC Robert F. McGiffen. *Furniture Care and Conservation*. 2d rev. ed. Nashville, Tenn.: AASLH Press, 1989.

FIRFOR Simon Pepper and Nicholas Adams. *Firearms and Fortifications: Military Architecture and Siege Warfare in Sixteenth-Century Siena*. Chicago: University of Chicago Press, 1986.

FLASH *Flash Art*. Milano: Giancarlo Politi, 1967-.

FLET19 Sir Banister Fletcher. *A History of Architecture*. 19th ed. London: Butterworths Press, 1987.

FLLWUH John Sergeant. *Frank Lloyd Wright's Usonian Houses: The Case for Organic Architecture*. New York: Watson-Guptill, 1976.

FMHE Frank J. Bruno. *The Family Mental Health Encyclopedia*. New York: John Wiley & Sons, 1989.

FMPTXT Florence M. Montgomery. *Printed Textiles: English and American Cottons and Linens, 1700-1850*. New York: Viking Press, 1970.

FOCII Henri Focillon. *The Art of the West in the Middle Ages*. 2d ed. 2 vols. Edited by Jean Bony. Translated by Donald King. New York: Phaidon Publishers, 1969.

FORTEA Peter Kent. *Fortifications of East Anglia*. Suffolk, England: Terence Dalton, 1988.

FRATER Alvin J. Schmidt. *Greenwood Encyclopedia of American Institutions*. Vol. 3, *Fraternal Organizations*. Westport, Conn.: Greenwood Press, 1980.

FRENCH Hollis French. *Silver Collector's Glossary, and a List of Early American Silversmiths and Their Marks*. Reprint. Architecture and Decorative Art, Da Capo Press Series, vol. 9. New York: Da Capo Press, 1967.

FRHLT F.W. Fairholt, ed. *A Dictionary of Terms in Art*. London: William Isbister, 1886.

FTFAA William Fagg. *Tribes and Forms in African Art*. New York: Tudor, 1965.

GALLO Italo Gallo. *Greek and Latin Papyrology*. Translated by Maria Rosaria Falivene and Jennifer R. March. Classical Handbook, vol. 1. London: Institute of Classical Studies, 1986.

GASKEL Philip Gaskell. *A New Introduction to Bibliography*. New York: Oxford University Press, 1972.

GAUR Albertine Gaur. *A History of Writing*. New York: Charles Scribner's Sons, 1985.

GBA *Gazette des Beaux-Arts*. Gap Cedex, France: Gazette des Beaux-Arts, 1859-.

GCCOP Carl Zigrosser and Christa M. Gaehde. *A Guide to the Collection and Care of Original Prints*. New York: Crown Publishers, 1965.

GCGAUD George R. Collins. *Antonio Gaudi*. New York: George Braziller, 1960.

GEOREF Crystal S. Palmer, ed. *Georef Thesaurus and Guide to Indexing*. 4th ed. Alexandria, Va.: American Geological Institute, 1986.

GEOSCO National Referral Center. *Geosciences and Oceanography: A Directory of Information Resources in the United States*. Washington, D.C.: Library of Congress, 1981.

GEOTEX Jean-Pierre Girond. *Geotextiles and Geomembranes: Definition, Properties, and Design, Selected Papers, Revisions, and Comments*. 3d ed. St. Paul, Minn.: Industrial Fabrics Association International, 1984.

GH *Garden History*. London: Garden History Society, 1972-.

GIRECH Mark Girouard. *Life in the English Country House: A Social and Architectural History*. New Haven, Conn.: Yale University Press, 1978.

GLASS Elizabeth Glass, comp. *A Subject Index for the Visual Arts*. 2 vols. London: Her Majesty's Stationery Office, 1969.

GLLIT Meyer H. Abrams. *A Glossary of Literary Terms*. 5th ed. New York: Holt, Rinehart & Winston, 1988.

GODDEN Geoffrey Godden. *British Porcelain: An Illustrated Guide*. New York: Clarkson N. Potter, 1974.

GOG3 Robert L. Bates and Julia A. Jackson, eds. *Glossary of Geology*. 3d ed. Alexandria, Va.: American Geological Institute, 1987.

GRAPAN *Graphis Annual*. Zurich: Graphis Press Corp, 1952-.

GREEND Avril Fox and Robin Morrell. *Green Design: A Guide to the Environmental Impact of Building Materials*. London: Architecture Design and Technology Press, 1989.

GROD Louis Grodecki. *Gothic Architecture*. Translated by I. Mark Paris. New York: Harry N. Abrams, 1977.

HAGGAR Reginald G. Haggar. *The Concise Encyclopedia of Continental Pottery and Porcelain*. New York: Hawthorn Books, 1960.

HAMMON Norman Hammond, ed. *Mesoamerican Archaeology: New Approaches*. Austin: University of Texas Press, 1974.

HARTMN Hartman Furniture Company. *Hartman's Supplementary Catalogue*. Furniture catalog. Chicago: Hartman Furniture Co., 1911.

HARTT Frederick Hartt. *Art: A History of Painting, Sculpture, and Architecture*. New York: Harry N. Abrams, 1976.

HASLAM Malcolm Haslam. *The Real World of the Surrealists*. New York: Rizzoli International Publications, 1989.

HEBARD Helen B. Hebard. *Early Lighting in New England, 1620-1861*. Rutland, Vt.: Charles E. Tuttle Co., 1964.

HENKLE *George J. Henkle's City Cabinet Warehouse*. Philadelphia: George J. Henkle, 1950.

HENZKE Lucile Henzke. *Art Pottery of America*. Exton, Penn.: Schiffer Publishing, 1982.

HEYD99 Heywood Brothers and Wakefield Company. *1898-1899 Illustrated Catalogue*. Furniture catalog. Gardner, Mass.: Heywood Brothers & Wakefield Co., 1899.

HIGG Dick Higgins. *Horizons: The Poetics and Theory of the Intermedia*. Carbondale: Southern Illinois University Press, 1984.

HIGPP Dick Higgins. *Pattern Poetry: Guide to an Unknown Literature*. Albany: State University of New York Press, 1987.

HILER Hilaire Hiler. *The Painter's Pocket-Book of Methods and Materials*. 3d ed. Edited by Jan Gordon and revised by Colin Hayes. New York: Watson-Guptill Publications, 1970.

HILLNA Jack Hillier. *The Japanese Print: A New Approach*. Rutland, Vt.: Charles E. Tuttle Co., 1975.

HILLSH Jack Hillier. *Suzuki Harunobu: An Exhibition of his Colour-Prints and Illustrated Books on the Occasion of the Bicentenary of his Death in 1770*. Philadelphia: Philadelphia Museum of Art, 1970.

HINDHI Arthur M. Hind. *A Short History of Engraving and Etching: For the Use of Collectors and Students*. 2d rev. ed. New York: Houghton Mifflin Co., 1911.

HISPUP George Speaight. *The History of the English Puppet Theatre*. 2d ed. Carbondale: Southern Illinois University Press, 1990.

HOED Peter J. Booker. *A History of Engineering Drawing*. London: Chatto & Windus, 1963.

HOLG Robert Schwartz. *Home Owner's Legal Guide*. New York: Collier, 1965.

HOLME Charles Holme. *Art in Photography*. New York: Arno Press, 1979.

HON1 William B. Honey. *Old English Porcelain: A Handbook for Collectors*. New York: Whittlesey House, 1946.

HON3 William B. Honey. *European Ceramic Art, from the End of the Middle Ages to About 1815*. London: Faber & Faber, 1952.

HOPSCP Jean-Claude Lemagny and Andre Rouille, eds. *A History of Photography: Social and Cultural Perspectives*. Reprint. Translated by Janet Lloyd. New York: Cambridge University Press, 1987.

HOWARD Alexander L. Howard. *Timbers of the World*. 3d ed. New York: Macmillan Publishing Co., 1948.

HOY Anne H. Hoy. *Fabrications: Staged, Altered, and Appropriated Photographs*. New York: Abbeville Press, 1987.

HPIOL Ruth L. Horowitz. *Political Ideologies of Organized Labor*. New Brunswick, N.J.: Transaction Books, 1978.

HSEI Charles Hudson. *The Southeastern Indians*. Knoxville: University of Tennessee Press, 1976.

HWAREN Peter Murray. *Renaissance Architecture*. History of World Architecture. Milan: Electa. New York: Rizzoli International Publications, 1985.

IDMB *International Dictionary of Medicine and Biology*. 3 vols. New York: John Wiley & Sons, 1986.

IEETWH Irene Emery and Patricia Fiske, eds. *Ethnographic Textiles of the Western Hemisphere*. Irene Emery Roundtable on Museum Textiles, 1976 Procedings. Washington, D.C.: Textile Museum, 1977.

IERAA Richard C. Dorf, ed. *International Encyclopedia of Robotics: Applications and Automation*. New York: John Wiley & Sons, 1988.

IESREF John E. Kaufman and Jack F. Christensen, eds. *IES Lighting Handbook* Vol. I, *Reference Volume*. New York: Illuminating Engineering Society of North America, 1984.

IESS David L. Sills, ed. *International Encyclopedia of the Social Sciences*. New York: Macmillan Publishing Co. and the Free Press, 1968.

IGOE Lynn M. Igoe and James Igoe. *Two Hundred and Fifty Years of Afro-American Art: An Annotated Bibliography*. New York: R.R. Bowker Co., 1981.

IHGACA Ivor N. Hume. *A Guide to Artifacts of Colonial America*. Reprint. New York: Alfred A. Knopf, 1976.

IMAGE *Image: Journal of Photography and Motion Pictures*. Rochester, N.Y.: International Museum of Photography at George Eastman House, 1952-.

INDMIN Max H. Hey. *An Index of Mineral Species and Varieties Arranged Chemically*. 2d rev. ed. London: British Museum, 1962.

INMINR *L'Industria Mineraria*. Rome: Associazione Mineraria Italiana. 1950-.

INNES Jocasta Innes. *Paint Magic*. New York: Pantheon Books, 1981.

INTERM Experimental Intermedia Foundation. *Theoretical Analysis of the Intermedia Art Form*. New York: Experimental Intermedia Foundation at the Solomon R. Guggenheim Museum, 1980.

IT+L *Information Technology and Libraries*. Chicago: Library and Information Technology Association, 1982-.

ITMARB O. Catella, A. Clerici, C. Costa, S. Pelizza and P. Piga. *The Italian Marble and Ornamental-Stone Industry*. World Mining Congress Proceedings 9: Exploitation and Beneficiation of Mineral Raw Materials. Dusseldorf, West Germany: Verlag Gluckauf, 1976.

ITRENG Claudia Lazzaro. *The Italian Renaissance Garden: From the Conventions of Planting, Design, and Ornament to the Grand Gardens of Sixteenth-Century Central Italy*. New Haven, Conn.: Yale University Press, 1990.

JB John Beckwith. *Early Christian and Byzantine Art*. Harmondsworth, England: Penguin Books, 1970.

JDEDS Jay D. Edwards. *Louisiana's Remarkable French Vernacular Architecture, 1700-1900*. Baton Rouge: Department of Geography and Anthropology, Louisiana State University, 1988.

JGLST *Journal of Glass Studies*. Corning, N.Y.: Corning Museum of Glass, 1959-.

JMLAUB Julian M. Laub. *Air Conditioning and Heating Practice*. New York: Holt, Rinehart & Winston, 1963.

JOURD8 Margaret Jourdain. *Furniture in England from 1660 to 1760*. London: B.T. Batsford. New York: Scribners & Sons, 1914.

JPH Penny Simpson. *Japanese Pottery Handbook*. New York: Kodansha International, 1979.

JRTWEN Jack Robertson. *Twentieth-Century Artists on Art: An Index to Artists' Writings, Statements, and Interviews.* Boston, Mass.: G.K. Hall, 1985.

JSAH *Journal of the Society of Architectural Historians.* Philadelphia: Society of Architectural Historians, 1940-.

JUMSAI Sumet Jumsai. *Naga: Cultural Origins in Siam and the West Pacific.* Singapore: Oxford University Press, 1988.

JWCI *Journal of the Warburg and Courtauld Institutes.* London: Warburg Institute, University of London, 1937-.

KAPROW Allan Kaprow. *Assemblage, Environments, and Happenings.* New York: Harry N. Abrams, 1966.

KCGAP Ralph Kovel and Terry Kovel. *The Kovel's Collector's Guide to American Art Pottery.* New York: Crown Publishers, 1974.

KENCAD E. Lee Kennedy. *CAD: Drawing, Design, Data Management.* New York: Whitney Library of Design, 1986.

KKPIT Kate P. Kent. *Pueblo Indian Textiles: A Living Tradition.* Sante Fe, N. Mex.: School of American Research Press, 1983.

KUBACH Hans E. Kubach. *Romanesque Architecture.* New York: Harry N. Abrams, 1975.

LAAA Samella Lewis. *Art: African American.* New York: Harcourt Brace Jovanovich, 1978.

LABARR Emile J. Labarre. *Dictionary and Encyclopaedia of Paper and Paper-Making: With Equivalents of the Technical Terms in French, German, Dutch, Italian, Spanish, and Swedish.* 2d ed., rev. and enl. New York: Oxford University Press, 1952.

LAPDW Paul Goldman. *Looking at Prints, Drawings, and Watercolours: A Guide to Technical Terms.* London: British Museum Publications in Association with the J. Paul Getty Museum, 1988.

LATAMS Bronx Museum of the Arts. *Latin American Spirit: Art and Artists in the United States, 1920-1970.* New York: Bronx Museum of the Arts in association with Harry N. Abrams, 1988.

LBAOP Leone B. Alberti. *On Painting.* Translated by John R. Spencer. New Haven, Conn.: Yale University Press, 1956.

LEEBK Marshall Lee. *Bookmaking: The Illustrated Guide to Design/Production/Editing.* 2d ed. New York: R.R. Bowker Co., 1979.

LGSURR J.H. Matthews. *Languages of Surrealism.* Columbia: University of Missouri Press, 1986.

LIGIMP Light Impressions Corporation. *Archival Supplies.* Product catalog. Rochester, N.Y.: Light Impressions Corp., 1970-.

LILLCH Meredith P. Lillich. *The Common Thread.* Studies in Cistercian Art and Architecture. Kalamazoo, Mich.: Cistercian Publications, 1982.

LIMTSC Oliver Andrews. *Living Materials: A Sculptor's Handbook.* Berkeley: University of California Press, 1983.

LIPCHA Lucy R. Lippard. *Changing: Essays in Art Criticism.* New York: E.P. Dutton & Co., 1971.

LIPEXP Helene Lipstadt, ed. *The Experimental Tradition: Essays on Competitions in Architecture.* New York: Princeton Architectural Press, 1989.

LISTER Raymond Lister. *Prints and Printmaking: A Dictionary and Handbook of the Art in Nineteenth-Century Britain*. London: Methuen, 1984.

LITG Michael C. Sansom, comp. *A Liturgical Glossary*. Grove Liturgical Study, no. 42. Bramcote, England: Grove Books, 1985.

LOFPM Shari Lewis and Lillian Oppenheimer. *Folding Paper Masks*. New York: E.P. Dutton & Co., 1965.

LOVEJ Margot Lovejoy. *Postmodern Currents: Art and Artists in the Age of Electronic Media*. Studies in the Fine Arts; The Avant-Garde, no. 64. Ann Arbor, Mich.: UMI Research Press, 1989.

LUCSYM Edward Lucie-Smith. *Symbolist Art*. New York: Praeger Publishers, 1972.

MAAS Trustees of the Museum of Applied Arts and Sciences. *Unravelling the Rug Puzzle*. Sydney, Australia: Trustees of the Museum of Applied Arts & Sciences, 1983.

MACUSE *MacUser*. Boulder, Colo.: Ziff-Davis Publishing Co., 1985-.

MAHWAP Merrily A. Smith, comp. *Matting and Hinging of Works of Art on Paper*. Washington, D.C.: Preservation Office, Research Services, Library of Congress, 1981.

MAPB05 *General Rules of Work for Housewrights in Newburyport*. Newburyport, Mass.: Angier March, 1805.

MARCH Benjamin March. *Some Technical Terms of Chinese Painting*. Reprint. New York: Paragon Book Reprint Corp., 1969.

MARLIS Frank A. Lent, comp. *Trade Names and Descriptions of Marbles, Limestones, Sandstones, Granites, and Other Building Stones Quarried in the United States, Canada, and Other Countries*. New York: Stone Publishing Co., 1925.

MCDPOL William A. McDonald. *The Political Meeting Places of the Greeks*. Baltimore: Johns Hopkins Press, 1943.

MEAD *Mead Art Museum Monographs*. Amherst, Mass.: Amherst College, Mead Art Museum, 1979-.

MEDAL *The Medal*. London: British Art Medal Society, 1982-.

MEGGS Philip B. Meggs. *A History of Graphic Design*. New York: Van Nostrand Reinhold, 1983.

MFAM Raymonde Moulin. *The French Art Market: A Sociological View*. Translated by Arthur Goldhammer. New Brunswick, N.J.: Rutgers University Press, 1987.

MGHEGS Daniel N. Lapedes, ed. *McGraw-Hill Encyclopedia of the Geological Sciences*. New York: McGraw-Hill Book Co., 1978.

MIAMAN Marble Institute of America. *Marble Design Manual I*. Washington, D.C.: Marble Institute of America, 1970.

MMARC David Black, ed. *The Macmillan Atlas of Rugs and Carpets*. New York: Macmillan Publishing Co., 1985.

MMAYAH Robert Wauchope. *Modern Maya Houses: A Study of Their Archaeological Significance*. Carnegie Institution of Washington Publication, no. 502. Washington, D.C.: Carnegie Institution of Washington, 1938.

MNAR Donald L. Miller. *The New American Radicalism: Alfred M. Bingham and Non-Marxian Insurgency in the New Deal Era*. Port Washington, N.Y.: Kennikat Press, 1979.

MOAD Helen Powell and David Leatherbarrow, eds. *Masterpieces of Architectural Drawing*. Edmonton: Hurtig Publishers, 1982.

MOREAU Charles Moreau-Vauthier. *The Technique of Painting*. London: William Heinemann, 1912.

MSJEGC Michael Schuyt, Joost Elffers and George R. Collins. *Fantastic Architecture: Personal and Eccentric Visions*. New York: Harry N. Abrams, 1980.

MTMPTG Daniel V. Thompson. *The Materials of Medieval Painting*. New Haven, Conn.: Yale University Press, 1936.

MYERS Denys P. Myers. *Gaslighting in America: A Guide for Historic Preservation*. Washington, D.C.: U.S. Department of the Interior, Heritage Conservation and Recreation Service, 1978.

NADEAU Luis Nadeau. *Encyclopedia of Printing, Photographic, and Photomechanical Processes: A Comprehensive Reference to Reproduction Technologies*. 2 vols. Fredericton, New Brunswick: Atelier Luis Nadeau, 1989.

NDAP Francis V. O'Connor, ed. *The New Deal Art Projects: An Anthology of Memoirs*. Washington, D.C.: Smithsonian Institution Press, 1972.

NEWIP Thelma R. Newman. *Innovative Printmaking: The Making of Two- and Three-Dimensional Prints and Multiples*. New York: Crown Publishers, 1977.

NGDMI Stanley Sadie, ed. *New Grove Dictionary of Musical Instruments*. 3 vols. London: Macmillan Press. New York: Grove's Dictionaries of Music, 1984.

NHNH Karen A. Franck and Sherry Ahrentzen. *New Households, New Housing*. New York: Van Nostrand Reinhold, 1989.

NJE David Bridger, ed. *The New Jewish Encyclopedia*. Reprint. New York: Behrman House, 1976.

NOC Philip Ward. *The Nature of Conservation: A Race Against Time*. Marina del Ray, Calif.: Getty Conservation Institute, 1986.

NYTFR *The New York Times Film Reviews, 1979-1980*. New York: New York Times and Arno Press, 1981.

ODEA William T. O'Dea. *The Social History of Lighting*. New York: Macmillan Publishing Co., 1958.

OED2 *Oxford English Dictionary*. 2d ed. Prepared by J.A. Simpson and J.C. Weiner. 20 vols. New York: Oxford University Press, 1989.

OHNF Gordon F. Streib, W. Edward Folts and Mary A. Hilker. *Old Homes—New Families: Shared Living for the Elderly*. Columbia Studies of Social Gerontology and Aging. New York: Columbia University Press, 1984.

OMDW *Old Master Drawings*. London: B.T. Batsford, 1927-1940.

ORR Peter F. Stone. *Oriental Rug Repair*. Chicago: Greenleaf Co., 1981.

OSTOIA Vera K. Ostoia. *The Middle Ages: Treasures from the Cloisters and the Metropolitan Museum of Art*. Los Angeles: Los Angeles County Museum of Art, 1969.

OXCTHE Phyllis Hartnoll, ed. *The Oxford Companion to the Theatre*. 4th ed. New York: Oxford University Press, 1983.

OXDPE John Pheby, ed. *The Oxford-Duden Pictorial English Dictionary*. Reprint. New York: Oxford University Press, 1984.

P&R *Parks and Recreation*. Alexandria, Va.: National Recreation & Park Association, 1966-.

PAA   David W. Phillipson. *African Archaeology*. Cambridge World Archaeology. London: Cambridge University Press, 1985.

PAPAT   Paulette Long and Robert Levering, eds. *Paper: Art and Technology; Based on Presentations Given at the International Paper Conference Held in San Francisco, March 1978*. San Francisco: World Print Council, 1979.

PCC   Carolyn L. Rose and D.W. Von Endt, eds. *Protein Chemistry for Conservators*. Washington, D.C.: American Institute for Conservation of Historic & Artistic Works, 1984.

PENCOO   Accademia Nazionale di San Luca. *Architectural Fantasy and Reality: Drawings from the Accademia Nazionale di San Luca in Rome, Concorsi Clementini, 1700-1750*. University Park: Museum of Art, Pennsylvania State University, 1981.

PETERD   Gabor Peterdi. *Printmaking: Methods Old and New*. rev. ed. New York: Macmillan Publishing Co., 1971.

PHOAA   Michel Melot, Antony Griffiths, Richard S. Field and Andre Beguin. *Prints: History of an Art*. Geneva: Skira. New York: Rizzoli International Publications, 1981.

PICON   Gaetan Picon. *Surrealists and Surrealism, 1919-1939*. Translated by James Emmons. Geneva: Skira. New York: Rizzoli International Publications, 1977.

PIPF   S.A. Smith et al. *Planning and Implementing Pedestrian Facilities in Suburban and Developing Rural Areas: State-of-the-Art Report*. National Cooperative Highway Research Program Report no. 294B. Washington, D.C.: Transportation Research Board, National Research Council, 1987.

PLANNB   American Planning Association. *Best of Planning: Two Decades of Articles from the Magazine of the American Planning Association*. Chicago: Planners Press, 1989.

PML   Pierpont Morgan Library. Word list. Document prepared for internal distribution. Pierpont Morgan Library, New York, 1990.

PPUS   Edwin A. Barber. *The Pottery and Porcelain of the United States: An Historical Review of American Ceramic Art from the Earliest Times to the Present Day*. 3d rev. ed. Combined with *Marks of American Potters* by Edwin A. Barber. New York: Feingold & Lewis, 1976.

PRAYER   Richard Ettinghausen, Maurice S. Dimand, Louise W. Mackie, and Charles G. Ellis. *Prayer Rugs*. Washington, D.C.: Textile Museum, 1974.

PRIMIT   William Rubin, ed. *"Primitivism" in Twentieth Century Art: Affinity of the Tribal and the Modern*. 2 vols. New York: Museum of Modern Art, 1984.

PROTO   Museum Prototype Project. "Medium of Objects Frequency Report." Document prepared for internal distribution. 1985.

PRTT   Jules Heller. *Printmaking Today: A Studio Handbook*. 2d ed. New York: Holt, Rinehart & Winston, 1972.

PVA   *Perspectives in Vernacular Architecture*. Columbia: University of Missouri Press, 1982-.

RACAR   *Racar: Canadian Art Review*. Quebec: Society for the Promotion of Art History Publications in Canada, 1974-.

RAMACH   R. Ramachandran. *Urbanization and Urban Systems in India*. New York: Oxford University Press, 1989.

RBGENR Association of College and Research Libraries. Rare Books and Manuscripts Section. Standards Committee. *Genre Terms: A Thesaurus for Use in Rare Book and Special Collections Cataloguing*. 2d ed. Chicago: Association of College and Research Libraries, 1991.

RBMSPA Association of College and Research Libraries. Rare Books and Manuscripts Section. Standards Committee. "Paper Terms: A Thesaurus for Use in Rare Book and Special Collections Cataloguing." Chicago, 1989.

RGSS *A Reader's Guide to the Social Sciences*. New York: Free Press, 1972.

RHBUN Agnesa L. Reeve. *From Hacienda to Bungalow: Northern New Mexico Houses, 1850-1912*. Albuquerque: University of New Mexico Press, 1988.

RICKEY George Rickey. *Constructivism Origins and Evolution*. New York: George Braziller, 1967.

RIESBS Heinrich Ries. *Building Stones and Clay-Products: A Handbook for Architects*. New York: John Wiley & Sons, 1912.

RISKAM Susan Rafter. *Risk Analysis and Risk Management: A Selected Bibliography*. Vance Bibliographies, Public Administration Series, P2218. Monticello, Ill.: Vance Bibliographies, 1987.

RJHGEO R.J. Johnston. *Philosophy and Human Geography: An Introduction to Contemporary Approaches*. 2d ed. London: Edward Arnold, 1986.

RLGGRP Research Libraries Group Government Records Project. "Rules for Choosing Function/Activity Terms." Document prepared for internal distribution. 1991.

RLIN Research Libraries Information Network, Research Libraries Group, Inc. Mountain View, California.

RYKAHP Joseph Rykwert. *On Adam's House in Paradise: The Idea of the Primitive Hut in Architectural History*. The Museum of Modern Art Papers on Architecture, v. 2. New York: Museum of Modern Art in association with the Graham Foundation for Advanced Studies in the Fine Arts, Chicago, 1972.

S&P Andre Breton. *Surrealism and Painting*. Translated by Simon W. Tyler. London: MacDonald and Co., 1972.

SAC84 Michael Sullivan. *The Arts of China*. 3d ed. Berkeley: University of California Press, 1984.

SAITZY Steven L. Saitzyk. *Art Hardware: The Definitive Guide to Artists' Materials*. New York: Watson-Guptill Publications, 1987.

SALHEL Mario G. Salvadori and Robert A. Heller. *Structure in Architecture: The Building of Buildings*. 2d ed. Prentice-Hall International Series in Architecture. Englewood Cliffs, N.J.: Prentice-Hall, 1975.

SBHS Ronald L. Coleman. *Sculpture: A Basic Handbook for Students*. 2d ed. Dubuque, Iowa: William C. Brown Co., 1980.

SCHARF Aaron Scharf. *Art and Photography*. London: Allen Lane, 1968.

SCHOUT Clara B. Lambert. *School's Out: Child Care Through Play Schools*. New York: Harper & Brothers, 1944.

SCSFS Carl D. Sheppard. *Creator of the Santa Fe Style: Isaac Hamilton Rapp, Architect*. Albuquerque: University of New Mexico Press, 1987.

SDA Dora Ware and Betty Beatty. *A Short Dictionary of Architecture*. New York: Philosophical Library, 1945.

SELZ81 Peter H. Selz. *Art in Our Times: A Pictorial History 1890-1980.* New York: Harcourt Brace Jovanovich and Harry N. Abrams, 1981.

SGMTC Siegfried Giedion. *Mechanization Takes Command: A Contribution to Anonymous History.* New York: Oxford University Press, 1948.

SIHLU Walter Hough. *Collection of Heating and Lighting Utensils in the United States National Museum.* United States National Museum Bulletin 141. Washington, D.C.: Government Printing Office, 1928.

SILACL Douglas H. Shaffer. *Clocks.* The Smithsonian Illustrated Library of Antiques. New York: Cooper-Hewitt Museum, 1980.

SIXCFP Carl Zigrosser. *Six Centuries of Fine Prints.* New York: Covici Friede Publishers, 1937.

SLINKS *Southern Links Magazine: The Magazine of Southern Golf, Travel, and Lifestyles.* Hilton Head Island, S.C.: Southern Links Magazine Publishing Associates, 1988-.

SOLDES John S. Crowley and L. Zaurie Zimmerman. *Practical Passive Solar Design: A Guide to Homebuilding and Land Development.* New York: McGraw-Hill Book Co., 1984.

SPONSH Carl V. Patton, ed. *Spontaneous Shelter: Intenational Perspectives and Prospects.* Philadelphia: Temple University Press, 1988.

STERRV *Stereo Review.* New York: Diamandis Communications, 1958-.

TANNER Clara L. Tanner. *Southwest Indian Craft Arts.* Tucson: University of Arizona Press, 1968.

TAUB Frederic Taubes. *The Painter's Dictionary of Materials and Methods.* New York: Watson-Guptill Publications, 1971.

TFNEL Ernest H. Roberts. *Treasures from New Eastern Looms.* Brunswick, Maine: Bowdin College Museum of Art, 1981.

THDMSC Trevor Faulkner. *The Thames and Hudson Manual of Direct Metal Sculpture.* London: Thames & Hudson, 1978.

THEOPH Theophilus. *On Divers Arts: The Foremost Medieval Treatise on Painting, Glassmaking, and Metalwork.* 2d ed. Translated by John G. Hawthorne and Cyril S. Smith. New York: Dover Publications, 1979.

THOAC Elaine Levin. *The History of American Ceramics, 1607 to the Present: From Pipkins and Bean Pots to Contemporary Forms.* New York: Harry N. Abrams, 1988.

THOMP Jon Thompson. *Oriental Carpets: From the Tents, Cottages, and Workshops of Asia.* New York: E.P. Dutton & Co., 1988.

THWING Leroy L. Thwing and Julius Daniels. *A Dictionary of Old Lamps and Other Lighting Devices.* Cambridge, Mass.: Thwing & Daniels, 1952.

TIME-S John H. Callender, ed. *Time-Saver Standards for Architectural Design Data.* 6th ed. New York: McGraw-Hill Book Co., 1982.

TIST Claire K. Schultz. *Thesaurus of Information Science Terminology.* rev. ed. Metuchen, N.J.: Scarecrow Press, 1978.

TOCCAB Harold B. Segel. *Turn-of-the-Century Cabaret: Paris, Barcelona, Berlin, Munich, Vienna, Cracow, Moscow, St. Petersburg, Zurich.* New York: Columbia University Press, 1987.

TOCOMO John S. Mills and Raymond White. *The Organic Chemistry of Museum Objects.* London: Butterworths & Co., 1987.

TPH Stan Smith and H.F. Ten Holt, eds. *The Painter's Handbook*. New York: Gallery Books, 1984.

TPRLST *The Thesaurus of Park, Recreation, and Leisure Service Terms*. Alexandria, Va.: National Park Service, Mid-Atlantic Region and National Recreation & Park Association, 1990.

TQWDSC Chaim Gross. *The Technique of Wood Sculpture*. New York: Arco Publishing, 1965.

TURKMN Louise W. Mackie and Jon Thompson, eds. *Turkmen: Tribal Carpets and Traditions*. Washington, D.C.: Textile Museum, 1980.

TYLER Kenneth E. Tyler. *Tyler Graphics: Catalogue Raisonne, 1974-1985*. Minneapolis: Walker Art Center. New York: Abbeville Press, 1987.

TYPO Ruari McLean. *The Thames and Hudson Manual of Typography*. New York: Thames & Hudson, 1988.

UHRAN Mark Uhran. *Solar Energy for the Northeast*. Old Saybrook, Conn.: Peregrine Press, 1980.

UMER Joan Gadol. *Leon Battista Alberti: Universal Man of the Early Renaissance*. Chicago: University of Chicago Press, 1969.

URBLND *Urban Land*. Washington, D.C.: Urban Land Institute, 1941-.

VABRIT Gwyn I. Meirion-Jones. *The Vernacular Architecture of Brittany: An Essay in Historical Geography*. Edinburgh: John Donald Publishers, 1982.

VAGEOR Victoria and Albert Museum. *Georgian Furniture*. London: Her Majesty's Stationary Office, 1958.

VLDFOR Eugene E. Viollet-le-Duc. *Annals of a Fortress*. Translated by Benjamin Bucknall. Boston: James R. Osgood & Co., 1876.

VTRANS Rodney R. Adler. *Vertical Transportation for Buildings*. New York: American Elsevier Publishing Co., 1970.

WANAI Carl Waldman. *Atlas of the North American Indian*. New York: Facts on File Publications, 1985.

WARCH *World Archaeology*. London: Routledge & Kegan Paul, 1969-.

WEICON Kurt Weitzmann. *The Icon: Holy Images, Sixth to Fourteenth Century*. New York: George Braziller, 1978.

WELLIN William B. Welling. *Photography in America: The Formative Years, 1839-1900*. New York: Thomas Y. Crowell Co., 1978.

WHITJP Frank Whitford. *Japanese Prints and Western Painters*. New York: Macmillan Publishing Co., 1977.

WITTSC Rudolf Wittkower. *Sculpture: Processes and Principles*. Icon Editions. New York: Harper & Row Publishers, 1977.

WNTPRT *Winterthur Portfolio*. Chicago: University of Chicago Press, 1964-.

WOODMH Margaret Wood. *The English Mediaeval House*. London: Phoenix House, 1965.

WPMICS Peter H. Wood, Gregory A. Waselkov and M. Thomas Hatley, eds. *Powhatan's Mantle: Indians in the Colonial Southeast*. Lincoln: University of Nebraska Press, 1989.

WSISRE Walter L. Williams, ed. *Southeastern Indians Since the Removal Era*. Athens: University of Georgia Press, 1979.

WWFRA   Martin Wackernagel. *The World of the Florentine Renaissance Artist: Projects and Patrons, Workshop and Art Markets*. Translated by Alison Luchs. Princeton, N.J.: Princeton University Press, 1981.

Art &
Architecture
Thesaurus

SUPPLEMENT 1

PART V:

Candidate Term
Form
Comment Form

These forms may be duplicated for the purpose of suggesting new terms or making comments on existing terms. Forms should be mailed or faxed to the AAT Editorial Office, 62 Stratton Road, Williamstown, MA 01267. FAX: (413) 458-3757.

AAT
Candidate Term
Form

FAX: 413-458-3757

AAT · Getty Art History Information Program · 62 Stratton Road · Williamstown, MA 01267 · 413-458-2151

Please use this form to submit Candidate Terms to the AAT office. Be sure to complete Section I. Section II is optional. Section III is for AAT staff use.

Submitting organization: _____

Contact person: _____ Date: _____

SECTION I

Suggested Term:

_____

Source of Term: (please give specific indication of at least one place where the term was found; if in text, give full citation, including page numbers; include photocopy if possible.)

_____

_____

_____

_____

_____

_____

SECTION II [Optional]

Suggested definition:

_____

Suggested Lead-in Term(s): _____

_____

Suggested Broader Term: _____

_____

Suggested Related Term(s): _____

_____

Comments: (continue on reverse or attach sheet if necessary)

_____

_____

SECTION III [For AAT Office Use]

AAT Editor(s): _____ Date: _____

☐ Accepted form of term: _____ AAT hier.: _____

    AAT Broader Term: _____ Spc. Thes.: _____

    AAT Scope Note:

☐ Accepted as Lead-in Term to AAT Term: _____

☐ Not accepted: ☐ Use existing AAT Term(s): _____

                ☐ Postcoordinate from AAT Term(s): _____

                ☐ Sufficient literary warrant not found. Please supply further information.

                ☐ Term is outside scope of AAT ☐ Other

AAT Comments:

rev. 10/88

219

AAT
Comment
Form

FAX: 413-458-3757

AAT · Getty Art History Information Program · 62 Stratton Road · Williamstown, MA 01267 · 413-458-2151

Please use this form to submit Comments on existing terms to the AAT office. Be sure to complete Section I. Section II is optional. Section III is for AAT staff use.

SECTION I

Submitting project: _____ Date: _____

Name of Contact: _____

AAT Term: _____ Status in AAT: ___ MT ___ Lead-in

Suggested Change:

☐ Add or Change Scope Note

☐ Change form of term to _____

☐ Move to different Broader Term _____

☐ Add Related Term(s) _____

☐ Delete term because _____

☐ Question relationship to AAT Term(s) _____

☐ Revise structure as noted on reverse or attached sheet

☐ Add qualifier   ☐ Delete qualifier

☐ Other

Comments: _____

_____

_____

SECTION II (For AAT Office Use]

AAT Editor(s): _____ Date: _____

☐ Accepted

   ☐ New Term Form: _____

   ☐ New AAT Broader Term: _____

   ☐ Add/Change Scope Note: _____

☐ Not accepted

☐ Other

AAT Comments: _____

rev. 10/88